of the Wealth Ancient World

of the Wealth Ancient World

The
Nelson Bunker Hunt
and
William Herbert Hunt
Collections

Kimbell Art Museum
Fort Worth, 1983

Published in association with
Summa Publications, Beverly Hills

This publication was produced for the exhibition
Wealth of the Ancient World

held at the Kimbell Art Museum, June 25–September 18, 1983;
Virginia Museum of Fine Arts, October 19–December 11, 1983;
Detroit Institute of Arts, February 1–March 24, 1984;
Dallas Museum of Art, April 25–June 10, 1984.

Essays by Dietrich von Bothmer, Jiří Frel, Arthur Houghton, and Margaret Ellen Mayo

Library of Congress Card Number 83-80661
ISBN (Cloth) 0-912804-13-0
       (Paper) 0-912804-14-9

Printed in U.S.A. by Alan Lithograph

General Editor: Janice Firth Tompkins

Design and Photography: Andrew Daneman

Photographs for [9] and [10] courtesy Metropolitan Museum of Art
Photographs for [7] and [8] in profile courtesy Bob Wharton Photography
Drawings for [17], Appendix A and all maps by Mary Beth Mackenzie
Drawing for Appendix B by A. B. Martinez

Cover: [6]   Attic Calyx-Krater
                 Signed by Euphronios, circa 510 B.C.
                 Death of Kyknos (detail)

Half-title: [134] Orichalcum Sestertius of Hadrian (obverse)
                 Attributed to the Alphaeus Master
                 Struck 135 A.D.

Frontispiece: [16] Etruscan Antefix
                 Maenad and Silen
                 Circa 500 B.C.

Contributors

Dietrich von Bothmer

Jane M. Cody

Jiří Frel

Arthur Houghton

Catharine Custis Lorber

Margaret Ellen Mayo

Photography

Andrew Daneman

[5] Attic Kylix
Signed by Euphronios, circa 520 B.C.
Death of Sarpedon (detail)

Contents

Contents <small>(continued)</small>

Foreword

Wealth of the Ancient World: The Nelson Bunker Hunt and William Herbert Hunt Collections offers an unparalleled opportunity to examine the art, attitudes and aspirations of classical antiquity—an age far removed from that of our own, but one that still impresses itself strongly upon ours, socially and culturally. The exhibition spans more than a thousand years, extending from the archaic period in Greece and Etruria through the rich style of Sicily and South Italy to the hellenistic and Roman periods; this epoch witnessed the shift in power from Athens to Rome and the final triumph of the east with the establishment of the new capital in Constantinople.

As the exhibition will demonstrate, the ancients converted even their most prosaic form of wealth—their coinage—into objects of great refinement and artistry. Of the 112 coins selected from the collection of Nelson Bunker Hunt—considered now one of the finest in private hands—many are notable for their rarity, condition or historical importance, but almost all exhibit qualities that distinguish them as works of art. Of particular importance is the group of eleven decadrachms, which forms the nucleus of the collection, including the Athens decadrachm [66], traditionally associated with the Greek victory over the Persian empire, and the decadrachm of Agrigentum [77], which celebrates a victory in the Olympic games of 412 B.C.

It is well known that Greek vases are among the greatest artistic legacy of antiquity. Their decoration derives from everyday life as well as from the rich tradition of Greek drama and literature. The fifteen examples that comprise the collection of Nelson Bunker Hunt, all of which will be exhibited, include both black- and red-figured pieces of Corinthian, Attic and South Italian workshops. The calyx-krater signed by Euphronios [6], the most famous of all Greek vase-painters, is the centerpiece of this distinguished group. Other outstanding examples have been attributed to the Epidromos Painter [7], the Proto-Panaitian Group [8], the Kleophrades Painter [9], and the Berlin Painter [10].

Bronze enjoyed a great importance in antiquity as the primary medium for "pure" sculpture, though today we can also appreciate the imaginative decoration of utilitarian objects in bronze. Both aspects of bronze artistry are reflected in the thirty-eight pieces of the William Herbert Hunt Collection. Among them are acknowledged masterworks of portraiture and small statuary. Of exceptional interest is a pair of life-size portrait heads of a young man [44] and old woman [43] cast during the Augustan or early Julio-Claudian period. A late sixth-century B.C. statuette of a horse [27] from the critical period of Etruscan art is also of the highest workmanship, as is a first-century B.C. statuette of a goddess with an excellent gilt finish [39].

As the first public showing of the majority of ancient works of art recently assembled by the Hunt brothers, this exhibition will demonstrate that the genius of classical art was not confined to monumental stone sculpture, but found eloquent and very refined expression in the labors of draftsmen, metalworkers and die engravers as well. Opportunities to see the arts of classical antiquity are unusual. Because of the many spectacular, rare, and, in several cases, unique pieces included in the selection, this show promises to make a major contribution to knowledge of the subject.

Ruth Wilkins Sullivan   Edmund P. Pillsbury
Curator of Exhibition   Director

[1] Corinthian Column-Krater
Circa 600 B.C.

[8] Attic Kylix
Proto-Panaitian Group
Circa 510–500 B.C.

Acknowledgments

Wealth of the Ancient World would not have been possible without the help and participation of many individuals. We are grateful, first and foremost, to Nelson Bunker Hunt and William Herbert Hunt for generously making their collections available for public viewing and for cooperating fully throughout this project. We are equally indebted to Bruce P. McNall, Chairman, Numismatic Fine Arts, Inc., who on behalf of the collectors first approached the Kimbell Art Museum about the exhibition.

In addition, our thanks go to Steve L. Rubinger, of the same organization, who helped with many administrative matters and to Janice Firth Tompkins, Director, the Summa Galleries Inc., who oversaw the loan arrangements and served as general editor of the catalogue. Catharine Custis Lorber, special consultant to Numismatic Fine Arts, Inc., labored tirelessly on this publication, writing the coin entries, compiling various supplementary materials for the end of the catalogue and making numerous editorial improvements. Professor Jane M. Cody of the Classics Department of the University of Southern California worked equally hard in writing and revising the bronze and vase entries and also contributed to the useful glossary.

We also deeply appreciate the participation of the four distinguished scholars whose introductory essays are included in the catalogue. We are particularly grateful to Dr. Dietrich von Bothmer, Chairman, Department of Greek and Roman Art, Metropolitan Museum of Art, who shared with us his great expertise of vase painting and contributed entries [9] and [10] on two recently acquired vases. We are also greatly thankful to Dr. Jiří Frel, Curator of Antiquities, the J. Paul Getty Museum, who reviewed the dating and attributions of the bronzes in the William Herbert Hunt collection. Arthur Houghton, Associate Curator of Antiquities, the J. Paul Getty Museum, and Dr. Margaret Ellen Mayo, Curator of Ancient Art, Virginia Museum of Fine Arts, authors of two further essays, also provided invaluable assistance with the catalogue and other aspects of the selection. Special thanks are finally owed to Dr. Stéphanie Boucher of the Centre National de la Recherche Scientifique in France who at our invitation offered valuable comments on the style, iconography, and dating of the bronzes and thereby contributed much to our knowledge of the collection.

Andrew Daneman is to be commended for his dual role as designer of this catalogue and photographer of the works of art in the show. Charles B. Froom, New York, contributed the thoughtful installation design which creates the visual environment for the exhibition.

The professionalism, dedication, and great interest of all the above were instrumental in realizing this exhibition and the handsome publication that accompanies it. The expected success of the undertaking is a tribute to their efforts.

Ruth Wilkins Sullivan
Curator of Exhibition

Edmund P. Pillsbury
Director

[39] Statuette of a Goddess
Greek (Asia Minor?)
First Century B.C.

[37] Anguipede Giant
Roman
Second Century A.D.

[42] Head of Zeus
Roman (Asia Minor?)
First–Second Century A.D.

[43] Portrait of a Woman
Roman (Spain)
Late First Century B.C. – Early First Century A.D.

[44] Portrait of a Man
Roman (Spain)
Late First Century B.C. – Early First Century A.D.

[48] Statue of a Youth (detail)
Roman
Second Century A.D.

[53] Pyx
Roman
Third Century A.D.

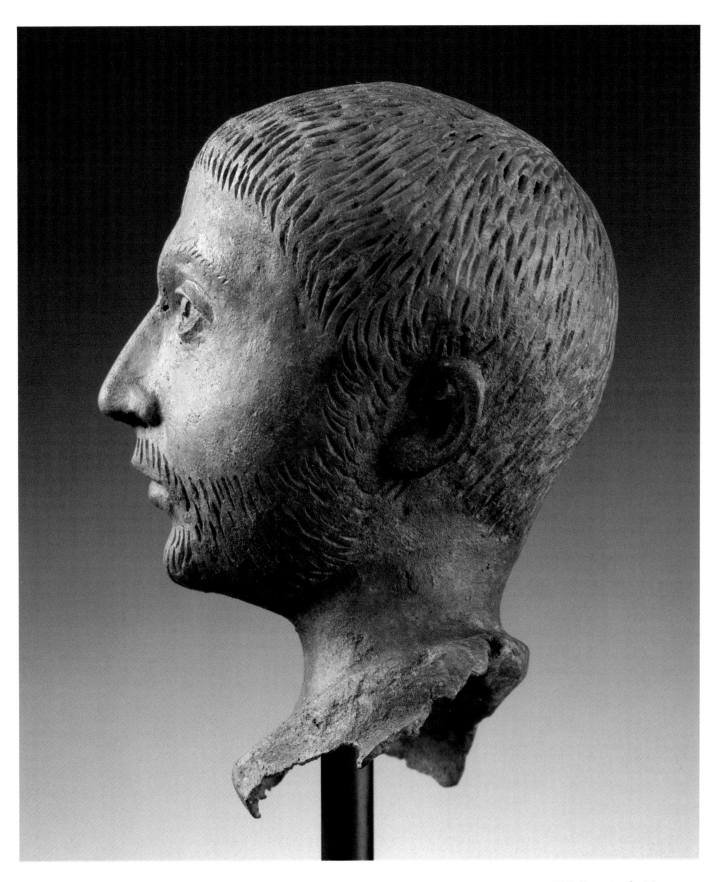

[54] Portrait of a Man
Roman (Spain?)
Late Third Century A.D.

[105] Gold Stater of Pyrrhus (obverse)
Struck at Syracuse
278 B.C.

[126] Orichalcum Sestertius of Galba (obverse)
Gallic Mint (Narbonne?)
68 A.D.

[153] Gold Medallion of Maximian (obverse)
Ticinum Mint
293 A.D.

[14] Lucanian Calyx-Krater
Circa 400 B.C.
Flight of Medea (detail)

Introduction

COLLECTING ANCIENT ART: AN HISTORICAL PERSPECTIVE

Margaret Ellen Mayo

In this century, especially during the last fifty years, a number of important collections of ancient art have been formed by American connoisseurs. Access to these collections has rarely been denied to scholars or interested laymen—rather, over the years there has developed a healthy tradition of collectors' sharing their treasures with the public through museums. Some collectors have enriched museums with long-term loans or with gifts; some, joining with other collectors and museums, have lent pieces to thematic exhibitions; and a few outstanding collections have merited their own exhibitions. With *Wealth of the Ancient World*, Nelson Bunker Hunt and William Herbert Hunt have joined this tradition.

Collecting ancient art itself has a long and distinguished tradition that began with the Greeks and Romans. Museums and, indeed, the world owe a great debt to those who have participated in this tradition, for until the advent of scientific archaeology in the nineteenth century, the discovery, recognition, and preservation of classical art were due largely to private collectors. The history of ancient art collecting is a vast and far-reaching subject touching on religion, history, politics, economics, and aesthetic sensibilities in the West for more than 2000 years.[1] It is a gold mine of information for those who want to know how we have obtained our knowledge and opinions of the past, why men have collected art, how works of art have been interpreted at various periods, and how works of art have fared physically through the thousands of years since their creation. Needless to say, the following brief account cannot answer all these questions; rather, it aims to provide some perspective for understanding the phenomenon of collecting ancient art in America in the twentieth century.

Today, when virtually all categories of art made in any period are so actively collected by so many private collectors and museums, it might be assumed that art collecting has always been a natural accompaniment to artistic creation. This is not the case. Although from the beginning of their history the Greeks obviously valued beauty and delighted in things made with art, there is no evidence of any Greek's collecting art for its own sake before the third century B.C. Part of the reason for this seems to lie in the uses the Greeks had for their art. While architects, sculptors, and painters were commissioned to create lavish public buildings, sumptuously decorated private homes were rare.[2] Private luxuries existed, of course, but these were mainly useful items made with art, such as fine dinnerware, decorated utensils, or tomb monuments; or they were items made as treasures and valued above all else for their raw materials, such as jewelry, vessels of silver or gold, and coins. Greek artists were far from anonymous—vase-painters, sculptors, even die-cutters of coins sometimes signed their work, and the names of contemporary artists are sometimes mentioned by authors of the fifth and fourth centuries; but it was not until the third century B.C. that the achievements of artists of the past were recorded by historians—the world's first art historians, Duris of Samos and Xenocrates. In the estimation of Xenocrates, the greatest art had been created in the fourth century, and in his time the quality of artistic creation was declining. Significantly, at the same period the world's first securely documented art collector began to collect masterpieces by Greek artists of past periods.

Attalus I inherited the throne of Pergamum, one of the kingdoms carved out of Alexander's empire, in 241 B.C. Vying with the Ptolemies who had established an enormous cultural complex at Alexandria, Attalus, and later his son Eumenes II, aimed to make Pergamum the most beautiful city in the Greek world and a major cultural center. To accomplish this, he became a patron of the arts on a grand scale: he endowed a library second only to the one in Alexandria and subsidized the scholars working in it; he commissioned artists for lavish public buildings (these artists formed the famous Pergamene school of sculpture); and he adorned the city with his personal collection of masterpieces by Greek artists of the past. What made this patron of contemporary art collect art of the past? It would seem likely that Attalus was familiar with Xenocrates' view of art history and that he agreed in admiring the art of the past centuries. It is also likely that he recognized the prestige of adorning his city with art that was so highly regarded by others; and it is possible that with the realization that this sort of art was no longer being produced may have come the consciousness of its limited availability, spurring the desire to gather it before it disappeared. Whatever his motives, Attalus enthusiastically acquired all of the masterpieces that he could, sometimes by purchase, sometimes by looting. When he purchased Aegina from the Aetolian League, he removed a number of sculptures dating from the fifth to the third centuries B.C., and when he helped Roman forces overpower the Euboean town of Oreus, he took as booty a number of works by a fourth-century artist. Attalus' descendants continued to collect, receiving the spoils that the Romans did not want from the sack of Corinth in 146 B.C., and finally in 133 B.C. they bequeathed to Rome their collection and the state of Pergamum, which became the Roman province of Asia.

The most avid collectors of Greek art were the Romans. Until the third century B.C. Rome had existed in relative isolation politically and culturally. Then, expanding her power in Italy and throughout the Mediterranean (264–133 B.C.), Roman forces conquered foreign states and absorbed much of their culture with lasting and dramatic results. Contact with Greek culture began with expansion into the wealthy Greek settlements in South Italy and Sicily. In 211 B.C. the Roman general Marcellus defeated the Carthaginians at Syracuse and returned in triumph with dazzling treasures: in addition to the usual money and slaves, he brought all the city's public statues and paintings. According to Plutarch (*Marcellus* 21), he was particularly proud of bringing back these works of art because they emphasized the importance of his victory and because they beautified Rome. The public was delighted, and Marcellus claimed to have brought art appreciation to Rome.

The destruction of Corinth in 146 B.C. also brought an overwhelming influx of the finest Greek art to Rome: the city was burned, its entire population was sold into slavery, and the best art works were sent to Rome, the rest auctioned off. According to Pliny (*N.H.* 34.24), the popularity of Greek paintings in Rome grew rapidly after the sack of Corinth because at this auction the first extraordinarily high bid in history was placed on a painting—which was then withdrawn from the auction and sent as booty to Rome on the premise that it must be very good if someone was willing to pay so much for it. The destruction of Corinth was also thought to have produced the craze for Corinthian bronze, supposedly an alloy invented by accident when the foundries burned (Pliny *N.H.* 34.6).

As Roman power expanded around the Mediterranean, the great wealth and luxury of the hellenistic kingdoms of the East made a particularly strong impression on Roman society. In 189 B.C. L. Scipio returned from the East with several thousand pounds of gold and silver vessels in his triumphal procession, and according to Pliny (*N.H.* 33.148–149) the Romans became so enamoured of foreign opulence that they bid wildly at the auction of Pergamene art in 132. Conquest did far more for Rome than bring great works of art back as public dedications; armies returned with private items that were exotic, old, or luxurious, and the upper classes acquired a taste for the trappings of Hellenic culture and the great wealth needed to acquire them. Although conservative Romans decried the detrimental effects of foreign culture on the Roman character, by the early Empire, virtually every aspect of Roman society showed its effect: oriental cults flourished, Roman children were taught Greek before Latin, Greeks were prominent in many professions (especially medicine and education), and Greek art was displayed publicly and avidly collected privately.

By the first century B.C. Rome had a true art market complete with dealers, high prices, and eager clients. Roman collectors bought silverware, Corinthian bronzes, murrhine vases, antique furniture, engraved gems and cameos, paintings, and marble sculpture. Julius Caesar was an avid collector of gems, statues, and old paintings (Suetonius *Divus Iulius* 47), and the emperor Augustus favored fine furniture and Corinthian vessels (*Divus Augustus* 68–70). The growth of the Roman building industry created a need for vast amounts of statuary as decoration. Private estates in the country, palaces in the city, gardens, baths, and other public buildings, all required decoration, and rather than commission work from contemporary artists, many Romans preferred to purchase old Greek sculpture, preferably by well-known artists. Cicero's letters about acquiring statuary for his Tuscan villa show the great quantity of statuary needed for such an estate, and they demonstrate that collecting well, even in the first century B.C., was not always easy.[3] Eventually the supply of good and appropriate pieces began to fall short of the demand and the copy industry was born: some copies were faithful reproductions of popular original works, others were made larger, smaller, or in mirror reversal as the client required.[4] Unlike today, copies, at least good copies, did not reflect poorly on the owner's taste or finances, for the emperor Hadrian, a well-bred connoisseur, made his famous villa near Tivoli a virtual museum of copies of famous Greek sculptures.

The Romans acquired their private collections in a number of ways. Cicero used dealers, such as the Greek Damasippus, or his friend Atticus who lived at Athens and acted as his agent in purchasing and shipping pieces to Italy. Art could also be acquired at auction. The most acquisitive Roman art collector used other methods, however. From 73 to 71 B.C. while proconsul of the wealthy province of Sicily, Gaius Verres systematically extorted and stole Greek art from temples, public buildings, and private collectors. He amassed great quantities of silver, bronze, statuary, and paintings, and he even set up his own workshop where the ornaments from plundered vessels could be reused on new vessels.[5] When Cicero brought him to trial for his crimes, he fled Rome, and refusing to hand over his prized Corinthian bronzes on order of Marc Antony, he was killed.

Collecting classical art seems to have persisted in some form into the later Roman period, although it was slowed by the rise of Christianity, which looked upon the figures of Greek mythology as the images of demons. Early in the fifth century a decree banned sacrifices at pagan altars in all Roman provinces. The last truly major collection assembled in antiquity was that of Lausus, Overseer of the Sacred Bedchamber of Emperors Arcadius and Theodosius II in the fifth century.[6]

The classical literature that survived the Middle Ages did so largely through the special interests of the Byzantine Empire and the Roman church, while the ancient art that had been collected in antiquity met a variety of fates. A great many pieces were melted in the foundries, burned in the limekilns, or mutilated by Christians. Some works of art literally went underground until the Renaissance or later: the followers of non-Christian cults often reverently and carefully buried their cult objects rather than allow Christians to deface them. Other pieces were preserved by being reinterpreted in Christian terms: the equestrian statue of the emperor Marcus Aurelius, for example, was mistakenly identified as Constantine, the first Christian emperor, and so was left unharmed at Rome. Some sculptures were "purified" so that they could be used as decoration in churches, and engraved gems, cameos, and coins were sometimes adapted to religious decoration. Privately, pieces of ancient sculpture might be built into homes or kept as curiosities. There was little active collecting, and the only real collector whose name we know before the thirteenth century was Henry of Blois, an Englishman, who in the twelfth century traveled to Rome to have himself named Archbishop of Western England. Failing at this, he consoled himself by buying a large collection of classical sculpture, which at the time was thought very eccentric.[7]

The Renaissance was marked by a revival of interest in the history, literature, philosophy, and art of classical antiquity. First in Italy, then throughout Europe, nostalgia for the classical past combined with a new sense of the importance of man to produce a shift of emphasis from the religious to the secular world and an outburst of creative activity in literature, painting, sculpture, and architecture. The humanists' intensified study of the classics contributed to the growth of important libraries. In trying to gain more reliable and direct knowledge of antiquity, they sought and collected lost or previously unknown manuscripts of classical works. In admiring ancient art for its beauty, style, and most especially for its subject matter, the humanists stimulated ancient art collecting.

The main sources for the supply of classical art in the Renaissance were chance discoveries in Italy and the very active commerce conducted by the Italian maritime republics of Venice and Genoa with the eastern Mediterranean. In the fourteenth century, the evidence for collecting classical art is fragmentary, but it reveals a rapidly growing interest. Some collectors were eager for anything ancient, others specialized in a few areas. Oliviero Forzetta, the earliest well-documented art collector of the period, included coins, medals, marble and bronze sculpture, and cameos in his collection, while the Italian scholar Petrarch, the first and greatest humanist, collected only coins and medals, which were especially satisfying to him because of his interest in famous men of the classical past.

Ancient coins were a major interest of Renaissance collectors, but unlike other categories of classical art, there is little or no evidence that coins were consciously collected in antiquity, and there is little evidence of what the ancients thought of them as works of art.[8] Suetonius (*Divus Augustus* 73) records that the emperor Augustus gave out foreign coins or coins with portraits of ancient kings as gifts on special occasions, but these may have constituted little more than curiosities or mementos.

In the Middle Ages, coin collecting seems to have been rare both because of the Christian suspicion of the pagan past and the shortage of mintable metal which was an encouragement to their being melted down. Amazingly, a few ancient coins survived in circulation until the nineteenth century: copper coins struck during the reign of Constantine in the fourth century after Christ were still in use in remote areas of southern France during the reign of Napoleon III.[9] Other coins have survived through being used in jewelry or as decoration on metal vessels, but the main source of the great number of coins available to collectors during and since the Renaissance is the discovery of hoards of coins that have been uncovered by accidental or deliberate excavation.

In the Renaissance, as today, coins were often the base upon which collections of other types of ancient art were built. They satisfied the humanists' desire for direct sources of information about the past, and connoisseurs were attracted by their beauty and intrinsic value. As the Renaissance progressed, coin collecting spread rapidly, and virtually every collection of ancient art included coins. Soon after the invention of the printing press in the fifteenth century, a number of treatises on coins were produced, and one scholar in the sixteenth century reported that his research on Roman coins had taken him to more than 380 collections in Italy, more than 200 in France, more than 200 in Holland, and more than 175 in Germany.[10]

The most important centers for collecting ancient art in the Renaissance were Florence, which was dominated politically, economically, and culturally by the Medici family, and Rome, where the great papal collections were assembled. From about the middle of the fifteenth century the Medici spent great amounts of money and energy in assembling spectacular collections of coins, cameos, engraved gems, and bronze and marble sculpture. The Medici collections did not survive the Renaissance intact, and we have only scanty information about how they came to be dispersed. The collection of Lorenzo the Magnificent (1449–1492), for example, had to be abandoned hastily when the French invaded Florence in 1494, and according to tradition some of the pieces were sold at auction. Today only a few pieces known to have belonged to the Medici remain in Florence.

Rome in the early Renaissance was a rather undistinguished city in comparison with the wealthier, more populous Florence and Venice. The city had suffered greatly from invasions and the plague during the Middle Ages, and even the popes had abandoned it for Avignon during the fourteenth century. When they returned and the economy became more vigorous, Rome began to share in the cultural life of the Renaissance already being enjoyed by the cities to the north.

One unexpected benefit of the intensive building activity in Rome in the late fifteenth and early sixteenth centuries was the discovery of great quantities of buried ancient art, especially large sculptures. As a consequence, private collections in Rome grew rapidly. Pope Paul II (r. 1464–1471), the first of many popes to collect ancient art, assembled a large collection of sculpture, coins, bronzes, gems, and cameos, but he seems to have considered the collections his private property, and since he did not leave any directions for their care after his death, his successor, Sixtus IV (r. 1471–1484), sold them to Lorenzo de'Medici.

Pope Julius II (r. 1503–1513), however, was one collector who did consider the future of his collections, and in so doing he founded the Vatican collections of ancient art.[11] Under his leadership the papacy regained its power in Europe, and with his patronage the arts flourished in Rome. He planned the rebuilding of St. Peter's and hired the finest architects and artists, including Bramante, Michelangelo, and Raphael. When he came to the Vatican, he brought his own collection of classical sculpture, including a marble statue of Apollo that had been found near Rome in the fifteenth century. To display this piece and others that he hoped to acquire, he incorporated the Belvedere Villa into the architectural complex of the Vatican and created a sculpture court, the "Belvedere Court." For the next 400 years the Apollo Belvedere was "the most admired piece of sculpture in the world,"[12] inspiring Michelangelo, Goethe, Canova, and countless other lovers of art. In 1506 Julius II purchased another impressive ancient sculpture, the Laocoon, discovered that year in the palace of Nero on the Esquiline, and this came to be admired equally with the Apollo.

Pope Julius II's successors continued to acquire ancient sculptures to fill the niches in the Belvedere Court, but their main interests lay in building their own family collections. The quality of the great collections in the Villa Medici (Popes Leo X, r. 1513–1521, and Clement VII, r. 1523–1534), the Palazzo Farnese (Pope Paul III, r. 1534–1549), the Villa Borghese (Pope Paul V, r. 1605–1621), and the Villa Ludovisi (Pope Gregory XV, r. 1621–1623) far exceeded that of any of the other private collections in Rome, of which there were many. The less powerful families sometimes did succeed in acquiring works that were widely admired (such as Francesco Fusconi's statue of Meleager, now in the Vatican), [13] but more often they had to be content with quantity rather than quality.

Competition for fine antiquities was keen from the sixteenth century on. Owing to the continued building activity in and around Rome, many pieces were found, but works of the highest quality remained relatively rare while the demand among collectors grew rapidly. Although the powerful families sometimes increased their collections with discoveries from their own estates, more often they had to vie with each other and foreigners for the best pieces, and so prices rose steeply. Even popes were not immune to competition, for Julius II had had to outbid other avid collectors for the Laocoon in 1506. Competition for lesser antiquities also increased later in the sixteenth century, as we learn from the report of Isabella d'Este's agent that prices of ancient coins in Rome had risen unreasonably high. [14]

In the sixteenth and seventeenth centuries, the popularity of collecting ancient art spread through Europe first among royalty, then among those who could afford "royal" prices. In this period also much attention began to be paid to the decorative display of sculpture collections. Many collectors constructed special galleries or sculpture gardens, and damaged works were often made more attractive to their owners by restoration (polishing surfaces, reworking contours, and supplying missing parts). About the middle of the sixteenth century Duke Albert V of Bavaria built an impressive gallery, the "Antiquarium," in Munich to house the large collection of classical sculpture that he had acquired through the notorious dealer Jacopo Strada, former court antiquary to the Hapsburg Holy Roman Emperors Ferdinand I and Maximilian II. (The best of the Antiquarium's pieces are now in Munich's Glyptothek.) In France, Francis I (r. 1515–1547) developed an intense interest in classical sculpture and acquired copies in bronze and marble as well as ancient pieces for Fontainebleau. Louis XIV (r. 1643–1715) also collected ancient originals and modern copies for display at Versailles, and he was so interested in his coin collection (inherited from his uncle) that he had it installed in the Louvre along with a specially appointed curator. However, Louis finally had the collection moved to Versailles so that he might have daily access to it. Other cabinets of ancient coins were assembled by James II of England, Frederick III of Denmark, Queen Christina of Sweden, and Frederick William I (1644–1688) of Brandenburg (the "Great Elector"). In Antwerp Peter Paul Rubens, the great Flemish painter, assembled a collection of over 18,000 ancient coins and more than ninety pieces of classical sculpture that he displayed in a specially constructed gallery-wing of his house. [15]

In England three major collectors of ancient art stand out in the first half of the seventeenth century. Thomas Howard, second Earl of Arundel (1585–1646), formed a large and important collection of sculpture, much of which is now in the Ashmolean Museum at Oxford and in the British Museum, and he built the first English gallery for display of his collection in his home, Arundel House. George Villiers, Duke of Buckingham (1592–1628), was greatly impressed by Arundel's collection and near the end of his life also began to collect. Charles I (r. 1625–1649) collected actively from early adolescence until about 1640 and knew both Arundel's and Buckingham's collections. The sources of these collections tell us much about the changing climate of collecting in this period. The major source for large sculpture was Rome, as it had been in the sixteenth century and as it continued to be in the eighteenth century. An important secondary market, however, was born when the many collectors throughout Europe began to sell to each other. In 1627 Buckingham purchased pieces of ancient sculpture from Rubens when the artist was temporarily in financial straits; and also in that year Charles I obtained paintings and ancient statues in Mantua from the Gonzagas, who were bankrupt. Arundel and Buckingham also opened a new avenue, to be used again in the eighteenth century by Lord Elgin, when they sent agents to the East Mediterranean in search of classical art and enlisted the aid of the British ambassador to Turkey.

As British commercial power grew in Europe and around the Mediterranean during the eighteenth century, British collectors rapidly became more numerous and more active, with the result that by the end of the century they could be considered second only to the Italians as collectors of ancient art. The excavations of Herculaneum, which began in earnest in 1738, and of Pompeii about ten years later caught the imagination of the public, inspiring renewed interest in all things classical, and producing a virtual mania among the English for classical art. All who could afford to do so traveled to Rome, where professional antiquarians could be hired as guides. Early in the century, these guides were usually Italians, but they were soon displaced by English artists and architects who needed another form of support while living in Rome. Inevitably, with easy access to excavations and Italian collections, the antiquarians became dealers. Gavin Hamilton, an English artist-dealer, James Byres, a Scot dealer-architect (who showed Gibbon Rome),[16] and Thomas Jenkins, a dealer who was the richest and most influential Englishman in Rome in the second half of the eighteenth century,[17] were instrumental in forming many of the greatest collections of ancient sculpture in England.

The classical art collections formed by Englishmen—both titled and untitled—in the eighteenth and early nineteenth centuries were often installed in special galleries in grand London houses or country estates where they became prestigious emblems of the wealth, power, and good taste of their owners. Early in the eighteenth-century Dr. Richard Mead, physician to George I and Sir Isaac Newton, formed a celebrated collection of Greek manuscripts, coins, gems, marbles, and bronzes, and he opened the "Museum Meadianum" in his London house regularly to visitors and students. Thomas Herbert, eighth Earl of Pembroke, installed his collection of ancient sculptures in Wilton House; Thomas Coke, later Earl of Leicester, made his collection in Holkham Hall in Norfolk one of the great sights in eighteenth-century England; and Henry Blundell, using Thomas Jenkins as his agent, acquired five hundred and fifty-three pieces of sculpture, the largest collection of the century, which he displayed in Ince Hall, Lancashire. William, Earl of Shelburne, first Marquess of Lansdowne, using Gavin Hamilton and Thomas Jenkins as agents, acquired one of the finest and most widely admired collections of classical sculpture, which he installed in impressive galleries in Lansdowne House in London. His collection remained intact until the early part of the twentieth century when it was sold.

Ancient art was also included in many of the miscellaneous collections of "natural and artificial curiosities" that were popular in England in the seventeenth and eighteenth centuries. Although the quality of the antiquities in these collections was usually not very high—a striking exception being the famous Portland Vase, purchased by the Dowager Duchess of Portland in 1784 for her museum and now in the British Museum—some of these collections played an important role in the survival and appreciation of ancient art when they became the basis upon which great public collections of ancient art were built. The Ashmolean Museum at Oxford began in the late seventeenth century as a "closet of rarities" purchased by Elias Ashmole from two eminent botanists. Ashmole added his own antiquities, coins, medals, paintings, books, and manuscripts, and in the nineteenth century the museum acquired its major collections of ancient art. The British Museum, founded in 1753, was based on the large, miscellaneous collection left to the nation by Dr. Hans Sloane. Objects of natural history predominated, but the collection also included 32,000 coins and medals, 700 cut stones, and 1,125 antiquities. The first classical art of importance, however, came to the British Museum later in the century when Sir William Hamilton sold his Greek vases to the museum in 1772, and the first important ancient sculptures entered the museum when it acquired the collection of Richard Townley in 1805.

The British Museum's acquisition of the Hamilton vase collection signaled a growing interest in Greek ceramic art among collectors, scholars, and the public. Before the second half of the eighteenth century, vases had received little attention. In the nineteenth century when systematic excavations in Italy and Greece uncovered great quantities of vases, they became a major component of most collections. The history of collecting Greek vases is surveyed by Dietrich von Bothmer in the following essay.

The Townley marbles came to the British Museum at an important juncture in the appreciation and collecting of classical sculpture. After the fall of Constantinople in 1453, the East Mediterranean was closed to European and British trade. As a consequence, mining for classical sculpture was limited mainly to Roman imperial sites in Italy, and so most pieces available to collectors were Graeco-Roman copies. The taste and admiration for Graeco-Roman art was so strong that when Greek originals were found, they were sometimes "doctored" by restorers to make them look more like the familiar copies. During the eighteenth century, the scholars Johann Richardson (father and son) and J. J. Winckelmann began to suspect that most known sculptures were Roman copies of Greek originals and that the Greek products were far superior; but it was not until the nineteenth century, with the defeat of the French and the rise of British power around the Mediterranean, that quantities of Greek art became available and the scholars' theories could be tested. When Lord Elgin brought the sculptures from the Parthenon in Athens to London early in the nineteenth century, so unfamiliar was the style of these fifth-century Greek works that Parliament agreed to purchase them for the British Museum only after much debate, and then for a great deal less than Elgin had spent on them. They were seen as the antithesis of the recently acquired Graeco-Roman Townley marbles, and for a time even their authenticity was called into question by those who found it difficult to synthesize the new understanding of Greek art with earlier assumptions about classical art. As the nineteenth century progressed, however, Graeco-Roman copies such as those in the Townley collection began to lose their appeal for collectors in favor of the growing number of original Greek works supplied through scientific archaeological excavations and chance discoveries.

The nineteenth century saw the rise of great public museums as major collectors of classical art. The British Museum's classical collection was already established when Napoleon invaded Italy in 1796 and began to send cartloads of paintings and classical sculptures back to the Muséum National (later named the Musée Napoleon) in the Louvre in Paris. In taking Italy's best art as booty, Napoleon was not unlike the Roman general Marcellus taking booty from Syracuse: he considered the art an important part of the material wealth of the conquered nation, he recognized the prestige it brought to his victory, and he considered it an appropriate patriotic adornment to the capital city. Like the Romans, the French were delighted, and the public's eagerness for classical art was further stimulated by the numerous plaster casts taken from the more famous pieces and circulated around the world. With Napoleon's defeat, the Musée Napoleon was dissolved in 1815, and while many of the pieces were sent back to Italy, others stayed in Paris or were sold to collectors. One of the lasting effects of the short-lived Musée Napoleon was to raise the consciousness of other states about the importance of major public collections. Prince Ludwig of Bavaria, who purchased a number of the Italian pieces left in France at the end of the Napoleonic era as well as Greek sculpture from the Temple on Aegina, directed the construction of the Glyptothek in Munich; an enormous museum was begun in Berlin early in the century; and both the Vatican and the British Museum undertook new construction to house their rapidly growing collections. In 1870 the United States joined the trend of public collecting with the founding of the Metropolitan Museum of Art in New York and the Museum of Fine Arts in Boston.

Early in the nineteenth century classical art began to have an attraction for Americans, and sets of casts, especially of pieces that had traveled from Italy to the Musée Napoleon, were brought to Boston, New York, and Philadelphia. Even earlier, one illustrious American had dreamed of assembling a private collection of classical sculpture: about 1771, as Thomas Jefferson was completing plans for Monticello, his mountain-top villa in Virginia, he recorded in his building notebook an ambitious wish-list of thirteen famous classical sculptures and seven well-known paintings to be installed in a gallery there. As the list included such unobtainable masterpieces as the Apollo Belvedere, the Medici Venus, and the Farnese Hercules, the project would appear to have been a pipe dream, conceived by an idealistic young architect and classical scholar. In Jefferson's time, however, casts of these works were available in England and Europe, and it is quite possible that his gallery was more practically conceived as an assembly of casts. In 1771, Jefferson had not yet traveled to Europe, so at this time he could have had firsthand knowledge of neither the originals nor probably even full-scale copies. Instead, he had very likely received his information and inspiration a few years earlier when he visited Philadelphia and made the acquaintance of Dr. John Morgan, who had traveled in Italy and had assembled a miscellaneous collection of natural curiosities, art objects, and books and prints on art and architecture.[18]

As the nineteenth century progressed, Greek vases, coins, and sculpture traveled to the United States in increasing numbers.[19] Undoubtedly many of these pieces were kept privately, but in the first part of the century, we know most about those that were installed in public places: in 1805 President Jefferson donated one hundred and fifty Roman coins to the American Philosophical Society in Philadelphia, and by 1811 the American Museum of the Tamany Society (in New York) had a collection of some three hundred coins; in 1836 a Greek vase was given to the American Philosophical Society in Philadelphia; and at various times tombstones, votive stelai, portraits, and sarcophagi were given to institutions in Boston, Brooklyn, Philadelphia, and Washington.

The great period of American collecting, however, did not begin until the last decade of the nineteenth century. In this period it was not unusual for wealthy collectors to acquire classical art primarily as decoration for their grand homes: Isabella Stewart Gardner bought a few Graeco-Roman sculptures for Fenway Court, her palazzo in Boston, as did James Deering for his Villa Vizcaya near Miami. For others collecting was a more serious passion. William Randolph Hearst amassed great quantities of Greek vases and Graeco-Roman sculpture from 1901 until his death in 1951, and while the collection was intended for his pleasure at his California castle, La Cuesta Encantada, it grew so large that at Hearst's death many pieces still lay unpacked in warehouses. The Hearst sculptures were donated to the Los Angeles County Museum of Art, and the vases have entered various private and public collections. Henry Walters, a railroad baron from Baltimore, formed another important collection of classical art in the first half of the twentieth century. Reportedly spending about a million dollars a year from 1899 until his death in 1931, Walters assembled an outstanding classical collection with major purchases in virtually every category of ancient art.[20] He installed the collection in the Walters Art Gallery, built by his father in Baltimore and now a public museum. Three other important collections formed in the early twentieth century are also now in public institutions through bequest or purchase: the vase collection of Joseph Clarke Hoppin, bequeathed to Harvard at his death in 1925; the vase collection of Albert Gallatin, purchased by the Metropolitan Museum of Art in 1941; and the vase and coin collections of David Moore Robinson, at Harvard and the University of Mississippi (the vases) and the American Numismatic Society (the coins) following his death in 1958.

From its very beginning in the nineteenth century, classical art collecting in America has been characterized by an atmosphere of cooperation between collectors and public museums. Contrary to British or European tradition, ancient art in the United States has rarely been handed down from generation to generation within a family. More frequently, American collections have passed to the public domain within a single generation by donation or bequest. Virtually every public collection in the United States has been created or enriched by private collectors: Wright Ludington, for example, has given real substance to the classical collections of the Santa Barbara Museum with donations and loans from his classical sculpture collection; Norman Davis, who has been collecting only since World War II, has created the core of the classical collection at the Seattle Art Museum with his donations of coins, sculpture, and vases; and Burton Y. Berry's collection of several thousand ancient objects (jewelry, bronzes, and glass), assembled over half a century and donated over a period ending in 1976, has become a major component of the Indiana University Art Museum's classical collection. His coin collection was donated to the American Numismatic Society and has been published in the first two American volumes of the *Sylloge Nummorum Graecorum*. The greatest donation by one collector, however, was made by J. Paul Getty, who in 1953 created a museum for his collections of antiquities, paintings, and decorative arts and at his death in 1976 left an enormous endowment to ensure their continued growth. Private collectors have also enriched public collections with long-term loans: Jeffrey Miller's Greek coin collection, on loan to the Virginia Museum since 1978, has added needed breadth to that museum's limited coin holdings, while Walter Bareiss' collection of Greek vases, on loan to the J. Paul Getty Museum, adds depth to that museum's already extensive holdings.

Since the 1950's, private collectors in America have been especially generous in making their art available to the public by lending to special exhibitions organized by museums. The success of thematic exhibitions such as *The Art of South Italy: Vases from Magna Graecia*, organized by the Virginia Museum in 1982, has often depended on the willingness of private collectors to share special pieces for which there is no near substitute in public collections. In the South Italy exhibition, for example, the name-pieces of several vase-painters (a column-krater attributed to the Maplewood Painter, collection of Joseph Veach Noble, and a bell-krater attributed to the Dechter Painter, collection of Hanita and Aaron Dechter) added a special dimension in illustrating the development of vase-painting in South Italy. In recent years, a particularly interesting phenomenon has been the proliferation of special exhibitions that focus on the private collections themselves. The pioneer exhibition *Ancient Art in American Private Collections* (The Fogg Art Museum, 1954) included pieces from collections in Canada and Cuba as well as the United States, while those since have been limited to collections in the United States (but often including public collections with the private ones). *Ancient Art from New York Private Collections* (The Metropolitan Museum of Art, 1959), the first of the exhibitions to focus on regional collecting, was followed by *Greek Art in Private Collections of Southern California* and *Etruscan Art from West Coast Collections* (The Art Gallery, University of California, Santa Barbara, 1963 and 1967, respectively), *Ten Centuries that Shaped the West: Greek and Roman Art in Texas Collections* (Institute for the Arts, Rice University, 1970), *Roman Art in West Coast Collections* (The Art Gallery, University of California, Santa Barbara, 1973), and *Classical Art from Carolina Collections* (North Carolina Museum of Art, 1974). Further specialization was introduced with exhibitions of only vases from collections in various regions: *Attic Vase Painting in New England Collections* (The Fogg Art Museum, 1972), *Greek Vase-*

Painting in Midwestern Collections (Art Institute of Chicago, 1979), and *Art, Myth, and Culture: Greek Vases from Southern Collections* (New Orleans Museum of Art and Tulane University, 1981). The few collections that have merited their own exhibitions, notably the collection of Norbert Schimmel at the Metropolitan Museum of Art in 1975, and the collections of Nelson Bunker Hunt and William Herbert Hunt in the present exhibition, have added a further refinement to the tradition of American collectors' sharing their treasures with the public through museums. While such exhibitions by definition can only be temporary, through their catalogues they have often continued to stimulate scholars and the interested public long after the objects have been returned to their owners.[21]

NOTES:
1. The literature on collecting is also vast. The following general works have been particularly useful in preparing this essay: Joseph Alsop, *The Rare Art Traditions. The History of Art Collecting and Its Linked Phenomena Wherever These Have Appeared* (New York, 1982); Elvira Eliza Clain-Stefanelli, *Numismatics—An Ancient Science*, Bulletin 229, *Contributions from the Museum of History and Technology*, Paper 32, Smithsonian Institution (Washington, D.C., 1965); Francis Haskell and Nicholas Penny, *Taste and the Antique* (New Haven, 1981); Niels von Holst, *Creators, Collectors and Connoisseurs* (London, 1967); J. J. Pollitt, *The Art of Rome c. 753 B.C.–337 A.D., Sources and Documents* (Englewood Cliffs, N.J., 1966); Cornelius C. Vermeule, *Greek and Roman Sculpture in America* (Malibu and Berkeley, 1981); John Walker, "1000 Years of the Art Trade," in *Experts' Choice: 1000 Years of the Art Trade*, catalogue of the seventh International Exhibition presented by C.I.N.O.A. at the Virginia Museum, April 22–June 12 1983 (New York, 1983); Roberto Weiss, *The Renaissance Discovery of Classical Antiquity* (Oxford, 1969).
2. Alsop, p. 190.
3. Cicero *Epistulae ad Atticum* 1.4.3; 1.1.5; 1.6.2; 1.8.2; 1.9.2; 1.10.3; *Epistulae ad Familiares* 7.23.1–3.
4. Cornelius C. Vermeule, "Graeco-Roman Statues: Purpose and Settings, I," *Burlington Magazine* 117 (1975): 204–211.
5. Cicero *In Verrem* I and II.
6. Alsop, pp. 209–210.
7. Alsop, p. 262.
8. Clain-Stefanelli, *Numismatics—An Ancient Science*, pp. 8–11; and Cornelius C. Vermeule, "Numismatics in Antiquity: the Preservation and Display of Coins in Ancient Greece and Rome," *Swiss Numismatic Review* 54 (1975): 5–32.
9. Clain-Stefanelli, p. 6.
10. Clain-Stefanelli, p. 19.
11. The history of the popes as patrons and collectors of art is the subject of the exhibition *The Vatican Collections: The Papacy and Art* at the Metropolitan Museum of Art, the Art Institute of Chicago, and the San Francisco Museums in 1983–1984. Works from the Belvedere Court, including the Apollo, are included in the exhibition.
12. Kenneth Clark, *Civilization: A Personal View* (New York, 1969), p. 2.
13. Haskell and Penny, *Taste and the Antique*, pp. 13 and 263–264.
14. Alsop, p. 425.
15. Jeffrey M. Muller, "Rubens's Museum of Antique Sculpture: an Introduction," *Art Bulletin* 59 (1977): 571–582.
16. On Byres, see Brinsley Ford, "James Byres, Principal Antiquarian for the English Visitors to Rome," *Apollo* 99 (1974): 446–461.
17. On Jenkins, see Brinsley Ford, "Thomas Jenkins: Banker, Dealer and Unofficial English Agent," *Apollo* 99 (1974): 416–425.
18. Seymour Howard, "Thomas Jefferson's Art Gallery for Monticello," *Art Bulletin* 59 (1977): 583–600.
19. For an excellent summary of the history of collecting classical sculpture in America, see Cornelius C. Vermeule, *Greek and Roman Sculpture in America* (Malibu and Berkeley, 1981), pp. 11–22.
20. Dorothy Kent Hill, "The Classical Collection and its Growth," *Apollo* 100 (1974): 352.
21. I wish to thank Dietrich von Bothmer, Amy Brauer, Elfriede Knauer, Pinkney Near, and William Peck for advice and suggestions in preparing this essay and Betty Stacy and Margaret Burcham of the Virginia Museum Library for research assistance.

[10] Attic Panathenaic Amphora
Attributed to the Berlin Painter
Circa 490–480 B.C.

The Vases of Nelson Bunker Hunt

NOTES ON COLLECTORS OF VASES

Dietrich von Bothmer

> *"Big money is now being paid for the Etruscan vases and of them many are certainly beautiful and excellent. There is no traveller who does not want to own some of them. Money is not valued so highly as at home: I am afraid I, too, shall be seduced."*
>
> (J. W. Goethe, *Italian Journey*, Naples, March 9, 1787)

When Goethe met Sir William Hamilton, the British Envoy and Plenipotentiary in Naples, Hamilton had already sold his first collection of vases to the British Museum some fifteen years earlier and professed not to be interested in starting another one. Yet, a few years later a second Hamilton collection of vases had come into being and was published under the supervision of Wilhelm Tischbein, recently appointed Director of the Academy of Paintings at Naples, in four folio volumes printed between 1791 and 1795. In 1798 Hamilton decided to ship his collection to England, but of the twenty-four packing cases, eight were lost when H.M.S. *Colossus,* a 74-gun man o'war on which they were transported, foundered off the Scilly Isles. The other vases that arrived on the *Foudroyant* were sold to Thomas Hope, a rich Amsterdam merchant who had emigrated to England in 1796. When the Hope collection was sold in London in 1917 the vases were dispersed all over the globe—from Lisbon to Los Angeles, from Stockholm to Dublin.

Hamilton had bemoaned the loss of the vases on the *Colossus,* for he considered his second collection even finer than his first and, in fact, had almost sold it to the King of Prussia in 1796. He could hardly have anticipated that in 1974 the wreck of the *Colossus* would be discovered off Samson, one of the Isles of Scilly, and that in several years of underwater excavations some thirty-odd thousand fragments of the "lost" part of his collection would be recovered.

While Hamilton was the most famous of the eighteenth-century collectors, others had preceded him, notably the Comte de Caylus (whose vases are now in the Cabinet des Médailles in Paris) and Cardinal Gualtieri who in about 1720 bought the collection of the Neapolitan lawyer Valetta. The Gualtieri vases were housed in the Vatican, since 1744 in a separate room (though by no means accessible to visitors).

The Golden Age of collecting vases, however, began in the nineteenth century, following the spectacular discovery of the cemetery of Vulci in the spring of 1828. In little over a year 3,000 painted vases were unearthed on the property of Lucien Bonaparte who in 1814 was created Prince of Canino by the Pope. It must be remembered that local patriotism encouraged the misnomer "Etruscan" for any vase found on Italian soil, even though some of the vases bore perfectly legible Greek inscriptions, recognized as such as early as 1754. Nor was the mania limited to Italy and Italians: Wedgwood called his pottery "Etruria" in 1769, and more than half a century later Prosper Mérimée entitled one of his short stories "Le Vase Etrusque." But quarrels of scholars over matters of dating and attribution have never discouraged collectors whose attraction to the objects of their particular passion has always been stronger than academic definitions. Canino did not keep his vases for himself for very long. He had seen to it that a catalogue of inscribed vases was published rather rapidly in an Italian and a French edition, dated respectively 1829 and 1830, and an English translation of his Italian catalogue was printed in the British periodical *Archaeologia* in volume twenty-three (1831), the labor of his son-in-law Dudley, Lord Stuart. Many of his vases, therefore, changed hands shortly after they had been found; others were sold at auction, mostly in Paris (1834, 1837, 1840, 1841, 1843, 1845, 1848, 1849: the last five sales after his death on June 29, 1840). One choice group of vases (now in Leyden) was sold in 1839 to King William I of Holland; many other vases entered the Louvre, the British Museum, the Berlin Museum and the Pinakothek of King Ludwig I of Bavaria, not to mention the large number of private collections that profited from sudden availability of fine Greek vases. Canino's discoveries at Vulci also gave an impetus to other explorers—Dorow, Candelori, Campanari, Basseggio, Fossati, Feoli—and went hand in hand with the formation of such private collections as those of E. Durand, Magnoncourt, the Duc de Luynes, the Vicomte de Beugnot, the Baron Roger, N. Revil, the Comte Pourtalès-Gorgier, and the Comte de Clarac in France, the Marquess of Northampton, the Earl of Pembroke, J. Millingen, W. W. Hope in England, and many more. If their names are still remembered today it is largely because so many collections were later sold at auction and provided with decent sale catalogues that made up for the lack of illustrations by ample descriptions.

The founding of an international Instituto di Corrispondenza Archeologica in Rome coincided with Canino's discoveries at Vulci. Frederick William, the Crown Prince of Prussia, had taken the Institute under his aegis, but the roster of associates, honorary members, full members, and corresponding fellows, numbering more than a hundred and fifty in its first year, was truly international and includes princes, ambassadors, scholars, artists and collectors. The publications of the Instituto, the *Annali*, the *Bulletino*, and the *Monumenti* furnished the interested community with a wealth of information, and it is enviable today to read of the ease with which new discoveries and acquisitions were discussed and communicated. Scholars and collectors were on the best of terms with one another, and corresponding fellows actually corresponded.

It is not surprising that in this enlightened climate collecting flourished, both in the public and in the private sector. There must have been some rivalry, but there also was much generosity: one thinks of C.L.F. Panckoucke whose heirs sold his vases to Boulogne in 1861 for a modest sum, of Antoine Vivenel whose gift to Compiègne dates from 1843 (he died in 1892), or of the Duc de Luynes who on October 28, 1862, gave his entire collection to the Cabinet des Médailles, noble examples that were soon followed elsewhere.

In the second half of the nineteenth century collecting of vases continued unabated, and again sale catalogues are our safest guide to the sequence in which private collections became available on the open market. Paris was still in the lead, and among the many collectors we should cite Raoul-Rochette (1855), Eugène Piot (1857, 1864, 1870, 1890), Louis Fould (1860), the Comte Pourtalès-Gorgier (1865), the Vicomte de Janzé (1866), A. Raifé (1867), Noël des Vergers (1867), the Prince Napoléon, "Plon-Plon" as he was called (1869), the Prince Paul Demidoff (1869), Paravey (1879), Rayet (1879 and 1886), R. Sabatier (1890), J. Gréau (1891), A. van Branteghem (1892), and the Count M. Tyszkiewicz (1898), while from sales in London, at the same time, we learn of Bram

Hertz (1851 and 1859), Emil Braun (1851), Samuel Rogers (1856), Matthew Uzielli (1861), Rev. J. Hamilton Gray (1888), and William Henry Forman (1899, 1900).

In Italy, meanwhile, a new generation of collectors and antiquarians had emerged, and the fabulous finds at Vulci of 1828 and 1829 were soon eclipsed by the even bigger collection of the Marchese Gianpietro Campana. No complete count of his vases has ever been made, but there are 3,791 in his printed catalogue of 1857 (which did not include the thousands of fragments). There must have been many a collector who in the pursuit of his passion ruined himself, but Campana is surely the first whose acquisitions led first to colossal embezzlements and then to a papal prison, from which he was released before he had served out his sentence by the intervention of Napoleon III. What was first a miracle and then a scandal has for over a hundred years become the pride of the Louvre, for there is no other museum in the world that can rival its collection of ancient vases. Among the antiquarians of this period the name of Castellani stands out. Alessandro and Augusto were the sons of Fortunato Pio Castellani, the founder of the famous jewelry workshop that specialized in reproductions or adaptations of ancient jewelry. Of the two brothers, Augusto took over the company but also collected and traded. In 1865 he sold 250 vases to Vienna. His own collection of vases was divided in three portions: one was given to the City of Rome and was allocated to the Palazzo dei Conservatori; another went to the Museo Artistico Industriale (now incorporated in the Conservatori). The rest he kept but was given long after his death by his son Alfredo to the Museo Nazionale di Villa Giulia. Alessandro meanwhile sold a large number of vases in Paris in 1866. An ardent Republican, he had been imprisoned in Rome by Pius X; after his release he settled in Paris and made frequent trips to England to stay in touch with Mazzini and other Italian exiles. He also established splendid relations with the British Museum and with the Ashmolean Museum in the seventies and even exhibited over 300 of his objects (though no vases) in three rooms of Memorial Hall during the centennial held at Philadelphia in 1876. After his death in 1883 his entire collection was sold in two separate sales: the antiquities (over one thousand lots) in Rome in the Palazzo Castellani (March 1884) and his post-classical objects in Paris two months later.

It is with this tradition in mind, sketched here in a few broad outlines, that the collectors of vases in this century can best be appreciated.

With the unification of Italy in 1870 private excavations in Etruria like those of Canino, Campana, Torlonia, and many others came to a standstill and there no longer could be any prospect of amassing thousands of vases by merely digging, as it were, in one's own back yard. At the same time knowledge of Greek vases, their origins, dates, and styles advanced considerably. Many more books on vases were published, and photographs often accompanied the descriptions rather than line drawings, engravings, or lithographs. Moreover, many more vases entered public collections, often thanks to the generosity of private collectors, and there is today hardly a country in Europe that does not have at least one respectable collection of Greek vases.

Nor has collecting been limited to Europe. As early as 1775 an American couple, Mr. and Mrs. Ralph Izard from South Carolina, was painted by Copley in Naples with a large Attic red-figured volute-krater in the manner of the Niobid Painter in the background. Ralph Izard's cousin, John Izard Middleton, likewise from South Carolina, traveled with Dodwell in Italy in 1808–1809. A vase of his, a red-figured lekythos found in Metaponto, was published by Millingen in 1822 in his *Ancient Unedited Monuments*. Middleton spent almost his entire life in Europe and died in Paris in 1849. It is, therefore, doubtful whether his lekythos ever crossed the ocean, just as it is not at all certain whether the volute-krater in the Izard portrait belonged to the sitters or was a prop in Copley's studio. We are, however, better informed about a red-figured kylix by the Penthesilea Painter that Joseph Bonaparte (or the Comte de Survilliers as he called himself in this country) gave to the Philosophical Society in Philadelphia in 1836. Another of his vases, a splendid red-figured stamnos by the Kleophrades Painter was given by him to his friend Dr. Nathaniel Chapman and entered first Memorial Hall (in 1899) and later the University Museum (in 1935). Throughout the nineteenth century more and more vases came to America, and they appeared even at public auctions as early as 1873. While the splendid collection of Greek vases in Boston is chiefly the result of E. P. Warren's great knowledge and efforts, it should not be forgotten that many came to the Museum of Fine Arts as gifts from Thomas G. Appleton, Henry J. and W. S. Bigelow, B. W. Crowninshield, Alfred Greenough, Henry P. Kidder, and George W. Wales. In 1890 the Union League Club of New York held an exhibition of American Landscapes and Greek Art. Of the sixty-nine vases there shown, sixty-one belonged to Thomas B. Clarke whose collections were sold in 1899, 1917, and 1925.

This increased interest in vases was by no means restricted to the East Coast. The Art Institute in Chicago got its first vases in 1889, and there were private collections in St. Louis before the turn of the century (now at Washington University). Farther west, Phoebe Apperson Hearst, advised by Professor Alfred Emerson, began to collect vases in the late nineties and the first years of this century with a view to establishing a strong classical section in the University Museum of Anthropology at Berkeley, while across the Bay M. H. de Young had given his vases to the San Francisco museum that now bears his name.

William Randolph Hearst, the son of Phoebe Apperson Hearst, began collecting vases at the age of thirty-eight in 1901 and continued for half a century until a few months before his death on August 14, 1951. Such a long period of collecting privately is in itself a record, as is, in this century, the sheer number of vases acquired. Some minor pieces were sold by him through H. A. Kende at Gimbel's in 1942, as were some from St. Donat's castle in Wales at Sotheby's in July 1939, and fifty-two of the vases acquired in London after the second war had been given by him to the Los Angeles County Museum of Art between 1948 and 1951, yet at the time of his death his collection numbered about four hundred vases displayed or stored at San Simeon. In a series of corporate reorganizations his collection and the castle at San Simeon had become the property of the Hearst Corporation that in 1956 sold sixty-five Greek vases to the Metropolitan Museum; twenty-seven were acquired by his son Randolph A. Hearst in 1962; five vases went to the Walters Art Gallery in Baltimore in 1958; ten vases bought by Hearst at the Earl Fitzwilliam Sale of 1948 never went to San Simeon but stayed in a warehouse in the Bronx. They were sold at auction in New York on December 7, 1951, and the corporation sold a hundred and thirty vases, again through Parke-Bernet, on April 5, 1963. A score had been either sold or given away privately, but the residue, over a hundred and fifty vases, was left in the castle, La Cuesta Encantada, which was given by the Hearst Corporation with its contents to the State of California on June 2, 1958.

Joseph Clark Hoppin, a few years younger than William Randolph Hearst, began collecting in Athens between 1893 and 1898 and continued in Rome between 1898 and 1901. After his retirement from Bryn Mawr, he lived in Pomfret, Connecticut, and on his death in 1925, at the age of fifty-five, his vases came to the Fogg Museum by bequest. In the preface to the first American fascicule of the *Corpus Vasorum Antiquorum* he speaks rather modestly of his collecting efforts: "No attempt was made to form a well balanced collection, as pieces were bought from time to time as they were offered, and consequently the collection is rather of a haphazard nature." His fifty-six vases printed on twenty plates would not have been enough to fill an entire fascicule, and he therefore decided to join forces with his friend Albert Gallatin, and it is indicative of the spirit of private enterprise that the very first American fascicule was produced and written by two private collectors.

Gallatin's first purchase was a minor Apulian chous connected with the Ugento Painter bought for five dollars at the H. de Morgan Sale of January 16, 1909 in New York, but his second vase, bought from Canessa in New York in 1911 was the splendid cup with a boar hunt in the tondo that Mary Swindler attributed to the Penthesilea Painter. After that the pace quickened, and soon after 1926 another fascicule was planned. In 1941 he contemplated giving up his townhouse, 7 East 67th Street, and he offered his collection, now grown to 275 vases, to the Metropolitan Museum of Art at less than half of what he had paid for them. The purchase was authorized on November 17, 1941, and three months later the Gallatin vases were shown in the Museum in a special exhibition.

The fourth American private collector of this century was David M. Robinson. He, like Hearst, collected for fifty years. At the Christmas meeting of the Archaeological Institute of America in 1916 he read a paper on vases in his collection at Baltimore. The example of Hoppin and Gallatin inspired him to publish his vases in the *Corpus Vasorum Antiquorum* in three fascicules. They contained not only objects in his possession, but also the much older collection of the Baltimore Society of the Archaeological Institute of America that was likewise housed at Gilman Hall on the campus of Johns Hopkins University in Baltimore. When Robinson became professor emeritus at Johns Hopkins in 1948, he continued for ten years teaching at the University of Mississippi, and it was to Oxford, Mississippi, that all his antiquities were moved. Following his death a division was made: half of his objects under the terms of his will went to the Fogg Museum and the other half to his widow, from whose estate the University of Mississippi acquired them subsequently. Though not a Harvard alumnus himself, Robinson, impressed by J. C. Hoppin's example, had wanted all his vases to go to the Fogg: the division was the result of his will being contested.

These four American collectors give us a fair cross section of the many different aims and attitudes that go into private acquisitions: Hearst, the powerful magnate whose romantic vision knew no bounds; Hoppin, the quiet scholar, always devoted to learning; Gallatin, the self-taught amateur who never went to college, but knowledgeable both on the stock market and the art market; Robinson, the prolific writer, excavator, and teacher, to whom collecting was an essential extension of his all-embracing archaeological activities. Their counterparts in Europe were few and far between. In England, especially after World War I, and again after the Second World War, the trend was rather to sell the family heirlooms, a policy that culminated in the sale of the Castle Ashby vases by the Marquess of Northampton in July 1980. Of the few British collectors in this century only Captain E. G. Spencer-Churchill of Northwick Park stands out, and his long friendship with Beazley prompted the bequest of his finest vases to the Ashmolean in 1965. No vase collectors of note emerged in France in this century (except perhaps for Maurice de Rothschild). In Germany, Munich fell heir to the collections of James Loeb (an American) and Hans von Schoen, while the vases of Adolf Preyss went to Mayence and Erlangen. More recently, the collection of Julius and Margot Funcke was donated to the Ruhr-Universität in Bochum, while the superb vases of Peter Ludwig in Aachen, once lent to Cassel and Basel, have now been donated to the Antikenmuseum in Basel that henceforth bears a hyphenated name. Another avid German collector, the late Landgraf Philipp of Hesse (son-in-law of Victor Emmanuel of Italy) established his own museum in Schloss Fasanerie in Adolphseck near Fulda. It is also worth remembering two great Dutch collectors, both equally public spirited, Jhr. Jan Six van Hillegom and C. W. Lunsingh Scheurleer, whose collections are now united in Amsterdam. In Greece, Michael Vlastos built up a formidable collection of Greek vases before World War II, which is now owned by Mme Serpieri, his daughter, and after the war Pavlos Kanellopoulos first collected and then installed a museum on the north slope of the Acropolis. At the same time a Cuban collector Dr. Joaquin Gumà, Conde de Lagunillas, created in about ten years a first-rate collection which he gave to the Museum in Havana in 1956, a collection first of its kind in Latin America.

But by far the greatest concentration of collectors emerged in Switzerland, after the second war. The generosity of Robert Käppeli, G. Züst, and Athos Moretti brought about a museum of ancient art in Basel that in the mere twenty years of its existence, thanks also to the help of Samuel Schweizer and a wise management, has achieved a degree of prominence that is the envy of sister institutions. As a museum totally dedicated to classical art, it resembles in many respects the Ny Carlsberg Glyptotek in Copenhagen. Before the war, the collections of Arnold Ruesch in Zurich and Ernst Pfuhl in Basel were sold at auction, mostly because there was in Switzerland no truly national museum of antiquities. Carl Hirschmann, a noted collector in Küsnacht near Zurich, brought together a choice collection in less than twenty years, and Ferruccio Bolla accomplished much the same in Lugano.

In Italy some of the great private collections formed in the nineteenth century have survived more or less intact: the Jatta collection, still in Ruvo, the Faina collection in Orvieto, and the Caputi collection (which changed hands three times in this century), now in Milan; Marchese Benedetto Guglielmi gave his antiquities to the Vatican in 1934, but most of the Giudice vases, formerly in Agrigento, were sold. The residue of the Spinelli collection is now in the Naples Museum. In this century Ignazio Mormino started a collection in Palermo for the foundation that bears his name some twenty years ago, and, more recently, an impressive collection of South Italian vases was formed by a doctor in Fiesole. Mario Astarita, "the sensitive lover of Greek vases" as Beazley describes him, died in 1980, thirteen years after he had donated his vast collection of vases and terracottas to the Vatican. The greatest number of his objects are incomplete or mere fragments, but, in a sense, the appreciation of fragments, especially in Attic red-figure, is a revealing proof of the intimacy a collector of pottery establishes with the styles and periods of his choice. Moreover, until fairly recently it was easier (and less ruinous) to buy fragments. The very incompleteness of the object poses a challenge that brings into play all one's knowledge of shapes, styles, and composition—

the ideal object for teaching and learning. This explains the extraordinary value of such university collections as Heidelberg, Goettingen, Tübingen, Erlangen, Mayence, Bonn, Greifswald, Leipsic, Vienna, Innsbruck, Strasbourg, Oxford, Cambridge, Reading, Newcastle, Philadelphia, Bryn Mawr, Chicago, and Bowdoin College.

Mrs. Gallatin once told me that she would not let her husband buy fragments, or "cripples" as she called them, but fortunately not every collector was similarly restricted. The collection of Sir John and Lady Beazley, mostly given to the Ashmolean Museum between 1912 and 1966, is particularly rich in fragments, and it is easy to see how Beazley's extraordinary eye for stylistic differences was sharpened by living with so many artistic examples that could be handled and studied with such ease.

Among the contemporary collectors who did not spurn fragments either is Walter Bareiss. At present all his vases and fragments are being shown at the J. Paul Getty Museum; an earlier exhibition held in the Metropolitan Museum of Art in 1969 comprised a selection of a hundred and twenty.

The willingness of private owners to share their treasures with a larger public so frequently demonstrated today by the ever increasing loan exhibitions mounted all over the world is an aspect of collecting that has become widespread only recently. In the field of vase-painting the first exhibition drawing on the private sector was held at the Burlington Fine Arts Club in 1888, and vases were also strongly represented in the exhibition of Ancient Greek Art held by the same organization in 1903. Shortly before the war Neugebauer organized in 1938 an exhibition in Berlin entitled "Antiken in deutschem Privatbesitz," and in this country Hanfmann staged at the Fogg Museum in 1954 an American counterpart, "Ancient Art in American Private Collections." The Metropolitan Museum of Art appealed to twenty-one members of the New York Society of the Archaeological Institute of America to lend 319 ancient objects to its exhibition "Ancient Art from New York Private Collections" (December 17, 1959–February 28, 1960). In the summer of 1960 Karl Schefold launched an enormous exhibition "Meisterwerke griechischer Kunst" in Basel which indirectly gave birth to the Antikenmuseum. In addition to thirty-three European and American museums, fifty-eight identifiable private collectors were represented. There had been an earlier exhibition of ancient art in Berne (1942), the work of Hansjörg Bloesch, who pulled together from private and public collections a considerable number of antiquities of which a selection was published by him in 1944. Anyone wishing to gauge the great advances made in private collecting in Switzerland in the short span of eighteen years need only compare the two catalogues.

Save for the 1888 Burlington Exhibition of Greek Ceramic Art, most exhibitions presented collections of different classes of ancient art grouped together, but in 1972 Diana Buitron published the first exhibition catalogue exclusively devoted to Greek vases (*Attic Vase-Painting in New England Collections*) and her idea of regional representation was taken up in 1979 by W. Moon for the Midwest (*Greek Vase-Painting in Midwestern Collections*) and in 1981 by H. A. Shapiro for the South (*Greek Vases from Southern Collections*). A year later Margaret Ellen Mayo went one step farther and undertook an exhibition in Richmond of 164 vases, all made in Southern Italy and Sicily (*The Art of South Italy: Vases from Magna Graecia*) which in scope and depth far surpassed any of the earlier shows of vases. Her catalogue is easily the best account of

South Italian in one volume, and perhaps the time has come to stage next exhibitions of individual painters.

In the forty-six years that I have studied vases I have witnessed a healthy change of attitude toward the ceramic art of the Greeks. As I began in Berlin in 1937 vase-painting was not taught as a subject, though visits to the Altes Museum were encouraged. When I moved to Oxford, however, in 1938 and became Beazley's pupil, there was no longer any need to apologize for my special interests, and the same benevolent climate prevailed in America, though not all museum directors (and by no means all professors of classics) shared my passion. What was unexpected, however, was the growing interest in vases on the part of private collectors of whom I came to know most, either in the course of my travels or, since 1946, in the Metropolitan Museum of Art. The survey that I have attempted above intends to underline the great tradition of collecting in the last two hundred years or more, and I think of collectors in terms of a family tree with its many branches.

Nelson Bunker Hunt has demonstrated in the few years since he took up collecting in earnest that the tree is strong and healthy. The many masterpieces that he has acquired are proof of a discriminating eye, and the spread of his collection—from Corinthian black-figure to South Italian red-figure—is evidence of a broad outlook. No collection, of course, is ever "complete," and one of the greatest attractions of collecting vases is perhaps the chance of constantly adding to it. Some of the vases here described and now exhibited were acquired even while this introduction was being written, which I take to be an auspicious mark of the true collector.

Catalogue

NOTES TO THE CATALOGUE OF VASES

Of the sixteen antiquities presented in this section, fifteen are terracotta vases. These pieces, which represent the whole of the Nelson Bunker Hunt Collection of vases at this time, are arranged in chronological order. The earliest piece was made at Corinth just at the turn of the seventh to sixth century B.C., and the last two pieces were produced in South Italy in the years between the last quarter of the fifth century and the end of the third quarter of the fourth century B.C. The other twelve vases are all Attic, and the greatest number of these [4–12] have been chosen to represent the high-point of all red-figured vase painting in the period from circa 520–480 B.C.

The one remaining piece included here, a fine terracotta antefix made in Etruria circa 500 B.C., is the latest addition to the Nelson Bunker Hunt Collection and marks a significant extension of the collection into a new and fascinating area of ancient art. It has been included, perhaps somewhat arbitrarily, at the end of this section to provide a bridge between the terracotta vases and the bronze sculptures.

The format of the catalogue entries has been determined by a desire for clarity and for the presentation of the essential facts about each piece. There is no attempt at providing an exhaustive publication of the pieces, an effort deemed inappropriate for the occasion of this exhibition. I do hope, however, that the entries will stimulate much further research and discussion.

Each catalogue entry begins with a section that provides the following information: (1) the important dimensions of the piece; (2) the condition of the piece, including any restoration and surface damage; (3) the place and date of manufacture. For the vases there is also, where possible, an attribution to a painter. Two of the vases (both by Euphronios) are signed by the artist. In the other cases the attribution is followed by the name of the person(s) who have attributed the vase (in parentheses). Many of these attributions have been given in conversation or correspondence; where published, the reference will appear in the bibliography that follows immediately; (4) publication data. Included here are published references to, or full publications of, the piece as well as public exhibitions in which the piece has been shown.

The main body of the catalogue entry is divided into two sections: (1) first, a detailed description of the piece and (2) a short commentary on selected features of the potting, subject(s) represented on the vase and/or (3) relevant material on the painter.

The notes that are appended to the commentary cover three areas, wherever this has been possible: (1) information for further reading on the shape and potting of the vase; (2) references to studies of the subject(s) of the vase painting and (3) bibliography on the painter and background to the attribution and dating of the piece.

I have received much help on this section from my colleague at the University of Southern California, Professor Kenneth Hamma. He read a very early draft of these entries, and continued to offer bibliographical references and to tolerate my nagging questions throughout the rewriting of the catalogue. Dr. Dietrich von Bothmer of the Metropolitan Museum of Art most graciously reviewed the final draft of the entries. He offered much parallel material and has edited the entries painstakingly for both content and style. He generously contributed the entire text for entries [9] and [10] as well. His collaboration on the catalogue has been invaluable. All errors and infelicities in which I have stubbornly persisted are my own responsibility.

1 COLUMN-KRATER

Height, as restored, 41.5 cm; diameter of the body 51.7 cm; diameter of the mouth 44.4 cm.

Recomposed from large fragments. The foot is modern, and there is restoration above the foot on side A; minor restoration on the lip and shoulder. Some surface abrasion.

Corinthian; near to the Painter of Vatican 88 (Amyx); circa 600 B.C. Unpublished.

Black-figured column-krater with details in incision and added red. The inside is entirely glazed. Added red is used extensively in the figured zones. There is also a band of red around the inside of the mouth, two bands around the body below the upper panels and the handles, and two bands above and below the lower pictures.

On the top of the mouth is a palmette and lotus festoon and on the top of each handle plate, a rooster. The pictures on the shoulders are set in panels; below, the subsidiary frieze runs all the way around the vase. Just above the foot the body is encircled with ten black rays.

SIDE A. On the shoulder, a combat of two hoplites accompanied by horsemen. The hoplites hold long spears in their raised right hands, and in their left hands they have large round shields (one decorated with a flying bird; the other seen from the inside). The hoplites are dressed in Corinthian helmets and greaves. The breastplate of the right-hand figure is incised and painted

red; on the left-hand warrior it is indicated only by added red paint. The warriors are flanked by mounted squires, who wear short chitons. In each of the upper corners, an eagle flies toward the combat. In the field, rosettes.

SIDE B. On the shoulder three horsemen proceed to the left on unnaturally stiff and long-legged horses, which are typical of the period. The horsemen wear crested helmets. They carry long spears and round shields with blazons of (from the left) a bull's head, a flying bird and the forepart of a lion. In front of and behind the procession flies an eagle. In the field, rosettes.

In the animal zone below the shoulder panels, six goats move to the left. Five of them face panthers with frontal heads and bodies facing right; one, in the center of side A, faces an owl. In the field, rosettes.

The krater is a bowl for mixing wine with water, as the Greeks customarily drank it. The column-krater is so named from its handles which, in the fully developed stage, are composed of two vertical column-shaped elements topped by a horizontal handle plate. This type of krater evolved from a Corinthian development of about 625 B.C. At this time the narrow lip of the earlier krater was extended by the addition of handle plates to cover the top of semicircular handles that formerly had been independent. This origin still is evident on the Hunt krater in the fully semicircular form of the handles. The massive invert-

ed dome of the body, the low neck and narrow lip are other characteristics of the early Corinthian column-krater.

At the height of the Greek orientalizing period in the seventh century B.C., Corinth was a major exporter of pottery. The Corinthian ware of this period is made of a very fine buff terracotta decorated with black glaze. Details are rendered with incision and with red and white paint added over the black glaze. On this vase there is no white, but the red appears extensively on all the decorated areas (with the exception of the rays above the foot). The general scheme of decoration with shoulder panels, an animal frieze, a broad band of black glaze and a series of rays at the base of the body is typical of the period in which this krater was made. There are, however, not many column-kraters extant from this intermediate phase between the Early and Middle Corinthian periods, and the Hunt piece seems to provide the earliest example yet published of the mounted horsemen who flank the two hoplites on side A.

NOTES: The most recent detailed discussion of the shape and decoration of similar vases is T. Bakir, *Der Kolonettenkrater in Korinth und Attika zwischen 625 und 555 v. Chr.* (1974). For parallels to the upper frieze on side A, see H. Payne, *Necrocorinthia* (1931), pl. 34, 8 (but the squires hold a void horse) and Bakir, *op. cit.* K31 and K63. In shape and decoration the Hunt krater is very close to a column-krater in the Vatican (no. 88): C. Albizzati, *Vasi antichi dipinti del Vaticano* (1925), pl. 10 (the picture with the riders is left and right reversed), p. 35, fig. 13. The Vatican vase also is mentioned by Payne, *op. cit.* no. 779 and J. Benson, *Die Geschichte der korinthischen Vasen* (1953), p. 58. The latter's attribution (with a question mark) of the Vatican vase to the Painter of the Hippolytus krater is not convincing.

Detail, handle plate

2 PANEL-AMPHORA

Height, as restored, 38.3 cm; diameter of the body 26.9 cm; diameter of the mouth 17.1 cm.

Recomposed from large fragments. The foot is modern; there is no significant restoration in the figured areas. Some chipping on the mouth.

Attic; attributed to the Painter of Berlin 1686 (Bothmer); circa 550–540 B.C.

Unpublished, but mentioned by K. Schauenburg, "Zu Repliken in der Vasenmalerei," *AA* 1977, p. 197 (erroneously called a neck-amphora).

Black-figured panel-amphora of type B with a flaring lip and round handles. The neck is glazed to a depth of 4.6 cm. Added red and white in the figured zones. There is one line of applied red around the neck and a double line around the body below the panels; another double line, just above the rays. On the side and bottom edges the panels are framed by a narrow line just inside the edge of the black glaze. At the top of each panel is a palmette and lotus festoon.

SIDE A. The palmette and lotus festoon has eighteen elements. Below, mounted hoplite and squire. The hoplite wears a crested Corinthian helmet and greaves, and carries a shield emblazoned in added white with the hindpart of a horse. The hoplite proceeds to the left, his horse walking slowly and in step with the horse of his squire. The squire, who is only partially visible behind the hoplite, wears a cap (pilos) and carries his hoplite's spear. An eagle flies above and behind the figures.

SIDE B. The palmette and lotus festoon is composed of nineteen elements. Below, the scene is similar to that on side A. On this side, however, the horses' heads are pulled in; on side A they are raised. The hoplite on this side is without greaves, and there is additional added white on the pilos of the squire and on the vertical bands of the crest of the hoplite's helmet. The most notable difference is the shield blazon, which on this side is the forepart of a horse, again in added white.

The amphora is a large storage vase. The neck and body of panel-amphorae are of one piece, and they are decorated on each side with a single figured panel. Type B panel-amphorae have round handles decorated only with the black glaze.

The Hunt vase is one of a number of black-figured panel-amphorae of the mid-sixth century that portray military life, often with the repetition of a single scene from one side of the vase to the other. Here the heavily armed hoplite rides to the field of battle accompanied by his assistant squire. Similar scenes from the life of a hoplite and squire on other sixth-century vases include their departure from home and scenes of actual combat where the warrior fights on foot while the mounted squire waits holding the warrior's horse. The heraldic and processional subject of the Hunt vase is reminiscent of orientalizing processions and battles like those on the upper panels of the Corinthian krater [1]. However, the effect here is that of a single figure extracted and monumentalized from the earlier treatment.

The Painter of Berlin 1686, who is named after a panel-amphora of type B in Berlin, has been identified as the painter of about thirty known vases, many of this shape. In general he painted scenes crowded with figures, and the simple uncluttered monumentality of this vase is unusual among his known works. The workmanship is some of the painter's best. Its high quality perhaps is most apparent in the precise delicacy of the palmette and lotus festoons and in the detail lavished on the horse trappings and the shields. Both the large size of the vase and the composition with the stiff-legged archaic horses that walk slowly and in step, alone but for the riders and the birds above, lend the piece a great formality and dignity.

NOTES: On the development of panel-amphorae, see R. Lullies, "Ein Amphora aus dem Kreis des Exekias," *AK* 7 (1964): 85ff.

For a good discussion (with parallels) of the scene on a very similar vase in a Swiss collection, see H. Metzger and D. van Berchem, "Hippeis," *Gestalt und Geschichte. Festschrift Karl Schefold* (1967): 155–158 and also Dörig, no. 159. Scenes of hoplite and squire alone on both sides of panel-amphorae are also found on Berlin inv. 4823 (*ABV* p. 80, Painter of Acropolis 606, no. 4; *CVA* Berlin 5 = Deutschland 45 [1980], pl. 1, 2 and pl. 3) and Naples 2770 (*ABV* p. 109, Lydos no. 23), but in this case with the squire on the outside. Closest in composition is perhaps the black-figured amphora of type B once on the Basle market: M & M *Auktion 26* (1963), pl. 27, 88. Cf. the fragment in G. Richards, "Vase Fragments from the Acropolis of Athens-I," *JHS* 13 (1892–1893), p. 289 and pl. 12 (B. Graef and E. Langlotz, *Die antiken Vasen von der Akropolis zu Athen* 1 [1909], Acr. 590, pl. 27.) For the Painter of Berlin 1686, *ABV* pp. 296–297, p. 692; *Para.* pp. 128–129; *ABVP* p. 63; and W. Moon, *Greek Vase-Painting in Midwestern Collections* (1980), nos. 31–32 (Bothmer and Moon).

3 KYLIX

Height 12.1 cm; diameter of the bowl 26.9 cm; width, including the handles, 34.2 cm; diameter of the foot 11.8 cm.

Recomposed from fragments with one handle and the area under it restored; minor restorations elsewhere on the bowl.

Attic; near the Kallis Painter (Bothmer); circa 540–530 B.C.

Published: Summa, *Auction 1* (1981), no. 4.

Kylix with a deep bowl and a disk foot on a short stem (proto-A type). The decoration is in a combination of outline and black-figured technique with much added red and white. There is a reserved circle around the inside of the lip and the insides of the handles also are reserved, as is the ring between the bowl and stem and the outer edge of the foot. The inside of the stem is covered with black glaze; the underside of the foot is reserved.

INSIDE. The inside of the bowl is black glaze except for the reserved circle just inside the lip and a reserved tondo (6.6 cm) with two concentric circles and a central dot in black glaze.

OUTSIDE–SIDE A. Between eyes, busts of DIONYSUS AND SEMELE(?) The large eyes and eyebrows are in outline technique; the pupils, in black-figured with added red and white. The two busts are side by side and facing left. On the near side and slightly to the right of the other figure, the Greek wine god Dionysus is rendered in black-figured technique. His hair is in long ringlets and decorated with a double wreath of ivy, the leaves in alternating red and black. His black mustache is decorated with incised dots; the locks of his beard are alternating red and black. The god wears a bordered red and black striped himation, and holds a forked ivy branch in his tiny right hand.

Behind Dionysus is a female bust (either Semele or Ariadne) in outline technique. She has short ringlets over her forehead, and around her head is a plain black fillet.

Four wreaths hang from the black glaze circle that runs around the bowl just below the lip. Behind Dionysus and above him on the black line are two partially obscured nonsense inscriptions.

OUTSIDE–SIDE B. Between the eyes, DIONYSUS AND SEMELE(?). The busts on this side are also side by side and facing left. The outer figure is again Dionysus in black-figured technique. His mustache and beard are similar to those on side A. On this side, however, he wears a plain red fillet; on the crown, his hair is incised in a zigzag pattern. Over his forehead are incised screw curls, and his short ringlets are alternating red and black. He carries a single ivy branch in his right hand. The female figure's fillet is red on this side, and she wears a simple beaded necklace. Again, four wreaths hang from the circle of black glaze just below the lip of the bowl.

Under the handles are addorsed palmettes and lotus with curling tendrils. There are four lines of glaze above and three lines of glaze below the fifty-four rays in outline technique that run around the base of the bowl.

This type of two-handled wine cup, or kylix, represents an early stage in the development of the type A kylix (with a molding between the bowl and the foot). The outline technique appears sporadically for female heads from the period when Attic black-figured ware was first produced up until the time this vase was made.

Dionysiac themes were very popular in late sixth-century vase painting, and Dionysus is a decoration most suitable for a cup for drinking wine. The accompanying female may be either his mother Semele or his bride Ariadne. Profile busts of several other divinities appear on Attic pottery, often without any clear indication of their identity. Their meaning is also unclear, but for the most part they seem to be merely abbreviated versions of full-length representations. The eyes are popular decoration on both black- and early red-figured cups, and seem to be present to watch over and ward off evil from the festive party-goer.

NOTES: On the shape of the cup, see H. Bloesch, *Formen attischer Schalen* (1940), p. 4.

The basic work on profile busts is O. von Vacano, *Zur Entstehung und Deutung gemalter seitansichtiger Kopfbilder auf schwarzfigurigen Vasen* (1973). Also, see E. Buschor, "Götterköpfe," *Feldmäuse* (*Sitzungsberichte der bayerischen Akademie der Wissenschaften* 1937.1), especially pp. 4–7; M. Milne's review of E. Langlotz, *Aphrodite in den Garten, AJA* 60 (1956), p. 204; K. Schauenburg, "Zu einigen böotischen Vasen des sechsten Jahrhunderts," *JRGZ* 4 (1957): 66ff.; "Ein spätkorinthischer schwarzbunter Aryballos in Wien," *JŒAI* 48 (1966–1967): 39ff.; K. Schauenburg, "Athenabüsten des Bowdoinmalers," *AA* 1974, pp. 150–151; E. Berger and R. Lullies, *Antike Kunstwerke aus der Sammlung Ludwig I* (1979), no. 18; D. Callipolitis-Feytmans, "La coupe à figures noires, Athènes 17873, et le peintre de Kallis," *BCH* 104 (1980): 322–325; and K. Schauenburg, "Zu einer Kleinmeister Schale in Privatbesitz," *AA* 1981, pp. 340–343.

On the meaning of the eyes, W. Deonna, *Le symbolisme de l'oeil* (1965).

For the identity of the female bust, note the head of Semele identified by legend on the cup Naples Sant. 172, attributed to the Kallis Painter (see below) and F. Matz, "Ariadne oder Semele," *Festschrift H. Drerup* (*Marburger Winckelmann-Programm* 1968), p. 115.

For the Kallis Painter, *ABV* p. 203; *Para.* p. 92; and D. Callipolitis-Feytmans, *op. cit.* pp. 317–332. The Hunt cup is closest to the proto-A kylix in Naples (Sant. 172) attributed to this painter (*ABV* p. 203, no. 1; *CVA* Naples = Italy 20 [n.d.], pl. 22).

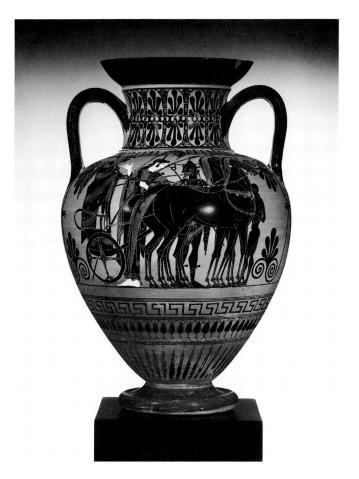

4 NECK-AMPHORA

Height 43.2 cm; diameter of the mouth 19.3 cm; diameter of the
body 29.3 cm; diameter of the foot 15.3 cm.

Intact and complete except for several repairs on the foot and three
small areas of restoration on the mouth. Excellent surface preservation.

Attic; attributed to the Three Line Group (Bothmer); circa 525 B.C.
Unpublished.

Black-figured neck-amphora with an echinus mouth, triple-
reeded handles and a spreading foot. There is much added red
and white paint, a reserved groove at the junction of the mouth
and neck and a raised red fillet at the junction of the neck and
shoulder. The bands above and below the ring at the junction of
the body and foot are also reserved, as are the insides of the
handles. The glaze does not extend to the base of the foot. On
the inside, the neck is glazed to a depth of 10.9 cm.

The neck is decorated with a palmette and lotus chain. There
are five and one-half pairs on side A, six on side B. On the
shoulder are tongues in alternating red and black. Under each
handle is an inverted lotus bud and four tendrils that terminate
in palmettes. Where the tendrils join, there are horizontal lotus
buds and, between the tendrils, a dotted cross. Below the figured
zone are three lines, a leftward key, three lines, a chain of upright lotus buds, three lines and, at the base of the body, rays.

SIDE A. HERAKLES' DEPARTURE FOR OLYMPUS. Herakles, wearing the lion skin that he won in his first labor, shouldering the
club with his left hand and holding the reins in his right hand,
stands in a four-horse chariot. Herakles' patroness Athena
stands on the ground to his right and turns her head to Hermes,
who stands on her right. The messenger god is dressed in a
pointed hat (petasus), traveler's cloak (chlamys) and boots. He
carries the kerykeion in his right hand. On the far right a groom
holds the chariot steady. All of the main figures wear garments
that are striped red and black and decorated with white rosettes.

SIDE B. MEMNON WITH AN ETHIOPIAN SQUIRE. The two central figures stand left and are flanked by frontal horsemen.
Memnon, on the outside, carries a large, round white shield and
long spear. He wears red greaves and a Corinthian helmet with
a high crest decorated with incision and added white paint.
Behind him, the Ethiopian archer carries a quiver. His right
hand is raised as if the painter intended to show him holding a
club or bow. His short bordered garment is decorated with incision and added white. There is added red for the horses' manes
and the riders' beards.

Herakles was a mortal hero who endured many labors, and
subsequently was admitted to the company of the gods. Much
has been written about the connection between Herakles' apotheosis and contemporary philosophical thought on the nature
of man and on the attempts of the Peisistratids, Athenian ty-

rants of the later sixth century, to associate themselves with Herakles. Whether these associations are valid or not, the introduction of Herakles to Olympus was one of the most popular mythological subjects of Attic vase painters from the middle of the sixth century onward. Schefold has counted about one hundred and fifty appearances of the theme. Most commonly Herakles is shown with Athena already in the chariot, or with Athena just stepping into the chariot where Herakles stands. The version of the subject on the Hunt amphora, which takes place moments before Athena steps into the chariot, is far less usual.

Memnon, the son of Eos and Tithonus, was king of Ethiopia. He came to help his uncle Priam of Troy in his war with the Greeks after the defeat of the Amazons, who had come to Troy after the death of Hector. A figure identified as Memnon appears several times on black-figured vases in battle with Achilles, while their mothers Eos and Thetis look on. Scenes of Memnon accompanied by negro squires are more rare, but he does appear elsewhere dressed as here and flanked by negro attendants who carry clubs, peltae and, at times, quiver and bow.

One of the characteristics of the Three Line Group to which this vase belongs is the sets of three lines that separate the friezes under the figured zones.

NOTES: For the scenes on both sides of the vase, see K. Schefold, *Götter- und Heldensagen der Griechen in der spätarchaischen Kunst* (1978): 35ff. and 238ff. On the introduction of Herakles to Olympus, also see P. Mingazzini, "Le rappresentazioni vascolari del mito dell'apoteosi di Herakles," *Atti Acc. Lincei* 6.1 (1925): 417–490, especially p. 425. For the possible political connections of Herakles, see J. Boardman, "Herakles, Theseus and Amazons," D. Kurtz and B. Sparkes, *The Eye of Greece* (1982): lff., with earlier bibliography. On Memnon, see F. Snowden, *Blacks in Antiquity* (1970): 151–153 and K. Schefold, "Memnons Auszug," *Forschungen und Funde. Festschrift B. Neutsch* (1980): 445–447. Parallels for the Memnon scene are in the British Museum B209 (*ABV* p. 144, no. 8, p. 686; *Para.* p. 60; *CVA* BM 4 = Great Britain 5 [1929], pl. 49, 1) and the Metropolitan Museum inv. 98.8.13 (*Para.* p. 62; *CVA* MMA 4 = USA 16 [1976], pl. 21). Also, a neck-amphora in Munich inv. 1507 (*ABV* p. 375, no. 207).

For the Three Line Group, see *ABV* pp. 320–321, pp. 693–694 and p. 700; *Para.* p. 140–141; *ABVP* p. 112.

5 KYLIX

Height 12.4 cm; diameter of the bowl 33.0 cm; width, including the handles, 42.1 cm; diameter of the foot 11.8 cm.

Recomposed from fragments. The foot was repaired in antiquity, and is recomposed with minor restoration. On the bowl there are some significant areas of restoration (in addition to several very minor ones). Side A: (1) the lower part of the left-hand lotus with the lower body and legs of Hypnos, the lower body of Sarpedon and the back of the right foot and lower leg of Thanatos; (2) the armpit of Thanatos; (3) the front of the left foot and ankle and the tip of the right foot of Akamas; (4) part of Akamas' shield, left arm and hand and right wrist; (5) much of the area under the right handle of which half is missing. Side B: (6) the tip of the hair and the wrists of the left-hand figure; (7) the right side of the shield of the second figure, his lower left arm and most of the flute player (third figure), except the lower arms and hands and the lower legs and feet. This break continues into the right-hand (fourth) figure, whose right shoulder and arm and left shoulder are also missing; (8) missing under the right handle, half of the palmette and part of the tendrils. Inside, a crescent-shaped area at the base of the palmette complex is missing.

Attic; signed by Euphronios; circa 520 B.C.

Published: M. Robertson, "Euphronios at the Getty," *JPGMJ* 9 (1981): 23ff. This cup also is discussed by D. von Bothmer, "Der Euphronioskrater in New York," *AA* 1976, pp. 511–512 and "The Death of Sarpedon," S. Hyatt, ed. *The Greek Vase* (1981): 63–80.

Red-figured kylix of type B with a wide shallow bowl and low foot. The edge of the foot is convex, with flat edges top and bottom. There is some use of added red. The inside of the handles are reserved, and the area under the handles is partially reserved (see below). The outside and outer edge of the underside of the foot are also reserved, and there is a reserved circle just below the edge of the bowl on both inside and outside.

INSIDE. Within a tondo formed by a reserved line there is a complex of eight palmettes. The main elements are two addorsed palmettes placed vertically and two horizontal palmettes. The vertical palmettes rest on dotted loops in four tendrils, as do two subsidiary horizontal palmettes. From the loops, the tendrils run out to the side in a lyre pattern and end in volutes, on which rest the larger horizontal palmettes. Above and below, the tendrils run from the loops along the sides of the vertical palmettes and enclose four more palmettes, two above facing upward and two below facing downward.

OUTSIDE-SIDE A. HYPNOS (SLEEP) AND THANATOS (DEATH) CARRYING THE BODY OF SARPEDON. The procession moves right and is led, on the far right, by Akamas. He is identified by the inscription ΑΚΑΜΑΣ (in front of his face). The letters, as on all the inscriptions on the bowl, are reserved. Akamas is bearded and wears a Corinthian helmet with a low crest. The rerebrace on his right upper arm is decorated with a Medusa head and tendrils. The shoulder flaps of his corselet are ornamented with stars, and the flaps (pteryges) at its lower edge are decorated with a band of dots between bands of rays. His short chiton is gathered up in front. He wears greaves, and carries a long red spear and a round shield (seen from the inside) in his left hand. A sheathed sword hangs on his left side held by a red baldric.

Thanatos and Hypnos follow with the body of Sarpedon. On the right, Thanatos, in profile, faces right and holds the upper body of Sarpedon over his shoulder, his right arm holding Sarpedon's right arm by the wrist above his head. Thanatos is bearded, and wears a Corinthian helmet decorated along the base of its low crest with dots. His chiton has short sleeves, and the short skirt is caught up in front. The corselet is decorated across the chest with a band of crenelation, around the waist with a dotted band. The flaps below are adorned with a band of rays between bands of chevrons. In his left hand Thanatos carries a long spear and a Boeotian shield. Over his shoulder is a red baldric, and his legs are equipped with greaves. The inscription before his face reads ΘΑΝΑΤΟΣ.

Sarpedon's head is shown in profile. He is bearded, and his long hair is rendered in wavy lines of dilute glaze on a reserved ground. The torso is shown frontally, with much detail in relief line. Blood, in added red, streams from two wounds, one on his chest, the other on his shoulder. The lower legs are turned in profile, still wearing greaves, the hero's only remaining armor. Above him is the inscription ΣΑΡΠΕΔΟΝ.

The figure to the far left, in profile and facing right, is Hypnos. He holds the legs of Sarpedon under the knees. Like the other figures he is bearded, and he wears a Corinthian helmet with a raised crest. His rerebraces are decorated with Medusa heads and tendrils. Over his shoulders, a mantle. The shoulder flaps of his

5 KYLIX (continued)

corselet are decorated with stars, the band across his chest with a key pattern to the right and the waistband with crenelations. On the pleats are a band of crenelation flanked by bands of rays. A sheathed sword hangs on his left side, and he carries a shield on his left arm. Behind him the inscription reads ΗΥΠΝ[Ο]Σ.

OUTSIDE–SIDE B. PYRRHIC (ARMED DANCE). The scene on this side consists of four figures, the two on the outside flanking and facing an armed dancer and a flute player. The armed youth, to left of center, wears a Corinthian helmet and greaves, and carries a long red spear in his right hand and a round shield (seen from the inside) on his left arm. He dances to the left and looks back over his shoulder. To his right, the flute player stands facing the dancer wearing a long chiton and playing a double flute.

The youth on the far left wears a red wreath and a mantle decorated with dot rosettes. He holds both hands upward before himself, and carries a flower in his left hand. The female figure on the far right wears a chiton girded at the waist and caught up around the hips. A mantle is draped over her shoulders. Her hair is caught up in a krobylos, and she holds a flower in her left hand. According to Bothmer, there is a trace of a second red flower that she would have carried in her right hand.

Under the handles, palmettes. Below each palmette are tendrils, one end of which loops and drops down, ending below the palmette. The other end turns out to the side where it encloses a horizontal palmette. From it branch three lotus buds, one below and two above.

The cup is signed on the outside of the foot, to the left of side A: ΕΥΦΡΟΝΙΟΣ ΕΓΡΑΦ[ΣΕΝ], Euphronios painted (this).

This cup seems to be the earliest extant work by Euphronios, and was probably potted by Kachrylion, who signed a cup painted by Euphronios in Munich and probably also made the Euphronios kylix with Ajax carrying the body of the dead Achilles now in the Getty Museum. Euphronios is certainly the most famous of all Greek vase painters, and he seems to have had a great reputation even among his peers. He is one of the "pioneer

group" who worked between circa 520 and 500, shortly after the introduction of the red-figured technique. This group of painters liked to work on large vases in a lively, personal and self-assertive style.

The red-figured technique was invented in Attica about 530 and lasted well into the fourth century. This type of painting reverses that of black-figured: the background is now black glaze and the figures, the red of the Attic clay itself. Details are drawn primarily in black relief lines or in a dilute form of the glaze that has a pale red-brown tone. In the beginning the incision of the black-figured technique continues to appear, as do the added red and white of the older technique.

On side A of this cup is the earliest extant representation of the removal of the body of the Lycian hero Sarpedon from the battlefield of Troy. The treatment seems to have been modeled on scenes of the removal of other dead heroes (especially Achilles), and reappears on the famous calyx-krater in New York, also painted by Euphronios. There Sleep and Death (both winged unlike here) are just lifting the body from the ground. Hermes appears with them, and they are flanked by two watching Trojan heroes. On the Hunt kylix the procession from the battlefield is already in motion with Akamas at the front, while Hermes is not present. The Akamas found on this kylix is perhaps the son of Antenor and one of the finest Trojan warriors. However, that Akamas died before Sarpedon (Homer, Iliad 16.342) and therefore would not necessarily appear at the head of the celebrated procession presented here.

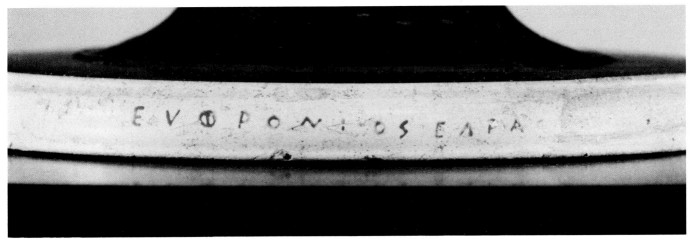

Detail, inscribed foot

The pyrrhic dance was a regular part of the competition at the Panathenaic festivals, but we know very little of how the event was actually conducted. Side B of this kylix has one of only four extant representations of pyrrhicists on early red-figured vases. The flute player and the dancer, dressed only in a helmet and carrying a spear and round shield, are usual for the extant representations, both the red-figured and the black-figured, which date from the late sixth and early fifth centuries. However, the two flanking figures, a male and a female onlooker with hands raised, the female bearing a flower(s), are unprecedented. On other representations only the participants in the action, such as singers or a judge, are present.

NOTES: In addition to the works cited in the bibliography above, see H. Bloesch, *Formen attischer Schalen* (1940): 45ff. and, on Euphronios, *ARV* pp. 13–19, p. 1619, and p. 1705; *Para.* pp. 321–322, p. 509; *ARVAP* pp. 32–33; W. Moon, *Greek Vase-Painting in Mid-Western Collections* (1980), no. 77 (L. Berge). The Munich and Getty cups and the New York krater are discussed by Bothmer and Robertson (above). Bothmer also discusses the treatment of side A in detail. On the pyrrhic dance, see J. -C. Poursat, "Les représentations de danse armée dans la céramique attique," *BCH* 92 (1968): 566ff. and Bothmer's commentary on the Panathenaic amphora [9].

Detail, palmette side B

6 CALYX-KRATER

Height, as restored, 45.0 cm; diameter of the mouth 55.1 cm; diameter of the foot 29.5 cm.

Restored on the basis of extant fragments.

Attic; signed by Euphronios; circa 510 B.C.

Published: M. Robertson, "Euphronios at the Getty," *JPGMJ* 9 (1981): 29–34.

Red-figured calyx-krater with a low foot in two degrees and a flaring body that rises above the set-off handle zone, or cul. The details are rendered with relief line (note especially the raised dots for the hair of Herakles and Athena) and dilute glaze. There are reserved circles on the inside just within the edge of the mouth and at the bottom of the rim and on the outside above and below the rim and at the top and bottom of the cul. The area under the handles also is reserved as is the outside edge of the upper degree of the foot. The foot is not glazed all the way to the bottom; on the underside, concentric glaze stripes.

Around the rim, palmettes. They alternately face upward and downward and are connected by tendrils. The upright palmettes are enclosed by the tendrils, which then turn outward to form volutes from which the inverted palmettes hang.

On the cul, side A, a chain composed of two festoons of alternating lotus buds and palmettes. In the chain the lotus are back-to-back with lotus and the palmettes with palmettes, the top one of the pair facing upward, the lower one downward. There are three loops between the palmettes and two loops between the lotus buds. On the cul, side B, palmettes facing right and enclosed by tendrils. In the area above the handle to the right of side A, addorsed palmettes with tendrils ending in three smaller palmettes on either side; the upper and lower side palmettes are enclosed, the central one unenclosed. Above the handle to the left of side A, a smaller but similar design (now mostly missing).

SIDE A. THE DEATH OF KYKNOS. The subject of side A is the death of Kyknos at the hands of Herakles, a hero apparently favored by Euphronios. Only the lower part of the garments and the feet of the left hand figure are extant. The figure, who is moving to the right, is not readily identifiable; perhaps it is Artemis, the sister of Apollo on whose behalf Herakles fights.

To the right, in the center of the scene, is Herakles. He has curly hair and beard, and is dressed in a lion skin carefully detailed with relief line and yellow-brown wash, a red baldric, sword belt and sheathed sword. The chiton under the lion skin has wavy lines of dilute glaze. He strides forward on the diagonal, holding his Boeotian shield (seen from inside) in the left hand and thrusting his long spear down into Kyknos' thigh. The inscription between his legs is ΛΕΑΓΡΟΣ ΚΑΛΟΣ; it names Leagros, a favorite among vase painters of the late sixth century, as beautiful.

6 CALYX-KRATER (continued)

The wounded hero Kyknos appears almost completely fallen, his left leg bent under him. His injured right leg is drawn up and shown in profile; his left leg, upper body and head are turned frontally. Kyknos wears greaves, a short chiton and a corselet magnificently detailed with scales and lions on the shoulder flaps in relief line. His Corinthian helmet has a transverse crest decorated below with dicing. It is pushed partly from his head, and he supports himself on his round shield (seen from the inside). In the throes of death he still reaches across his body to pull the sword from its scabbard which is attached to a decorated belt and a red baldric. His teeth are clenched, his face wrinkled and his eyes turned up in agony. Above his head is his name, written retrograde, ΚΥΚΝΟΣ.

Above and behind Herakles and the fallen Kyknos the goddess Athena, protectress of Herakles, strides vigorously to the right. She wears a long chiton and crested Attic helmet. The aegis, her protective breastplate with the head of Medusa and snakes around the edge, is draped over her extended left arm. Her right hand is raised to thrust a long spear at her opponent Ares. Next to her face is her name ΑΘΕΝΑ.

Facing her is Ares, the god of war and father of Kyknos. He strides left, thrusting his raised spear toward Athena. The god wears a Corinthian helmet with low crest decorated below with dots, a corselet over a chiton and greaves. He carries a Boeotian shield emblazoned with a Medusa head between two lions. He is identified as ΑΡΕΣ by the retrograde inscription above.

On the far right is Aphrodite. She wears a chiton, a himation bordered with crenelation and a red bracelet and stands facing the battle with her right hand raised before her. Issuing from her face is her name, written retrograde, ΑΦΡΟΔΙΤΕ. The vase is signed ΕΥΦΡΟΝΙΟΣ ΕΓΡΑΦΣΕΝ, Euphronios painted (this), between the heads of Athena and Ares.

SIDE B. ATHLETES. In contrast to the mythological subject of side A, the reverse side of the Hunt krater has a scene from contemporary life in the palaestra, a popular theme among early red-figured vase painters. The five overlapping figures in various poses are preparing for exercise. To the left is a naked figure who strides forward with a pick used for loosening the ground. Next, the back foot of another athlete; then, a youth in a long chiton playing the aulos, the musical accompaniment for the exercise. To his right is a second athlete tightening the cords of his javelin and by him, the inscription [ΑΝ] ΤΙΑΣ, Antias. The last figure also has a javelin, and is identified by an inscription now mostly lost, but beginning with Σ.

The calyx-krater, said to be an invention of Exekias in the latter half of the sixth century, is a large bowl for mixing wine and water [14, 15]. It is so named from the shape of the body which, with its convex handle zone and flaring body, resembles the cup-like shape of a flower.

The story of Kyknos' death, told at some length in the short epic attributed to Hesiod and called *The Shield of Herakles*, is a very popular subject among black-figured vase painters in the later sixth century, including those contemporary with Euphronios. Euphronios, however, has given us an exceptionally vivid, detailed and full representation of the battle in which Herakles

Detail, rim side A

Detail, cul side A

met Kyknos, who had been stealing the animals intended for sacrifice to Apollo, and defeated him in single combat.

The careful workmanship is of extraordinary quality. The details of the eyes and lashes of the important figures, Herakles, Athena, Kyknos and Ares (but not Aphrodite or the flute player on side B), and the intricacy and color of the breastplate of Kyknos and the lion skin of Herakles are excellent examples. The composition is also outstanding, juxtaposing as it does the strong rightward diagonals of the victorious figures with the very stable triangular element in the center of the scene. The latter is composed, at its base, of the foot of Herakles and the left leg and foot of Kyknos; on its left side, by the body of Herakles; on its right, by the hero's spear. The figure on the left and the fallen body of Kyknos reinforce the rightward thrust of victory, while the upright figures of Ares and Aphrodite resist it from the right of the scene.

NOTES: On the Kyknos myth, see F. Vian, "Le combat de Héràkles et de Kyknos d'après les documents figurés du VIe et du Ve siècle," *REA* 47 (1945): 4–32; K. Schefold, *Götter- und Heldensagen der Griechen in der spätarchaischen Kunst* (1978): 136–138; *Vasenlisten* pp. 102–108; K. Stähler, "Schwarzfigurige Hydria der Sammlung Socha," *Boreas* 1 (1978): 194–199.

On Euphronios, see the bibliography cited above on the kylix [5].

7 KYLIX

Height 10.4 cm; diameter of the bowl 25.7 cm; width, including the handles, 33.1 cm.

Recomposed from fragments and augmented in 1979–1980 with two fragments near the rim of the bowl identified by J. Frel. There are two restorations on side A and one on side B. The foot was reattached in antiquity, and there are holes for ancient repairs on side B.

Attic; attributed to the Epidromos Painter (Bothmer); circa 510 B.C. Unpublished.

Red-figured kylix with a shallow bowl and low spreading foot (type B). There is some use of added red; reserved circle just inside the edge of the bowl and reserved areas on the inside and under the handles. Two reserved lines articulate the join of the stem and foot. The glaze does not extend to the bottom of the foot.

INSIDE. Within a tondo bordered by a net pattern there is a running huntsman. He is naked except for a pointed, wide brimmed hat with a red tie and a short mantle, which is draped over his shoulders and his extended left arm. He runs left, looks back over his shoulder and holds his spear at waist level directed, as is his head, to the right. The inscription in the field reads ΕΠΙΔΡΟΜΟΣ ΚΑΛΟΣ, Epidromos is beautiful.

OUTSIDE–SIDE A. SCENE OF REVELRY. Above a net pattern bordered by a thicker (top) and thinner (bottom) line of glaze that run around the bowl under the figured zone are four figures, naked but for short mantles and red laurel wreaths. The figure to the left carries a long staff and a krotalon, the next plays a double flute. The third figure holds two krotala (one now missing), as does the right-hand figure. The inscriptions, now mostly gone, read ΝΟΝΝΟΣ (?) ΚΑΛΟΣ, Nonnos (?) is beautiful.

OUTSIDE–SIDE B. THE SCENE OF REVELRY CONTINUES. On the left a youth leans on a staff and balances a large wreathed amphora on his left knee. To the left of center a bearded and apparently inebriated man, bent over, walks forward with the help of his stick. To his right a youth, walking right, looks back and holds a skyphos (wine cup) aloft behind him. On the far right another youth plays a lyre. The inscription ΝΟΝ[ΝΟΣ](?) reappears on this side.

The Epidromos Painter, so named from the kalos name commonly found on his cups, is generally believed to have been Apollodoros in an early stage of his career. Less than twenty kylikes have been attributed to this painter; they are character-

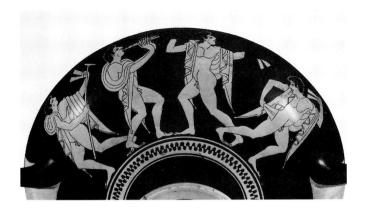

ized by his long pointed beards (note the inebriated man on side B), the straight line of the nose and forehead and the precise rendering of the little lines of hair around the forehead and neck (note the inside and side A, but not side B).

In the tondo the painter has accommodated the figure to the round space with great skill. The huntsman's feet run around the border, and impart a vivid sense of movement. This movement, however, is carefully restrained and balanced by the strong horizontals of the turned head, the extended left arm and the spear, as well as by the vertical lines formed by the edges of the mantle to the left and right of the figure.

On the outside, the exercise in rendering the postures of the human figure is reminiscent of side B of the Euphronios krater [6]. On side A the composition is carefully balanced over the two central figures, who stand knee to knee and toe to toe. The outer figures, inner legs overlapping with the central figures, step outward to follow the curved line of the cup's bowl. On side B the rightward movement of the figures is balanced by the central vertical of the skyphos and the second figure's staff, a composition different from, and perhaps not as effective as that on side A. No two postures on the outside of the cup are the same and, taken together, they constitute a skillful study in human motion, one of the most prominent themes of early red-figured vase painting.

The following information has been provided by Bothmer: The net pattern on the *inside* is rare in red-figure but occurs on the bilingual cup signed by Andokides as potter in Palermo (*ARV²* p. 5, no. 14), on the coral-red cup in Palermo by Skythes (*ARV²* p. 85, no. 21) as well as on a cup by the Painter of Berlin 2268 in the Louvre (Cp 11282 and 11243, *ARV²* p. 155, nos. 35–36, belonging to the same cup) and on two fragments in the Villa Giulia. As the ground frame on the outside of red-figured cups it is somewhat more frequent: *ARV²* p. 19 (Freiburg S 131, Halle, Goettingen); *ARV²* p. 125, no. 17 (Louvre G 4, Nikosthenes Painter); *ARV²* p. 129, nos. 20–22 (Würzburg 471, London 1907.10–20.1, London E 11—all connected with the Nikosthenes Painter and signed by Pamphaios as potter); Basle, Cahn 615 (Herakles in Centauromachy).

In Attic black-figure the net pattern framing a tondo on the *inside* first occurs on a cup by the Lysippides Painter in Munich (*ABV* p. 256, no. 22) and, at about that time, on a cup belonging to the Group of Walters 48.42 in Dallas (1972.5; *Greek Vases from Southern Collections* [1981] p. 75). In each case the net pattern frames a gorgoneion, and perhaps the inside of the bilingual cup in Palermo, signed by Andokides, may have been black-figure, showing, as Beazley (*ABV* p. 256, no. 21) surmised, a gorgoneion.

NOTES: On the painter, see *ARV* pp. 117–118; p. 1627; *Para.* p. 509; *ARVAP* p. 62; M. Ohly-Dumm, "Schale mit Theseus und Sinis," *Münchner Jahrbuch der bildenden Kunst* 22 (1971): 7–22, especially 14ff.; K. Schefold, "Pammachos," *AK* 17 (1974): 137ff., especially p. 140; T. Blatter, "Eine neue Schale des Epidromos-Malers," *HASB* 2 (1976): 5–9; and D. Williams, "Apollodoros and a New Amazon Cup in a Private Collection," *JHS* 97 (1977): 160–168, especially 163ff.

8 KYLIX

Height 8.2 cm; diameter of the bowl 23.9 cm; width, including the handles, 30.9 cm.

Recomposed from fragments with very minor restoration.

Attic; attributed to Onesimos by Ohly-Dumm, but to the Proto-Panaitian Group by D. Williams, Bothmer and Guy; circa 510–500 B.C.

Unpublished, but mentioned by M. Ohly-Dumm, "Medeas Widder-zauber," *JPGM* 9 (1981), p. 21, n. 62.

Red-figured kylix with a shallow bowl and a low foot (type B). There is some use of added red. On the rim of the bowl, reserved circle. The areas inside and under the handles are reserved, as is the molding between the stem and the foot. The glaze does not extend to the bottom of the foot.

INSIDE. On the inside of the cup the tondo is formed by a double reserved circle. There is a small reserved exergue on which two figures stand. A taller youth, his staff propped behind him, is engaged in affectionate conversation with a younger boy. Both figures wear red wreaths, and the younger one's hair is rendered by a triple row of tiny pellets of glaze. The older male wears only a loosely wrapped himation. The younger, who is naked, returns his affectionate gaze. He holds a hoop and

the stick used to roll it along in a favorite Athenian boys' game. In the field above hang everyday implements of the Greek bath, an aryballos (round container for rubbing oil) and, on top, a sponge. To the right hangs a strigil (metal scraper for rubbing down). Also in the field is the inscription ΑΘΕΝΟΔΟΤΟΣ ΚΑΛΟΣ, Athenodotos is beautiful.

OUTSIDE–SIDE A. ARMING SCENE. The scenes on the outside of this cup appear on a double reserved ground line; both are composed of four figures putting on, or wearing, armor. The left-hand figure on side A is bearded and wears a Corinthian helmet with horsehair crest and a short mantle with a plain black border. He holds a long spear upright before him, and steps toward the central figure. In his left hand is a round shield (seen from inside). The second (and central) figure is dressed in a short chiton worn below the waist and a wide red fillet. He is shown in profile leaning over to put on his right greave.

The two right-hand figures face toward the center. The nearer is naked, but for his crested Attic helmet, and he holds a long spear in his right hand and a round shield with a maple leaf blazon in his left hand. The figure on the near plane wears a

loose mantle with a plain black border over his shoulders and arms, and carries a round shield emblazoned with a prancing horse. In his right hand is a spear. In the field the inscription is HO ΠΑΙΣ ΚΑΛΟΣ, the boy is beautiful.

OUTSIDE–SIDE B. CONTINUATION OF THE ARMING SCENE. The figure on the left continues the pair on side A. He stands left, wearing a crested Attic helmet and a black bordered himation. In his right hand he holds a spear; in his left, a round shield with a lion blazon. Next, a youth with one leg in profile and one frontal, his body twisted with movement, has just slung his red baldric over his right shoulder. On his head, a wide fillet.

Next on the right a youth twists his upper body toward the ground to lift his crested Chalcidian helmet (with a nose piece and cutout sections for the ears) and his round shield with a dog blazon. He wears a short pleated chiton with a plain black border.

On the far right a warrior, naked except for his crested Attic helmet, holds a round shield with a leaf blazon. His head and upper body are twisted to the right, as he looks at the long spear held point downward in his right hand. Under the handle to the left of side B, the inscription ΚΑΛΟΣ, beautiful, and, above the figures, HO ΠΑΙΣ ΚΑΛΟΣ, the boy is beautiful.

This cup is painted with great care and delicacy. As on the reverse of the Euphronios krater and the outside of the Epidromos Painter's cup [6, 7], much of the interest here lies in the experimentation with human postures. Aside from the simple profile view, there is a three-quarter view from behind (the third figure on side B) and several three-quarter views from the front with torsion of the upper body and legs that are either shown both in profile, or one in profile and the other fully frontal.

The composition on side A expertly emphasizes the young warrior putting on his greave. The two figures to his right are close together and balance the single figure to his left. The left- and right-hand groups are united by their crossed spears that meet near the ground line directly under the central youth, and the triangular area thus formed serves to focus attention on the central figure.

This cup is most convincingly attributed to the late sixth-century Proto-Panaitian I Group which shares kalos names (the names of favored youths) with Euphronios and the Epidromos Painter. Proto-Panaitian cups, mostly with athletic and party scenes, are the immediate forerunners of the famous early fifth-century artist Onesimos, some of whose vases formerly were attributed to a "Panaitios Painter."

NOTES: For the gesture of the older male in the tondo, see the cup by Peithinos (to whose cups this piece is very close), *ARVAP* fig. 214. The portrayal of the two figures in the tondo is similar to representations of Zeus and Ganymede (see H. Sichtermann, "Zeus und Ganymede in frühklassischer Zeit," *AK* 2 [1959]: 9ff.; S. Kaempf-Dimitriadou, *Die Liebe der Götter in der attischen Kunst des 5. Jh. v. Chr.* [*AK* Beiheft 11, 1979]: 7ff.), but the lack of divine attributes (especially a sceptre) in connection with the elder or a rooster in connection with the younger makes this identification doubtful. On the various types of armor, see A. Snodgrass, *Arms and Armour of the Greeks* (1971), *passim*. On the kalos name Athenodotos, see *ARV* pp. 1567–1568, nos. 1–14. The name appears on cups of or near the Proto-Panaitian Group (three), Onesimos (seven), Peithinos (one), Colmar Painter (one) and somewhat akin to the early work of Douris (one).

For the Proto-Panaitian Group, *ARV* pp. 314–315, p. 1605, p. 1701; *Para.* p. 358; *ARVAP* pp. 133–134.

9 PANATHENAIC PRIZE AMPHORA

Height 65.8 cm; diameter 40.4 cm; diameter of mouth 17.9 cm; width of lip 1.7 cm; diameter of foot 12.5 cm; width of resting surface of foot 1.2 cm.

The vase is broken and repaired with minor missing portions restored (notably part of the shield and left leg of the stooping man on side B). The vase has misfired, with much of the glaze on side B red, instead of black, and the glaze has been abraded in many places and is totally gone from the foot. In addition there are many scratches and several spalls, as well as nicks along the edge of the mouth.

Attic; attributed to the Kleophrades Painter (compilers of *Catalogue of Antiquities*); circa 500–490 B.C.

Published: Sotheby's, *Catalogue of Antiquities* (December 13, 1982), pp. 64–65, no. 221.

Black-figured Panathenaic prize amphora. Echinus mouth, top flat and reserved. Neck glazed inside to depth of 4.6 cm. Ring at junction of neck and body, set off by incised line below. Round handles, oval in section, entirely glazed.

Echinus foot with steep curve. Slight flare of body above foot; twenty-eight rays above foot joined at base by black band. Palmette lotus chain on neck (seven lotuses and seven palmettes on side A, seven lotuses and six and a half palmettes on B). Tongue pattern below (twenty-two on A, of which three are obscured by Athena's helmet; twenty-one on B). The pictures are in panels with ground lines in diluted glaze and lateral frames in glaze.

The subject on the obverse is the statue of Athena Polias between two Doric columns surmounted by cocks. Inscribed, between the left-hand column and Athena: ΤΟΝ ΑΘΕΝΕΘΕΝ ΑΘΛΟΝ one of the prizes at Athens. Athena is shown wearing a belted peplos, an aegis, a high-crested Attic helmet, an earring and a spiral bracelet, as well as a fillet on her helmet. An incised line on her neck may stand for a necklace. In her right hand she holds a spear; on her left arm a round shield emblazoned with a Pegasus.

The reverse shows the competition for which the vase was awarded, the pyrrhic. On the left a bearded judge or trainer clad in a himation gestures toward a nude, bearded contestant who carries *two* shields on his arms and looks back. Both wear fillets in their hair. The near shield has a hoplitodromos as a device. On the right another bearded man, a garment wrapped around his middle, carries a shield on his left arm and bends over, looking up. His shield is without device.

The accessory colors are white and red. White is applied to the flesh of Athena, dots on her peplos, dots along the border of her aegis and along the support of her crest, the shield devices, as well as the outlines of the shield strap and shield-staple of the man's left shield, its tassels and connecting cords. Red is used for the alternate tongues on the shoulders, the comb, wattles and wing bows of the cocks, the fillet and belt of Athena, a stripe

along the edge of her peplos, and the fifty-three dots on her shield rim.

On the reverse red is used for the fillets and beards of the judge and the contestant, stripes along the edges of the judge's himation and the rims of the shields. There are also red lines on the ring or fillet between neck and shoulder, on top and bottom of the frame of the panel on the reverse, along the edge of the mouth, and above the rays.

There is much variety in the treatment of Athena's peplos on the Panathenaics by the Kleophrades Painter, and it is not always easy to recognize chronological criteria based on the garments alone. Other considerations should include the treatment of the rim of Athena's shield and the drawing of the Pegasus, the Kleophrades Painter's constant shield device. While the obverse is by necessity rather traditional if not stiff, the artist has bestowed his own personality on the profile of Athena's head, with the big ear and the full lips so well known from his red-figured heads. The reverse allowed him greater freedom, especially in those events that show athletes (as opposed to chariots). The Kleophrades Painter favors three-figure compositions (cf. *ABV* p. 404, nos. 5 bis [*ARV*² pp. 1632 and 1705], 7, 8, 9, 15, 16), even in foot races.

The representation of a pyrrhic dancer with *two* shields is of special significance, for we know very little of the pyrrhic competition at the Panathenaic festival. Lysias wrote a defense for an unnamed Athenian who had been accused of taking bribes (XXI) and we learn that this man had spent eight hundred drachmae on pyrrhic dances at the Great Panathenaea in the archonship of Glaukippos (410–409 B.C.); a few years later at the small Panathenaea under Eukleides (404–403 B.C.) he expended seven minae on a chorus of boy pyrrhicists. The pyrrhic

dance was a dance in armor and the normal equipment was a shield, a helmet, and a spear, but Xenophon mentions in his *Anabasis* (VI,I.9–10) a Mysian who performed with two peltae in 400 B.C. when the Greeks entertained the envoys of King Korylas of Paphlagonia at Kotyora, in the country of Tibarenes. Two peltae, of course, weigh much less than two regular round shields; dancing with two heavy shields must have been quite strenuous, and it is even more astonishing that on occasion two shields were used for acrobatic feats, of which the earliest representation occurs on a pseudo-Panathenaic amphora in the Cabinet des Médailles (*CVA* Bibliothèque Nationale pls. 88–89). There an acrobat with *two* shields, greaves, and a helmet has run up a ramp and jumped on the croup of a horse, while a youth seated on a second horse next to it looks on. This vase of about 540 B.C. is the earliest that shows a man dressed as a hoplite, but with two shields, performing in front of an audience. Beazley had surmised (*BABesch* 14 [1939], p. 11) that this acrobatic feat was "not one of the official events at the games, but a side show," but the appearance of a Panathenaic prize amphora with a man holding two shields suggests that perhaps there was a competition involving two shields at the Great Panathenaea. In spite of the visible shield device on Mr. Hunt's amphora, a hoplitodromos, the scene cannot be interpreted as the preparation for the race in armor with one of the contestants having merely picked up a second shield to be handed to a friend, for the shield device faces *right* and suggests that the shield should be carried on the *left* arm, just as on the red-figured skyphos of about 470 B.C. in Mr. Noble's collection (*Ancient Art from New York Private Collections* [1961] pp. 63–64, no. 248, pl. 90) on which an acrobat with helmet and *two* shields is about to turn a somersault. There the visible device is a crouching dog, also facing *right*. DvB

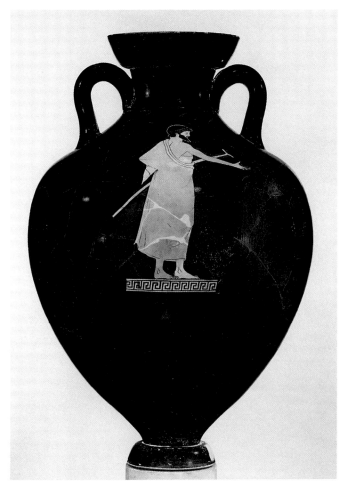

10 PANATHENAIC AMPHORA

Height 64.7 cm; diameter 43.3 cm; diameter of mouth 19.7 cm; diameter of foot 13.74 cm; width of lip 1.83 cm; width of resting surface of foot 1.6 cm.

The vase is broken and repaired, with some pieces missing, notably a section of the kithara with the right hand and part of the right forearm and the heel and ankle of the left foot, as well as the shin of the kithara player. The heel and ankle of the left foot are restored, as is the knee of the right leg. The glaze, as often on vases by the Berlin Painter, is less well preserved on the reverse where it has fired reddish and where it has flaked off from some of the relief lines in the himation.

Attic; attributed to the Berlin Painter (Bothmer); circa 490–480 B.C. Unpublished.

Red-figured Panathenaic amphora. Echinus mouth, slightly beveled top, glazed. Neck glazed to depth of 5.4 cm. Ring at junction of neck and body. Round handles, oval in section, entirely glazed. Echinus foot. The pictures are unframed; each figure stands on an ornamental strip that begins on the obverse at the height of 27.0 cm and on the reverse at the height of 28.05 cm.

The subject is a concert. On the obverse a bearded kithara player is singing as he plays the kithara. He wears a voluminous festive robe with short sleeves. His head is thrown back, beard and hair are reddish brown, and in his hair he wears a wreath. The

kithara is equipped with a long sash that terminates below in a tasseled fringe. The reverse is occupied by an attentive judge or listener. His beard and hair are black, but he wears a similar wreath on his head. His garment is a normal himation worn over his left shoulder; his right arm is stretched out as in a greeting; with his left hand he holds a staff. The pattern below the figures is, on the obverse, a key pattern in which the stopt key alternates between a rightward and a leftward direction. Each key, in turn, is followed by a saltire cross set in a square which, in turn, either sits on the ground line or is suspended from the upper border. This sequence of ornamental elements has been dubbed "ULFA" by Beazley: "short for upper, lower, facing alternately" as he explains his abbreviation in his last article on the Berlin Painter (Melbourne University Press, Occasional Paper No. 6 [1964], p. 7); on the reverse the ornamental band is a simple stopt key pattern of ten elements. A matte red accessory color is used for the wreaths, the fasteners of the kithara chords and the string of the plektron. There are also two red lines on the foot, one near the junction of foot and body; the other at the lower edge.

Amphorae of Panathenaic shape are in the tradition of the full-sized *black-figured* amphorae that, filled with oil from the sacred olive groves of Athens, were awarded at the great Panathenaic festivals every four years. The earliest prize amphorae date

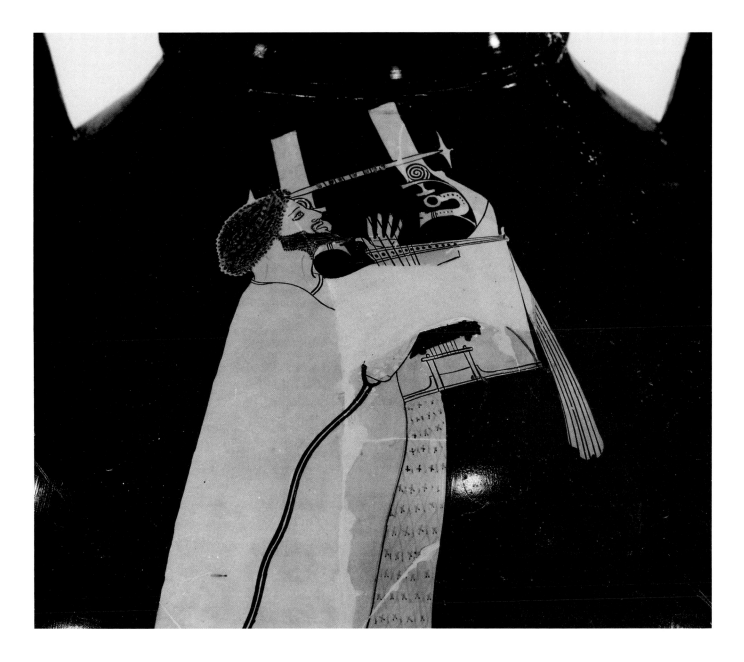

from 570–550 B.C. but the custom continued well into Hellenistic times, long after the black-figured technique of vase-painting had been replaced by the red-figured technique. This Panathenaic by the Berlin Painter is unusual in that it is of the same size (and holds presumably the same liquid content) as the black-figured prizes, and it must have been made by a potter who normally made the standard vases that were painted in black figure and endowed with the official legend "one of the prizes at Athens."

There are other red-figured vases of the distinctive Panathenaic shape by the Berlin Painter, but all of them are smaller, ranging in height from 32.4 to 53.5 cm.

Musical competitions were part of the Athenian festival; and there are many kithara players by the Berlin Painter, notably the bearded performer on a Panathenaic in Montpellier, the similar kithara player on an amphora recently in the London

market and two young musicians, one in New York on an amphora of type C and one in Leningrad on a neck amphora with twisted handles. No two of his citharodes are alike, but they all share a certain rapture. The player on the amphora of type A once in the London market bends over as if still tuning his kithara before the concert has begun and the young musician on the New York vase has his feet wider apart with the body in swaying motion, also conveyed by the fluttering kithara sash. Beazley (*op. cit.* p. 6) aptly remarks that the scene in New York "is not a performance, but practice or instruction." The youth on the New York vase has the same diluted glaze in his hair, rendering the color reddish brown, as does the kithara player on the Panathenaic amphora. A special feature of the latter is his beard: since the head is thrown back, the underside of the beard is revealed and we observe that it grows to about the middle of the throat, a touch of realism not visible on other red-figured beards.   DvB

11 KYLIX

Height 9.8 cm; diameter of the bowl 23.7 cm; width, including the handles, 31.1 cm.

Recomposed from fragments. There are restored areas on side B: (1) from the left-hand handle across to include part of the upper body, face and the himation of the figure on the left and (2) the right shoulder and upper body of the central figure. There is marked abrasion of the surface on sides A and B.

Attic; attributed to the Triptolemos Painter (Knauer, Bothmer and Guy); circa 490–480 B.C.

Published: Summa, *Auction 1* (1981), no. 10, but with an attribution no longer held.

Red-figured drinking cup with a shallow bowl that runs smoothly into the stem of the foot (type B kylix). The lip is offset on the inside only (2.4 cm). There is some use of added red and reserved areas on the inside of and under the handles. The glaze does not extend to the bottom of the foot.

INSIDE. DOG TRAINER. Within a tondo formed by a maeander border within circles of glaze, a youth and a dog that bites him stand on a reserved exergue. The youth wears a red apicate fillet and is infibulated. He holds a long and knotty staff in his right hand and turns three-quarters left to place his left hand on the

back of the unruly animal. The dog, whose body is shown in profile with his head sharply rotated, defecates while he bites the youth on the thigh. Above the figures hang implements of the bath: an aryballos and sponge. The scene graphically illustrates the beginning of the dog's training, which is shown completed on the outside of the cup.

OUTSIDE–SIDE A. DOG TRAINER. The scenes on the outside of the cup appear on a double reserved ground line. To the left on this side a youth wearing a red apicate fillet, his lower legs crossed, leans on a long knotty staff and watches dog and trainer perform. The now well-behaved animal stands in profile and lifts his left forepaw to "shake hands" with his successful trainer. The trainer, naked except for the same fillet, leans with his right foot forward toward the dog. In the field above hang an aryballos with sponge, a strigil and a pair of sandals (the upper parts in added red).

OUTSIDE–SIDE B. BATHING SCENE. The central figure in this side also wears the red fillet and carries a staff like the trainer in the other two scenes. He may be the same man at his bath. He carries an aryballos strapped very high on his arm and reaches for a folded himation that the youth to his left, naked but for the fillet, holds out to him. Behind the central figure a third naked youth with a similar fillet holds a scraper toward him, as if to help with the bath. Above the scene are an aryballos suspended by a strap, a pair of sandals (added red for the straps) and a pair of shoes (added red for the upper part).

The Triptolemos Painter is named after the subject of a stamnos in the Louvre attributed to his hand. He decorated both large vases and a number of cups. He seems to have spent his early years in the workshop of Euphronios, and some of his early cups were potted by that master. Many of his works show the same novelty of theme that appears here in the bold and unusual treatment of the athletic motif, which along with other subjects from everyday life were among the painter's favorites.

NOTES: For the subject of dog training, see D. Hull, *Hounds and Hunting in Ancient Greece* (1964): 50ff. For the Triptolemos Painter, *ARV* pp. 360–367, p. 1648, p. 1708; *Para.* pp. 364–365, p. 512; *ARVAP* pp. 139–140; E. Knauer, *Ein Skyphos des Triptolemosmalers* (125. Winckelmannsprogramm, 1973), especially pp. 17–18; "Fragments of a Cup by the Triptolemos Painter," *GRBS* 17 (1976): 209–216; R. Guy, "A Ram's Head Rhyton Signed by Charinos," *Arts in Virginia* 21.2 (1981): 2–15.

12 STAMNOS

Height 36.5 cm; diameter of the body 29.3 cm; width, including the handles, 38.3 cm; diameter of the mouth 20.7 cm; diameter of the foot 14.6 cm.

Recomposed from fragments. There are several areas of restoration on both obverse and reverse. Side A: (1) part of the rump of Odysseus' ram and the door of the cave; (2) the upper legs and lower body of Odysseus and part of the rock below; (3) most of the head, right arm and sword of Odysseus along with his upper body and part of the lower legs of his companion; (4) one foreleg of Odysseus' ram and one hindleg of the leading ram with part of the right foot of the Kyklops and (5) the left ankle and foot of the Kyklops along with the right elbow of Odysseus' companion and one foreleg of the leading ram. Side B: (1) the lower part of the male figure along with the bottom left-hand corner of the frame extending into the foot of the laver; (2) part of the upper torso, left hip and arm of the youth along with much of the left side of the bowl of the laver and the upper part of its foot; (3) the left elbow of the girl in the center; (4) the right-hand shoulder, upper arm and part of the breast of the girl on the right. Several minor fills; ancient repairs on side A.

Attic; attributed to the Siren Painter (Greifenhagen); circa 480 B.C.

Published: C. Isler-Kerényi and F. Causey-Frel, *Stamnoi. An Exhibition at the J. Paul Getty Museum* (1980), no. 15 (with incorrect dimensions); D. von Bothmer, "A New Kleitias Fragment from Egypt," *AK* 24 (1981): 66–67; A. Greifenhagen, "Odysseus in Malibu," *Pantheon* 40 (1982): 211–217. The fragments he speaks of as lost (215) were not ancient, but modern restoration.

Red-figured stamnos of the shape standard for the early fifth century with a downturned lip, a high and slightly concave neck, a broadly ovoid body and a disk foot. There is a raised fillet at the junction of the neck and shoulder. The horizontal handles are triple-reeded. The glaze does not extend to the bottom of the foot. The top edge of the fillet is reserved, as are the insides of the handles. The figured panels are framed above by tongues (which run all the way around the shoulder of the vase), on the sides by a net pattern and below by maeanders and cross-squares (side A) and maeanders and checkerboard squares (side B). In each case there are two maeander elements flanking the squares.

SIDE A. ESCAPE OF ODYSSEUS FROM THE CAVE OF POLYPHE-MUS. The bearded giant with long ringlets, his single eye closed and bleeding from the wound inflicted by Odysseus, dominates the scene. He stretches diagonally across the picture from foreground to background to close the huge rock door of his cave. In the middle ground are two rams carrying the Greeks to safety. The rear one, Polyphemus' best (Homer, *Odyssey* 9.432), nuzzles the giant's beard in the upper center of the scene. A bearded Odysseus is bound to this ram's belly with two straps. He holds the rump with his left hand, and carries a drawn sword in his right. Like his companion, he wears a short chiton with buttoned sleeves. On the right, the companion clings to his ram in the same manner as Odysseus, but is beardless and wears a scabbard over his shoulder. All three characters are identified by inscriptions: ΚΥΚΛΟΠΣ (Kyklops); ΟΔΥΣΕΥΣ (Odysseus) and ΙΔΑΜΕΝΕΥΣ (for Idomeneus, otherwise unknown as a companion of Odysseus).

SIDE B. BATHING SCENE. On the left is a youth. He wears a himation draped below his waist, and leans on a staff. His right hand is on his hip; with his left, he reaches across the basin to fondle the breast of the woman in the center. The woman's body is turned frontally, her head to the left. With her right hand she adjusts her diadem. Her left hand rests on the rim of

the basin below. The torsion of the body is suggested by the raised right shoulder, profile right breast and by the three-quarter view of the legs (one in profile, one in three-quarter view). To the right a woman, naked but for the sakkos (net) on her head, holds a sponge and steps on a board(?).

On the underside of the foot, graffiti ⊢ε and ⋏7.

Odysseus' escape from Polyphemus is one of the best-known events in Homer's *Odyssey* (9.413–479). It appears in vase painting in the mid-seventh century, and becomes especially popular in the later sixth and early fifth centuries. This version, one of the earliest Attic representations to include a portrayal of the cave, is unique among paintings of the legend in that it shows Polyphemus in the act of closing the cave. Usually he sits or stands by, holding his club and groping for his surroundings, but here he dominates the entire scene. A pathos, somewhat comic perhaps, is established by the left-hand ram, who at the same time affectionately acknowledges his master and carries his enemies to safety.

The Siren Painter, so-called from a stamnos in the British Museum with Odysseus listening to the Sirens on side A, also painted a well-known stamnos in the Louvre. Both are very similar in shape, subsidiary decoration and style to the Hunt stamnos. On both sides of the Hunt vase the artist has rendered his theme with an innovation, life and humor that is most appealing.

NOTES: On Attic red-figured stamnoi, see B. Philippaki, *The Attic Stamnos* (1967), especially pp. 97ff. and C. Isler-Kerényi, *Stamnoi* (n.d.), especially p. 70 for a similar bathing scene, but with all women. On the theme of Odysseus' flight from the Kyklops, O. Touchefeu-Meynier, *Thèmes odysséens dans l'art antique* (1968): 42–78; *Vasenlisten* pp. 437–439 with Bothmer's commentary, *op. cit.* p. 67, n. 5; B. Fellmann, *Die antiken Darstellungen des Polyphemabenteuers* (1972): 79ff. There is much general information on the Greek bath in R. Ginouvès, *Balaneutiké* (1962).

On the Siren Painter, *ARV* p. 289, p. 1642; *Para.* p. 355; *ARVAP* p. 113.

13 PELIKE

Height 38.2 cm; diameter 26.7 cm.

Intact and complete. Very slight chipping of the surface and some incrustation.

Attic; attributed to Hermonax (Bothmer); circa 470 B.C.

Unpublished.

Red-figured pelike with a torus lip, flat handles and a disk foot. The body is globular, heavy at the bottom. There are touches of added white, and the glaze does not extend to the bottom of the foot.

On the handles are addorsed palmettes; between them, tendrils ending in volutes. On the neck, a laurel band facing left and broken at the handles; below, lotus and enclosed palmettes. Around the body below the picture zone, a band of maeander and cross-squares in an irregular sequence.

SIDE A. THESEUS' BATTLE WITH THE MINOTAUR. In the center Theseus, dressed in a white wreath and short belted chiton and carrying a scabbard on his left side, draws his sword back from the wound he has just inflicted in the Minotaur's right armpit. With his left hand he holds the Minotaur by one of his horns. The very human and somewhat comic Minotaur steps forward to defend himself (far from threateningly). In his extended right hand is a stone; his left arm is stretched out behind him. Between the two central figures is a rock which probably represents the landscape of the labyrinth in which the Minotaur lived.

To the left a youth, wearing a white wreath and a himation draped over his left shoulder and arm, holds a lyre ready to celebrate Theseus' victory. To the right a maiden wearing a fillet with leaves, a chiton with dotted borders and a himation steps forward and holds a white wreath out toward Theseus.

SIDE B. YOUTHS AND MAIDENS. The celebrants, two youths and two maidens rescued from the Minotaur, continue the scene from side A onto the reverse of the vase. The youths, the first and third figures from the left, wear wreaths and himations and carry lyres. The second and fourth figures are maidens who wear decorated fillets, long full chitons and himations. The second figure carries a wreath.

Under the handle on the right of side A, a rock seat; under the handle to the left, a rock seat with a backrest (cf. *ARV* p. 485, no. 24).

The deeds of the early Attic king Theseus are among the most popular themes of red-figured vase painters in the early fifth century. By the time this vase was painted the theme of Theseus' battle with the Cretan monster had long been popular, as had the particular form of representation with the celebrants present, albeit anachronistically, at the encounter. The portrayal, however, makes up for what it lacks in novelty and strength by its rather humorous and certainly very graceful execution of the traditional theme.

NOTES: On the shape, see R.-M. Becker, *Formen attischen Peliken von den Pionier-Gruppe bis zum Beginn der Frühklassik* (Diss. Tübingen 1977) with the review of D. von Bothmer, *AJA* 83 (1979): 361–362. In size and shape it is closest to Becker's earliest group including the two pelikai in the Villa Giulia (*ARV* p. 485, nos. 27, 33). In pattern work it is also close to the pelike in Basle (*ARV* p. 485, no. 26; S. Kaempf-Dimitriadou, "Zeus und Ganymed auf einer Pelike des Hermonax," *AK* 22 [1979]: 49–54). Several early pelikai have a scene continuous from obverse to reverse.

On the legend of Theseus and the Minotaur, see H. Herter, s.v. 'Minotauroskampf,' *RE* Suppl. 13 (1973): cols. 1117ff. Also, F. Brommer, "Mythologische Darstellungen auf Vasenfragmenten der Sammlung Cahn," *Studien zur griechischen Vasenmalerei* (*AK* Beiheft 7, 1970): 50ff. and *Vasenlisten* pp. 226ff. I have not seen E. Young, *The Slaying of the Minotaur* (Diss. Bryn Mawr 1972). For a political interpretation, see J. Neils, *The Youthful Deeds of Theseus: Iconography and Iconology* (Diss. Princeton 1980). There is a more general treatment of Theseus in art in C. Dugas and R. Flacelière, *Thésée. Images et récits* (1958).

On Hermonax, see *ARV* pp. 483–492, p. 1655, p. 1706; *Para.* pp. 379–380; *ARVAP* pp. 193–194; G. Richter and L. Hall, *Red-figured Athenian Vases in the Metropolitan Museum of Art* (1936): 115–116; M. Pallottino, "Studi sull'arte di Hermonax," *Atti Acc. Lincei* 7.1 (1941): 1–76; F. Johnson, "A Pelike Painted by Hermonax," *Classical Studies in Honor of W. A. Oldfather* (1943): 73–81 and "The Late Vases of Hermonax," *AJA* 49 (1945): 491–502 and "The Career of Hermonax," *AJA* 51 (1947): 233–247; G. Richter, *Attic Red-figured Vases* (1958): 108–109; N. Weill, "Un cratère d'Hermonax," *BCH* 86 (1962): 64–94 (important, as this krater also has a scene of Theseus and the Minotaur, but with a very different composition); F. Johnson, "A Note on Hermonax," *AJA* 73 (1969): 73ff.; E. Dusenbery, "Two Attic Red-figured Kraters in Samothrace," *Hesperia* 47 (1978): 236–243; J. Oakley, "Athamas, Ino, Hermes and the Infant Dionysus: A Hydria by Hermonax," *AK* 25 (1982): 44–47, especially pp. 46–47. I have not seen H. Langenfass, *Hermonax. Untersuchungen zur Chronologie* (Diss. Munich 1972).

14 CALYX-KRATER

Height 51.4 cm; diameter of the mouth 49.9 cm; diameter of the foot 22.0 cm.

Intact and complete. Minor incrustation and very minor chipping on the surface.

Lucanian; near to the Policoro Painter (Trendall); circa 400 B.C. Unpublished.

Red-figured calyx-krater [6] with a torus mouth, deeply tapering offset rim, tall narrow body and a high disk foot. There is a fillet at the junction of the body and the foot. The decoration is rich in added white, yellow and red. Reserved circles on the inside of the lip and inside at the base of the rim. On the outside, reserved

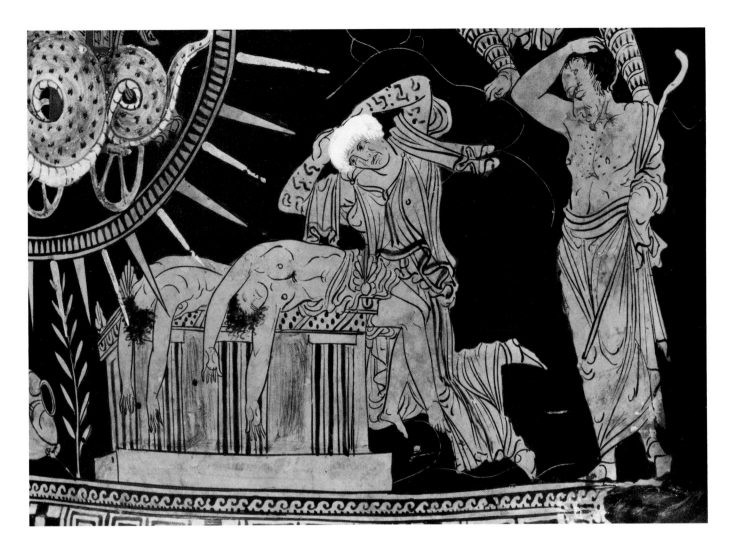

circles above and below the rim, above and below the fillet and on the concave molding on the top of the foot. The glaze does not extend to the bottom of the foot. The insides of the handles and the areas under the handles are also reserved.

On the rim is a chain of diagonal addorsed palmettes connected by tendrils. Around the roots of the handles are tongues. The patterns on the cul are, on side A, wave pattern, followed by maeander to the left and checkerboard squares, above five and one-half diagonal addorsed palmettes bounded below by a narrow band of small rays. On side B, maeander to the left and two checkerboard squares, bordered below by a somewhat broader band of small rays.

SIDE A. MEDEA'S DEPARTURE. In the upper center Medea rides off in a chariot drawn by two crested, bearded and spotted serpents. She is dressed ornately in a Phrygian helmet and a cross-girded chiton under which is a tight-fitting long-sleeved garment in a pattern of light and dark diamonds. Around her is a large and boldly colored nimbus, which is perhaps present as an attribute of her grandfather Helios who had given her the chariot she drives and/or as a symbol of her ascent into another realm, a function of the nimbus in several other South Italian vase paintings.

To the left and right of Medea are Furies, female spirits of vengeance with hawk noses, sagging breasts and large wings. They are clad in short belted chitons worn over sleeved undergarments and trousers, all finely ornamented. Their feet are bare and gnarly, and they sit upon large rocks rendered with incision.

All three figures in the upper register gaze at the scene of carnage below. To the right an old nurse and paedagogue have raised their hands to their heads in mourning for Medea's two dead children, whose partly clad bodies are draped over the altar before them. To the left, Jason with high boots, a staff and himation draped loosely around his waist looks up at Medea, while to the right a Maltese dog and upset bronze hydria appear in the landscape, rendered by incision and flanked by small shrubs.

SIDE B. TELEPHUS AND AGAMEMNON. The central figure is Agamemnon, drawing his sword against Telephus. His mantle is draped over his left arm and he wears high laced boots. On the left, Telephus takes refuge at an altar. He holds Orestes in one hand and a sword to kill him, if Agamemnon should approach, in the other. His wounded leg is bandaged and blood drips on the altar. The child looks toward his parents and holds out his

14 CALYX-KRATER (continued)

arms to them. To the right a crowned Clytemnestra holds out her own hands and looks toward her husband and young son in the arms of Telephus.

The story of Medea, a woman with magical powers who left Colchis on the Black Sea with Jason, but was deserted by him

and in revenge killed her children, is one of the most popular and enduring of Greek legends. Side A is a representation (or artistic elaboration) of the final scene of Euripides' *Medea*, a tragedy produced in 431 B.C. Scenes such as this with Medea and her dead children are known to appear only on vases that were produced in South Italy. On this vase it receives a rich, exceptionally full and ornate treatment.

The legend of Telephus and Orestes is another favorite of Greek legend and the subject of a Euripidean tragedy presented in 438. The stories about this son of Herakles and Auge appear in many variations. At the beginning of the Trojan War he fought against the Greeks, who mistakenly had landed in Mysia, and was wounded by Achilles. When the wound did not heal, he consulted an oracle which told him he would be healed by the one who wounded him. Telephus accordingly went to Greece, where the Achaeans had returned, and consulted Clytemnestra. With or without her consent he took her child Orestes as a hostage to force Agamemnon to help. Agamemnon was at first angered, and it is this critical point in the action that is portrayed on side B of the Hunt krater. Subsequently Agamemnon relented, and Telephus was cured not by Achilles himself, but with the rust from his spear.

In the later fifth century the Greeks of South Italy developed a red-figured pottery industry of their own. At first very close to its Attic models (and perhaps employing Attic artists), it soon developed its own very rich, colorful and ornate style, both in potting and painting. This vase is a large and fine example of this incipient ornate style.

The Policoro Painter is an early Lucanian artist who is named after the town in southern Italy where many of his vases were found. Favorite subjects of the painter and those around him were Greek tragedies, and the Policoro Painter himself painted a version of the same episode in the Medea story that appears on the Hunt krater. It is far simpler in composition, but stylistically similar to the rendition on the Hunt piece and the Policoro Painter's vase itself is of a far less refined shape. The elaboration of both painting and potting suggest that the Hunt painter is a successor of, rather than the Policoro Painter himself.

NOTES: For versions of the Medea story in vase painting, see E. Simon, "Die Typen der Medeadarstellung," *Gymnasium* 61 (1954): 203–227; *Vasenlisten* p. 494; A.D. Trendall and T.B.L. Webster, *Illustrations of Greek Drama* (1971): 96ff. D. Page's edition of Euripides' *Medea* (1952) is often wrong or outdated, but has some useful material. For the Policoro Painter's krater with Medea, see *LCS* 2, pl. 26, 3 and pl. 27, 3. On the meaning of the nimbus, J. Beazley, *Etruscan Vase Painting* (1947), p. 38; Keyssner, s.v. 'nimbus,' *RE* 17 (1937): cols. 591ff., especially pp. 599ff.; *LCS* 1, p. 689 and K. Schauenburg, "Gestirnbilder in Athen und Unteritalien," *AK* 5 (1962): 51ff. For Helios with a nimbus very similar to that around Medea on the Hunt krater, see W. Hornbostel, *Aus Gräbern und Heiligtümern* (1981), no. 115. For the naked Furies, cf. a bell-krater with the Orestes myth in K. Schauenburg, "Die nackte Erinys," *Festschrift Brommer* pp. 247–254; E. Wüst, s.v. 'Erinys,' *RE* Suppl. 8 (1956): cols. 138ff.

For Telephus in vase painting, see C. Bauchhenss-Thüriedl, *Der Mythos von Telephos in der antiken Bildkunst* (1971); *LCS* 1, pp. 103–104; *VMG* no. 20 (M. Mayo); There is a reconstruction of the plot of Euripides' *Telephus* with some relevant material on vases in T.B.L. Webster, *Tragedies of Euripides* (1967): 43–48.

On the Policoro Painter, *LCS* 1, pp. 50–51 and pp. 56–59.

15 CALYX-KRATER

Height 57.1 cm; diameter of the mouth 53.4 cm; diameter of the foot 25.4 cm.

Intact and complete; minor surface abrasion.

Apulian; attributed to the Darius Painter; circa 350–325 B.C.

Published: *RVAp* 2, 18/64a; Summa, *Auction 1* (1981), no. 26.

Red-figured calyx-krater with torus lip, concave offset rim, narrow body and high disk foot. There is a fillet at the junction of the body and the foot. This krater, manufactured some fifty to seventy-five years after the preceding vase [14], exhibits a later, more exaggeratedly elegant shape. The body is slim and tall.

The elongated handles lie close against the body and thus reinforce this profile.

The decoration has much added white, yellow and red. There is a reserved circle on the top of the lip and another on the inside of the rim. There are also reserved circles on the outside below the rim and above and below the fillet, as well as on the concave molding on the top of the foot. The foot is not glazed to the bottom. Also reserved are bands just above the cul on A and B and the areas under the handles.

On the rim, a laurel band facing left. On the cul, side A, upright palmettes separated by stylized lotuses and a narrow egg and dot frieze. Side B, maeanders (four to the left, four and one-half to the right) interrupted by a single cross-square. Below, a narrow band of waves.

SIDE A. BELLEROPHON'S ARRIVAL AT THE COURT OF IOBATES. To the left in the upper register Bellerophon rides the winged horse Pegasus toward the center of the scene. He wears a petasus and short mantle, and carries a sealed letter in his right hand. To the right the sea god Poseidon, holding a trident, is seated and gestures in Bellerophon's direction. Above him is a sacrificial bull's skull (bukranion) and a sacrificial plate. In the center of the upper register, the lower part of a shield is flanked by wheels.

In the lower register King Iobates is seated on an ornate pillowed couch with his feet on a stool decorated with a Medusa head. He wears an ornate Phrygian helmet and holds a royal scepter surmounted by an eagle. The king glances toward the arriving

Bellerophon. His wife (or daughter) to his right is dressed in chiton and himation and also gestures toward Bellerophon. To her right is a large laver. To the left of Iobates, an Eastern soldier in a Phrygian helmet, a cross-girded chiton, mantle, long-sleeved garment and trousers, holds a spear in his left hand and raises his right arm to the arriving horse and rider. Below, an oinochoe, kantharos, plates and a schematized plant rest on the ground indicated with dotted lines.

SIDE B. DIONYSIAC SCENE. In the center of the top register Eros is seated holding a plate with offerings. In the field far to his left is a window and, to his right, a sash. The figures in the second register stand to the left and right of Eros on ground indicated with dotted lines. On the left, a wreathed young satyr stands with one leg raised on a rock with a schematized plant at its base. He carries a kantharos and a lighted torch. To the right stands a woman dressed in a long chiton and holding a diadem and long branch.

The two figures in the lowest register sit closer in, but still to the left and right of Eros, below and between the flanking figures of the middle register. To the left a woman holds an offering plate and branch and, to the right, Dionysus, wreathed with ivy, has a gnarled staff and another large plate. Both figures are seated and rest their feet on ground indicated by dotted lines. The woman wears a long chiton; Dionysus is half-naked, his mantle draped across his back and thigh. On the ground below (again indicated by dotted lines) there is a flower and, to the left, a plant; to the right, a plant and plate.

15 CALYX-KRATER (continued)

Bellerophon was falsely accused of seducing Stheneboia, the wife of the Argive king Proitos. His royal host thereupon sent him to the Lycian king Iobates with a letter that, unbeknownst to him, contained an intended death warrant. Bellerophon, however, did not die; but, after completing a number of difficult tasks set him by Iobates (including the defeat of the Chimaera), he married the king's daughter.

Although representation of Bellerophon's arrival at Iobates' court are common in South Italian vase painting, this is one of the most detailed of extant versions. Unusual features are the presence of the woman at Iobates' side and the actual appearance of the sealed letter in Bellerophon's hand.

NOTES: For other examples of Bellerophon's arrival in vase painting, see K. Schauenburg, "Bellerophon in unteritalischen Vasenmalerei," *JDAI* 71 (1956): 59ff., especially pp. 81ff.; J.-M. Moret, "Le départ de Bellerophon sur un cratère campanien de Genève," *AK* 15 (1972): 99ff. For more general bibliography on Bellerophon, see *VMG*, no. 32 (K. Hamma). The treatment is especially close to that on a Campanian lekythos in Naples, 147868 (*LCS* 1, 2/781); a Campanian bell-krater in Winterthur, 364 (*LCS* 1, 3/360); and, most notably, to an Apulian column-krater in the Hearst Collection (*RVAp* 1, 1/116; I. Raubitschek, *The Hearst Hillsborough Vases* [1969], no. 27).

On the Darius Painter, see *RVAp* 2, pp. 482–506 (with full bibliography); M. Schmidt, *Der Dariosmaler und sein Umkreis* (1960); M. Schmidt, A. D. Trendall and A. Cambitoglou, *Eine Gruppe apulischer Grabvasen in Basel* (1976): 94–108; J. Chamay and A. Cambitoglou, "La folie d'Athamas par le peintre de Darius," *AK* 23 (1980): 35–43.

16 MAENAD AND SILEN

Height 54.2 cm; length of the base, as preserved, 29.4 cm.

Mold-made terracotta recomposed from five pieces. The right side is missing including the left shoulder, left side of the body and left leg of the silen, and the corner of the base below. One further piece is missing from the garment of the maenad. Excellent preservation of the color.

Etruscan (Città Castellana); circa 500 B.C.

Unpublished.

Large terracotta antefix with a maenad and silen hurrying to the right on a rectangular base. On the back are the remains of the rounded cover tile and a flying strut. On the left the maenad, her legs in profile and her body and face turned frontally, has her left arm over the shoulder of the silen. In her right hand, which is held over the right hip, she carries krotala. On her head is a cylindrical diadem. Her black hair hangs in waves over her forehead and down to her shoulders. The maenad wears a deep red chiton decorated with white rosettes and bordered with black stripes. The chiton clings to the maenad's body and falls into multiple graceful pleats between the legs. Over her shoulders in front and flaring out to her left side and below the hem

of the chiton there is a red himation bordered with black zig-zags. The maenad's feet are bare, her toenails outlined in black.

The silen also strides to the right, his legs in profile and his body and head turned frontally. On his head is an ivy wreath. He looks back and up into the face of the maenad, and has his right hand over her right shoulder. His body is naked except for a lion skin, which still is visible below his left thigh. He has hooved feet (only one extant) and pointed animal ears. His face, a masterpiece of characterization in the archaic Etruscan style, has quizzically arched brows, round protruding eyes and an upturned nose, very pudgy at the tip. He wears a mustache and large round black beard. In his left hand (the arm is now almost entirely missing) he holds a rhyton over his torso.

On the base the decoration is red and black checkerboard between flanking lines of black (top) and red (below).

This antefix, a decorative cover for the ends of the roof tiles, is very similar to two other pieces with the same function and decorative motif, one in the Villa Giulia and the other in the Metropolitan Museum of Art. They all, along with several other fragments extant, seem to have decorated the roof of the smaller temple at Città Castellana (the ancient Falerii). The Hunt piece, however, is significantly larger than either of the other two (54 and 43 cms respectively). Its original brilliant color is preserved over much of the surface; the other two pieces have none.

The motif of maenad and silen was very popular in archaic art, and there are several other Etruscan sites where it was employed for temple antefixes. Silens with hooved feet are especially popular in Etruria (and Ionia), as are the reveling, unresisting maenad figures.

NOTES: For the other two well-preserved antefixes from Città Castellana, A. Andren, *Architectural Terracottas from Etrusco-Italic Temples* (1940): 100–101, no. 1:1; G. Richter, *The Metropolitan Museum of Art. Handbook of the Etruscan Collection* (1940), p. 22 = R. Teitz, *Masterpieces of Etruscan Art* (1967), no. 34. There is a silen head from the same mold in Cleveland: Teitz, *op. cit.*, no. 10. For a slightly later antefix with the same motif from another site at Falerii: M. Pallottino et al., *Il Museo Nazionale Etrusco di Villa Giulia* (1980), no. 329. Another well-preserved maenad and silen antefix of about the same period as the Hunt piece comes from Satricum to the south: Brendel, fig. 173; cf. pp. 247–248.

[51] Balsamarium
Roman (Asia Minor?)
Late Second Century A.D.

The Bronzes of William Herbert Hunt

CLASSICAL BRONZES: SOME NOTES ON THE WILLIAM HERBERT HUNT COLLECTION

Jiří Frel

When Pliny the Elder wrote about sculptors working in bronze in his *Naturalis Historia*, he included it in a passage dealing with bronze technology, similar to his discussion of marble sculptors which he dealt with as part of a treatise on mineralogy. Pliny's approach to art follows the best Greek traditions. The Greek word for art was *techne*—the root for our words *technique* and *technology*—in the same way as the Latin word *ars* reappears today in *artificial* or *artisan*.

For the ancients, art stemmed from craft; the union of both was natural and inevitable. Before there could be any possibility of making sculpture from bronze, it was first necessary to master the composition of the alloy and the process of casting. Such techniques were developed over time in the production of bronze arms, instruments and implements. These were often works of art in themselves; often they could carry further artistic decoration. One example is the eighth-century B.C. Villanovan dagger in the William Herbert Hunt collection [17], which was carried in the bronze sheath decorated with an elaborate incised pattern. Another is the third-century A.D. bronze inkpot [53] inlaid with colorful enamel, anticipating the taste of late antiquity. Few such exquisite objects are known but their places of origin, which range from the limits of ancient Gaul to southern Russia, confirm their popularity throughout the Roman world. The Hunt inkpot was found in the Rhineland. Although the dagger and the inkpot were utilitarian objects, their practical function for the ancient users was inseparable from the aesthetic satisfaction they continue to provide to the modern viewer.

By the same token many small sculptures viewed today as "pure" art originally formed an integral part of some utilitarian object. The small archaic bronze youth [25], for example, was designed as the handle of a pan; the hellenistic Alexander-Herakles [38] was originally a relief-appliqué on a vase; and the splendid Etruscan horse [27] decorated the rim of a cauldron or another similar vessel.

The development of artisanal technology was a precondition for the creation of large bronze sculpture. Ancient tradition credits Theodorus, a sixth-century B.C. court artist in Samos, with landmark innovations in metallurgy and in the creation of freestanding bronze statues. While bronze sculptures of notable size had existed in the previous century, they were laboriously constructed products formed from beaten metal mounted on a wooden core. Casting was limited at the time to the production of small-scale sculptures. In the early fifth century there was a further development of technological processes such as the lost wax technique and the use of the composite casting form which resulted in the predominance of bronze for freestanding statuary that lasted throughout antiquity.

Our vision today of classical sculpture is hampered by several difficulties. The literary sources are scarce and cannot always be related to the available monuments. Very few Greek bronze originals survive—the preserved marbles are considerably more numerous—which is opposite to the situation in antiquity when the majority of works were in bronze. Only three extant life-size bronzes can be directly associated with famous names: the two Riace statues with Phidias, and the Getty bronze with Lysippos. The works of many other masters who sculpted exclusively in bronze are lost. Many famous bronze artists are only names. The works of others, like the masterpieces of Myron or Polykleitos from the fifth century, exist only in Roman marble copies, which dilute their art even more than do marble reproductions of marble originals. Under such circumstances every large bronze is a treasure; for example, one can divine in the gauche Roman youth with inlaid silver eyes [48] some of the inspiration from the classical ephebic beauty, even if its true starting point was the widespread image of Antinous, the emperor Hadrian's favorite.

The situation is similar in regard to Roman portraits. The large collections of the great museums around the world contain countless marble busts and heads. The majority of the few extant ancient bronzes was found in Pompeii and Herculaneum (they are now in the Naples museum) providing a limited insight into the real history of Roman portrait art. But this is not the only reason why the three bronze portrait busts in the Hunt collection assume a special interest, however.

Two of the Hunt portraits [43, 44], unquestionable masterpieces, open new horizons. They evidently belong together, however different they may appear. The woman looks like a Roman matron from the late Republic. The merciless realism of her wrinkled face dried with age stamps her as a farmer's wife, while the urbane appearance of the man is marked by the classicism established in Augustan portraiture. What was the real link between the aging matron and the still young man? Could they have been husband and wife? The busts appear to have been cast as pendants, to be included in the same family gallery. They were created in the same workshop, if not by the same man. A closer examination reveals that the differences are superficial, involving the description of the exterior. Deep down both share the same nature, tough towards the world, hard towards oneself, with silent pride and controlled susceptibility. A similar presentation may be found in Roman portraits from southern Spain, particularly in the museums of Seville or Malaga, but especially in numerous marble heads from the excavations of Merida, which unfortunately are mostly still unpublished. The Hunt bronzes add a new dimension. The local sculptor overcame his provincial limitations and the portraits successfully capture something of the fierce Hispanic nature of the sitters. Something of the same human condition reappears in Spanish painted portraits of the sixteenth and seventeenth centuries.

The third bust [54], also from Spain but of a reduced scale, represents a man from the same stock. While the treatment of the facial structure is more summary than that of the first two busts, the expression is stronger and the psychological characteristics are more marked. In Hispania, the abandonment of classical traditions appears more strikingly than in Rome. The spiritualization of the third century endows the simplified features with a tragic anxiety. A bronze head from Eravisca of larger size in the museum of Cuenca, Spain, belongs to the same current.

Among the other bronzes in the collection deserving special attention is a statuette of a woman holding an object [39], most probably an apple. The figure may represent the goddess Hera, or possibly Eris; the apple would be hers, inscribed "to the most beautiful one," thrown into the midst of goddesses assembled at the wedding of Peleus and Thetis, which started a ruthless competition that brought endless sorrows to mortals. The statuette was found in Antiochia on the Orontes with other material from the first half of the first century B.C. It entered the Hunt collection covered with extensive corrosion, but careful conservation has restored much of the original gilding while removing the corrosion. The execution of the piece is superb, with the exception of two carelessly drilled holes in the bottom edge intended for its mounting on a pedestal, done by an incompetent local craftsman and indicating that the piece was brought to Antiochia from a more important art center. Some large late hellenistic marble statues from Pergamon and the islands of the Aegean (Cos, Delos) show comparable treatment of the volumes, a similar use of the transparent drapery of the himation superimposed over the chiton which enhances the elaborate torsion of the body. The final impression is that of a large statue, demonstrating once again a basic tenet of Greek art: monumentality does not necessarily involve big scale.

While the "golden lady" represents the classical tradition, a smaller statuette of a fully armed Athena [33] introduces a completely different world. Greek ideas underlie her conception, but the forms used in creating her shape are considerably less Greek. She maintains strength, but her wisdom and grace have disappeared. The craftsman must have come from an indigenous community in Sicily; her nearest kin is a small bronze Athena from Selinos, a more ferocious and barbaric goddess of slightly earlier date in the Ortiz collection in Geneva.

Alexander the Great is represented twice in the Hunt collection. One is the already mentioned appliqué [38] of the second century B.C., which recalls the iconographic tradition from Alexander's lifetime of the assimilation of the ruler with Herakles. The concept, Alexander's own, appears already on Alexander's own coin types. The appliqué was found in the Negev desert, but it may have been produced in Alexandria. The other piece which bears Alexander's likeness without involving his identity is an already famous Etruscan statuette of notable size, with a votive inscription [36]. This is not an isolated phenomenon. The features of the great conqueror impressed the Etruscans no less than they did other peoples; perhaps even more, judging by his "presence" in various works of Etruscan art, including large size architectonic sculptures, such as the tufo head of Medusa on the crown of a gable in the J. Paul Getty Museum.

Two Greek statuettes are closely associated by the subjects. The walking satyr [23] was cast apparently in Tarentum still in the sixth century B.C., while the flutist dancing to the sound of his own music [29] must be considerably later, perhaps already from the mid-fifth century B.C. despite its old-fashioned style. His rustic appearance corresponds well to similar products of Arcadia in the central Peloponnese.

Among the Roman bronzes several are particularly attractive. The charming infant Herakles [41] preserves the original base with silver encrustation. The miniature Hermes of Polykleitan inspiration [45] is a masterpiece of Augustan classicism and bears a patina that has won admiration from expert collectors for centuries. The composition and modeling of the fighting giant [37] are so accomplished that one is tempted to consider the statuette an original of the Pergamene school; however, its execution points indisputably to a Roman date.

Animal statuettes are particularly well represented in the Hunt collection. Chronologically, a protome of a griffin [21] opens the series. It was cast in Samos in the first half of the sixth century B.C. and decorated the rim of a large cauldron. Next comes the flat appliqué of a heifer [26] probably made in Tarentum in the early fifth century B.C. intended to be affixed to the neck of a bronze krater. The style remains that of Spartan bronzes, which is not surprising since Tarentum was Sparta's only colony, maintaining close relations with its metropole. Another bovine, a powerful bull [28] also from Magna Graecia, belongs to the decades around the middle of the fifth century B.C. The comparison with the heifer clearly illustrates the change which occurred from the light and pleasant style of the late archaic period to the monumentality of the first stage of classicism.

The two last animal sculptures are Etruscan. A pair of lion protomai [22] served as finials on wooden cylindrical handles of an instrument or a piece of furniture. Their rather barbaric archaic style enhances successfully the ferocious appearance of the beasts. The horse [27] has already been mentioned. A companion piece, formerly in the Bomford collection, is well known; another appeared recently on the art market. All three may have been mounted on a single bronze vessel, but they were certainly cast in the same workshop. Their beautiful patina, workmanship and art point unequivocally to Vulci, and this provenance seems to be confirmed for the Bomford horse is said to have come from this location. Vulci bronzes, famous already in antiquity, were exported outside of the Etruscan world, even beyond the Alps in the far North. The small horse represents well not only the masterful bronze work of Vulci. Gracious, strong and very lively, however stylized in every detail, the noble animal radiates the vitality of the Etruscans and the genius of all classical art.

Other important and valuable pieces could be mentioned. Nonetheless, even this small selection shows the importance of the William Herbert Hunt collection and its potential to become a major ensemble of classical bronzes.

NOTES ON THE CATALOGUE OF BRONZES

Included in this section is the entire William Herbert Hunt Collection of ancient bronzes. The thirty-eight pieces, which are arranged in chronological order, have been chosen to represent in as much variety as possible the major artistic trends in Greek and Roman art. They cover the entire span of classical art from the Italian bronze age in the eighth century B.C. through the art of the Roman provinces in the third century A.D.

The catalogue entries in this section are arranged in much the same way as those for the vases. Each entry begins with introductory material on: (1) the dimensions of the piece; (2) the method of manufacture (i.e., hammered, solid cast, hollow cast, etc.) and condition of the piece, including repairs, restorations and the patina (I have given the patina in terms of color only, and tried to refrain from subjective judgements upon its quality); (3) the place and date of manufacture and (4) data on previous publication and/or public exhibition of the piece.

The body of the catalogue entries is arranged in two sections: (1) a technical description of the piece and (2) a short commentary. Here I have tried to include relevant material on the style of the piece as representative of the culture and period from which it comes, on the function of the piece and on similar pieces that provide a basis for stylistic comparison and dating.

The notes provide parallel pieces for comparison of provenance, style and dating. I have included only pieces that seem to me to provide especially close or interesting parallels. Also included here is background information that I have found especially pertinent to my studies of the pieces. I have not tried to give a complete bibliography; that the reader can obtain by consulting the references provided.

Professor Kenneth Hamma, my colleague at the University of Southern California, read an early draft of these entries, and has continued to discuss them with me during my revisions. I owe him many thanks. Stéphanie Boucher of the Centre National de la Recherche Scientifique in France has most kindly read the same draft of the entries, and has offered many valuable comments on dating and on iconographical and stylistic details that I otherwise would have missed. I am also grateful to Dr. Jiří Frel of the J. Paul Getty Museum for his advice and assistance in cataloguing the collection. However, the views expressed here, especially as regards the dating of the pieces, more than once differ radically from those of others and are my own. They are in no way responsible for these dates or for any errors that may remain in the text.

17 SWORD AND SCABBARD

Length of the scabbard 26.2 cm; length of the handle 12.4 cm.

The scabbard is a hammered and incised sheet of bronze folded so that the ends are aligned down the center of the back side. The knob on the sheath and the sword handle are cast. The iron sword blade has perished except for incrustation on the lower edge of the handle and small spots of incrustation elsewhere. Eight notches have been carved on the left of the scabbard. Light green patina.

Villanovan; late eighth century B.C.

Unpublished.

On the long sides of the scabbard is a border of parallel lines decorated with zigzags flanked by triangles shaded with diagonal lines. Within these, the central decoration consists of three trapezoidal elements decreasing in size toward the point of the sheath. Each of these elements is made up of a smaller trapezoid bordered with shaded parallel lines within a similarly bordered trapezoid that terminates on the left side in shaded triangles and on the right side in a maeander pattern. In each of the smaller trapezoids is a stag in the geometric style. The heads are trapezoids, the bodies rectangles and the legs, tails and antlers simple straight lines. At the narrowest point of the sheath there is a larger and smaller stag without the surrounding trapezoidal and maeander elements. The separately made knob decorated with a molding and horizontal lines slips over the pointed end of the scabbard and holds it in place.

The very unusual and decorative sword handle is spool-shaped with moldings that articulate the narrowest and widest points. The top of the spool forms a platform on which stand two horses in a geometric style that is considerably less angular than that on the scabbard. The legs are stiff and straight, but the rectangle of the body is broken by the curve of the rump. The faces are trumpet-shaped and the manes and tails are half-circles. Two short struts support the horses' heads.

In the absence of literary evidence, what little we know of Villanovan culture comes from archaeological finds. Excavations indicate that the Villanovans were an agricultural and hunting people (the latter reflected in the stag motif on the scabbard), and bronze implements discovered in their tombs lay heavy emphasis on a military life style. Characteristic are helmets, shields, fittings for horse-drawn chariots, spears and short swords like the one to which this handle and scabbard originally belonged.

The Villanovan style, so named after a site in northern Italy once erroneously believed to have been the cradle of this civilization, is characterized by geometric ornamentation in the Greek style which often appears on pottery and metal objects of native types. Especially common decorative patterns include parallel lines, zigzags, hatched triangles and maeanders.

The decoration of this scabbard is a combination of maeander ornament and the metope and triglyph pattern found on Greek pottery of the geometric period. In the Greek pattern the rectangular metope sections with painted decoration are flanked by narrow triglyphs composed of vertical lines. On this piece the

maeander takes the place of the triglyph element, and the metope becomes a trapezoid adapted to the tapering form of the piece. The resulting pattern is ornamental, but not integral to the piece itself, and the delicate balance of the horizontal and vertical elements of the Greek metope and triglyph has been lost. Nonetheless, the piece is an excellent example of the creative imitation for which the Villanovans, Etruscans and Romans are well known.

NOTES: For very similar scabbards, from the same hand or at least the same workshop (Tarquinia?), see H. Hencken, *Tarquinia and Etruscan Origins* (1968), p. 41, fig. 11c and p. 59, fig. 22a, d. For the decorative horses on the handle, cf. *Master Bronzes* no. 154 and Å. Akerström, *Der geometrische Stil in Italien* (1943): 106–107 and pp. 112–113 for a discussion of the short sword and the theory that the decoration of the scabbard is a maeander "filled" with a hunting motif. H. Hencken, *Tarquinia, Villanovans and Etruscan Origins* (1968): 510–511 argues that the same decoration is eastern European in origin.

18 HELMET AND SHIELD

Height of the helmet 19.9 cm; diameter of the helmet 25.4 cm.
Diameter of the shield 34.0 cm.

The shield is hammered sheet bronze with repoussé decoration. The helmet is also hammered, and decorated with repoussé cutout and incised ornament. The helmet is intact with several minor breaks and some pieces of the crest missing. The shield is intact and complete except for a few cracks that have been repaired on the back. Olive-green patina.

Villanovan; late eighth century B.C.

Published: Summa, *Catalogue 5* (1979), no. 41.

The helmet, of a very unusual type, is made of bronze hammered into a round rather than pointed cap as is customary for this style of helmet. Near the rim it is decorated with a row of incised zigzags flanked by rows of hatched triangles. At each side near the rim are three holes for the attachment of protective ear pieces.

The double crest, possibly a support for a more prominent horsehair crest, is hammered from sheet bronze and riveted into place on the cap. The crest originally terminated at front and back in oval sections that lay flat against the helmet, but only traces of these now remain. On the crest cutout triangles are flanked by rows of bosses. Above them is a double, below them a single row of bosses flanked by lines of very small dots.

The small bronze shield appears to come from the same burial. It has the same patina and is decorated with a pattern similar to that on the crest of the helmet. In the center of the shield is a raised disk decorated with a central boss and, around it, concentric rings of small dots. A strap handle is riveted to the back of the shield on either side of the central disk.

Villanovan burials often contain helmets, shields and other military equipment. Larger shields (over 50 cm) from these burials have been the subject of much study and classification, but to date there has been no comprehensive treatment of these smaller shields.

Shields of all sizes are found in tombs, sometimes arranged around the walls. Because of their small size and fragility, many believe that at least some of the shields were ceremonial rather than functional, but the question is still open. The small size and the very simple decoration without animals or other figures indicate that this piece is among the earliest yet found.

The decoration of bosses on both helmet and shield imitates the appearance of the rivets that were used to hold sheets of metal together (note the attachment of the helmet crest and the shield handle), a technique of metalworking that the Villanovans shared with the central Danubian cultures that flourished in this period.

NOTES: For parallels to both pieces, see P. Stary, *Zur eisenzeitlichen Bewaffnung und Kampfeweise in Mittelitalien* (1981). Similar helmets, but with conical caps, are published in H. Hencken, *The Earliest European Helmets* (1971): 163ff. For bibliography and discussion of the larger shields, see I. Strøm, *Problems Concerning the Origin and Development of the Etruscan Orientalizing Style* 1 (1971): 19ff., especially Group A.V (p. 47).

19 HORSEBIT

Length, including the shanks, 35.9 cm; length of the bit itself 21 cm;
length of the cheekpieces 11.1 cm; height of the cheekpieces 9.2 cm.
Solid cast in six pieces. The pendants that hung from the two lower
rings are missing. Blue-green patina.
Villanovan (Volterra); late eighth century B.C.
Unpublished.

The mouthpiece of the bit consists of two twisted pieces of
bronze joined by interlocking loops. They pass through the
cheekpieces, and end in reinforced flat rings through which
pass one end of the shanks. At the other end of each shank is a
rectangular opening for the leather reins.

On the cheekpieces there is a large horse standing forward. On
his back is a small, but similarly stylized horse with typically
Volterran pricked ears, high-arched neck and trumpet-shaped
face. The front and back legs of the large horse are joined by a
strut on which stands another small horse, facing backward,
and a bird, facing forward. The feet of the large horse end in
rings from which ornate pendants originally hung.

Horsebits with flexible mouthpieces and highly decorative
cheekpieces are some of the best-known finds from Italian
tombs of the geometric period. They are found along with other
equipment for horses and chariots in pairs and double pairs in
the graves of relatively few, apparently upper class, men and
women. They were placed there seemingly to serve the dead in
the afterlife, much as they did in their former existence.

The form of the cheekpieces derives ultimately from similar
pieces made in ancient Iran. However, the style of the horses,
with long legs and trumpet-shaped faces, and the presence of the
birds, with long flat bills and arched bodies, are influenced by
Greek art of the geometric period. From these derivative elements Villanovan artists created a typically Etruscan form. This
is especially clear in the preference for a nearly two-dimensional rendering and in the highly decorative pattern of balanced
curved and straight lines on the cheekpieces.

NOTES: The standard work on these bits is F.-W. von Hase, *Die Trensen
in der früheisenzeit in Italien* (1969), especially pp. 11–12 and pl. 4. For
examples of Near Eastern bits from Luristan, see P. R.S. Moorey, *Catalogue
of the Ancient Persian Bronzes in the Ashmolean Museum* (1971),
especially pl. 22. For Greek imitations of the eastern bits, quite unlike the
Villanovan creations: H.-V. Herrmann, Frühgriechischer Pferdeschmuck
vom Luristantypus," *JDAI* 83 (1968): 1ff.

Good parallels for the bit in the Hunt collection are *Master Bronzes* no. 154;
M & M, *Auktion 56* (1980), no. 34; *Mildenberg Collection* no. 84 ("ranks
among the finest known examples of these masterpieces of Villanovan
metalwork"). Two examples with the pendants preserved are *Pomerance*
no. 118; Dörig, no. 115.

20 TWO YOUTHS

Height 9.9 cm; width, at the widest point, 6.5 cm.
Solid cast bronze. Intact and complete. The strut between the heads is an ancient addition to the piece. Green and red patina.
Villanovan (or more generally Italic); eighth–seventh century B.C.
Unpublished.

Solid cast bronze statuette of two male figures standing on a rectangular plinth. The plinth is of one piece with the conical section below. This, in turn, flares out to form a circular base by which the statuette was attached, possibly to the lid of a bronze vessel. The two identical figures stand frontally, their inner arms interlaced (but represented by a single round bar); their outer arms are bent outward with the hands placed palm down over their abdomens. They have no hair. Their faces are formed schematically with mere hollows for eyes, bulbous noses and slit-like mouths. On their bodies little except the gender of the figures is defined.

As with the Villanovan horsebit [19], these little figures are so shallow that their appearance is almost that of two-dimensional relief; the interest of both lies in the articulation of line and formal elements rather than anatomical detail. On this piece there is a carefully constructed interplay between the curves of the outer arms and the straight lines of the triangular sections formed by the inner arms and edges of the bodies.

From this very early period of Italic art there are several other, though quite rare, examples of the combination of symmetrically placed figures, a characteristic of Etruscan art that is best known from the much later (fourth- and third-century) lid handles for cosmetic boxes connected with the city of Praeneste. On these handles figures with interlaced arms appear dancing or wrestling with their outer hands on their hips. Whether the two youths are brothers or twins, or whether they were coupled in the interest of symmetry, is unclear.

Whatever the exact meaning of the outer hand placed over the abdomen, it appears often in funerary contexts. Here, as often in later Etruscan art, the importance of symbolic gesture is emphasized by the disproportionately large size of the hands.

NOTES: The anatomical details and faces are best compared with contemporary human figures that formed the decorative element of so-called candelabra: F. Messerschmidt, "Die 'Kandelaber' von Vetulonia," *SE* 5 (1931): 71–84, especially pl. 5, 1. The base of the Hunt piece, however, indicates a different function.

Early examples of symmetrically placed figures are a statuette of a couple in Syracuse: A. Giuliano, *Les Etrusques et l'Italie avant Rome* (1978), pl. 25 and figures on seventh-century Etruscan urns: M. Cristofani, *L'arte degli Etruschi* (1978), fig. 87. For the later cistae, *Master Bronzes* nos. 204, 208–210; cf. no. 205, and D. Mitten, *Rhode Island School of Design. Catalogue of the Classical Collection. Classical Bronzes* (1975), no. 38 with the bibliography in n. 3. Also, the lid of the Ficaroni cista with three figures with interlaced arms: Brendel, fig. 276. On symmetry as a characteristic of Etruscan art, see the brief comments of C. Robert, *Oidipus* 2 (1915), p. 156, n. 102.

21 GRIFFIN PROTOME

Height 13.0 cm; diameter of the base 2.5 cm.

Hollow cast bronze with incised locks and punched scales on the neck. Most of the left ear is missing, and there is some damage to the left side of the base. The eyes originally were inlaid. Dark gray patina.

Greek; late seventh–early sixth century B.C.

Published: *Master Bronzes* no. 67; H.-V. Herrmann, *Die Kessel der orientalisierenden Zeit* (Olympische Forschungen 11, 1979), no. 171.

This hollow cast head and neck of a griffin is flanged at the base and perforated there with three holes for attachment to the shoulder of a bronze cauldron. The pointed ears stand fully upright above the prominent chin roll. The beast's pointed beak is open wide, his pointed tongue curving upward inside the mouth. On the forehead, a round knob is elevated on a stem. The prominent eyes are surmounted by lines. The neck is covered with scales; on each side, a long curling lock.

In the late eighth and seventh centuries many Near Eastern motifs were established in Greek art. Among the exotic or fantastic mythological creatures thus imported was the griffin which, in the form first adapted by the Greeks, combines the head and wings of an eagle with the body of a lion. The knob on the head, the roll under the chin and the spiral lock(s) on the neck (both perhaps derived from the lion's mane) and the upright pointed ears (of a horse, bull or lion?) are standard features of the Greek hybrid.

This griffin protome was one of several that were attached to the shoulder of a large bronze cauldron. Although other explanations have been suggested, these griffins probably stood as alert sentinels, guards of the valuable vessel to which they were attached.

The bronze cauldrons, which rested on tall conical stands, were one of the favorite dedications at major shrines of the Greek world in the orientalizing period. They were presented by victors in the games or by wealthy men, and were also extraordinarily fine gifts of friendship. As such, the commission and/or dedication of these cauldrons was the prerogative of the highly honored or very wealthy in late eighth- and seventh-century Greece.

Although this type of dedication (like the griffin itself) is derived from Near Eastern models, the adaptation of the griffin protome to this position on the shoulder seems to have been a Greek invention. At first these protomes were hammered with round bulging eyes, short ears and short straight necks. Subsequent pieces, like this one, are among the first hollow cast bronzes produced by the Greeks.

Protomes of the class to which the Hunt griffin belongs are characterized by their broad upright head, round eye, thick chin roll and heavy serpentine neck. They frequently are praised for their monumentality and for the careful balance between the erect vertical thrust of the knob and ears and the rounded curves of the beak, tongue and neck.

NOTES: The two standard works on these protomes are U. Jantzen, *Griechische Greifenkessel* (1955), where this piece fits into the first cast group, and Herrmann, *op. cit. supra* (cf. the first part of this work [Olympische Forschungen 6, 1966]), where it is published as part of his second group of cast protomes. There are two useful supplements to Jantzen's monograph: U. Jantzen, "Greifenprotomen von Samos. Ein Nachtrag," *MDAI (A)* 73 (1958): 26ff. and J. Benson, "Unpublished Griffin Protomes in American Collections," *AK* 3 (1960): 58ff. For another close parallel, see Rolley, *Bronzes*, nos. 135ff.

22 PAIR OF LION PROTOMES

Length of each piece 10.5 cm; height of each piece 8.1 cm.

Hollow cast bronze with details in incision and separately made ears. Both pieces are intact, but one has several breaks and two small ancient holes on the shoulder to better secure the fitting. Green patina.

Etruscan; sixth century B.C.

Published: Summa, *Auction 1* (1981), no. 49.

The two crouching lions, represented only to mid-body, have tiny forepaws extended and heads turned to the side. Their mouths are opened wide revealing prominent teeth and a protruding tongue. The ears are laid back; the eyes, large and round. The hair of the mane, lines on the forehead and nose wrinkles are all rendered with deeply cut parallel lines.

Lions were not native to Italy. They came in the late eighth or seventh century along with the griffin and sphinx as part of the Near Eastern artistic repertoire, and remained common through the archaic period of the sixth and early fifth centuries.

These lion protomes are designed to fit neatly on the ends of wooden poles, probably of a sedan chair or litter. On each, one side of the open back end is flattened to fit over the pole, and there is a bronze dowel that runs from the top to bottom of the opening to secure the fitting to the pole which is now completely missing.

In general these fittings are similar to lion protomes on large Italian bronze cauldrons of the same type as that to which the Greek griffin protome [21] was attached, but of a significantly more developed stylistic stage. As is typical of much Etruscan art, there is little attention to anatomical realism, as evidenced by the oversized heads and diminutive legs. Instead of fierce and noble beasts with large jaws, flowing manes and strong legs, these lions are decorative, amusing and slightly grotesque.

NOTES: For the Etruscan cauldron protomes, compare especially W. L. Brown, *The Etruscan Lion* (1960), pl. 8, c (from the Regolini-Galassi tomb). For comparable lion sedan chair fittings, see Doeringer, pp. 196–197 and Brown, *op. cit.* pl. 10, b.

There are Etruscan griffin protomes with the same function as the Hunt lions: D. Mitten, "Two Griffin Protomes," *Fogg Museum Acquisitions 1964* (1965), p. 16. For a griffin protome with diminutive paws like those on the Hunt lions, see A. de Ridder, *Les bronzes antiques du Louvre* 2 (1915), pl. 120, 3684 and, for another griffin protome with a similar treatment of the shoulders, note C. Hopkins, "The Origin of Etruscan Art," *Archaeology* 11 (1958), p. 96, fig. 8, b.

For discussion and bibliography on the Etruscan lion in the orientalizing period, see Brown, *op. cit.* and G. Camporeale, "Considerazioni sui leoni etruschi di epoca orientalizzante," *MDAI(R)* 72 (1965): 1ff. There are some comments on the style of similar stone lions by M. del Chiaro, "An Etruscan Stone Winged Lion," *JPGMJ* 10 (1982), p. 123.

23 SILEN

Height 7.1 cm; length at the feet 6.1 cm.

Solid cast bronze. Intact; the nose and right thumb are slightly chipped. There are two ancient perforations on the head. Green-brown patina.

Greek (Tarentum?); third quarter of the sixth century B.C.

Unpublished.

Although it is fully worked on all sides, this solid cast silen was once an attachment. There are two holes in the head to secure the piece, each about half a centimeter deep. One is round and nearly at the center of the crown; the other where the right ear should be, and shaped accordingly. That the piece also was attached from the back is clear from the rough edges on this side of the feet and from the small semicircular holes there that must have aided in fitting.

The silen strides vigorously to the right. The head and legs are shown in profile, the body turned three-quarters front. His arms are in a swastika-like position, the archaic gesture of running. The palms are open. Although stylized and unnatural, the gesture vividly imparts an impression of rapid movement.

The silen has horse's ears and is bearded. His long ringlets, which are divided into horizontal sections, fall over his shoulders in front and behind. His face is broad with wide-open eyes, arched brows, a pudgy nose and fleshy lips.

The silen is a rustic creature part man, part horse that was especially popular among artists of the archaic period. In later times silens quite commonly were identified with satyrs, or thought of as young satyrs. Like them, silens appear with horse's tails, legs and ears, with beards and the facial features of this piece. Not all of these characteristics necessarily are present on any one representation. Only the typical face and horse's ears appear here.

NOTES: For parallels, see Jantzen, pl. 2, 4–5 (for the pose of the silen); pl. 15, 59–60 and pl. 11, 44–45 (for the style); Charbonneaux, pl. 21, 1.

General treatments of silens in art are F. Brommer, *Satyroi* (1937) and H. Bulle, *Die Silene in den archaischen Kunst* (1893).

24 SPHINX

Height 6.3 cm.
Solid cast bronze. Complete; the tail is recomposed, and there is some damage on the right leg. Red and green patina.
Greek (Metapontum); circa 530 B.C.
Published: *Das Tier in der Antike* (1974), no. 157.

This solid cast sphinx is seated in profile with the front legs held stiffly before her, paws forward. The back legs are bent; the feet not rendered in detail, but as a simple block on which the weight of the piece rests. The sphinx's face is turned frontally. She wears a polos (the round hat of eastern fertility goddesses) and a plain necklace. Her hair is done in screw curls over the forehead; it falls in ringlets divided horizontally into sections onto the shoulders in front and in a long flat section in back. The eyes are large and almond-shaped, the ears protruding and the lips upturned. The wing arches upward with the feathers arranged spirally below a fillet that runs from under the shoulders to the center of the wing tip. Above this line the wings are undecorated. The tail, which rests on the "ground" and against the rump, is S-shaped.

The sphinx with a human head and lion's body originated in Egypt where it was usually male and often wingless. These sphinxes, like the one that still rests among the pyramids at Giza, are sometimes thought to be representations of pharaohs. In Greek art the sphinx almost always has a female human head, the wings (and often the breast) of a bird and the body of a lion. Archaic Greek sphinxes are spirits of death who attend fatal battles and make off with men too young to die. Perhaps because of their fatal power, they appear as protective figures on

shields, votive monuments and tombs. The Hunt sphinx is seated with her head turned frontally in exactly the same pose as on sixth-century grave markers. However, the alert and watchful sphinx is sometimes merely decorative (as on Corinthian pottery, mirrors and other bronze objects), as is the present example.

Much of the bronze work from South Italy in this period is of very high quality, and Tarentum, a colony of mainland Sparta just east of Metapontum, is especially noted for its metalwork in a style very similar to that of this sphinx. The artist who produced this piece had an unusually fine sense of line and form, as is clear from the pleasing juxtaposition of the solid triangular outlines of the piece as a whole and the two carefully balanced uplifted curves of the tail and wing.

NOTES: Parallels for this piece are *Rép. stat.* 5, p. 408, 2 = Jantzen, p. 3, no. 6 = *Master Bronzes* no. 42; Jantzen, *op. cit.* p. 3, no. 3 and p. 27, nos. 11 and 12 = M. Maass, *Griechische und römische Bronzewerke der Antikensammlungen* (1979), no. 30; Jantzen, *op. cit.* p. 70 with pl. 33; L. von Matt and U. Zanotti-Bianco, *Magna Graecia* (1962), pl. 106 (all from South Italy); cf *Rép. stat.* 3, p. 706, 4 (from Crete); M. Grbič, *Choix de plastiques grecques et romaines au Musée National de Beograd* (1958), pl. 12 (from Trebenischte).

For stylistically similar figures from Tarentum, see Jantzen, *op. cit.* p. 27, no. 19 with pl. 13, 51 (a siren) and p. 27, no. 18 with pl. 15, 59–60 (a reclining silen).

In general on sphinxes, see J. Ilberg, s.v. 'Sphinx,' *Roscher* 4 (1909–1915), cols. 1298–1408; G. Hanfmann, "On Sphinxes," *Archaeology* 6 (1953): 229–230; A. Dessenne, *Le sphinx. Étude iconographique 1. Des origines à la fin du second millénaire* (1957), for Egyptian and Near Eastern precedents only; R. Hampe, *Ein frühattische Grabfund* (1960): 64ff.

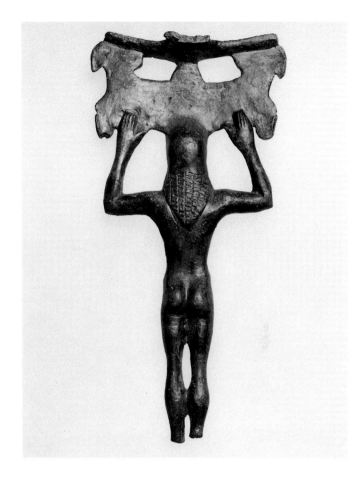

25 YOUTH

Height 17.4 cm.
Solid cast bronze with incised detail. Intact, but broken at the ankles.
The attachment to the bowl is missing. Green and red patina.
Greek (South Italy); late sixth–early fifth century B.C.
Unpublished.

During the archaic period an interest in the portrayal of the human figure in individual, monumental form manifested itself in the production of kouroi (youthful naked male figures) and korai (youthful draped female figures). This kouros is a miniature version of those that appear in archaic monumental sculpture.

The youth stands fully frontal, legs together and arms raised to the side and upward. The hair over his forehead is arranged in vertical waves and decorated with a beaded band. On the sides and back the hair falls in stiff horizontal waves. The eyes are almond-shaped, the lips slightly upturned. Bone structure and muscles of the torso are carefully detailed.

The youth's head and hands, which are not fully worked, support a flat molding that ends on the outside in volutes. On this lie addorsed rams. They are shown in profile, their forelegs tucked under them; between them, a palmette. A curved element rests on top of the palmette and over the heads and shoulders of the rams, where it terminates in volutes.

This kouros was originally the handle, and main decorative element, of a small frying-pan-like dish known as a patera which was used for libations, funeral gifts and perhaps as a serving piece. The back (underside) is fully worked with the exception of the upper part of the hair, the rams and volutes. The curved upper section of the handle once fitted to the edge of the patera bowl, and the legs of the youth terminated in a palmette.

There are several varieties of patera handle with kouros figures. The class to which this handle belongs (Gjødesen's IIA) is characterized by the rams with volutes that rest on their shoulders.

Design and balance are carefully executed, even at the cost of a realistic rendering of anatomy. The unnaturally extended arms balance the horizontal lines of the palmette, ram and volute decoration above, and play against the slim vertical lines of the youth's body and head.

NOTES: M. Gjødesen, "Bronze Paterae with Anthropomorphic Handles," *AArch* 15 (1944): 101–197; P. Amandry, "Manches de patère et de miroir grecs," *Mon. Piot* 47 (1953): 47–70; U. Jantzen, *Griechische Griff-phialen* (114. Winckelmannsprogramm, 1958): 5–29, especially pp. 24ff.

For individual parallels, *Man in the Ancient World* (Exhibition at Queens College 1958), no. 130 = D. von Bothmer, *Ancient Art from New York Private Collections* (1961), no. 135 = *Pomerance* no. 93; *Master Bronzes* no. 26; Doeringer, p. 156, fig. 18; S. Boucher, *Bronzes grecs, hellénistiques, et étrusques des Musées de Lyon* (1970), no. 18.

26 HEIFER

Height 8.6 cm; length of the base 7.9 cm.
Cast bronze with incised detail. Intact and complete. Green patina.
Greek; late sixth–early fifth century B.C.
Unpublished.

This piece is worked only on the outside; the back is hollow. It originally was an appliqué, almost certainly one of several (six?) affixed to the neck of a bronze volute-krater. Five similar and nearly contemporary pieces have been found in Bulgaria and survive along with the krater to which they belong. Other heavier bodied parallels from the Greek mainland are also extant.

The heifer walks right on a base decorated with a horizontal beaded frieze. The body and back three legs would have appeared in shallow relief against the background to which they were attached; the head, neck, upper part of the dewlap and the left foreleg are in high relief. The body, except for the dewlap, shoulder and left foreleg, is in profile; the head is turned fully frontal. The young cow has upturned horns and ears that extend prominently to the sides. Details of the slim face are carefully worked. The treatment of the figure is orientalizing, descended from Near Eastern, especially Persian, art of the seventh and sixth centuries.

Although the head of the young cow is portrayed quite realistically, other anatomical details contribute more to the formal effect than to an accurate rendering of the animal. This is especially marked in the lack of bone structure and musculature and in the treatment of the folds of the dewlap and shoulder as decorative concentric lines rather than anatomical realities. It

also appears in the displacement of the tail, which falls to the rear against the background, rather than between the legs of the heifer.

NOTES: For the heifer appliqués from Trebenischte, B. Filow and K. Schkorpil, *Archaische Nekropole von Trebenischte am Ochrida-See* (1927): 39ff. and pl. 7; republished with parallels and more recent bibliography by W. Hitzl, *Die Entstehung und Entwicklung des Volutenkraters von den frühesten Anfangen bis zur Ausprägung des kanonischen Stils in der attischen schwarz-figurigen Vasenmalerei* (1982): 43ff. with pls. 21–23 and 31. Also cf. Charbonnèaux, pl. 2, 1 (a horse attachment of a very similar style found at Pesaro); Jantzen, pl. 9, 39 (a heifer attachment for a tripod in a different style).

27 HORSE

Height, including the base, 10.4 cm; length 10.7 cm; width of the base 3.0 cm.

Solid cast bronze decorated with incision. Intact and complete. Green patina.

Etruscan (Vulci?); circa 500 B.C.

Published: S. Boucher, "Deux petits bronzes à Malibu," *JPGM* 10 (1982): 130–132.

This solid cast horse walks slowly forward on a flat rectangular plinth. His right foreleg is slightly raised with the hoof pointing toward, and nearly touching, the base. The bridle is carefully worked with the loops for the reins represented fully in the round and extending out to each side of the face. The horse's ears are pricked, and the details of his face carefully rendered. The mane consists of a series of overlapping tile-like sections. The largest section is over the face; the others diminish in size toward the back. Over the head and shoulders, a curved border provides a transition between the lines of the horse's body and his mane. Bone structure and muscles are indicated with lines incised on the nearly flat surface of the body. The tail is long, reaching almost to the ground, and incised with vertical wavy lines.

The horse is worked fully on all sides, but is very shallow. There are two holes on the base for the attachment of the piece to a larger object. Like the almost identical horse in the Bomford Collection, it may have been a dedication attached to an inscribed base or a decorative attachment for a bronze stamnos, tripod, small table or some other object.

The function of the very prominent loops for the (leather) reins is not certain. There is no trace of a rider who once may have sat on the horse, although Haynes suggests that there was such a figure on the Bomford piece. Boucher rejects this idea in favor of a groom who would have stood in front of the horse (on a separate base) and held him by the reins. Both of these suggestions present problems, and it is possible that no rider or groom, simply leather reins, would have supplemented the piece as we now have it.

The modeling of the hocks and tendons of the hindlegs and the details of the face and bridle are extraordinarily accurate, but the horse still exhibits much archaic abstraction of form. The body is too slender and cylindrical through the mid-section, the legs too stocky and the hooves oversize. The interplay between decorated and undecorated surfaces, between the highly decorative treatment of the mane and the carefully incised tail and the smooth undecorated surfaces of the body, is a hallmark of archaic art that is unusually effective on this piece.

The posture of the head, the pointed foot, the accurately rendered face and expressive eyes all capture the fine delicacy of a well-bred and well-trained horse.

NOTES: For the Bomford horse, S. Haynes, "Neue etruskische Bronzen," *AK* 9 (1966): 101ff.; *Antiquities from the Bomford Collection* (1966), no. 343. Haynes calls the nearly identical mate "one of the finest representations of animals known to me in Etruscan art" (p. 103). S. Boucher (in correspondence) points out the following parallels for the horse (and groom) on paintings from Tarquinia: M. Sprenger and G. Bartolini, *Die Etrusker* (1977), pl. 78; M. Pallottino, H. and I. Jucker, M. Hürlimann, *Etruskische Kunst* (1955), pl. 61.

28 BULL

Height, without the casting tenon on the rear foot, 13.1 cm; height of the tenon 2.7 cm; length 21.5 cm.
Solid cast bronze. The lower left front leg is missing, and there is a small rectangular hole in the forehead. There is some minor incrustation, but otherwise the preservation of the surface is excellent. Light green patina.
Greek (South Italy); 480–450 B.C.
Unpublished.

The finely modeled bull walks slowly, facing straight ahead. His right foreleg and left hindleg are forward. The body is fully rounded and worked on all sides. His small head is held low, continuing the horizontal line of the back. The dewlap is rendered with a scalloped edge. The body itself is very heavy, with the ribs and bone structure of the rump carefully modeled. The long tail hangs between the bull's legs, neatly twisted at its lower end. The sex of the animal is clearly indicated.

Much detail is lavished on the head of the bull, who has almond-shaped eyes, short horizontal horns and large ears that turn up gracefully under the horns. The insides of the ears are modeled in an elaborate star-like pattern; the lines above the eyes and wavy hair on the forehead and between the horns are also worked with much attention to detail.

This exceptionally large and heavy, solid cast statuette was once a very expensive dedication to some deity. It originally stood on a base as the extant fitting on the right rear foot (now inserted in the modern base) shows. Since the bull is one of the most common sacrificial animals in antiquity and, thus, appropriate to many gods, it is impossible to tell to whom the statuette was dedicated.

The bull belongs to a long series of votive statuettes, many of which have been found in archaic and early classical Greek sanctuaries. Earlier, sixth-century pieces lack the definition of musculature and bone structure of this piece, nor do they have the careful detailing of the head. However, the schematic rendering of the dewlap, inner ears and tail, as well as the stiff-legged walk of the beast, indicate that this piece should precede the fully classical examples. On those the bull is more active, often with his tail twirling up onto his back and his foreleg pawing at the ground.

NOTES: For several hundred examples of Greek votive bulls from the archaic and early classical periods, B. Schmaltz, *Metallfiguren aus dem Kabirenheiligtum bei Theben* (1980), especially pls. 20–21. For other bronze bulls of similar date, *Metropolitan Bronzes* no. 97; C. Rolley, *Musée des Delphes. Bronzes* (n.d.), no. 28; A. Furtwängler, *Olympia* 4 (1890), p. 151, no. 960 and pl. 56; M. Maass, *Griechische und römische Bronzewerke der Antikensammlungen* (1979), no. 21; M&M, *Auktion 22* (1961), no. 55; Jantzen, pl. 9, 38; cf. pl. 8, 36–37 and *Mildenberg Collection* (1981), no. 158.

29 SATYR

Height 6.7 cm.

Solid cast bronze. Intact, but the left forearm and hand are missing as is the right hand, left leg from mid-thigh and the right leg from the knee. Brown patina.

Greek (Arcadia?); first half of the fifth century B.C.

Unpublished.

The solid cast satyr faces straight ahead, and is worked fully on all sides. He hops, or skips, forward in one of the steps typical of dancing satyrs. He supports his body on his left leg and kicks high into the air with his right leg, which is held slightly to the right and bent at the knee.

The satyr has a short beard. His hair is cut short and straight, and he has pointed ears, round cheeks, a pudgy nose and prominent belly, as is typical of his race. He wears a phorbeia, the strap used for holding the double flute that provided musical accompaniment for the satyrs' festivities. One part of the phorbeia runs from the mouth around the crown of the head. The lower part runs over his beard and just above the nape of the neck. The satyr's arms are raised to hold the two parts of the instrument. The left hand was almost directly in front of the mouth; the right hand extended to the side.

Satyrs, like the silens from whom they are often undifferentiated, are woodland creatures, attendants of the wine god Dionysus. Also like the silens, satyrs appear with a variety of animal traits. This little satyr has only the pointed ears derived from a horse. His pug nose and beard are also typical of both silens and satyrs. The prominent stomach and generally pudgy proportions are quite common for satyrs, and seem to be related to the paunchy, padded dancing figures on seventh-century Corinthian pottery and its sixth-century successors made at Athens (the so-called komasts).

This single figure has been excerpted from one of the revels of wine, song and dance that are prominent in Greek art for both humans and their mythological counterparts, the satyrs, maenads and Dionysus. The workmanship of this small piece is very careful. The detail of the head and face and the soft, unmuscled body capture all the picturesque jollity of the satyr's race.

NOTES: For representations of satyrs, F. Brommer, *Satyroi* (1937): 20ff. and *Satyrspiele* (1959).

On the dance step, see the copious photographs in G. Prudhommeau, *La danse grecque antique* (1965) especially 1, pp. 53ff. and 2, pls. 23–24 and 34. Also, L. Lawler, *The Dance in Ancient Greece* (1964).

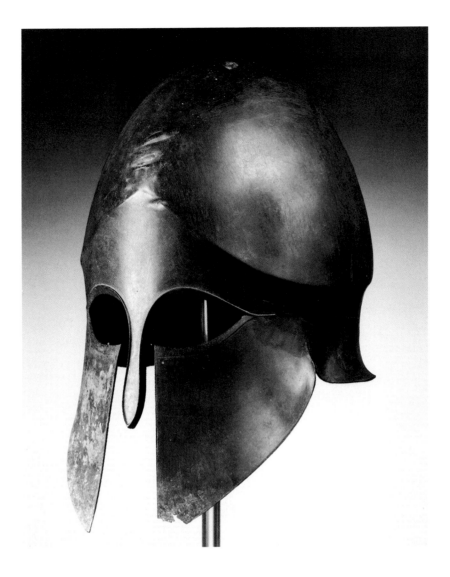

30 HELMET

Height, from the base of the neck protector to the crown, 23.1 cm;
length at the base 28.6 cm.

Hammered bronze. Complete except for a small area at the bottom of
the left cheek protector; a piece is missing from the back of the
crown. Some cracking elsewhere. There are repairs and reinforce-
ments in several places and two dents above the forehead.

Greek (mainland); circa 500–480 B.C.

Unpublished.

Hammered bronze helmet of the Corinthian style. The cap is
tall and elongated with sharply raking cheek pieces. A visor-like
ridge runs from a peak over the eyes around and above the
cheek pieces and the short, offset concave neck protector at the
back. There are single holes at the joins of the cheek pieces and
neck protector, probably for the attachment of a chin strap or
lining. The archaic almond-shaped openings for the eyes and
the tongue-shaped nose protector are finished decoratively with
an offset flat border that continues in an abbreviated form
around the other edges of the helmet.

This type of Corinthian helmet with notches for easy fitting on
the shoulders and pointed cheek pieces is the latest form of the
Corinthian style. It evolved by stages from a much more restric-

tive form in which the cap itself extended straight down to
serve as both cheek pieces and neck protector, and ended in a
straight edge just above the shoulders of the warrior.

The best-known varieties of Greek helmet in the classical period are the Corinthian, the Attic and the Phrygian. The Phrygian is so named from its similarity to caps worn by easterners
with a high crown that flops forward. The Attic, cut high over
the face, lacks a nose protector and cheek pieces and often has a
visor and protective flaps for the ears. The Corinthian helmet,
the only one of the three varieties that has a modern name
based on ancient literary evidence (Herodotus 4.180), is a development of the late eighth century. It appears to have been in
common use down to the time of the Persian Wars (490–480),
when it was supplanted by the Attic variety, which was less
restrictive of sight and sound.

NOTES: For a very similar example, D. Mitten, *Rhode Island School of
Design. Catalogue of the Classical Collection. Classical Bronzes* (1975), no.
14, with bibliography. Other good parallels: E. Kunze, *Bericht über die
Ausgrabungen in Olympia* 3 (1938–1939), pls. 44–45 (a more exaggerated
form) and 5 (1956), pls. 34–39; T. Shear, "Excavations at Corinth in 1930,"
AJA 34 (1930), p. 425, fig. 17.

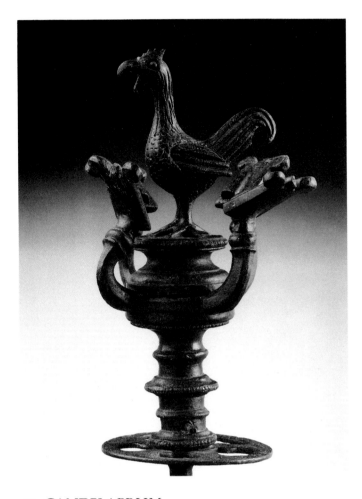

31 CANDELABRUM

Height 115 cm.
Solid cast bronze. Intact and complete. There is some incrustation and abrasion on the candle holders. Red and green patina.
Etruscan; early fifth century B.C.
Unpublished.

The candelabrum is composed of several separately made parts. The curved legs of the tripod base end in lion feet which rest on small round bases. Between the legs are inverted palmettes and, at the top of the base, an echinus molding. The tall polygonal shaft is made from another piece of bronze and fits into the center of the base. It is undecorated except for the flaring ends at both top and bottom. Over the top of the shaft fits a wheel-like openwork disk and a double spool element with decoration of egg and dart on the three most prominent moldings. It is held in place by a metal pin. From the upper edge of this element spring four arms, arching upward and terminating above a bead and reel molding in a flattened lotus blossom with a raised triangular section near the base on the upper side.

The uppermost element is a cock, of abstract late archaic design, with much punched and incised detail. He stands on a spool-shaped pedestal decorated on the upper edge with egg and dart. The bird has a small crest, a prominent wattle and small beady eyes. His prominent tail stands erect and is notched near its upper end. The large feet each have four spurs.

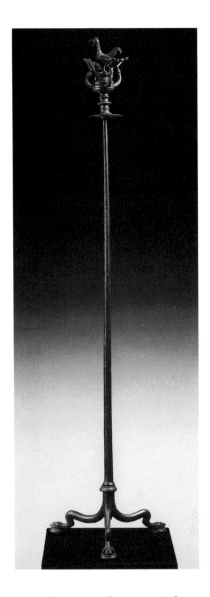

Throughout most of antiquity houses in Italy were lit by candles (or oil lamps) supported on tall stands. This Etruscan candelabrum from the late archaic period is of a particularly well-known form, not very different from stands for oil lamps found in first century A.D. Pompeii. Characteristic of the early Etruscan candelabra are the separately made statuary elements that stand between the candle holders on their own bases, and form the decorative focal point of the pieces.

Human figures in various poses are the usual decorative elements of this class of Etruscan candelabra, and both the unusual animal figure and the lotus-shaped candle holders make this piece an interesting addition to the known candelabra of its type.

NOTES: For comparable pieces, G. Giglioli, *L'arte etrusca* (1935), *passim*; Brendel, pp. 299–301; K. Neugebauer, "Reifarchaische Bronzevasen mit Zungenmuster," *MDAI(R)* 38–39 (1923–1924): 436–438; T. Dohrn, "Zwei etruskische Kandelabra," *MDAI(R)* 66 (1959): 45–64.

A similar Etruscan cock has been discovered recently: P. Bocci Pacini, "La stipe della Veneziana ad Arezzo," *SE* 48 (1980), p. 88 and pl. 32, b. For a comparable Greek cock, also fifth century: S. Haynes, *Antiquities in the Bomford Collection* (1966), no. 317.

32 THYMIATERION

Height 41.1 cm; diameter of the base on which the silen stands
11.2 cm.

Solid cast bronze. Intact except for pieces of the bowl which is almost
entirely missing, but recomposed in small part. Very minor chipping
and incrustation on the base for the silen. Brown patina.

Etruscan; early fifth century B.C.

Unpublished.

This thymiaterion (incense burner) stands on a tripod base. The
legs are gracefully arched; each foot is in the form of a lion's
paw and stands on a small, undecorated circular plinth. Between the legs are inverted palmettes that descend from a calyx
that has three sections, each ending in an upward curve over
one of the legs.

The main decorative element of the thymiaterion is a finely
crafted silen. He stands above the foot on a circular base decorated around the edge with egg and dart. The silen is a slender
bearded figure with long ringlets, wide-open eyes with hollow
pupils, quizzically arched brows and snub nose. His only horse-
like features are the prominently pointed and pricked ears. He
wears, as do many silens and satyrs, a lion skin. It is tied with a
"knot of Herakles" over his shoulders. The frontal head of the
lion, jaws splayed and ears folded forward, appears on the silen's
left side. The woodland creature stands on tiptoe and raises his
arms in one of the gestures typical of ancient dance. His right
arm is held almost straight from the shoulder, palm out and
thumb up; the left hand, palm inward and thumb extended,

falls vertically from the elbow. Poised ready to whirl into motion, the figure embodies the primitive aspect of man, close to
nature and the world of animals.

Above the silen is the bottom half of a globe surmounted by a
disk. On this rests a stem ending in a downturned floral calyx
that is balanced by the lotus buds that arch outward and upward
from below it. The upper half of the globe at the top of the piece
was originally the central part of a phiale (bowl) which held the
incense.

NOTES: For other Etruscan thymiateria of similar date, G. Giglioli, *L'arte
etrusca* (1935), pls. 210–213; Brendel, pp. 216ff.; M. Sprenger and G.
Bartolini, *Die Etrusker* (1977), pl. 78.

For the gestures, see the bibliography to [29]. On thymiateria in general, M.
Besnier, s.v. 'Turibulum,' C. Daremburg and E. Sagliou, *Dictionnaire des
antiques grecques et romaines* 5.1 (n.d.): 542–544.

33 ATHENA

Height 12.0 cm.
Solid cast bronze. Intact. Green patina.
Greek (Sicily?); early fifth century B.C.
Unpublished.

The goddess stands on a stepped rectangular plinth with two holes for attachment to a larger base. She steps forward on her left foot. Her right arm is raised above her shoulder, and the hand is positioned to brandish a long spear (there is a hole, but the spear is missing). Her left arm, bent at the elbow and held before her, once carried a shield (the hole for attachment remains, but not the shield).

Athena wears an Attic helmet (there is a hole for the attachment of a crest, now missing) and a long straight chiton belted at the waist. The few folds on the slim skirt are indicated with incised lines. On her upper body she wears an aegis adorned in front with small incised crosses with short-footed cross bars. It hangs low over her back and, from all around its edges, serpents encircle the goddess's body.

The goddess Athena, a virgin warrioress, patron of craftsmen and of the city of Athens, was represented in archaic times by the palladion, so-called after one of the goddess's epithets, Pallas. In these early representations Athena appears strictly frontal, legs together and wearing a close-fitting belted chiton. Her attributes are a shield held in her lowered left hand and a spear held horizontally above her head in her right hand.

During the sixth century the palladion type developed into the Athena Promachos, a representation of the goddess striding forward and using, rather than just holding, her spear and shield. The best-known representation of this type is the Athena Promachos of Phidias made for the Acropolis at Athens from the spoils of the victory over the Persians at the Battle of Marathon (490 B.C.).

This statuette retains the early plain chiton with a few simple engraved folds and facial features that are notably archaic. The forward step, however, is common to later Attic representations of Promachos. A date for the statuette in the early (even toward the mid-) fifth century is probable because of the generally conservative features of cult or votive objects such as this and because of its stylistic affinities with works from Dorian Sicily, an area colonized by the artistically provincial city of Sparta.

NOTES: For a substantial number of parallel pieces, H. Niemeyer, *Promachos. Untersuchungen zur Darstellung der bewaffneten Athena in archaischer Zeit* (1960). For some Spartan Athenas that are very close to the Hunt piece, note especially p. 61 and figs. 17–18. More recent discussion of the Promachos type: H. Herdejurgen, "Bronzestatuette der Athena," *AK* 12 (1969): 102–110 and M. Jost, "Statuettes de bronze de Lykosoura," *BCH* 99 (1975): 345ff. Cf. *Master Bronzes* no. 36; E. Kunze, *Bericht über die Ausgrabungen in Olympia* 7 (1961): 160–163; *Pomerance* no. 92.

34 HYDRIA

Height 48.1 cm; diameter of the body 31.9 cm; diameter of the mouth 17.8 cm; diameter of the foot 13.7 cm.

The body of the hydria is raised from hammered sheet bronze; the lip, handles and foot are cast. The body has been reinforced in several places, and there are some chips in the edge of the foot. Green-brown patina damaged in several places.

Greek; mid-fifth century B.C.

Unpublished.

Hydria with a tall concave neck, ovoid body and flaring foot. The upper edge of the lip is beaded; the outside of the lip is decorated with a plastic frieze of egg and dart. The neck is decorated near its base with a double molding. On the wide shoulder are tongues, and in the handle zone is a cable frieze between double moldings. On the foot there is a lotus and palmette frieze between narrow beaded bands.

34 HYDRIA (continued)

The three solid cast handles are the main decorative elements of this hydria. The two round and arched horizontal handles are encircled at the central high point with a ring of large beads flanked by borders of tiny beads. The attachments on either side of the handles are palmettes facing outward and ending on the inside in volutes with a flat molding. At the base of the molding serpent heads curve back inward toward the handle. At the junction of the attachments and the handles are tongues and a border of small beads that repeats the motif on the lip and at the center of the handles.

The vertical handle arches up over the lip of the hydria. Round extensions of the handle spread over the lip and end on either side in rotelles decorated on the edges with beads and, on the outside, with rosettes. Over the neck stands an intricately detailed lion head rendered frontally and in the round. In a clever allusion to contemporary water spouts in fountain houses and on the roofs of buildings, the lion overlooks—and symbolically empties water into—the hydria below. The lion has stylized teeth and a protruding tongue; he is wide-eyed with ears pricked. The details of his wavy mane are incised all around the head and up the handle above.

The back side of the handle has a central rib. There is a line of large beads down the center, and lines of smaller beads along each side. The base of the handle, where it joins the attachment, is decorated with large beads. The attachment is the forepart of a lion skin with the mane on both sides folded over the paws. The mane over the forehead ends on both sides in volutes.

The hydria is a vessel used to carry and pour water. The horizontal side handles are for lifting; the vertical rear handle, for

pouring. Although none of the elements of this bronze hydria is unique, the combination of the two lions on the vertical handle is very rare. Such expensive bronze vases as this would have been used as votive gifts, as prizes, funeral dedications or as ash urns.

NOTES: The basic work on hydriai is E. Diehl, *Die Hydria* (1964). This hydria is an unusual example of her class b (vertical handles with lion heads facing inward), some of which have siren attachments at the base of the handle. The earliest bronze hydria with a lion head above the rim is Olympia inv. 13199 (Diehl B86). Parallels for the two lions are a handle from Dodona (Diehl B93) and one in Toledo (D. van Bothmer's review of Diehl in *Gnomon* 37 [1965]: 601–602 and *Museum News. The Toledo Museum of Art* 7 [1964], p. 80). Bothmer notes (in correspondence) that the tongue pattern on the shoulder occurs on this type first on a hydria from Paestum (Diehl B87) and a hydria in Naples (Diehl B94). The convention of the lion skin at the root of the back handle that terminates above in a lion head is also known from bronze oinochoai (cf. New York inv. 1981.11.23; Bothmer in *Notable Acquisitions 1981–1982* [1982], p. 10). Also, cf. *Mildenberg Collection* nos. 113–115 and A. Andriomenou, "Vases et lampes de bronze dans des collections privées d'Athènes," *BCH* 99 (1975): 535ff. For the serpent motif on the horizontal handles, D. Kent Hill, "Palmette with Snakes: A Handle Ornament on Early Metalware," *AK* 10 (1967): 39–40.

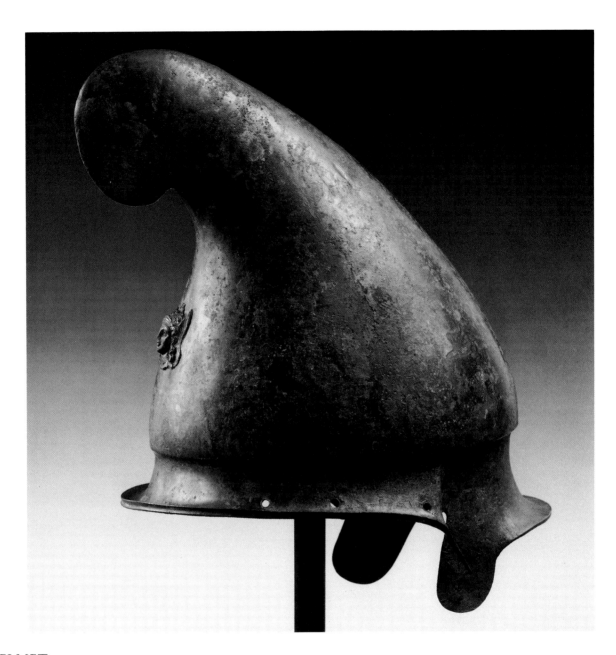

35 HELMET

Height from the rim to the top of the crest 28.0 cm; length at the base 20.8 cm.

Hammered sheet bronze with cast appliqué. Complete. There are repairs in several places, and one of the projections of the neck protector is reattached. Dark green patina.

Greek; fourth century B.C.

Published: Summa, *Auction 1* (1981), no. 43.

Phrygian (or Thracian) helmet of the standard type. The high crown arches and falls forward, ending in a rounded peak above the forehead. At the base of the cap there are offset bands that form a protector for the forehead in front and a deeper neck protector behind. At its front ends the neck protector terminates in rounded projections that guard the area behind the ears. The forehead protector has a narrow horizontal rim to keep the sun off the wearer's face. On each side of the cap near the rim are three holes for the attachment of cheek pieces.

Several examples of Phrygian helmets from the late classical and hellenistic period are decorated with appliqués. The one on this helmet, mounted above the forehead, is a frontal head of the warrior goddess Athena in a triple-crested helmet.

This type of helmet is fashioned on the model of a soft cap with a peak that falls forward in a similar way. In art it is a headdress characteristic of figures from the north, especially Thrace, and from the east. In spite of its unwieldy size and shape, it seems to have been used in the fourth-century Macedonian army, especially among the infantry.

NOTES: The standard work on these helmets is still B. Schröder, "Thrakische Helme," *JDAI* 27 (1912): 317–344. For a similar piece from Epiros, N. Yalouris et al., *The Search for Alexander. An Exhibition* (1981), no. 103. Less similar is M. Comstock and C. Vermeule, *Greek, Etruscan and Roman Bronzes in the Museum of Fine Arts, Boston* (1971), no. 589A.

36 ORANT

Height 31.6 cm.

Hollow cast bronze. Complete and intact except for ancient repairs on the left shoulder, legs and back. There are casting tenons under both feet. Light green patina.

Etruscan; third century B.C.

Published: *Master Bronzes* no. 187; Brendel, p. 411.

The youth stands facing forward with his weight on his left leg, his right leg placed back and out with the knee slightly bent in a variation of the traditional late fifth-century Polyclitan pose. He wears only a toga draped over his left shoulder, around to the back and right hip and in front again over his extended left arm.

The figure's head is tilted to the right; the hair is parted in the center and tapers from the two arching locks above the forehead over the ears and onto the nape of the neck. The youth's hands are extended, the left one in front and slightly to the side just

below waist level; the right one is held higher, but in basically the same position. On both hands the palm is exposed.

There are two inscriptions in Etruscan, here transliterated. Below the left wrist on the drapery is LEL MATUNAS TURCE (Lar Matunas a gift), and on the drapery in the back is (left) ERA and (right) LUR MUTLAC (gave to the god?).

The pose, dress (with toga and bare feet) and gesture of the youth are those of a notable series of Etruscan figures of priests and of sacrificing and praying youths of the fourth through first centuries B.C. This statuette, as the dedicatory inscription shows, is a votive gift and the youth, with his hands in this position but apparently without sacrificial implements, is in the act of praying. In antiquity (as now) the statuette was affixed to a base with the two casting tenons still in place on the bottom of the feet.

36 ORANT (continued)

The treatment of the head and face has a strong resemblance to the portraits of Alexander the Great. This is evident not only in the rightward tilt of the head, but in the deep-set eyes, the large straight nose and the full mouth. The particular form of the features (especially the contours of the face and the lips) and the rendering of the hair that tapers in a series of large locks from the forehead where the anastole rises in two steeply arched locks above the face is markedly similar to the Roman imperial Alexander portrait of the Azara Herm in Istanbul and the Fouquet type in the Louvre.

The feet and the hands of the youth are very large, way out of proportion to the rest of the figure. This common feature of Etruscan art is a symbolic shorthand used to communicate the essential elements of a man's position, character and profession or function.

NOTES: For the Etruscan priest, sacrificing and orant figures, S. Haynes, "The Bronze Priests and Priestesses from Nemi," *MDAI(R)* 67 (1960): 34–47, especially pl. 19, 2; A. Krug, "Eine Etruskische Perseusstatuette," *Festschrift Brommer* pp. 207–208 and pl. 58, 1; Brendel, fig. 251.

The essential bibliography on the portraits of Alexander is extensive, but note: G. Kleiner, "Das Bildnis Alexanders des Grossen," *JDAI* 65/66 (1950/1951): 206–230; E. Harrison, "New Sculpture from the Athenian Agora," *Hesperia* 29 (1960): 382–389; Bieber, *Alexander*, especially pls. 8–9 for the Azara Herm; E. Schwarzenberg, "Der lysippische Alexander," *BJ* 167 (1967): 58–118; T. Hölscher, *Ideal und Wirklichkeit in den Bildnissen Alexanders des Grossen* (1971); E. Berger, "Ein neues Porträt Alexanders des Grossen," *AK* 14 (1971): 139ff.; J. Siebert, *Alexander der Grosse* (Erträge der Forschung 10, 1972); R. Corchia, "Una testa di efebo del Museo Provinciale S. Castromediano di Lecce," *AFLL* 6 (1971–1973): 133ff.; V. von Graeve, "Ein attisches Alexanderbildnis und seine Wirkung," *MDAI(A)* 89 (1974): 231–239; E. Scwarzenberg, "The Portraiture of Alexander," *Alexandre Le Grand* (Entretiens Fondation Hardt 22, 1976): 223ff.; K. Fittschen, *Katalog der antiken Skulpturen in Schloss Erbach* (Archäologische Forschungen 3, 1977): 21ff.; H. Niemeyer, "Alexander in Sevilla," *AA* 1978, pp. 106ff.; G. Schwarz, "Triptolemos-Alexander," *Forschungen und Funde. Festschrift B. Neutsch* (1980), pp. 449–455; W. Radt, "Der 'Alexanderkopf' in Istanbul," *AA* 1981, p. 588; N. Yalouris et al., *The Search for Alexander. An Exhibition* (1981), nos. 1ff.

For the emphasis on gesture in Etruscan art, R. Brilliant, *Gesture and Rank in Roman Art* (1963), *passim*.

37 ANGUIPEDE GIANT

Height 14.9 cm.

Solid cast bronze. Intact. The right arm is corroded badly, as is the end of the right serpent leg. The left arm is missing below the shoulder. Gray-green patina.

Roman; second century A.D., after an original of the second century B.C.

Unpublished.

The solid cast giant has a hole for mounting in his left knee. The heroic, but nearly defeated figure crouches low on the "knees" of his serpent legs, which writhe out and up around him. The upper sides of the legs are decorated with a series of

overlapping horizontal bands of scales that point upward and are incised in a leaf-like pattern. The underside duplicates the appearance of a serpent's belly with a series of deep horizontal lines. Each leg terminates in a dragon-like head with large beady snake eyes, a prominent "beard," an open mouth with fangs and a protruding tongue.

The torso and face of the giant stand in direct contrast with the ferocious animal legs. The giant, his head tilted back, looks up with pathetic eyes and partially open, downturned mouth to plead with the conquering power who (we must imagine) stands above him. His right arm is raised above his head in weak

37 ANGUIPEDE GIANT (continued)

defense. His left arm (worked for insertion above the elbow) reaches out behind him. One or both hands originally may have held stones (now missing).

The torso itself is modeled with much attention to realistic portrayal of the bone structure and musculature and a decorative treatment of the surface. There are four incised whirligigs on the chest, shoulder and raised right arm, and the same pattern is repeated on the hair in the center of the chest and around the navel. The back of the torso is, if anything, even more carefully modeled. On the left buttock is an incised K.

The small, but influential and wealthy kingdom of Pergamum in central Asia Minor was ruled in the hellenistic period by the Attalid kings. In the early second century, under Eumenes II, there was ever increasing artistic activity there. The Pergamene style of this period stems from the classical tradition, but this heritage is transformed by an often highly emotional, almost baroque, spirit. The best-known monument of this Pergamene style is the Great Altar of Zeus (now in East Berlin) which in part depicts the mythological battle of the Gods, led by Zeus, and the Giants, sons of Earth. In the battle the gods were victorious and thus established themselves on Mt. Olympus. The giant in the Hunt Collection is related to the Great Altar not only in subject, but in style. The flowing treatment of the hair, the highly pathetic emotion and the strong, twisting diagonal movement of the body and legs are all very typical of the second-century baroque style. But the deep carving of the hair and

the exaggerated pathos of the face indicate that the giant is an Antonine copy of a hellenistic original.

NOTES: For the Great Altar, Bieber, *Hellenistic Sculpture*, figs. 459ff.; H. Kähler, *Der grosse Fries von Pergamon* (1948); E. Schmidt, *The Great Altar of Pergamon* (1962); cf. G. Kleiner, *Das Nachleben des pergamenischen Gigantenkampfes* (1949). For the treatment of the torso, head and the same overall conception, Rolley, *Bronzes*, no. 127. S. Boucher (in correspondence) notes the similarity of the treatment of the hair and pathetic expression to that of hellenistic fauns.

38 HERAKLES

Height 10.3 cm; length of the base 5.4 cm; depth of the base 1.0 cm.
Solid cast bronze. Intact and complete with some surface abrasion.
Deep green patina.
Greek (South Italy?); second–first century B.C.
Unpublished.

Herakles stands on a very low, and roughly rectangular base. This piece originally was an appliqué. There is a deep hollow running vertically down the center of the back and a small piece for attachment remains at waist level. The back of the piece is completely unworked.

The hero lunges to the left, his right leg bent at the knee. His torso is shown frontally, his legs in three-quarter view. Herakles' face and gaze follow the line of motion. In his raised right hand he brandishes the club (which is joined to the top back side of his head). The well-muscled body is naked except for the lion skin which is worn on his head, tied over his shoulders and tightly twisted around his left arm. This arm is held stiff, diagonally behind, and the end of the lion skin flares out with the motion of Herakles' attack.

The base on which Herakles stands resembles the rough terrain appropriate to the hero's labors, but the actual enemy remains unseen. This type of striding god or hero with a weapon raised above his head originated in archaic Greek art, when Herakles appears striding forward with his club in his raised right hand and his bow in his left hand, which is extended forward. By the

hellenistic period this type was often much altered, though far from unrecognizably, and it became a favorite for small statuettes in Italy and the western provinces of the Roman Empire. In this particular version, the well-muscled body and the pathos of the face appear to derive from the Pergamene art of Asia Minor in the second century B.C.

The youthful features of Herakles, although somewhat pinched, bear a definite resemblance to those of Alexander the Great. The type of portrayal, however, is distinctly different from the one that lies behind the head of the orant in the Hunt Collection [36]. The hair around the forehead is rendered in a mane-like crown, which arches smoothly upward all around the forehead under the lion skin. Much more leonine than the type of the Etruscan youth, it is one of several ways in which the hair of the great king was portrayed in posthumous portraits.

The kings of Macedonia traced their ancestry back to Herakles, and the hero is a common type on coins of Alexander and his father. It is possible that even during Alexander's lifetime these numismatic representations began to assume the features of the king. In any case, after Alexander's death the artistic identification of king and hero took hold, and there are many extant examples both on coins and in monumental sculpture.

NOTES: Examples of similar, usually far less fine, Herakles types from Italy and the Roman Empire: A. Maiuri, "Sepino," *NSc* 1926, pp. 248–250; *Metropolitan Bronzes* nos. 153ff.; E. Espérandieu and H. Rolland, *Bronzes antiques de la Seine-Maritime* (1959), pls. 14ff.; cf. *Rép. stat.* 6, pp. 56–57.

For earlier Greek types, Charbonneaux, pl. 12; *Metropolitan Bronzes* no. 62; Rolley, *Bronzes*, no. 124. More generally on hellenistic Herakles types: F. Brommer, *Herakles* (1953), p. 66 and H. Cassimatis, "Herakles et Lysippe. La descendance," *BIAO* 78 (1978): 541–564.

For identification of Alexander and Herakles, Bieber, *Alexander*, 48–52; C. Vermeule, "Commodus, Caracalla and the Tetrarchs: Roman Emperors as Hercules," *Festschrift Brommer*, p. 289. Also see the literature cited under [36]; for the Herakles types on coins issued during Alexander's lifetime, see Hölscher, *op. cit.* pp. 46–48; Berger, *op. cit.* p. 40, n. 9.

39 GODDESS

Height 25.3 cm.
Hollow cast, bronze completely gilt. Intact and complete. The bronze is visible through the gold over much of the surface.
Greek (Asia Minor?); first century B.C.
Unpublished.

This large statuette is probably a votive dedication. The two holes at the hem of the figure's garment indicate that at some time in antiquity (perhaps not originally) the statuette was mounted on a base.

The female figure stands facing the viewer, her weight resting on her right leg and her left leg bent at the knee. She wears a long, full chiton which falls out around the feet on all sides. Her feet, dressed in deep-soled sandals, protrude only slightly from under the chiton. The mantle is wrapped tightly around her shoulders and upper right arm. Her lower right arm is bent across her body, and with her right hand, she firmly holds the mantle on her left hip. Her left arm, covered by the chiton to just below the elbow, is raised up in front of her face, and in her hand there is a small oval object. The figure's head is tilted to

the left to gaze at the object before her. The hair is treated in the classical manner, drawn back in a loose roll from the center part to an uptwisted bun behind. On her head is a round diadem. The features are small and angular, crowded toward the center of the face.

The small head and genre pose in which the figure gazes thoughtfully at the object in her hand are typical features of hellenistic art. The basic type of the statuette, however, originated in the fourth century, perhaps in the hands of Praxiteles or one of his followers. This so-called Herculaneum woman type (named from the find spot of one of the most famous examples), heavily draped in a very long, full chiton and closely wrapped himation, stands with her arms held close to her body.

In the second century the Herculaneum woman type developed into the so-called Pudicitia (Latin for chastity) figure that was popular throughout the early Roman Empire for portraits of matrons. There is a long series of these figures to which the Hunt statuette may be compared. The short waist, narrow upper torso and large hips, as well as the wrapping of the mantle and the position of the arms, all closely resemble the "Cleopa-

tra'' of Delos, one of the best-known Pudicitia types which dates to the late second century B.C.

The round diadem and idealized features identify the figure as a goddess, but which one is uncertain. The only attribute, aside from the diadem, which is common to many female divinities, is the object in the figure's hand, and this is not clearly identifiable. If the object is an apple, the figure could be Hera, Aphrodite or Eris. If it is a pomegranate, she would be Persephone. Boucher suggests (in correspondence) that, because of the position of the arms, it is Hygeia and that the object in the figure's left hand is food for a serpent which would have encircled the arm of the goddess.

NOTES: For the Herculaneum woman type, Robertson 1, pp. 479–480. For the Pudicitia, Bieber, *Hellenistic Sculpture*, pp. 131ff.; C. Havelock, *Hellenistic Art* (1968), fig. 116 (with commentary and bibliography).

Roman imperial portraits of this type from Asia Minor are discussed by D. Pinkwart, ''Weibliche Gewandstatuen aus Magnesia am Mäander,'' *Antike Plastik* 12 (1973): 149ff. For comparable Hygeia types: *Rép. stat.* 2, p. 298; 3, p. 91.

40 TYCHE

Height 43.0 cm.

Hollow cast bronze. The eyes originally were inlaid, probably with silver. Intact. Both lower arms, which were made separately and attached, are missing. There is a hole in the left arm just above the elbow, and the second toe on the left foot is corroded. Light green patina.

Roman (Asia Minor?); late first century B.C.–early first century A.D. Unpublished.

On this large statuette Tyche (Fortune) wears a round diadem and a tall, carefully detailed mural crown. Gates and blocks of the city walls and sections of the walls themselves all are delineated. Tyche's hair is rendered in a classical style, waving in loose curls from a central part to a high, large chignon in back. Originally she wore earrings, though only the holes for their insertion remain.

The goddess wears a very long, high-girded chiton. It falls off her right shoulder leaving one breast bare in the manner of an Amazon or young maiden, and is rendered with much transparency below the belt in the center of her body. A himation is draped loosely and gracefully over her left shoulder, around her right hip and up in front over her extended left arm. Her feet, which are visible at the front edge of the chiton, are dressed in elaborate deep-soled sandals. Her right arm extends down and slightly outward from the shoulder. Just above the elbow, where the lower arm was inserted, there is an armlet. Her left arm is also extended down, but close to the body and outward from the elbow. The hands, now both missing, originally carried further attributes. Given the immense variety in the extant representations of Tyche, it is perhaps dangerous to suggest a reconstruction of these, but a plate or wheat ears in the left hand and a rudder in the right are not unlikely.

The Greek Tyche was personified in literature from the early classical period, and in the less stable hellenistic age she was deified and attached to many Greek cities and to the people of Rome as a divine protectress. Among artistic representations of the goddess the best known is the Tyche of Antioch, who was given sculptural form by Eutychides in the early third century, but many other cities and even leading men had their own representations. Common to many of these are the mural crown; the cornucopia; the rudder, since she was thought of as helmsman of the state; and wheat ears, symbolic of fertility.

In style this Tyche is marked by the elegant, if slightly mannered, neoclassicism of the first centuries before and after Christ. The treatment of the hair and face, the long neck, the graceful treatment of the drapery and the classical proportions of the figure all indicate a date of circa 50 B.C.–50 A.D.

NOTES: Cf. *Rép. stat.* 3, p. 81, 8 and, more generally, J. Szilagyi, s.v. 'Tyche,' *EAA* 5 (1963): 1038ff.; W. Kaiser, "Die Göttin mit der Mauerkrone," *SM* 18 (1968): 25–30.

41 HERCULES

Height 9.9 cm; height of the pedestal 3.5 cm; diameter of the pedestal 4.8 cm.

Solid cast bronze statuette with hollow cast pedestal. The eyes are inlaid with silver. There is also silver inlay for the rosettes on the pedestal and some further inlay—perhaps gold—has perished. The two inlaid teeth of the lion are also missing; otherwise intact and complete except for the right jaw of the lion on the headdress. Dark green patina.

Roman; first century A.D.

Unpublished.

The infant Hercules is shown frontally, walking forward with his weight on his left leg. His head is turned slightly to the right, and he gazes upward and to the right. The pupils are hollow; the rest of the eyes inlaid with silver. The face, like the rest of the body, is chubby and thoroughly childlike.

Over Hercules' curly hair is the lion skin won in his first labor (in anticipation of his future deed). The head is worked with much detail, and there originally were two inlaid teeth over the young hero's forehead. The upper part of the skin is tied over Hercules' shoulders in front; the rest is draped over his back and wound around his left arm in front. In the back the full, wavy mane appears beautifully detailed between the upturned edges of the underside of the skin, which also appears over the left arm in front. In his right hand the young hero once held his club (now missing); in his left are the apples of the Hesperides won in his last labor.

The cylindrical pedestal is decorated around its upper edge with a band of small beads and, just below, a plastic band of tongues. The base of the pedestal is bell-shaped and decorated with acanthus leaves between bands of small beads. The central decoration of the pedestal is inlaid with silver (partially missing) in a pattern of eight-petaled rosettes linked by diamonds flanked by horizontal lines.

In Greek myth the infant Herakles, prodigious son of Zeus and Alkmene, single-handedly fought off the huge snakes sent to his cradle by Hera, the jealous wife of Zeus. In the hellenistic period, when an interest in the representation of children blossomed, images of this exceptional child became popular. They remained so throughout the Roman Empire, and among them this representation is notable for its rich inlaid decoration and wealth of detail.

NOTES: For comparable representations of the infant Hercules, *Master Bronzes* no. 253 (different attributes and style) = C. Vermeule, *Greek and Roman Sculpture in America* (1981), no. 149; "Commodus, Caracalla and the Tetrarchs: Roman Emperors as Hercules," *Festschrift Brommer* p. 292; pl. 77, 2–3; cf. *Rép. stat.* 5, p. 80, 7.

More generally, D. Hill, "Ancient Representations of Heracles as a Baby," *GBA* 36 (1948): 193ff.

There is a very similar base for a statuette of Mercury: *GR Bronzes* pl. 87.

42 ZEUS (?)

Height 21.1 cm.

Hollow cast bronze. Intact. There is an area missing in the hair above the forehead and several small perforations in the metal elsewhere. The sides of the base of the head are slightly damaged. Green patina.

Roman (Asia Minor?); first–second century A.D.

Unpublished.

The god faces forward, his head surrounded by loose, flowing locks of hair and a prominent beard. Above the forehead the hair rises in a series of waves and falls in loosely curled locks both front and back. The beard has tighter curls and is parted down the center with rows of curls twisting back to each side. The mustache is full and wavy, and turns out at the ends in two small locks that merge with the similar curls of the beard. The pupils and irises of the eyes are incised. There are small pouches under the eyes and shallow laugh lines above the mustache. The nose is straight, slightly flattened down the central ridge, and the lips are full.

One of the most influential statuary types developed in the hellenistic period is the so-called Father God, a type used for Jupiter Capitolinus as he appeared in the cult statue made by Apollonius in the first century B.C. The Father God type was used for many other divinities as well. Since there are no specific attributes on this head, we cannot be certain of the god portrayed. Zeus is most likely, Poseidon or Asclepius a little less so.

The facial type ultimately is based on the high classical Zeus of the fifth-century sculptor Phidias, much transformed by the spirit of a later age. The god's expression is still majestic, but the distance is somewhat tempered by a benign and concerned expression in the eyes and by the light smile of the full, expressive mouth. This feeling is reinforced by the signs of age and weariness around the eyes and mouth and by the soft full waves of the hair.

NOTES: E. Thiemann, *Hellenistische Vatergottheiten* (1959) is basic on the type. Among numerous variations, see J. Sieveking, *Die Bronzen der Sammlung Loeb* (1913): 41ff. (Poseidon); K. Neugebauer, "Zwei Jupiterstatuetten in Berlin und Weimar," *AA* 1935, pp. 321ff.; A. Liebundgut, *Die römischen Bronzen der Schweiz 3. Westschweiz, Bern und Wallis* (1980), no. 3; S. Boucher, *Musée de la Civilisation Gallo-Romaine à Lyons. Bronzes antiques* (1976), no. 40.

For a centaur head of similar style, H. Menzel, *Die römischen Bronzen aus Deutschland 1. Speyer* (1960), no. 14.

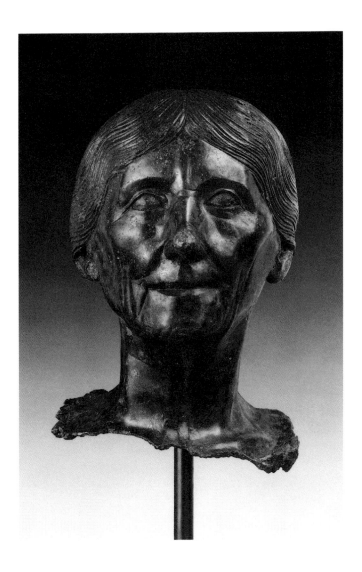

43 PORTRAIT OF A WOMAN

Height 29.3 cm.

Hollow cast bronze. There is minor damage to several small areas on the hair and right eye. The tip of the nose is abraded, and the lower part of the bust is broken on all sides. Red-brown patina on the face and neck; dark green patina on the hair.

Roman (Spain); very late first century B.C.–early first century A.D.
Unpublished.

Life-size bust of an old woman. Her head is held straight and proud, and she looks out shrewdly to the right of the viewer. The hair is rendered in low relief. It is parted down the center and pulled back to the ears with only a very few waves. Behind the ears there are two low braids, one above the other. They end in a pony tail, which is flat and held in place by a double twist of hair at the top. The woman has high cheek bones, a straight nose with a prominent upturned tip and a thin-lipped mouth. There are deep frown lines, and the skin is sunken and furrowed over the rest of the woman's face.

The characteristics of Roman portraiture of the late Republic and early Empire are the result of the influence of a number of trends: the formal structural features of Etruscan art, the idealizing portraits of the hellenistic Greeks and the Roman tradition

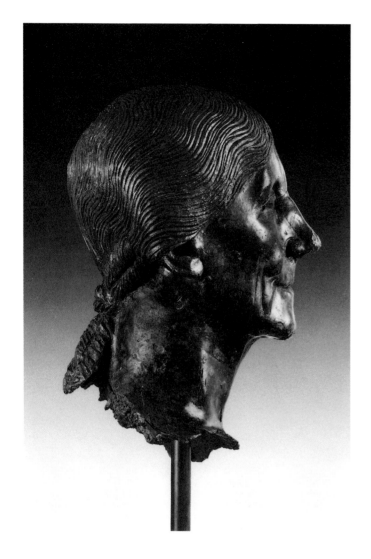

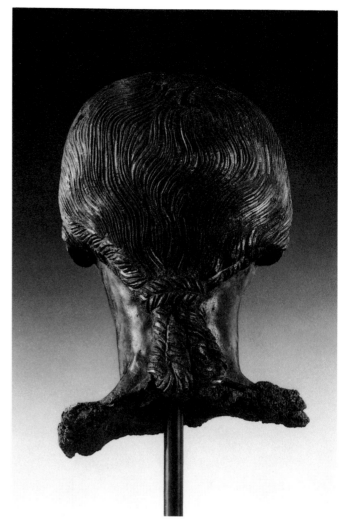

of making realistic death masks, images made of wax at the time of death that were kept in the houses of a noble's descendants and paraded in public on special occasions.

In Roman society, much respect was accorded to the elderly for their wisdom and experience. In this portrait there is no attempt to conceal age; in fact, there is a set of stylized features that emphasize it. The frown lines between the eyes, the crow's feet, the laugh lines and wrinkles on the cheeks and below the corners of the mouth all can be paralleled on portraits of other old women from the period. The nose and mouth, however, are very much those of a single individual, though not one readily identifiable on the basis of other extant portraits.

Another important characteristic of Roman society in this period is a rigid set of moral values. Severity, austerity and chastity were the governing ideals for the conduct of the Roman matron. These qualities are suggested by the tight-lipped mouth with no hint of a smile, the penetrating—even hard—gaze and the simple, severe treatment of the hair.

A date for the portrait in the Augustan or early Julio-Claudian period (until about 54 A.D.) is indicated by the treatment of the hair and by the unrelieved emphasis on the age of the subject.

NOTES: For the hairstyle, G. Giacosa, *Ritratti di Auguste* (n.d.), pl. 4 and a portrait that has been identified as Antonia Minor (the niece of Augustus and mother of the emperor Claudius): Poulsen 1, pl. 42. For a general treatment of the subject (without plates): H. Bartels, *Studien zum Frauenporträt der augusteischen Zeit* (1964); and, on male and female portraits, *Roman Portraits: Aspects of Self and Society* (1980): 8–18 and 107; A. Hekler, *Greek and Roman Portraits* (1912); A. Zadoks-Josephus Jitta, *Ancestral Portraiture in Rome* (1932).

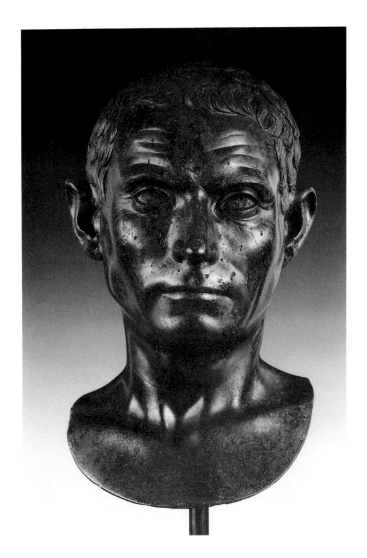

44 PORTRAIT OF A MAN

Height 32.6 cm.

Hollow cast bronze. The inlaid pupils of the eyes are missing. Red-brown patina on the face and neck; dark green patina on the hair.
Roman (Spain); very late first century B.C.–early first century A.D.
Unpublished.

The similarity both in style and patina of this life-size portrait bust of a middle-aged man to that of the old woman preceding [43] indicates that the two pieces come from the same workshop and that they were found together. It is possible that they represent mother and son.

The man, who appears to be in young middle age, looks steadily outward, his head turned slightly to the left. The pupils are incised. His short hair is rendered with small locks in low relief. Above his forehead the hair turns out to left and right just to the right of center, as is typical of portraits in the Augustan and early Julio-Claudian period. The hairline is slightly receding, the nose is straight with a fleshy tip not at all dissimilar to the old woman's, the lips are thin, and the chin pointed. There are prominent vertical ridges between the nose and mouth. The ears are prominent, a feature perhaps modeled on the emperor Augustus.

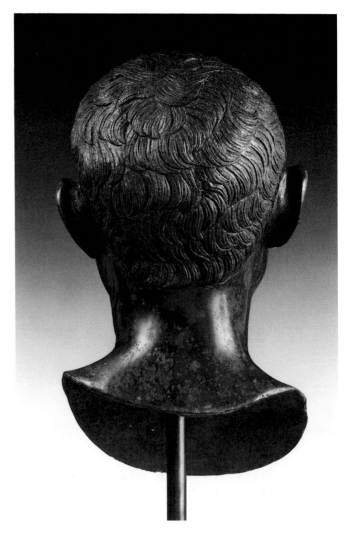

Two seemingly contradictory styles are combined on this portrait, and together they transcend and transform the individualized features such as the nose, lips and chin.

The deeply furrowed brow, the sunken care-worn eyes and the wrinkles in front of the ear and neck on the right side of the piece convey, in a quite standardized manner, the hallmarks of a seasoned Roman statesman, his gravitas and severitas (seriousness and austerity). The unsmiling mouth with firmly set lips and eyes directed into the distance in thought reinforce this image.

In contrast to these features are the contours of the lower half of the face and the left side of the head and neck. Here the sitter is youthful and wrinkle-free, traits that reflect the idealizing trend in Roman portraiture prominent in the Augustan period.

NOTES: There is a very similar bronze portrait of an older man: *Roman Portraits*, no. 8. For other bibliography, see portrait of woman [43].

45 MERCURY

Height 12.8 cm.
Solid cast bronze. Intact. One wing on the hat and the right foot below the ankle are missing. Dark green patina.
Roman; first century A.D.
Unpublished.

The god stands at rest with his weight on the right leg, his right hip raised and his left leg bent, a posture ultimately based on a late fifth-century B.C. original of the sculptor Polyclitus. The hair style, with locks turned away from a central part and lying flat over the forehead, is derived from the same source.

Mercury wears a traveler's hat (petasus) with wings on the top and a broad and gracefully wavy brim. His traveler's cloak (chlamys) is fastened at the neck, but draped only from the god's left shoulder. In his right hand he holds an animal skin money bag, a typically Roman attribute of Mercury. In his left hand, which is open with the palm tilted upward, he probably once held the caduceus. On his feet are Mercury's characteristic winged endromides.

Commerce and business were primary concerns of the Roman upper middle classes, especially from the late third century B.C. when Rome's conquests in the Mediterranean yielded progres-

sively more territory for expansion and trade. Along with these interests, symbolic of them, comes the prominence of the god Mercury in his capacity as god of trade.

There are a very large number of Mercury statuettes that survive from the Roman Empire, especially from the provinces in western Europe north of Italy, and some of them resemble the emperor Augustus. Among these the Hunt statuette stands out both for its excellent state of preservation and for the pure classicism and delicacy with which the figure is modeled.

NOTES: For a synthetic treatment of this type, S. Boucher, *Recherches sur les bronzes figurés de Gaule pré-romaine et romaine* (1976): 81–84 and 116. Cf. S. Boucher, *Musée de la Civilisation Gallo-Romaine à Lyon. Bronzes antiques* (1976), no. 45, cf. no. 51; *GR Bronzes*, pl. 87; M. Comstock and C. Vermeule, *Greek, Etruscan and Roman Bronzes in the Museum of Fine Arts, Boston* (1971), no. 110; Doeringer, 229–231; R. Fleischer, *Die römische Bronzen aus Österreich* (1967): 56–57 and E. Espérandieu and H. Rolland, *Bronzes antiques de la Seine-Maritime* (1959): 28–32.

For an example much closer to the fifth-century original, Robertson 2, pl. 110c.

For Augustus and Mercury-Hermes, I. Ryberg, *Rites of the State Religion in Roman Art* (1955), p. 38; O. Brendel, "Novus Mercurius," *MDAI (R)* 50 (1935): 213–259 reprinted in *The Visible Iden: Interpretations of Classical Art* (1980) with the review of R. Smith, *JRS* 72 (1982), p. 199.

46 MERCURY

Height, including the loop for hanging, 11 cm.
Hollow cast bronze with inlaid silver eyes. Intact and complete. Dark green patina.
Roman (Alexandria); first century A.D.
Unpublished.

At the top of this steelyard weight is a loop for hanging it on the arm of the scale. On the underside there is a square opening (1.5 cm on each side) for the insertion of lead weight into the hollow interior. Around the lower edge of the bust there are seven evenly spaced holes that must have been used to secure a garland of leaves or some other decoration.

Mercury faces straight forward and wears his characteristic messenger's hat (petasus), fashioned with a wavy brim and tiny flattened wings that do not impede the hanging of the weight. A chlamys, which is gracefully draped around the narrow shoulders of the god, terminates the bust.

The facial features and short curly hair, although generally Polycleitan bear a marked resemblance to portraits of the Ptolemies who ruled Egypt from the death of Alexander until the reign of Augustus. The wide-open eyes and long upper lid, the pointed nose, small downturned mouth and contour of the cheek all have a family resemblance to the Egyptian kings [107]. The pupils and irises are incised and the irises are inlaid with silver.

The Roman steelyard scale (with unequal arms and a movable weight) was called a statera, and the weights used to balance the object to be weighed were made in many decorative forms. There are busts of satyrs, maenads, of actors, negroes, children, emperors and gods. As the god of commerce, for which the scale was used, Mercury was one of the most popular of these types.

NOTES: For the form and operation of steelyard weights, W. Hornbostel, *Aus Gräbern und Heiligtümern* (1981), no. 154; H. Philipp, "Zu einer Gewichtsbüste aus dem Kerameikos," *MDAI(A)* 94 (1979): 137ff. I have not seen H. Menzel, *Mitteilungen des historischen Verein der Pfalz* 58 (1960): 56ff. For other Mercury weights, C. di Stefano, *Bronzetti figurati del Museo Nazionale di Palermo* (1975), no. 157; E. Babelon and J. Blanchet, *Catalogue des bronzes antiques de la Bibliothèque Nationale* (1895), no. 361; V. Barbu, "Bronzes romains de Constantza," *Dacia* 2.9 (1965), p. 393; A. de Ridder, *Les bronzes antiques du Louvre* 2 (1915), no. 3269 (very similar, but without petasus); P. Ducati, "Sarsina," *NSc* 1911, pp. 123-124. For portraits of the Ptolemies, Kyrieleis.

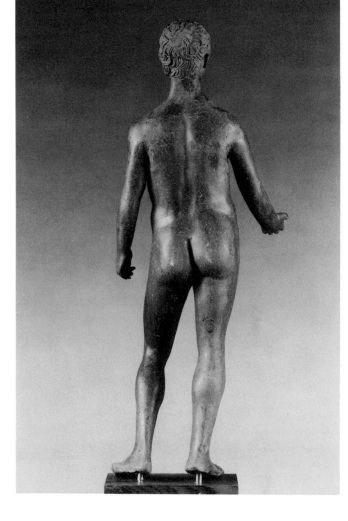

47 YOUTH

Height 67.4 cm.

Hollow cast bronze. Intact and complete. There are ancient repairs on the right foot, the shoulders (a large number) and upper arms. Gray-green patina.

Roman; second century A.D.

Unpublished.

The naked youth, approximately half life-size, stands facing forward with his weight on his right leg, his left leg bent back and slightly out from the knee. Both heels are raised slightly. His head is turned three-quarters right and he gazes off into the distance, a very slight smile playing on his lips.

The youth's right arm is held out from the elbow, the hand extended with the palm open and facing upward. The left arm is extended straight down with the palm of the hand turned upward and the fingers curled in toward the body.

The small head and features of this young man are derived ultimately from a Polyclitan treatment of the popular fifth-century type of a victorious athlete sacrificing [71], but the details have been much modified over time. The cap-like treatment of the hair with short curls and the treatment of the face are generally classicizing, but adapted to the features of an un-known individual with close-set, almond-shaped eyes and a small mouth.

The body and stance also are Polyclitan in origin, but the whole is far softer, the torso shorter and thicker through the hips, and the arms shorter than those typical of the Greek sculptor. The stance and the position of the hands and feet are almost identical to those of the early first century A.D. (and far more classical, though the exact origin is much disputed) bronze youth in Florence known as the Idolino. Both figures may have held a libation plate in their outstretched right hand. In the left hand, if anything, there was perhaps a lamp or a palm branch.

NOTES: On the Idolino and related Roman types: A. Rumpf, "Der Idolino," *Critica d'Arte* 4 (1939): 17–27; P. Zanker, *Klassizistische Statuen* (1974); C. Blümel, "Idolino, Apollon Kitharista, Münchner Knabenkopf," *AA* 1974, pp. 247–254.

For fifth-century examples of the young athlete sacrificing, W. Fuchs, "Die verschollene Kleinbronze aus Tegea," *AA* 1956, pp. 1ff.; H. Niemeyer, "Attische Bronzestatuetten der spätarchaischen und frühklassischen Zeit," *Antike Plastik* 3 (1964), p. 262 and pl. 20; Langlotz and Hirmer, pls. 81, 84, 85. For the successors of Polycleitus, D. Arnold, *Die Polykleitnachfolge: Untersuchungen zur Kunst von Argos und Sikyon zwischen Polyklet und Lysipp* (*JDAI* Ergänzungsheft 25, 1969), especially pp. 93–96.

 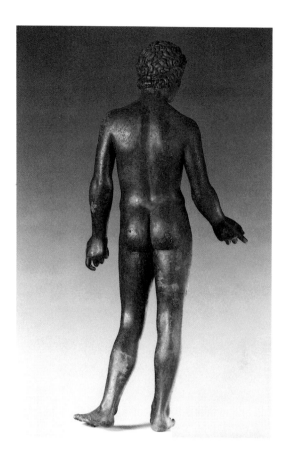

48 YOUTH

Height 117 cm.

Hollow cast in six parts: (1) the head and upper neck; (2) the lower neck, torso, arms to above the elbows and legs to mid-thigh; (3–4) the rest of the arms and (5–6) the lower part of the legs. The eyes are inlaid with silver. Intact and complete. There are ancient repairs on the buttocks and upper legs. Some minor surface corrosion. Dark green patina.

Roman; probably second century A.D.

Unpublished. This piece has been exhibited in the CINOA exhibition in Amsterdam (1972) and New York (1973), in the André Emmerich Gallery in New York (1975) and in the Boston Museum of Fine Arts (1978–1979).

This approximately three-quarter life-size youth is naked and stands facing forward with his weight on his right leg and his left leg bent back and out from the knee. The left foot is tilted up to the outside. The head is turned three-quarters right, and the youth looks out in the distance. The eyes are incised and inlaid with silver. On the short curly hair is a narrow fillet. The left hand is extended straight down, the hand palm up with the fingers curled into it. The right hand is extended out from the elbow, the thumb and index fingers extended, the rest of the fingers curled up into the hand.

Like the previous piece in this exhibition [47], this figure is inspired by a Polyclitan original. It also differs markedly from the classical ideal, but in a different way. Most unusual is the treatment of the hair. It has an almost wig-like appearance with deep tufts tapering around the face to cover the ears. The face itself is idealized, lacking individualized features or expression.

The stance and proportions of the body also deviate from the Polyclitan standard: the left leg is bent in an exaggerated way, the arms are too long, the ankles too heavy and the modeling of the torso too smooth and unmuscled.

This figure may have originally served as a lychnouchos, or lampbearer, of the type found at Pompeii and have held a branched candle holder in each hand. Or, according to Boucher (in correspondence), he may have held the attributes of an athlete: the palm, as a reward for victory, in his right hand and, perhaps, a discus in his left.

NOTES: See the literature cited under [47], especially Zanker, pl. 74 (an Apollo); Blümel, fig. 4 (a lamp bearer in Naples); Arnold, pp. 94ff.

49 BACCHUS

Height 14.7 cm.

Solid cast bronze. Intact, but both feet are missing from the ankle down and the support is lost from a point just below Bacchus' knee. Dark green patina.

Roman; second century A.D.

Published: Summa, *Catalogue 5: Ancient Art* (1979), no. 1.

The slim young Bacchus, Roman god of wine, stands forward with his weight on his right foot, his right hip raised and slung far to the right and his left leg bent at the knee. His lower left arm rests on a "support" in the form of a grape vine twining upward in an openwork pattern decorated with leaves and clusters of fruit. The vine is not fully worked on the back of the piece. The god's right arm is raised and the wrist and back of the hand rest on the top of his head. In this hand Bacchus holds a rhyton, or drinking horn.

The god wears high skin boots (embades) and an animal skin which is draped gracefully around his upper body under his right arm and fastened on his left shoulder. One of the large (and unusual) bear-like paws falls onto his left arm in front, the other behind. Over his forehead there is a narrow fillet and on his hair is a wreath of leaves and fruit clusters. The hair is parted in the center and falls in two long ringlets onto his shoulders in front. Behind, the long hair is drawn up into a chignon. On the forehead, flanked by deep grooves, are two small protuberances like the budding horns of a goat [51].

In inspiration this representation of the god standing in repose with his weight on the right leg and his left leg slightly bent is Polyclitan, but more specifically the figure is a version of the so-called Apollo Lykeios, which is attributed by modern scholars to the fourth-century sculptor Praxiteles or one of his followers. On extant copies and adaptations of this work Apollo rests his left hand on a lyre (originally a bow) which stands on a pedestal. His right hand, holding the pick for the lyre, rests at ease on the top of his head.

The relaxed and sensuous pose of the Apollo Lykeios seems suitable to less aggressive and physically powerful divinities, and was used for later Apollo, satyr and Dionysus-Bacchus figures. Here the vine support, as unnecessary as it is on a piece of this size, appears in place of Apollo's lyre and the pedestal. In the raised right hand a drinking horn replaces the pick for the lyre.

The god's features are modeled in a very linear style (especially the line of the brow and nose) with deeply carved pupils, wide round eyes and prominent lids. The mouth is downturned, almost pouting. These non-classical features and the overly pronounced swing of the hips, even though well balanced by the support, indicate that this statuette was made in the second century A.D.

NOTES: For the Apollo Lykeios and some imitations, Bieber, *Hellenistic Sculpture*, figs. 17, 19–23, 678–681. For Dionysus-Bacchus figures with this placement of the right arm, E. Pochmarski, *Das Bild des Dionysos in der Rundplastik der klassischen Zeit Griechenlands* (1974): 127ff., 159ff.; C. Vermeule, *Greek and Roman Sculpture in America* (1981), no. 268; J. Pedley, "A Dionysus in Ann Arbor," *Bulletin. Museums of Art and Archaeology, The University of Michigan* 1 (1978): 16–25; K. Lehmann-Hartleben, "Bellerophon und der Reiterheilige," *MDAI(R)* 38/39 (1923/1924), p. 271 and fig. 3; C. Picard, "Statues et ex-voto du 'Stibadeion' dionysiaque de Délos," *BCH* 68–69 (1944–1945), p. 246, p. 248 and figs. 5–6; C. Clairmont, *Die Bildnisse des Antinous* (1966), pl. 29, 38; cf. W. Helbig, *Führer durch die öffentlichen Sammlungen klassischer Altertümer in Rom* 2 (1966), no. 1383 (H. von Steuben); H. Hoffmann, *Ten Centuries that Shaped the West* (1971), no. 15; B. Andreae, "Archäologische Funde im Bereich von Rom 1949–1956/57," *JDAI* 72 (1957), p. 235 and fig. 48, with no head. On the derivation and meaning of the gesture, B. Ridgway, "A Story of Five Amazons," *AJA* 78 (1974): 9ff.

For a Praxitelean satyr with a similar treatment of the body and skin, Bieber, *Hellenistic Sculpture*, fig. 16.

50 SILVANUS

Height 29.5 cm.
Solid cast bronze; the left arm and skin are made separately. Intact.
The left foot and part of the wreath are missing, as is the silver inlay
for the eyes. Dark green patina.
Roman (Asia Minor?); late second century A.D.
Unpublished.

The woodland god Silvanus stands forward with his weight on
his right foot, his left leg bent well back at the knee. He wears a
prominent wreath of wheat, arranged like a crown of rays, on
his head. It is grooved in front, undecorated on the back side.
The hair of this older god is full and wavy, as are the mustache
and beard. Above the forehead two locks rise on either side of a
central part, and the curls of the beard turn back from another
central part.

A goatskin laden with various fruits is draped from Silvanus'
right shoulder, where it is tied by the front feet, and falls over
most of his left arm. The main body of the skin appears on the
left side of the god's back where the finely detailed head, the
wavy coat and the back hooves all are rendered. In his left hand

Silvanus carries a goat's foot drinking horn, and in his right
hand he holds a pruning knife. On his feet are high skin boots
(embades).

Silvanus is a native Italian woodland deity, a protector of agricultural fertility who was identified with the emperor Hadrian's favorite Antinous, and thus became very popular in the art
of the second century A.D. In general type, this statuette derives
from representations of the most important Greek gods—Zeus,
Poseidon and several others—made in the fifth and fourth centuries B.C. Typically these "father gods" have the same stance
as the Hunt Silvanus, as well as the full, long hair and beard and
a majestic expression at times tempered with benignity [42].

NOTES: In general on Silvanus, *Rép. stat.* 2, pp. 43–44; 3, p. 14; 6, p. 12; C.
Saletti, s.v. 'Silvanus,' *EAA* 7 (1966), p. 297. For parallels, H. Walters,
*Catalogue of the Bronzes, Greek, Roman and Etruscan in the Department
of Greek and Roman Antiquities, British Museum* (1899), no. 1523; E.
Babelon and J. Blanchet, *Catalogue des bronzes antiques de la Bibliothèque
Nationale* (1895), no. 90; *Badisches Landesmuseum. Bildkatalog* (1968), no.
D77.

51 BALSAMARIUM

Height 19 cm.

Hollow cast bronze. Intact. The left shoulder, the back below the shoulder and the front of the lower right shoulder are missing as is the entire bottom of the container. The rings for the attachment of the handle are broken, and the handle itself is lost. There once was silver inlay in the eyes and on the lips. Green patina.

Roman (Asia Minor?); late second century A.D.

Published: A. Birchall, *The Brummer Collection* 2 (1979), no. 577.

This large and very finely worked balsamarium has no foot, but rests directly on the base of the body. The attachments for the handle are stationary and rise straight out of the hair on the crown of the head. The swinging handle is now missing. The lid is cut in the top of the head between the handle attachments and hinged for easy opening.

The body of this container is in the form of the bust of a satyr, whose face is turned three-quarters left. From his right shoulder is draped an animal skin. It is fastened at the shoulder and folded back to form a border along its inner edge. The diminutive head and forepaws hang decoratively to the front. The animal characteristics of the satyr are his pointed ears and the horn-like projections that seem just to be budding on his chin. In antiquity the goat often is associated with Dionysus and his attendant satyrs, and here one of the animal's most characteristic features is assumed by the satyr himself.

The representation of the satyr, of a type developed in the hellenistic period [29], has shaggy, short tufts of hair that are tousled, as if wind-blown up and back from the face. The contours of every part of the face are soft and fleshy. The hooded eyes protrude markedly from the sockets and look up and off to the left. The downturned nose has large, flaring nostrils; the lips are thick and sensuous with just the hint of a smile to come. Although the features apart from the ears and goat-like budding horns on the chin are human, there is a marked quality of animality about the bust.

The balsamarium is a lidded container that, judging from the expense of the container itself, was used for such precious commodities as incense or balsam (thus the name). Such containers have been found over much of the outer reaches of the Roman Empire—in the Nile delta, in North Africa, in Thrace and up the Danube valley to the Rhine. Probably they were produced originally in Egypt; later in Asia Minor, Thrace and Gaul.

NOTES: For a general treatment of balsamaria, K. Majewski, "Brazowe balsamaria anthropomorficzne w Cesarstwie Rzymskim," *Archeologia* (Warsaw) 14 (1963): 95–126; also, *Master Bronzes* no. 310.

There is a faun of comparable style, S. Boucher, *Bronzes romains figurés du Musée des Beaux-Arts de Lyon* (1973), no. 40.

52 BALSAMARIUM

Height, without the handle, 13.4 cm; diameter of the foot 5.9 cm.
Hollow cast bronze. Intact. There is chipping on the top of the
handle and the end of the nose. Some incrustation. Emerald green
patina.
Roman (Alexandria?); late second–early third century A.D.
Published: Summa, *Catalogue 5: Ancient Art* (1979), no. 46.

This balsamarium stands on a low round foot that is decorated
with three incised circles. The swinging handle is attached to
the body by hinged loops on either side of the head. The handle
is cast in a floral pattern with a schematized calyx as its central
section. From either side of the calyx emerges a tendril that
curves downward, passes through the hinged loop and turns up
again on the outside.

The body of the container is in the form of the bust of a young
man that emerges from a band of acanthus leaves. In turn, the
leaves emerge from a molding that forms the lowest part of the
body. The underside of the body is flat and rests directly on the
foot. The top of the youth's head is cut to form a lid, which is
hinged at the back to provide easy access to the contents of the
container. Long, wavy hair curls around the face and tapers
downward at the back. Single locks curl onto the forehead. The
eyes are close set with prominent lids and deeply incised pupils.
The sensuous, full lips are slightly parted.

Balsamaria were cast in many forms which seem to be drawn
from the same repertoire of figures that was used for steelyard
weights [46]. The treatment of the head of this youth with
close-set languid eyes, heavy cheeks, full mouth and wavy tapering hair recalls portraits of Antinous, Hadrian's young favorite who drowned in the Nile in 130 A.D. There were hundreds
of monuments erected to him, and the characteristics of his
portraits permeated nearly every type of artistic representation
including the balsamaria.

NOTES: For similar pieces: J. Sieveking, *Die Bronzen der Sammlung Loeb*
(1913), p. 73; A. Zadoks-Josephus Zitta, W. Peters, W. van Es, *Roman
Bronze Statuettes from the Netherlands 2. Statuettes Found South of the
Limes* (1969), no. 14.

On portraits of Antinous, see the literature on [50]; also, H. Jucker, *Das
Bildnis im Blätterkelch* 1 (1961): 87–89, 189ff.

53 PYX

Height 5.7 cm.
Bronze panels soldered together and inlaid with glass. Several of the corners of the top and bottom are repaired, and the (three) rings on the top are missing as is the lid. Some of the outer glass band on the top is lost; there is a chip in one of the side panels.
Roman (Rhineland); third century A.D.
Unpublished.

The box stands on three solid cast bronze feet, and is made of eight bronze panels soldered together. Each of the six sides and the top panel is decorated with millefiori glass (made with tiny tubes of colored glass within a background) fused into place.

On the six sides the decoration is four squares of glass inlay that form a larger square and are flanked, top and bottom, by three inlaid horizontal bands. The flanking bands are blue with a red and white cross pattern on the outside, red with a blue and white checkerboard pattern in the middle and white with a blue floral pattern on the inside. The four central squares are composed of sixteen smaller squares arranged in a checkerboard pattern. On alternating sides they are: (1) blue and red with a white and blue checkerboard pattern and (2) blue and blue with a white floral pattern. On the top there are three concentric circles in the same patterns as the horizontal bands on the body: on the outside blue, in the middle red and inside, white. The top of the box has a circular opening notched to hold a lid (now missing), and there were several loops for hanging the box that also have vanished.

Colorful glass enamel was very popular among the provincials of the Roman Empire almost everywhere in Europe north of Italy, and this hexagonal box is a fine, well-preserved example of the type of enamel work popular in the third century. Such boxes, or pyxides, probably were used as inkstands, for perfume, incense and other valuable commodities.

NOTES: There are only three other fairly complete examples of this type of checkerboard pyx with square decoration on the panels: one in the Metropolitan Museum of Art, one in Cologne and a third, fragmentary piece in St. Germain-en-Laye. See W. Forsyth, "Provincial Roman Enamels Recently Acquired by the Metropolitan Museum of Art," *ABull* 32 (1950): 296–300; *Römer am Rhein* (1967), p. 237, no. C169 (P. la Baume) = D. Strong and D. Brown, *Roman Crafts* (1976), p. 47 and fig. 43; N. Thierry, "A propos d'une nouvelle pyxide d'époque romaine à decor d'email 'millefiori'," *AK* 5 (1962): 65ff. For more general information on enamel work in this period, F. Henry, "Emailleurs d'occident," *Préhistoire* 2 (1933): 65–146; H. Maryon, *Metalwork and Enamelling* (1954).

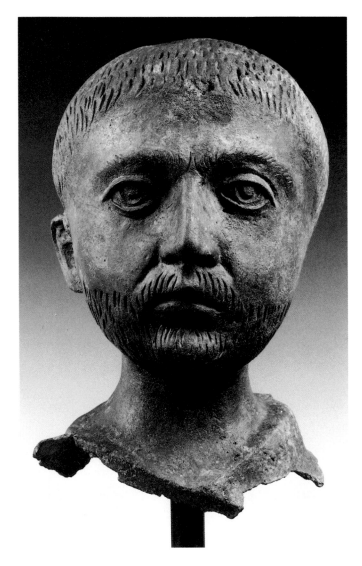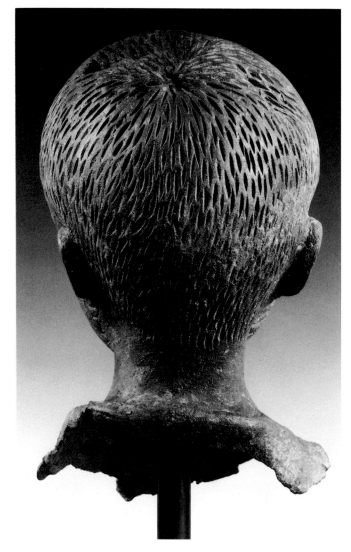

54 PORTRAIT OF A MAN

Height 20.8 cm.

Hollow cast bronze. There is some incrustation and perforation of the surface. The bottom of the bust is broken on all sides. Light green patina.

Roman (Spain?); latter half of the third century A.D.

Unpublished.

The subject of this under-life-size portrait has a broad, smooth forehead, but narrow lower face and a mouth that is downturned with a very thin and off-center upper lip. His very short hair, mustache and beard are rendered in a hard, expressionistic style with a simple series of straight, short slashes into the metal. The eyebrows and deep furrows between the eyes are represented in the same manner. The eyes are large and careworn, hooded by prominent upper lids. The irises and pupils are deeply worked.

The features are individualized with an almost brutal realism, and the eyes demandingly engage the viewer in the sad, troubled and very practical day-to-day existence of a man living in the age of the soldier emperors. At any moment power, based as it was on raw military force, could change hands.

The style of the hair, mustache and beard, rendered in slashes with very low relief, as well as the treatment of the face in general, resembles the portraits of the emperor Trebonianus Gallus (251–254 A.D.). Although at first glance the subject appears to be quite a young man, the furrows between the eyes and the deep laugh lines deny this. The face bears no real resemblance to that of any of the prominent figures of the mid- to late third century, and for now the identity of the sitter remains unknown.

NOTES: For close parallels, Wiggers-Wegner, 83–91 and pls. 34–35; Poulsen 2, pl. 181.

More generally on the portraits of this period, *IRI* 2; B. Haarløv, *New Identifications of Third Century Portraits* (1975); M. Bergmann, *Studien zum römischen Porträt des 3. Jahrhunderts n. Chr.* (Antiquitas 3.18, 1977); K. Fittschen, *Katalog der antiken Skulpturen in Schloss Erbach* (1977), no. 35; J. Balty, "Trébonien Galle et Volusien," *Eikones. Studien zum griechischen und römischen Bildnis H. Jucker . . . gewidmet* (1980): 49–56; "L'iconographie romaine du IIIe siècle," *AC* 49 (1980): 269–285.

[81] Silver Tetradrachm of Syracuse
Signed by Eucleidas
Struck 410 B.C.

The Coins of Nelson Bunker Hunt

COINS OF THE ANCIENT WORLD

Arthur Houghton

Coins are essentially nothing more than metal pieces of predetermined value, usually struck between dies with designs engraved on their surfaces. This simple definition, however, obscures both the revolutionary transformation of the ancient world's economic systems caused by the invention of coinage, and the rapid evolution of ancient coins, once invented, from formless metal shapes to brilliant examples of contemporary art and powerful vehicles of state and personal ideology.

The Beginning of Coinage
The cradle of coinage lies in the extreme western part of Asia Minor, along the Ionian coast where in ancient times Greek and Near Eastern Asiatic peoples intermingled. The date when coins first appeared is not certainly known, but at some point toward the middle of the seventh century B.C. pieces of precious metal with values established systematically according to their weight began to be used in transactions, partially replacing what must have been an exceedingly cumbersome system of payment in kind. The earliest metal objects used for payment were not, in fact, true coins. They were instead primitive, unstruck round or ovoid shapes, proto-coins bearing one or more punch marks on their reverses but lacking design of any kind. The first struck coins were also very crude and represented little technical advance in their shape and articulation. They, too, carried formless reverse punch marks while the other, obverse side was marked by striations impressed by a summarily but consciously worked die. At about the same time the first struck coins appeared with obverse types, usually depicting a simple animal or floral motif. All seem to have circulated at about the same time.

For at least the first fifty years after their inception the coins of western Asia Minor were struck exclusively in electrum, a natural alloy of gold and silver strained from the silt of Anatolian river beds. The composition of the alloy itself varied considerably, but the weight of individual coins was standardized in a manner that permitted their use at more or less fixed values. The stater, weighing between 14 and 16 grams depending on the area of circulation, was the standard unit of reckoning.

Few complete early staters have survived, but fractions as small as one-ninety-sixth stater (no more than a peppercorn in size, weighing about .13 gram) have been recovered. Despite their size such coins were very valuable, representing as much as a full day's pay for a skilled laborer, and it has been generally believed that they may have been intended as bulk pay for state or private employees, rather than as payment in retail transactions. Whatever the case, the use of metal rather than payment in kind soon became attractive to civil administrations; the evolution toward a true monetary economy in which coinage became the accepted means of executing even small transactions followed inevitably.

Public Money
By the early part of the sixth century, most cities with operating mints had begun to place symbols of local significance on their coin issues. Coins of Phocaea, for example, show seals (in Greek, *phokai*) on their obverses. Cyzicus used differing obverse types, almost always in conjunction with the city's symbol, a tunny fish. Lydia employed at

first the device of a lion's head, then in the middle of the sixth century changed its types to show the foreparts of both a lion and a bull, first joined back to back, then facing. Politically, the obverse symbol served as an advertisement for the community, the visual sign of its identity as an independent city. A significant period of time passed before communities universally placed unequivocal visual or epigraphic political statements on their currency, but by the beginning of the sixth century the trend was clearly in that direction.

A fundamentally important monetary reform occurred in western Asia Minor around the middle of the sixth century. Whereas electrum had been universally used for coinage throughout the region, the Lydians began to strike a bimetallic currency in nearly pure gold and silver at their capital city of Sardes. The change has generally been ascribed to the proverbially rich king of Lydia, Croesus (560–546 B.C.), after whom the coin type is named. The monetary parity of silver to gold was set at 13 ⅓:1, but the size of the individual issues was adjusted so that a gold stater was initially worth twenty silver staters, simplifying commercial calculations. This first known use of silver for coinage, combined with its division into small fractions, also provided change for retail use.

The same Croeseid gold and silver types were still being produced as late as the reign of the Achaemenid ruler Darius I (521–485 B.C.), testifying to the strength of the currency reform and the exceptional authority of the coinage. Darius himself struck the first true Persian issues, also at Sardes, but while the types were changed to show a representation of the Great King [59] instead of the Lydian facing lion and bull, the similarity of concept and technique between the late gold issues of the Croeseid type on one hand and their Persian gold and silver successors on the other, is evident. The chronological gap between the issuance of these coinages was probably quite short, if it existed at all.

The Spread of Coinage to the West: Central Greece
About the middle of the sixth century the island of Aegina may have become the first community in the area of central Greece to strike its own coins. These were of silver only (the mainland Greeks did not discover gold in quantity until the time of Philip II of Macedon) and carried the obverse device of a sea turtle, an appropriate symbol for a seafaring people. Because Aegina was an important center of Aegean commerce whose economic reach extended throughout the eastern Mediterranean, its "turtle" coins were broadly accepted in international trade. Aeginetan staters were produced and exported in vast quantities; their use spurred the development of a monetary economy in the Aegean and set a standard against which many other cities of Greece later regulated their own currencies. At some point around the middle of the sixth century, perhaps shortly after the appearance of Aegina's first turtle issues, Athens and Corinth, then other cities with which the mainland Greeks maintained contact, began to strike their own coins. Athens' earliest issues, also of silver, carried on their obverses various heraldic devices such as a wheel, a horse forepart, or a gorgon. Late in the sixth century these diverse types were replaced by a single coin design carrying a vigorous head of Athena in high relief on its obverse. These new coins bore true types on both sides, an evolution of technique that had reached other areas of the Greek world. In the case of Athens, their reverse became a field for a second motif, an owl, Athena's own symbol after which the coins themselves were called.

In the century and a half after the appearance of the first coins in Asia Minor, a transformation had occurred in the function of coinage itself. Metal pieces which had initially simply facilitated payment and exchange had become objects with both artistic and political significance which used the coin's type as a vehicle of expression. The idea of type, the principal design on a coin, almost certainly emerged from the long Near

Eastern tradition of seals—stone or some other hard material into which a design had been engraved or impressed—and it is very possible that early die engravers had been gem or stone cutters who had already worked in intaglio. Early coin designs, in any event, closely resemble those of Near Eastern seals and draw many of their motifs from the repertoire of Near Eastern art current in the seventh century B.C. The griffins [55, 60], sphinxes, lions, and lionesses [56] which throughout the archaic period adorned the obverses of coins struck in Asia Minor, come from the mainstream of Mesopotamian and Anatolian iconographic and decorative tradition. As coinage was adopted by the cities of central Greece and other communities further west toward the end of the sixth century, however, coin designs moved away from the heraldic concept prevalent in Asia Minor toward a new perception of both form and substance, one which on one hand shows a greater sense of plasticity, on the other a heightened awareness both of the importance of volume and of the relationship of a design to the size and shape of the coin's flan.

The Athenian owls [such as 58] are a case in point. Their obverse relief is high, their surface richly modeled; even in profile view the face of the goddess gives a strong sense of volume. The goddess's forehead and the bowl of her helmet both echo and develop the outline of the coin's rim in sweeping curves. The effect is very different from that of earlier Ionian coins, which seem by comparison stylized and two-dimensional. Stylistically, the Athena heads on Athens' archaic owl coins have a strong relationship to freestanding sculpture of the period. The best can be placed alongside the korai of the Acropolis as outstanding examples of late sixth-century Attic art.

The Fifth Century: Stereotype and Evolution
By the end of the sixth century, the use of coinage had spread widely across the Mediterranean into almost every corner of the Greek world. Greek colonies in Asia Minor and Cyprus, communities of the Greek mainland and islands, Greek cities in Italy and Sicily, and other areas which had seized upon the advantages of coinage, were all issuing coins in profuse variety. A brief look at the mint history of the two cities of Athens and Syracuse in Sicily, serves to illustrate separate developments in the function and form of money in the fifth century B.C.

In a sense, the issues of these two cities are contrasting opposites. The numismatic evidence strongly suggests that the production of the Athenian owls, which were primarily tetradrachms and therefore of a size and value which made them unusable for retail transactions, was primarily intended to support the city's foreign trade, and not for internal consumption. They have been found in hoards from locations as diverse as South Italy and Sicily in the west, to southern Turkey, Syria, Egypt and other parts of the Middle East, and it seems clear that by the end of the sixth century few areas of the Mediterranean were not familiar with these coins, which evidently flowed abroad in enormous numbers and had begun to take on the function of an international currency.

The production of archaic owls may have ended with the capture of Athens by Xerxes in 480 B.C. Within a decade of the city's liberation, however, the output of the Athenian mint was resumed. Emerging from its victories over the Persians, Athens soon launched itself into a program of rebuilding and rearming which, combined with a ruthlessly aggressive foreign policy, had by the midpoint of the fifth century made the city a dominant, even overpowering force in central Greece and the Aegean. The requirement for money to finance its activities must have been considerable; after the beginning of the Peloponnesian War in 431 B.C., enormous. In a deliberate effort to maintain the acceptance of its currency abroad, Athens continued the production of coins of the same basic type as those it had issued in the archaic period. Whereas considerable experimentation in style and variation of decorative detail is evident in the archaic owl series, however, now the elements of the type (including Athena's helmet, which had acquired an olive-leaf diadem and a floral design [see 66]) became set and remained virtually unchanged for the next century and a half. The evolution of style—the gradual transformation of Athena's eye from archaic frontality to profile view, for example—introduced minor variations into a design which had begun as a significant artistic creation but which in time had become stereotyped. By contrast the coins of Syracuse, which were not exported extensively, reflect a process of stylistic change and iconographic inventiveness which culminated in examples of numismatic art unsurpassed for their brilliance of design and execution, and which became rich sources of inspiration for almost all other Sicilian mints of the period.

The mint of Syracuse itself opened toward the end of the sixth century B.C. It adopted for its first tetradrachm issue the obverse type of a charioteer in a quadriga, probably reflecting the equestrian interests of the city's aristocracy. The issue's reverse was at first a simple four-part incuse punch. Like Athens' coins, however, it was soon given a motif on its reverse, the head of a local fountain goddess, Arethusa, framed within a small central medallion.

Like the Athenian owls, the basic type of a quadriga and the goddess Arethusa remained constant in concept for an extended period after its initial appearance, but unlike Athens' coinage it underwent a continuing process of development and change. An early tetradrachm [63] struck after the city was seized by the Sicilian tyrant, Gelon, shows the first major evolution of the type. In addition to the quadriga, which is rendered in a far more naturalistic manner than it was on Syracuse's first issues, the small figure of Nike hovering with outspread wings has been placed above the chariot's horses, symbolizing Gelon's own victorious race at the Olympic games in 488 B.C. On the coin's reverse, the Arethusa head has been dramatically enlarged to fill the central portion of the flan, and is now surrounded by four swimming dolphins, a metaphor for the sea. The new design shows a keen eye for unity and detail, the latter most apparent in the special care given to the figure of Nike above the horses and in the precision of Arethusa's individual features.

An exceptional silver issue, the so-called Demareteion, was struck before the midpoint of the century [64]. The figure of Nike above the horses now flies, and a small running or leaping lion has been placed in the lower field; the effect of the composition is one of motion, a departure from the stasis of earlier series. The Arethusa head on the issue's reverse is bound with an olive-leaf diadem, symbolic of victory. As important as this enrichment of the goddess's iconography, however, is the execution of her features, which have been rendered with extraordinary precision and endowed with remarkable feeling and life. Several artists, clearly superior to their contemporaries, must have been specially commissioned to engrave the dies of these coins. Syracuse continued to produce the basic quadriga/Arethusa tetradrachm type in a profusion of different styles and compositional arrangements, but the quality of the Demareteion Master's work was not equaled for many years.

An unusual example of innovation at Syracuse appeared toward the end of the century, when an issue of tetradrachms was struck showing a richly detailed reverse with the head of Athena in three-quarter view [81]. The artist Eucleidas, who signed his dies, was among the few coin engravers in antiquity to have successfully represented a facing head with convincing spatial depth. He also attempted to give a sense of dimensionality to the obverse by showing the horses of the quadriga appearing to leap out of the coin's background.

At about the same time, possibly in connection with a major military victory won by the city over Athens, Syracuse commissioned the execution of an impressive series of decadrachms by two famed artists, Cimon and Euainetus who, like Eucleidas, signed their dies. The Arethusa heads of this series were drawn with close reference to classical models, but differ stylistically in important respects. Cimon's design [85] is a study in tranquillity. Smoothly modeled, the goddess's face has been caught in a moment of calm reflection; her hair is bound up in a net, represented as a richly embroidered but static tapestry. The fuller and more plastic expressiveness of Euainetus' Arethusa [86] is echoed by the animated, liquid flow of her curls, woven through with a crown of reeds. These brilliant examples of coinage mark the pinnacle of Syracusan numismatic art. Famous even in antiquity, the Arethusa head of Euainetus inspired copies and reinterpretations on coinage struck elsewhere in the Greek world.

Hellenistic Coins: Portraiture and Propaganda
The hellenistic period—the years between the reign of Alexander the Great (336–323 B.C.) and Rome's victory over the Egyptian fleet at Actium in 31 B.C.—witnessed the institutionalization of coins as instruments of imperial power, characterized by the introduction and systematic use of royal portraiture to project the authority of the ruler and state. As such, it marks a point in the evolution of coinage as important as any since the first figural motifs began to appear on the archaic issues of Asia Minor.

The change was effected by Alexander's able and cunning father, Philip II, who managed to attain military dominance first over all of Macedonia and northern Greece, then over the independent cities of the Greek mainland. Shortly after his accession in 359 B.C., Philip reformed the Macedonian monetary system, introducing the first bimetallic currency (in gold and silver) in mainland Greece. He initially struck tetradrachms with a magnificent head of Zeus on their obverse based on the local weight standard. The reverses of this early issue appear to show what may be the first contemporary image of a ruler on a Greek coin, that of Philip himself, riding a horse and with his hand upraised in the unmistakable pose of a victorious Greek general.

Perhaps a decade later, Philip initiated an extensive issue of gold staters whose obverse head of Apollo probably relates to Philip's victory at the Delphic games in 348 B.C., but also suggests an attempt by Philip to appropriate universally understood imagery to further his political ambitions in Greece. Significantly, the gold staters were adjusted to the more generally used Attic weight system, and may have been designed to fill the role of a panhellenic currency, supporting Philip's own vision of a union of Greek states under Macedonian leadership.

Soon after his accession, Alexander reformed Philip's coinage in a manner which suggests far-reaching monetary and political objectives. He first adopted coin types whose symbolism was, like Philip's, generally understood throughout Greece, but which became at the same time allegories of his own move into Asia; their design may also have been meant to appeal to the non-Greek populations which lay in his path of conquest. In addition, Alexander adjusted the weight of Macedonian silver to conform to the Attic standard, establishing its utility as a broadly-based currency.

The silver series which includes the decadrachm from the Babylon mint [100] is an example. The obverse head of Heracles, which appears on Macedonian coins late in the fifth century B.C. and also some of Philip's issues, refers to Alexander's claim to descent from the mythological hero. Heracles also symbolized the elemental struggle of the forces of civilization against barbarism, and could be seen as a visual metaphor for Alexander's own civilizing struggle against the Persians. Appearing on coinage which was intended to be issued along Alexander's line of march, moreover, the Heracles type may well have been meant as a forward-looking reference to Asiatic deities or heroes with whom the Greek hero had been syncretically assimilated: Sandan at Tarsus; Melqart at Tyre; and Gilgamesh of Assyrian legend. Although the Heracles head has sometimes been identified as a portrait of Alexander himself, the relationship between the coins and the visual representations of Alexander is neither clear nor convincing. But for a very few issues produced under exceptional circumstances [such as 101], Alexander struck no coinage with his own likeness.

Coins of Alexander's types were issued long after his death. Like the Athenian owls, they became a currency readily accepted in international commerce with a strength of their own. Well into the third and second centuries, cities of Asia Minor continued to produce tetradrachms bearing Alexander's types and name in profuse quantity. The location of the issuing mint was indicated only by the use of symbols or monograms.

Within a few years of Alexander's death, his empire was divided. His most powerful successors established themselves in separate satrapies and began to strike coinage of their own. Initially these issues were of Alexander's types, but they were gradually replaced by coinage which reflected the growing independence of their issuing authorities.

A major break with tradition occurred in 305 B.C. when Ptolemy I, who had claimed Egypt on Alexander's death, declared himself king and began to strike coins at Alexandria with his own name and bearing his own deified portrait [103]. Ptolemy's portrait was, in fact, the first to appear on the coinage of any of Alexander's successors. It has occasionally been seen as a true likeness of the aged ruler, yet it is quite clearly a study in exaggeration, reflecting a deliberate effort to emphasize heroism at the expense of reality. The dramatic and forceful representation of the aged king, with outthrust forehead and chin, sagging brow, distended eye and hair flowing around his head in a sea of curls, is far more a contrivance than the realistic portrait of a living man. The stylistic formulae employed by the die artists of Alexandria were not confined to Ptolemy's image, but were used in connection with many ruler portraits of the early hellenistic period. Similar baroque elements may be seen, for example, in Lysimachus' romantic representations of Alexander [102] or the portraits of Seleucus on tetradrachms struck at Pergamum in the first half of the third century B.C. [104].

Hellenistic artists were beneficiaries of a variety of different—even opposing—stylistic traditions, and hellenistic taste was anything but static. On one hand, hellenistic coin reverses tended to be conservative, retaining forms which had been developed in the fourth century and adhering to standard Greek mythological themes except where they adopted the symbolism of local cults. On the other, royal coin portraits ranged across a broad array of styles, depending on both the location and period of their execution. At Alexandria, for example, the intensification of features which characterizes early Ptolemaic portraits gave way in the middle of the third century to studiedly serene representations of Ptolemaic kings and queens whose classicism was drawn directly from the wellsprings of Attic art; by the end of the century, Egyptian coin portraits had begun to degenerate into a series of stereotyped images of the dynasty's founder. Macedonian mint artists began to explore the possibilities of realism in representations of Alexander's successors, anticipating the sometimes brutal verism of Roman Republican portraiture. In Asia Minor an attenuated baroque style continued in use at Pergamum into the second century, while artists of other mints fell back completely upon classical motifs and style. From the early part of the third to the middle of the second century, a number of outstanding examples of royal portraiture were executed by die artists working at various city mints of the Seleucid and Bactrian kings. Their style fluctuated at first between drama and idealization, finally devolving into a weak classicism, further undermined by a decline of artistic skill. The ability and imagination of the mid-second-century Seleucid court artist who engraved the archaistic head of Zeus on coins of Alexander Balas [112] is an exception which underscores the vacuity of the general trend.

Roman Coins: The Republic

In the Greek world, coins evolved from typeless and anepigraphic pieces of electrum into highly sophisticated currencies, struck in a variety of metals, often bearing complex iconographies. Roman coins developed from an extant but unwieldy system of exchange into a multidenominational coinage which, over its course, provided an astonishing range of information and commentary on contemporary political, social, military, economic and religious affairs.

A systematized medium of exchange appears to have existed in central Italy as early as the fifth century B.C., when pieces of bronze were made exchangeable with cattle, according to their weight. In time, these crude metal shapes were replaced by uninscribed cast bronze bars with designs on both faces. About 300 B.C. the city of Rome, which already possessed a highly developed political and military system, began to issue bars bearing figural devices and the inscription *ROMANOM*: "of the Romans." Such ingots were currency but not coinage, regulated according to value. The first true Roman coin appears to have been a small bronze issue inscribed in Greek with the same legend and bearing the types of the Greek colony of Neapolis (Naples), where it was probably struck.

About 289 B.C., Rome formally established a monetary board and authorized coinage to be issued at a mint on the Capitoline. The currency system which eventually emerged from this reorganization was derived on one hand from the city's traditional use of bronze, of which the *as* now became a standard unit; on the other from its need for silver for external trade, primarily with the Greek communities located to the south. Rome's first silver coins were, in fact, probably produced in southern Italy under Roman authority, but it could not have been long before the mint of Rome began to strike its first silver didrachms, which held to the Greek weight system and were suited for bulk transactions in foreign trade. The dies for these early Republican issues appear to have been executed by Greek artists: both in style and quality they are much closer to coins struck by the Greek cities of southern Italy than to the parallel cast bronze issues of the mint of Rome.

The requirements of an economy under strain from virtually constant warfare, demands imposed by the state's own territorial expansion and the need for usable specie in domestic retail transactions, forced major readjustments in Rome's currency system in the latter half of the third century. In a series of changes linked to the First Punic War (264–241 B.C.), the Greek-style didrachms were eventually abandoned in favor of a silver coin of Roman type, the quadrigatus, and Rome's bronze coinage was unified by the use of a single reverse motif, a ship's prow [117]. A second, more far-reaching change occurred during the Second Punic War (218–201 B.C.), when the quadrigatus was supplemented and eventually replaced by an array of new silver issues. One, the victoriate, so called because its reverse displayed the figure of Victory crowning a trophy of arms, was evidently intended for use in foreign trade as silver coinage with guaranteed bullion value. For use within the Roman state three other silver issues were struck: the denarius, quinarius and sestertius, respectively equaling ten, five and two and a half bronze *asses* in value.

In time both the quadrigatus and the victoriate disappeared. The denarius remained, and became a standard denomination of Roman currency for the next four and a half centuries. Unlike the victoriate, which bore no marks of value, the Roman denarius and its fractions explicitly indicated their value relative to the as. Bronze gradually became a subsidiary coinage with generally unchanging types. At about the same time, Rome suppressed the production of all non-Roman silver coinage in the areas it ruled. Except for coinage struck by military commanders for their own payment needs and a few instances where coins were issued in the provinces, the mint of Rome supplied all money for the Republic from that point onward.

For the next century and a half changes in Rome's monetary system primarily involved technical adjustments; coin types continued to evolve, however. The denarii in particular were struck in an increasing number of varieties. Often these were of a retrospective nature, referring to the city's legendary past or commemorating specific events in Roman history, but Republican moneyers began to use coin types as political advertisements, recording their own achievements and the deeds and histories of their families. The proliferation of Roman coin types was accelerated in the early first century when silver propaganda issues emphasizing themes of military victory were struck in vast quantity by competing political factions in Rome and the provinces, most extensively by Sulla and his lieutenants during their various campaigns. Sulla also struck a regular coinage in gold, the aureus, which in the past had been issued for emergency reasons only or under exceptional circumstances by Roman commanders in the field. Under Julius Caesar, the aureus became a regular issue, varying in type along with Roman silver.

Caesar himself ordered a change in coinage of profound iconographic significance. Disregarding deeply-rooted Roman tradition, he placed his own image on issues struck during his last months of rule, in 44 B.C. Caesar's was the first portrait of a living person to appear on any Roman coin. After his death the portraits of living Romans, aspirants to power as well as rulers and their families, began to appear on coins as a matter of course [118, 119, 120]. In a sense, Caesar's portrait issues mark the beginning of a truly imperial Roman coinage, although they predate the establishment of the Empire itself.

The Empire

The intense political turbulence which followed Caesar's death saw the mint of Rome superseded by the production of coins at provincial centers, which issued gold and silver in vast quantity. After establishing his authority Octavian, Caesar's heir and adopted son, did not reverse the process of decentralized mint operations. Not wishing to risk Senate opposition to the opening of an imperial mint in Rome, he maintained mint operations in the provinces, where they continued even after he assumed the title Augustus. About 23 B.C., a reorganized Rome mint opened with the issuance of gold and silver, and the production of lower value coins in the base metals of orichalcum (a natural alloy of copper and zinc) and copper for ordinary retail trade. The provincial center of Lugdunum (Lyons), however, began to strike the vast bulk of Augustan gold and silver from about 15 B.C. and a significant proportion of the aes (bronzes) from 10 B.C.

Since the late Republic, gold and silver coinage had been dated by the years of office of Roman consuls; under Augustus, the years of the emperor's tribunician power as well as those of his consulship were sometimes included on state coinage, indicating with considerable precision when an issue was struck.

Augustus' state coinage was controlled in a manner which permitted the orchestration of its propaganda content. Careful attention was given to both the presentation of the emperor's achievements, status and powers and the style of the imperial portrait. In many cases, coin types and inscriptions associated the emperor with divinities and abstract virtues, all with special political significance (Jupiter, for example, was both lord of the world and the emperor's protector; Venus, the mythological ancestor of the

Julian family, etc.). Coin portraits were also rendered in a manner suggesting divine association; in Augustus' time, they were modeled on sculptural prototypes commissioned and officially sanctioned by the central government. Augustus' own portraits reflect the influence of a single classical ideal, but show considerable diversity nevertheless; a generation was to pass before imperial portraiture on Roman coinage achieved significant consistency.

In the last years of Augustus' reign the Rome mint, which had issued bronzes of standard variety and generally inferior workmanship, saw a marked improvement in the technique, style and quality of its product. Roman bronze began to develop an increasing range of types, in time becoming the preferred coinage for displays of epigraphic or pictorial imagination. Bronze issues struck late in Nero's reign (54–68 A.D.) became bold exploratory ventures into new compositional arrangements; some show an interest in perspective and spatial depth which had been part of a long-standing tradition of hellenistic and Roman landscape painting, but which was startlingly innovative in numismatic art. A remarkable sestertius of Nero which shows a view of the harbor of Ostia with ships, docks and warehouses arrayed as if seen from the air [125], is an example of this new direction.

Through the first century A.D., important coinage reforms had been instituted by Nero's predecessor Claudius (41–54 A.D.), by Nero himself, and by Vespasian (69–79 A.D.). The result was threefold. First, the government rationalized the currency system by readjusting the weights of gold, silver and bronze coins, and reissuing coinage linked to the new parities. Secondly, virtually all coinage was centralized at the Rome mint with the exception of provincial issues struck principally for local circulation in Asia Minor, Syria and Egypt. Finally, the output of gold and silver was systematized by its regular production on an annual basis.

During the second and third centuries, Roman currency markets became increasingly disrupted by political and military strife, and by financial mismanagement. The effect can be seen in the evolution of Roman silver coinage, which was progressively devalued by successive reductions in weight and the debasement of its metal content. Various devices were employed to maintain the optical integrity of the currency system: under Caracalla (212–217 A.D.) for example, a new issue was struck, the antoninianus, which was nominally worth two denarii but weighed only one and a half. Even the gold aureus, which had remained unchanged since the time of Nero, fell in value from the beginning of the third century onward. The secession of Gaul (circa 259 A.D.) and the decision of the empire's "legitimate" emperors to establish a series of new mints, moreover, scattered a system of production which had, since the Augustan period, remained generally centralized at Rome.

A major change was instituted by Diocletian (284–305 A.D.), whose virtually total reform of imperial administration under a tetrarchic system extended to a complete overhaul of Roman currency. In an attempt to return stability to Rome's financial markets, Diocletian and his partners established new relative values for all metals and introduced new coinage which, consistent with the decentralization of the Empire, was issued by a number of mints located at various centers across the Roman state. For the first time, the reverses of Roman silver and bronze became regularized, the former generally depicting military themes or showing the tetrarchs, while the standard large bronze coin, the follis, was inscribed with the statement GENIO POPVLI ROMANI, the "Genius of the Roman People." The new epithet reflects an important directional shift that had taken place in the message content of Roman coin issues since the early imperial age, from propaganda related to the person of the emperor toward a broader more abstract conception of the Roman state itself.

During the imperial period, the style of Roman coinage remained fully within the mainstream of Roman art forms. The delicacy and grace of Augustan portraits gave way in time to a variety of styles and modes of representation, depending on the preference of the emperor and the perceived political requirements of imperial portraiture. The summit of Roman numismatic art occurred in the period which embraced the reigns of Nero and Hadrian (approximately the second half of the first century A.D. through the first half of the next), when the die engravers of the Rome mint produced a series of magnificent imperial portraits, elaborately modeled to show the subtlest details of character. The skill exhibited by Hadrian's artists [134] was never matched afterwards, although individual engravers of later coin dies produced occasional masterpieces of imperial portraiture.

From the middle of the second century onward, there was a general decline in both technical and stylistic quality of Roman coinage. The change becomes most marked after the Severan period, when the modeling of imperial portraits suffers a loss of plasticity, and the facial features become flatter and less expressive. Hair and drapery, too, become more linear and stylized. From the middle of the third century, there is increasing lack of variation in the portraits themselves; elements of individuality are suppressed and representations of human form take on an increasingly abstract character. At times, the portraits of different emperors merged into a single image, equally valid for one as for the other. Even during periods of innovative change, such as that of the tetrarch when Roman art accepted the intrusion of cubistic forms, imperial portraiture, both three-dimensional and numismatic, tended toward abstraction. In the tetrarchic period itself imperial portraits on coins struck at various mints were often conditioned by the portrait type of the tetrarch in whose territory they were issued, no matter which emperor they purported to represent. As time passed, the perceived reality of the human face was further modified, the ruler's image increasingly portraying less of its subject's material form while striving toward a representation of imperial spirituality. In the end, the emperor's face had become an iconic image with only the most distant relationship to the individual.

Human heads, in essence, have been reduced to emblems; and it is in this context that the portraits of late Roman coinage are related to the griffins, lions, and other obverse coin designs of the Greek archaic period. The rules of abstraction govern both. A thousand years after the first appearance of coins in western Asia Minor, the heraldic concept has reappeared. A thread has returned to complete the circle.

NOTES TO THE CATALOGUE OF COINS

Nelson Bunker Hunt has formed one of the most impressive collections of ancient coins in private hands today. It is a collection of star pieces, coins which would be the highlights of a great museum collection. Many are splendid examples of varieties made famous by the literature and familiar to all numismatists. Virtually all are remarkable for their beauty, rarity and/or historical interest. The 112 coins following represent a selection from the Hunt Collection. Because they were to be displayed with other art objects, the coins were chosen for their aesthetic merit and their relation to stylistic trends in ancient art. The catalogue order was determined by the same considerations. Thus the Greek coins are grouped by style, approximately chronologically, ignoring the geographical arrangement which has become traditional in this field. There follows a small group illustrating the adaptation of Greek coinage by non-hellenic peoples. The Roman coins are ordered chronologically, as is usual.

Ancient coins have been studied most thoroughly as historical documents, illuminating local history and religion in the case of Greek coins and the development of propaganda techniques in the case of royal hellenistic and Roman imperial coins. Such information is summarized in the essay accompanying each coin description. Often there follows an iconographical or stylistic analysis. In the case of the Greek coins the discussion focusses on their relation to Hellenic art as a whole, demonstrated by unity of style, sharing of motifs and intentional echoes of famous masterpieces. With portrait coins, whether hellenistic or Roman, artistry and iconography are closely entwined with the propaganda function of the coinage. Another most important aspect of coinage is its role in economic life. This interesting topic has been touched upon only superficially here, because the selection of artistic coins is not especially illustrative of economic history, a field in which common and unattractive coins are often of greater significance.

The major sources of numismatic and historical information are listed in the notes at the end of the catalogue. This is not intended as an exhaustive bibliography. In the same place I have provided references for the artistic parallels cited in the text. Extensive art historical bibliography would be irrelevant in this context, but I have attempted to provide access both to reproductions of high quality and to sound authors, whose own footnotes and bibliographies can be profitably consulted.

Most of the coins are illustrated by an actual-size photograph, but their dimensions are also indicated by a diameter measurement taken at the broadest point across the flan. In most entries a small arrow follows the diameter measurement. This is the die axis, indicating the relation, often skewed, between the verticals of the obverse and the reverse of the coin. The variability or control of the die axes is an aspect of ancient minting technique of interest to specialists; the problem of die axes also explains why only one side of most coins is exhibited. Another technical factor, the weight standard, is explained in Appendix E.

Coins differ from most other art objects in being mass produced, even though struck by hand, and they therefore bear various degrees of relation to other, similar coins. Two coins struck from the same dies will be virtually identical from the artistic point of view, though their weight, shape and state of conservation may vary. This relationship is indicated in the descriptions by the term "same dies." Much of the older literature contains detailed descriptions of the coins with few or no photographs, and some issues of coinage are so voluminous that the full range of dies is not yet published. Thus in many cases it is possible to identify a coin by a printed description without necessarily matching the dies. This relationship is expressed in the text by the somewhat infelicitous term "equivalent coin(s), various dies." In the case of a very rare coin it may be impossible to find a matching description, but the piece may still be dated by comparison with coins which are similar in most important respects though different in some detail. This relationship is indicated in the catalogue by the term "variant."

It is with particular warmth that I acknowledge my debt to various scholars and colleagues. Arthur Houghton read the manuscript, offered suggestions and in general made collaboration a pleasure. Silvia Hurter read the manuscript at an early stage, corrected it at many points and provided valued bibliographical help. Pierre Bastien applied his vast expertise in late Roman coinage to the latter half of the Roman section, drawing my attention to many important publications. Martin Price and Nancy Waggoner generously shared their profound knowledge of the Alexandrine coinage. Francis Campbell, librarian of the American Numismatic Society, kindly supplied photocopies of numerous articles unavailable to me in Los Angeles. I was stimulated throughout my research by conversations with David Sear, who also reviewed and amended the supplementary materials at the end of the catalogue. Their kindness in assisting me does not necessarily imply agreement with what I have written; I alone am responsible for the use I made of the information they provided.

55 EARLY ELECTRUM STATER

OBVERSE:
   Griffin head right with rounded finial on forehead and two spiral locks behind ear.
REVERSE:
   Square incuse with irregular raised pattern.

Phocaic standard, weight 16.38 gm; diameter 22 mm.

Struck at an uncertain mint in northern Ionia (Phocaea?), circa 600–575 B.C.

Published: E.S.G. Robinson, "Some Electrum and Gold Greek Coins," *ANS CentPubl*, p. 589, 7 and pl. 39; *Kunstfreund* lot 2. Mentioned: C. Boehringer, *SNR* 53 (1974), p. 20 (review of *Kunstfreund*).

Variants: *Traité* 1 (1907), 170ff, pl. 5, 1–4 (later issue with fractions).

Ex Wéver collection, Paris.

Unique.

Coinage as we know it originated in western Asia Minor in the second half of the seventh century B.C. It evolved from nuggets of electrum or white gold, an alloy of silver and gold which occurs occasionally in nature. The lumpy shape of the early electrum coinage advertises its relation to nuggets. Another primitive feature is its one-sidedness. Only the obverse of these early coins bears a pattern or recognizable image, often related by style and subject matter to other contemporary artistic media. The reverse invariably has one or more deep incuse punch marks left by the tool used to force the lump of annealed metal into the obverse die, which was fixed into an anvil. A last distinctive feature of the early electrum coinage is a multiplicity of subdivisions, encompassing denominations as small as 1/24, 1/48 and even 1/96 stater. The fractional denominations far outnumber extant specimens of the full stater, which is in fact very rare. It is not clear whether these proportions represent the structure of the primeval monetary system, or whether they are an artifact of unequal survival rates.

This specimen and the following are probably the two earliest staters which can be appreciated primarily as aesthetic objects.

Their distinction lies in a felicitous combination of style and superb condition. The griffin head of this stater naturally invites comparison with [21], the cast bronze griffin protome. Similarities include their sturdiness; the smooth line of the skull; the large, protruding eye; the rounded finial on the forehead; the heavy roll under the chin; short ears attached to the roll by a knob; and two spiral locks on the neck. The short neck places the electrum griffin in even closer relation to the earliest *hammered* bronze griffin protomes, Jantzen's Group One. Its proportions are inherited from Hittite prototypes, and indeed it is easier to imagine this upright head upon the standing human body of the Hittite griffin demon who supported the heavens than upon the lion's body of a Greek griffin.

A second major difference between the two Hunt griffins involves matters of texture. There is no attempt here to indicate scales, and the spiral locks on the neck gain enormous prominence from being modeled rather than incised. The inherent softness of electrum makes the coin griffin less ferocious than its bronze counterpart, its weaker silhouette less decorative.

56 EARLY ELECTRUM STATER

OBVERSE:
  Lioness walking right, head reverted.
REVERSE:
  Two square incuse punchmarks of unequal size with irregular
  raised pattern.
Phocaic standard, weight 16.36 gm; diameter 20 mm.
Struck at an uncertain mint in northern Ionia (Phocaea?), circa 600–
  575 B.C.
Published: E.S.G. Robinson, "Some Electrum and Gold Greek
  Coins," *ANS CentPubl*, p. 588f, 6 and pl. 39; *Kunstfreund* lot 1.
  Mentioned: C. Boehringer, *SNR* 53 (1974), p. 20 (review of
  Kunstfreund).
Variants: *BMC Ionia* 43, pl. 2, 4 = *Traité* 1 (1907), pl. 5, 6 (hecte of
  same issue with lioness' head).
Unique.

The earliest coinage is characterized by an untrammeled diversity of types and by the absence of any indication of the mint city or issuing authority. It has been hypothesized that these multifarious types were derived from the personal seals of the magistrates or dynasts responsible for the coinage. This theory gains some support from the rare inscriptions on early electrum coins which invariably record personal names, in one instance with the specific formula, "I am the seal of Phanes." Furthermore the glyptic artists who engraved gemstones had skills closely related to those of the die cutter and are by far the most likely craftsmen to have undertaken the new assignment.

The lioness is quite a scarce subject in most artistic media. The exception is gemstones: the lioness together with her variant the pantheress is rather common on Minoan-Mycenaean gems and again on scarabs and scaraboids of the archaic and transitional periods. Inconveniently, however, she seems to have been absent from the gem engraver's repertory at the time the Hunt stater was struck. Instead, contemporary gems feature combat scenes in which lions with reverted heads battle heroes or a Gorgon-faced goddess equivalent to the *Potnia Theron*, mistress of wild beasts, who appears with lions in orientalizing jewelry, ivories and decorative metalwork. One such gem, thought to be from Cyprus, features maneless lions which bear a strong resemblance to the lioness here. Walking felines however do not appear on gems until perhaps the middle of the sixth century, and the vogue for lionesses belongs to an even later date to judge from their advanced style.

Walking animals, including lions and panthers, are on the other hand the chief subject matter of orientalizing ceramics; see for example the Corinthian crater in the Hunt Collection [1]. The Corinthian approach to these animals is rather stiff and abstract, and in their elongated, low-slung proportions they are quite different from the tall, slender lioness on the stater. However East Greek and especially Rhodian ceramics are decorated with long-limbed, graceful and often vivacious animals which share with our lioness a lifelike charm despite a high degree of stylization.

The lioness displays several traits which are old-fashioned rather than forward-looking, finding their parallels in the art of the seventh century and even earlier. These include the slim body, definitely an early feature in the orientalizing style; the absence of a mane, which is a stylistic consideration rather than an observed sexual difference; the alert, pricked ear; and a lack of artificial subdivisions or decorative detail. This last feature—fidelity to an organic rather than abstract conception of animal form—remains relatively characteristic of gemstones alone among the orientalizing art forms. Each individual feature of the lioness, as well as her general proportions, can be matched in other media; but the total configuration is not formulaic and must be considered a unique statement of a common theme.

The use of two or more incuse punchmarks, applied separately, is an early practice in the production of coinage. It was superseded by a single incuse at several major mints in the first quarter of the sixth century. The double incuse may possibly indicate that the lioness stater is to be dated slightly earlier than the griffin stater.

57 SILVER STATER OF POSEIDONIA

OBVERSE:
ΜΟΠ, Poseidon, diademed, striding right and brandishing trident, chlamys falling vertically over each shoulder, dot and cable border.

REVERSE:
ΜΟΠ in relief, obverse type reversed and incused as if viewed from behind, chlamys draped across back, trident in relief, incuse cable border.

Campanian (Phocaic) standard, weight 7.54 gm; diameter 29 mm.↑

Struck circa 520 B.C.

Published: Leu 2 (1972), lot 40.

Same dies: S. Pozzi, "Ripostigli di monete greche rinvenuti a Paestum," *AIIN* 9–11 (1964), pl. 1, 3; *SNG ANS* 613.

This is an example of one of the earliest coinages in silver, a metal which all but superseded electrum in the Greek world. A notable feature of Greek silver coinage is the use of fixed types, which generally had profound significance for the mint city.

The Achaean colonists of southern Italy minted their earliest coinage using a novel technique found nowhere else in the Hellenic world. Their silver staters are wafer thin, and the reverse is rendered in intaglio. Usually the reverse type is a mirror image of the obverse, a *trompe-l'oeil* creating the illusion that the coins were manufactured by a repoussé technique. The deception is enhanced by the fact that the intaglio reverse is invariably a bit crude. In fact, however, these staters were struck from two dies like other coins.

The South Italian incuse fabric involved great technical difficulties, yet there is no evidence of evolution or experimentation: the earliest coins are both technically and artistically mature. It has been argued that the incuse technique may have been the most effective means of overstriking the foreign currency which constituted the only supply of silver for this mineless region. It is even possible that the motive behind this ingenious development was primarily aesthetic, for the intaglio fabric is believed to have developed at Sybaris, a city known for its love of luxurious refinement.

Poseidonia, a colony of Sybaris, made exceptionally witty use of the incuse fabric. Its obverse types show the city's patron Poseidon, the sea god, in a militant stance, brandishing his trident over his head. The reverse shows him as if viewed from behind, his long lovelocks streaming down his neck and his shawl looped across his shoulder blades. The "swallowtail" folds of this garment are one of the most characteristic details of the archaic style. The striding posture, one arm raised behind his head and the other extended in front of him, is also a commonplace of early Greek art [1] and long retained an association with this particular god. Famous examples include the bronze Poseidon from Creusis; the slightly later bronze from Cape Artemision, with pose a bit altered; and the deliberate archaic revival of the Cypriote tetradrachms of Demetrius Poliorcetes. At Poseidonia the aggressive stance is balanced in such a manner that it loses its forward propulsion and achieves the static, heraldic quality typical of early South Italian coin types.

If Poseidon's stance is traditional, the more detailed treatment on the obverse nevertheless shows an awareness of the advances toward realism in late archaic art. The ancient formula of frontal shoulders on profile hips and legs is modernized by the oblique placement of the abdominal muscles, denoting the necessary twist of the torso. The exaggerated, knotted musculature of many archaic works is here smoothed down and made relatively graceful. The long limbs and small head contribute to an impression of height and elegance.

58 SILVER TETRADRACHM OF ATHENS

OBVERSE:
  Head of Athena right in crested Attic helmet with spiral
  ornament behind ear.

REVERSE:
  ΑΘΕ, owl standing right, head facing, olive sprig behind, outline
  of square die visible around.

Attic standard, weight 17.02 gm; diameter 26 mm. ↓

Struck circa 520–510 B.C.

Published: Sotheby's (Warren collection, 5 July 1910), lot 13; Seltman
  302d (A196/P247); *Kunstfreund* lot 25; H.A. Cahn, "Dating the
  Early Coinages of Athens," *Kleine Schriften zur Münzkunde und
  Archäologie* (Basle, 1975), p. 94, fig. 5a.

Same dies: two specimens in London, *TrésAth* pl. 6, 21, 22 = Seltman
  302a, 302b = *AGC* figs. 69, 70; the Cambridge specimen, *TrésAth*
  pl. 6, 23 = Seltman 302c = McClean 2 (1926), 5799, pl. 206, 20.
  Same obverse die: Seltman 299, 300a, 300b, 301.

Ex E.P. Warren collection.

One of three specimens from these dies, with four others from the
  same obverse die.

The coinage of Athens is anomalous in several respects. Unlike other silver coinages it underwent an early phase involving variable types, reminiscent of the practice of the early electrum coinage. Only around 520 B.C. did it settle down with fixed types, the city's patron goddess Athena and her familiar animal the owl. More surprising, even shocking, is the fact that the coinage of Athens, the artistic center of the Hellenic world, is for the most part aesthetically insignificant. The two exceptional periods of artistic coinage at Athens are both represented in this exhibit [66].

This tetradrachm belongs to the first decade after the introduction of regular types, when there was considerable experimentation with the style of the coinage. The reign of Peisistratus' sons Hippias and Hipparchus (527–514/510 B.C.) was the heyday of Attic votive statuary, but this head of Athena instead shows powerful links with sculpture of the middle of the sixth century. The strongly receding plane of the cheek as it passes the mouth can be observed in many early kore heads and results from the attempt to depict a serene smile. The subtle modeling of Athena's cheek and chin is extremely close to that of the Peplos Kore (circa 530 B.C.), generally regarded as the finest sculpture of its period. Other similarities to this famous masterpiece include the outlining of the eyelids, the treatment of the ear and the jutting chin, which is however heavier here. The large, frontal eye is universal in black-figured vase painting and bas reliefs of the period. The latter medium offers a comparison piece fully as striking as the Peplos Kore, the profile of a discus thrower from a funerary stele. Though in flatter relief than the Hunt Athena, it shows the same placement of the frontal eye, the same connection of brow line to nasal bone, the same bumpy bridge on a pointed nose, the same short upper lip and long chin and the same size and angle of the mouth. Some authorities have attributed the discus thrower to the same hand as the Peplos Kore, and indeed these works share a rare expressiveness and vitality also captured on the tetradrachm.

The owl of the reverse has a traditional pose, wings folded and head cocked facing; the Corinthian crater [1] offers a typical example. The subject does not have the artistic possibilities of the obverse type, but the engraver has taken pains to distinguish it by delicate engraving and imaginative detail. Especially fine is the treatment of the downy breast, whose speckled coloration is suggested by a dot-in-crescent pattern shading seamlessly into small dots around the legs. Some elaboration of the breast feathers is standard for Athenian tetradrachms, but the subtlety of this die suggests it is one of the earliest. Another virtually unparalleled detail is the almond shape of the eyes, which gives expression to a normally blank stare.

59 GOLD DARIC OF ACHAEMENID PERSIA

OBVERSE:
  Great King kneeling right and drawing bow.
REVERSE:
  Oblong incuse.

Persic standard, weight 8.27 gm; diameter 15.5 mm.

Struck at Sardes, circa 500 B.C.

Equivalent coins, various dies: E.S.G. Robinson, "The Beginnings of
  Achaemenid Coinage," *NC* 1958, p. 189 and pl. 15, 10–13; *ACGC*
  81.

Of the highest rarity: four specimens known to Robinson.

The Achaemenid Persians acquired an existing sytem of coinage when they conquered the Lydian kingdom of Croesus in 546 B.C. Croesus' currency was innovative, for he had substituted coins of pure gold and pure silver for the primitive electrum which then circulated in Asia Minor [55, 56]. The Persians were content to issue coins on the Croeseid model for about half a century. It was only toward the end of the sixth century that their coinage was given a specifically Persian character, probably in connection with the financial and administrative reforms of Darius I. A new type was introduced, an archer in Persian garb. Over the years he was presented with minor variations in his pose and attributes. This is the very first version to appear on the Persian gold: the archer kneeling and drawing his bow. It was soon replaced by a different variant and is thus extremely rare. The variety is also highly significant for the history of Persian numismatics, because it is known in two weights, one corresponding to the gold stater of Croesus and the other to the slightly heavier standard of the majority of Persian darics. It thus forms the metrological link between the inherited Croeseid coinage and a truly Persian one.

The archer is a typical subject of Achaemenid glyptic art, occurring on cylinder and stamp seals, of which Croesus' capital city Sardes was probably a center of production. On seals the figure is often shown hunting or slaying mythical beasts. He represents the Great King, assimilated to the long Near Eastern tradition of

guardian heroes who protect their land from malevolent forces. The running-kneeling attitude is an old oriental device but was perhaps reintroduced to this coinage from archaic Greek art. The attempt to depict the folds of the drapery may be observed also in the Persepolis reliefs but in both cases probably reflects Greek influence. The style of the coinage is distant from the elegant but immobile precision of the court art and even from the crispness of Achaemenid seals. Its vigor and sense of motion surely result from contact with Greek art, while the low relief and somewhat scratchy technique are typical of the Croeseid mint at Sardes which produced the Persian coinage.

The Persians themselves did not use currency. This coinage was employed primarily in transactions between the central government and the restless Greeks. Its fundamental purpose was to pay mercenary soldiers. But it did not take long to discover that golden darics made effective ambassadors, buying support for Persian interests among key politicians on the Greek mainland. Thus the royal Persian coinage was very much an instrument of official policy. Its Persian character was made explicit by the distinctive battle dress of the archer, so different from Greek armor, and also by his bow, an oriental weapon despised by the Greeks as cowardly because the bowman did not risk his life in hand-to-hand combat. Their colloquial and slightly derisive name for these coveted coins was "archers."

60 SILVER OCTODRACHM OF ABDERA

OBVERSE:
   Griffin seated left atop column, off foreleg raised, grape cluster in lower left field, dotted border.

REVERSE:
   Quadripartite incuse.

Abderite standard, weight 29.78 gm; diameter 27 mm.

Struck circa 490 B.C.

Published: S. Hurter and E. Paszthory, "Archaischer Silberfund aus dem Antilibanon," *Essays in Honor of Leo Mildenberg* (forthcoming), 2.

Equivalent coins, various dies: *Asyut* 137 (possibly same reverse die). Variants: J.M.F. May, *The Coinage of Abdera*, RNS Special Publication no. 3 (London, 1966), close to 37 (delta and grapes on obverse), stylistically comparable to A35, A36.

Very rare variant of a rare coinage.

Abdera was a colony of refugees from Asia Minor who fled to the Thracian coast in 544 B.C. rather than submit to Persian domination. Its coin type, the griffin, had strong Ionian associations and was apparently the civic badge of Abdera's mother city Teos, which also used the type on its coins. The griffin ultimately derived from Persian art, where it generally fought a Persian hero. The Greeks therefore thought of the griffin as the enemy *par excellence* of the Persians, an ideal visual symbol for their own resistance to Achaemenid imperialism.

The griffin depicted here is a later archaic version of the Ionian type exemplified by the bronze griffin protome [21]. It has a similarly strong serpentine neck, but the ears are longer and the head has a more complex and rather studied profile. The body is exceptionally delicate and graceful, both in its outline and in its modeling; compare, for example, the exquisite articulation of the legs and haunches with the more solid conception of the

Hunt sphinx statuette [24]. The griffin on the octodrachm is decorative rather than ferocious, and in this respect it differs from the majority of heavy, expressive griffins on Abderite coinage. Perhaps the most admirable feature of this specimen is

the artist's abstraction of detail and restraint in its use. The empty, concave wing, of standard archaic shape, is adorned only by two curved lines which echo the twin spiral locks on the neck. This striking and unusual treatment of the wing is found on other early Abderite coins. But on many coins contemporary with the Hunt specimen, this appealing simplicity is vitiated by the indication of a second wing. The crest which appears on many Abderite griffins has been omitted to enhance the powerful outline of the neck. The ruff below the chin, equivalent to the roll on the bronze cauldron attachments, is here reduced to a sickle-shaped line. In fact the only touches of contrasting texture are the fur of the ears and the fine spraying lines of the ribs.

The half-visible grape cluster in front of the griffin is a control symbol intended to distinguish this issue of coinage and presumably also the magistrate responsible for it. Abdera was the first mint to intrude its administrative concerns into the designs of the coinage, a practice which did not become widespread until the fourth century.

61 SILVER DODECADRACHM OF THE DERRONES

OBVERSE:

DE⊬ON, ox cart driven left by bearded teamster wearing petasus and holding whip, above large crested Corinthian helmet, dotted border.

REVERSE:

Triskeles and lotus blossom.

Thasian standard, weight 39.17 gm; diameter 39 mm.

Struck at an uncertain Thraco-Macedonian mint, circa 470 B.C.

Published: *Hellénisme primitif* p. 9, 15, and pl. 2, 1; Jameson 3 (1924), 1946; *Kunstfreund* lot 38. Mentioned: *IGCH* 355 with supplemental information from W. Schwabacher, "Zur Silberprägung der Derroner," *SM* 3 (1952), p. 1; C. Boehringer, *SNR* 53 (1974), p. 22 (review of *Kunstfreund*).

Same dies: Egger 39 (1912), lot 235 = *Hellénisme primitif* p. 13, 20 and pl. 2, 7.

Ex Stip hoard, circa 1912 (*ICGH* 355); R. Jameson collection, Paris.

This large coin is as heavy as a decadrachm, but it lacks the artistic inspiration and commemorative intent of these special coins [64, 66, 77, 84ff]. Heavy silver coins were produced on a regular basis by the inhabitants of the ore-rich Thraco-Macedonian region following the example of Abdera (see preceding). Most of these coins seem to have found their way to the manufacturing centers of the Persian empire in Egypt and the Levant. Presumably they were exported as payment for oriental luxury goods or perhaps in the case of Egypt for foodstuffs. It is also suspected that some of this coinage may have been minted as a form of tribute.

The populations which produced these export coinages included warlike Indo-European tribes which still preserved the values and social organization of the Mycenaean Greeks; that is to say, they were peasant societies dominated by a warrior aristocracy. Several of these tribes are known today only from their coinage, among them the Derrones who issued this piece.

The repertory of tribal coin designs was quite limited, and most were shared by several tribes. It is possible in fact that some or all of the tribes made use of a single mint. The same pattern of mint- and type-sharing is found among some other non-Greek peoples, for example the Lycians and Carians [67] and the Persian satraps of Asia Minor. It is of course quite opposite to the normal practice of the Greeks, whose unique civic types reflect their intense local patriotism.

The obverse design of this rare coin is often described simply as a local peasant at work. But the content of archaic coinages is so strongly symbolic that the figure is more likely to be a god or hero engaged in an act of peculiar significance, possible plowing. The helmet above the ox may imply an assimilation to the war god Ares, for the tribal religion was very susceptible to syncretism. The reverse type is a radiate figure composed of three running legs and known as a *triskeles*. It was a common design element of archaic art and often functioned as a solar symbol. Here it is accompanied by stylized flowers, recalling the fusion of the solar and vegetative deities which was an important feature of North Greek religion.

The style of this coinage is obviously barbarous. The stocky ox is a stiff relation of the bull on the tetradrachm of Macedonian Acanthus (see following), even down to the division of the neck into three columns. The stick-like arms of the driver, so different from the powerfully muscled limbs of Greek archaic art, are a common feature of the Thracian figure style. This coin also displays an undeveloped minting technique, for the flatness of the reverse is not due to wear but to the method of production.

62 SILVER TETRADRACHM OF ACANTHUS

OBVERSE:
   Lion right attacking bull kneeling left on triple exergual line of dots between parallel lines, θ above, stylized flower in exergue, dotted border.

REVERSE:
   Shallow quadripartite incuse.

Attic standard, weight 17.43 gm; diameter 27 mm.

Struck circa 470 B.C.

Published: J. Ward, *Greek Coins and Their Parent Cities* (New York, 1902), 375; Sotheby's Zurich (Metropolitan Museum 2, 4 April 1973), lot 325.

Variants: J. Desneux, *Les tétradrachmes d'Akanthos* (Brussels, 1949), 69–79.

Ex J. Ward collection, New York; Metropolitan Museum of Art.

This tetradrachm is an issue of Acanthus, a Greek colony on the three-fingered Chalcidian peninsula of Macedon. Like the octodrachm and dodecadrachm preceding it was essentially an export medium, and it shows the influence of the Abderite coinage in its flat, spread fabric and quadripartite incuse reverse. Its type belongs to a regional system featuring a different animal combat scene for each of the participating mints.

Lions attacking their prey are a favorite subject of ancient oriental art. The compositional possibilities are numerous, but the Minoans developed a compact grouping which emphasized the power of the theme and which became the basis for the later Greek approach. The motif of animal combat subsequently disappeared, then reentered the Greek artistic repertory in the orientalizing period, becoming a popular subject in the second quarter of the sixth century. Numismatic representations show a particularly close relationship to the schemata adopted for gemstones. Both reduce the number of combatants to two and typically place the lion on the back of his prey, which often staggers or kneels under the force of the assault. The original Acanthine coin type of the last quarter of the sixth century shows striking stylistic similarities to the finest scarab of the

Group of the Munich Protomes. Shared details include the stippled or dotted mane, the bristles running down the length of the lion's spine (an East Greek feature) and the bull's exaggerated dewlap.

This original type is little changed on the Hunt tetradrachm over half a century later. What marks this as an archaizing work is its repudiation of the struggle toward realism which propelled genuine archaic art. The flat, massive character of the original type is exaggerated here. The body shapes are no longer organically conceived but appear concocted of geometric elements. The most remarkable feature of this geometric abstraction is the extensive and systematic use of pellets. Elongated dots are arranged in neat, parallel rows to create textured areas for the lion's mane and bull's neck. The latter is arbitrarily divided into three vertical columns which ignore the twist of the animal's head. Dotted lines comprise the ground line and circular border besides indicating the hair on the tip of the bull's tail. Pellets of varying size denote joints and muscles.

The abstract flower in the exergue may be an example of the Greek fondness for visual puns on their coins [65, 69, 88]. It has been identified by some authorities as an acanthus flower, a clear reference to the name of the mint city.

63 SILVER TETRADRACHM OF SYRACUSE

OBVERSE:
  Slow quadriga driven right by male charioteer in long chiton, above Nike right alighting on backs of horses with wreath to crown them, dotted border.

REVERSE:
  ΣΥ—PAϙ—OΣI—ON, filleted head of Artemis-Arethusa right with wire choker and beaded neck truncation, beaded hair cut in bangs around face, combed over ear and falling free down back of neck, four dolphins around.

Attic standard, weight 17.25 gm; diameter 25 mm. ↖

Attributed to the Master of the Large Heads. Struck circa 485 B.C.

Published: K. Schefold, *Meisterwerke griechischer Kunst* (Basle, 1960), 432; Käppeli F21.

Same dies: Boehringer 46 (V27/R30); Rizzo pl. 34, 13; H. Scharmer, "Die Meister der spätarchaischen Arethusaköpfe," *AK* 10 (1967), pl. 28, 7; Kraay-Hirmer 75; Gulbenkian 250.

Syracuse, the greatest city of Greek Sicily, was noted both for its wealth and for its love of high culture. Its coinage is the most artistic of the fifth century, and it ultimately exercised a dominating influence on other western coinages which aspired to be beautiful. The earliest Syracusan coin types seem prosaic enough: on the obverse a quadriga or four-horse racing chariot, on the reverse a shallow quadripartite incuse with a tiny female head in the center.

These types were enriched about 485 B.C. when the Geloan tyrant Gelon made Syracuse the capital of his considerable Sicilian empire. A small figure of Nike was added to the obverse, symbolizing Gelon's racing victory at the Olympic games of 488 B.C. The reverse type was profoundly transformed, with the female head enlarged to comprise the principal type and the four quarters of the incuse replaced by playful dolphins. The goddess represented is Artemis, mistress of wild beasts. At Syracuse she was assimilated to the local goddess Arethusa, spirit of the fresh-water spring which still bubbles today among the breakers on the island of Ortygia, site of the original eighth-century foundation. The dolphins thus represent the salt water surrounding the spring but also, on a grander scale, the two harbors which embrace the city.

This tetradrachm was issued not long after the introduction of the elaborated types. The quadriga of the obverse conforms to an ancient formula also exemplified on the black-figured amphora [4]. The head of Arethusa bears a striking resemblance to the admirable terracotta goddess from Agrigentum now at Palermo, which has the same narrow eye, blunt nose, thin lips with protruding chin and simple modeling. The shoulder-length hair brushed behind the ears is found on numerous West Greek terracottas and also on the slightly later Ludovisi Acrolith at Rome. The rendering of the hair, beaded with a subtle change of scale at the diadem, belongs to the Ionian tradition. The unity of form underlying the diverse media of this transitional age may be suggested by two more comparisons. The narrow three-quarter eye, straight nose and strong chin bring Arethusa's physiognomy close to a basic facial type of Attic red-figured vase painting: see for example the youth holding helmet and shield on the exterior of [8] and the tondo figures of [7] and [11]. An even stronger kinship exists with the famed kore of Euthydikos (kore 686), one of the latest of the Athenian korai and practically contemporary with this tetradrachm. She displays the same profile, the same heavy-lidded eyes, the same simplified modeling and grave, inward expression. The Euthydikos kore prefigures the severe sculptural style developed under Peloponnesian influence, and it should be no surprise to find related qualities in the art of the Dorian cities of southern Sicily.

64 SILVER DECADRACHM OF SYRACUSE

OBVERSE:
Slow quadriga driven right by charioteer in long chiton, above
Nike flying right to crown horses, lion running right in exergue,
dotted border.

REVERSE:
ΣΥ—ΡΑΚ—ΟΣΙΟ—Ν, head of Demarete-Arethusa right, wearing
olive wreath, hoop earring and necklace with pendant, hair waved
at temples and dressed in krobylos, long wavy lock behind ear,
nimbus surrounding head, four dolphins around.

Attic standard, weight 42.42 gm; diameter 35 mm. ↗

Attributed to the Demareteion Master. Struck circa 470 B.C.

Same dies: *de Luynes* 1 (1924), pl. 8, 1–2; Boehringer 378 (V193/R267);
Demareteion p. 27, 7 and pl. 3, V3/R5.

One of seventeen specimens now known, four from these dies.

This great rarity has traditionally been known as the "Demare-teion" on the basis of an episode from Sicilian history recounted by Diodorus Siculus (11.26.3). The first historical confrontation between the Sicilian Greeks and the Carthaginians ended in the total defeat of the latter at the battle of Himera in 480 B.C. The leaders of the victorious Greeks were Gelon, tyrant of Syracuse, and his father-in-law Theron, tyrant of Agrigentum. Gelon's wife Demarete interceded in the peace negotiations on behalf of the vanquished invaders. In gratitude for the generous terms which she obtained for them, the Carthaginians presented her with a golden diadem of exceeding value. It was converted into an exceptional ten drachma coin called the "Demareteion" after Queen Demarete.

The types of the Demareteion derive from those of the Syracusan tetradrachms (see preceding) but with significant changes and additions. Instead of the usual diadem, the female head of the reverse wears an olive wreath, symbol of victory. Her rather individual features have sometimes been regarded as a portrait of Queen Demarete. The nimbus around her head is in fact merely a development from a faint line drawn on earlier tetradrachms to guide the lettering of the legend; it is barely visible on the preceding example. The lion in the exergue of the obverse has traditionally been explained as a symbol of the African power Carthage. More recently it has been pointed out that the lion was the seal of the Emmenid family of Demarete and her father Theron. It may thus pay homage to the alliance which enabled Syracuse to repel the Carthaginian invasion.

Recent scholarship has emphasized epigraphical and technical numismatic considerations which suggest a later date for the Demareteion. The years around 470 B.C. witnessed a constellation of festive events celebrated by the Syracusan tyrant Hieron, brother and successor of Gelon, for which he commissioned commemorative works by the most brilliant literary men of the day. 470 was the year of the formal dedication to Zeus of Hieron's colony of Aetna, which was probably actually founded around 476. Both Syracuse and Leontini were associated in the festival, which was immortalized by Pindar's First Pythian Ode and by a lost play of Aeschylus, "Women of Aetna." In the same year Hieron won a panhellenic chariot race at the Pythian

64 SILVER DECADRACHM (continued)

Games, also celebrated in Pindar's First Pythian Ode and in the Fourth Ode of Bacchylides. A further chariot racing victory at the Olympic games of 468 occasioned Bacchylides' Third Ode and apparently also Pindar's Second Pythian. The latter contains a metaphor which seems to describe the reverse type of the decadrachm (lines 9ff):

> Hieron of the fair chariot, who rules her,
> Has crowned Ortygia with wreaths,
> The dwelling place of Artemis of the rivers
> (author's translation)

Hieron's extravagant patronage of works celebrating his achievements creates a context into which a commemorative decadrachm fits most comfortably. Its artistic distinction and unique courtly style can then plausibly be attributed to an important artist, no doubt the most celebrated engraver of his day. In this revisionist view the Demareteion decadrachm should be renamed the Hieroneion.

This first Syracusan decadrachm issue was struck from three obverse and five reverse dies, indicating a quite restricted coinage not intended for general disbursement. The style of these decadrachms and the associated tetradrachm issue at Leontini is discussed under the next entry. Of the five decadrachm reverse dies, this one is the closest in form and feeling to the mainstream of the severe style.

65 SILVER TETRADRACHM OF LEONTINI

OBVERSE:
  Slow quadriga driven right by charioteer in long chiton, above
  Nike flying left to crown him, lion right in exergue, dotted border.

REVERSE:
  ΛΕΟ—ΝΤΙΝ—Ο—Ν, head of Apollo right wearing olive wreath,
  hair braided and pinned to back of head, lion right under neck
  truncation, three laurel leaves around.

Attic standard, weight 17.11 gm; diameter 28 mm. ✓

Attributed to the Demareteion Master. Struck circa 470 B.C.

Same dies: Rizzo pl. 22, 14; *Götter Griechenlands* pl. 2; "Syrakus und
  Leontinoi" pl. 1, 5; Kraay-Hirmer 19; Gulbenkian 211. Same
  reverse die: Pfeiff *Apollon* pl. 43.

Rare.

Leontini was located only twenty miles away from Syracuse. It was captured by the Geloan tyrant Hippocrates in the later 490's and made part of the Deinomenid empire. In the time of Hieron it had the distinction of being virtually the only subject city which was neither destroyed nor abused by the tyrant: instead it was enlarged by the resettlement of the populations of Catana and Naxos and made into the Ionian metropolis of eastern Sicily in much the same manner that Syracuse was its Dorian metropolis. Leontini was governed either by Hieron directly or by a dependent tyrant with strong personal ties to the dynasty.

This tetradrachm, only the second issue in Leontini's history, is clearly modeled upon the Syracusan Demareteion (see preceding) and has long been recognized as a work of the same hand. The occasion of issue is of course dependent upon the date assigned the decadrachm. It is worth noting that the relations between Syracuse and Leontini were particularly close under the Deinomenids but unfriendly after the establishment of democracy. The production of a small and especially beautiful tetradrachm issue, symbolically linked to the Syracusan decadrachm and executed by the same major artist, can be most persuasively dated to Hieron's reign and should probably be associated with his festival for the foundation of Aetna.

The obverse type, the Syracusan quadriga, had already been employed on Leontini's earliest tetradrachms. Apollo, who appears on the reverse, was worshipped as civic founder at Leontini as at many cities because his oracle at Delphi had authorized the settlement of the original colonists. In place of the Syracusan dolphins he is surrounded by laurel leaves, tokens of his oracular powers: the Pythian priestess ate laurel leaves to achieve the state of mystic transport in which she delivered her oracles. The lion, carried over from the Demareteion to both sides of the tetradrachm, is Apollo's special animal and also a pun on the name of Leontini.

With the Demareteion Master we are in the presence of one of the truly individual stylists of Greek numismatics. His hallmarks are an enormous, heavy-lidded eye in three-quarter view, generally complete with iris and pupil, under a high arching eyebrow, drawn rather than modeled; a small, fine-boned nose with flaring nostrils; thick lips rendered without defining the corner of the mouth; long upper lip and smallish pointed chin; and a long, wavy lock falling loose behind the ear. Certain famous works of West Greek manufacture share the same air of courtly refinement, notably the Ludovisi Throne and the Apollo of Piombino, if indeed the latter is of the fifth century. The basic facial type too seems to have been popular in West Greek art during the first half of the fifth century, though these forms are only dimly reflected in the well-known monumental sculpture of the Greek homeland. The braided hair pinned to the back of the head is a typical coiffure of severe style sculpture, frequently accompanied by wavy bangs ending in little hook-like curls. But the loose, wavy lock behind the ear belongs to the lighter repertory of vase painting.

This tetradrachm issue at Leontini was even smaller than the Demareteion issue at Syracuse. It employed two obverse and two reverse dies. Of the reverse dies the one represented here is less idiosyncratic and thus closer to the general stylistic trends of the day. It is also the only head of the Demareteion group whose eye lacks iris and pupil.

66 SILVER DECADRACHM OF ATHENS

OBVERSE:
  Head of Athena right in crested Attic helmet ornamented with three olive leaves over visor and spiral palmette on bowl, dotted neck truncation.

REVERSE:
  A—Θ—E, owl standing facing with spread wings, olive sprig to upper left, all in shallow incuse square.

Attic standard, weight 42.67 gm; diameter 36 mm. ↘

Struck circa 465 B.C.

Published: Seltman 447; C. Seltman, *Greek Coins* (London, 1933), pl. 13, 2; C.G. Starr, *Athenian Coinage 480–449 B.C.* (Oxford, 1970), p. 35, no. 55 and pl. 6, 55; *Kunstfreund* lot 147. Mentioned: C. Boehringer, *SNR* 53 (1974), p. 20 (review of *Kunstfreund*).

Equivalent coins, various dies: *Traité* 1 (1907), 1141–1142, pl. 36, 8, 11; *TrésAth* pl. 8, 8, 13–17; F. Mainzer, "Das Dekadrachmon von Athen," *ZfN* 36 (1926), p. 37f; Kraay-Hirmer 357, 358.

Found at Spata, Attica, 1922; ex C. Seltman collection, Cambridge.

One of twelve specimens known and the only example from these dies.

The decadrachm denomination was minted only once in Athenian history. Traditionally it has been associated with the Persian Wars of the early fifth century B.C., in which Athens played the leading role in repelling the Persians from Europe. This is considered one of the crucial turning points in world history, for it saved a budding western civilization from being swamped by oriental influences. The decadrachm has been connected with the ten-drachma largess paid to all Athenian citizens from the bonanza of the Laurian silver mines until 483 B.C., when the bullion was diverted to the construction of a navy—Athens' "wooden walls" (*Ath. Pol.* 22.7; Herodotus 7.144). It has also been regarded as a victory piece celebrating the defeat of Xerxes' invasion force at Salamis and Plataea in 480 and 479 B.C. This would make the Athenian decadrachm an exact contemporary of the Syracusan Demareteion [64]. Indeed the two would seem to constitute sister issues, the one celebrating the repulse of the barbarian in the east, the other in the west. However these traditional theories have faced a formidable challenge from the modern school of numismatics which places great emphasis on hoard contents, die sequences and other scientific data. The latest scholarship dates the decadrachms to the 460's B.C., when Athens carried the war into Persian territory.

The types of the decadrachm are traditional for Athenian coinage [58], while the style mirrors that of contemporary tetradrachms. A new feature of the postwar coinage is the three olive leaves which appear over the visor of Athena's helmet. They are reminders of the goddess's gift of the olive tree to her people but also, in this context, tokens of victory and peace. They call to mind the olive wreath of the Demareteion, reinforcing the parallelism suggested above.

The Attic mint was generally conservative in artistic matters, and that tendency is apparent in the archaizing style of the Athena head. The frontal eye, archaic smile and beaded hair are old-fashioned in feeling. But the simplified modeling, low forehead and general heaviness are related to the sculptural severe

style and mark this head unmistakably as a transitional work. Also contemporary is the monumental feeling despite the miniaturist medium. The owl of the reverse is conceived with similar expansiveness. The frontal pose with wings spread was first introduced on the decadrachm and gives the bird a majestic, perhaps even militant air totally lacking from the usual side view.

67 SILVER STATER OF AN UNCERTAIN CARIAN MINT

OBVERSE:

Eros kneeling right, winged at shoulders and heels, holding wreath in right hand, ⚲ above left shoulder.

REVERSE:

Large ⚲ , small [8]—M—ᴠ, lion standing left, head reverted, off foreleg raised, all within shallow incuse square with dotted border.

Aeginetic standard, weight 11.70 gm; diameter 21 mm.↑

Struck circa 465 B.C.

Same dies: E.S.G. Robinson, "A Find of Archaic Coins from South-West Asia Minor," *NC* 1936, p. 269, 12 and pl. 14, 12.

This stater was produced by an unidentified mint in southern Asia Minor along the border of Caria and Lycia. Each of these regions was inhabited by a non-Greek people speaking a different language. The Carians and the Lycians were both open to Greek artistic influence, but our inability to decipher their languages makes it difficult to interpret the native religious ideas which may underlie the borrowed Hellenic types.

Winged figures were popular artistic subjects in this area and on nearby Cyprus. Those on coins mostly appear to be solar or heavenly divinities, but the young male with winged shoulders and heels who appears consistently on the coins of this mint resembles the figures of Eros which commonly occur on gemstones from this same south Anatolian-Cypriote axis. Eros was the god of sexual desire, winged to symbolize his sudden, fleeting nature. His popularity in this region may be linked to the cult of Aphrodite, a major deity of the Levant. Eros was also a favored subject in Attic vase painting, where he had dual aspects as a love god and as a death god.

The chief interest of the Carian Eros lies in his intriguing pose, which is perhaps intended to capture the action of the body alighting from flight. The pose is not found in other depictions of the god either on gemstones or on Attic vases. However a large class of transitional gemstones uses similar if not identical poses, with western examples in particular illustrating the use of slack muscles and oddly twisted members to depict slain heroes. The figure on the stater thus embodies major concerns of transitional art in its contrived posture and in the new sensitivity to muscle tone. The twisted torso achieves a fairly successful three-quarter view with both abdomen and shoulders foreshortened, although the latter still recall the archaic preference for a frontal view [57].

The lion of the reverse is another characteristic subject of this region. The crouching S-pose with reverted head and one raised paw is a typical configuration in East Greek art inherited from the orientalizing period. The strong serpentine neck with mane indicated only as rows of pellets is another holdover from hittitizing prototypes [22] and was long retained at certain Carian mints. Another local peculiarity is the impossible angle of the raised foreleg. There may be a thematic connection with the obverse type, suggested by the conjunction of Eros and a lion on a plastic vase in the shape of an astragalos or knucklebone, the ancient gambling token which itself symbolizes the unpredict-

able nature of love. It has been suggested that the lion like Eros can belong to the realm of the dead.

The sign which appears on both obverse and reverse of this coin is also found on Lycian coinage. Here it is usually regarded as a mint mark. The legend on the reverse is written in Carian script, a variant of the Greek alphabet. It is suspected of naming a local dynast who authorized the coinage. The existence of an alternate legend with the same types and mintmark would seem to indicate a situation in which two petty rulers shared a single mint, whose coin types reflect the traditions of the town rather than of the dynasts. Such practices have been demonstrated for neighboring regions in Lycia, but at a later date around the end of the fifth century.

68 SILVER TETRADRACHM OF SICILIAN NAXOS

OBVERSE:
  Head of bearded Dionysus right, crowned with ivy, hair tied in krobylos at back of neck, dotted border.

REVERSE:
  N—AXI—ON, nude ithyphallic silen seated facing, head turned left, lifting cantharus to his lips.

Attic standard, weight 17.24 gm; diameter 27 mm.←

Attributed to the Aetna Master. Struck circa 460 B.C.

Published: *SNG Spencer Churchill* 46; Cahn 54, example 29; *Kunstfreund* lot 95.

Same dies: Regling pl. 17, 395; Rizzo pl. 28, 12; *Götter Griechenlands* pls. 48, 50; Kraay-Hirmer 6; *AGC* figs. 366–367.

Ex E.G. Spencer Churchill collection, Northfield Park.

Cahn lists 56 specimens.

The Syracusan tyrants of the earlier fifth century indulged in grandiose schemes of colonization which involved the forcible resettlement of whole populations. One city so affected was Sicilian Naxos, a coastal town at the foot of Mt. Aetna. Its citizens, deported in 476 B.C., recovered their homes in 461. The Naxian mint had not previously issued so large a denomination as the tetradrachm. But one of exceptional brilliance was now commissioned to celebrate the homecoming, doubtless from an outside artist. The same supremely gifted hand has been recognized in a unique tetradrachm of Aetna at Brussels, probably the foundation issue of Aetna as reconstituted at the mountain fortress of Inessa after 461. The anonymous artist has therefore been dubbed the Aetna Master.

The god Dionysus was the traditional obverse type at Naxos, perhaps because of his association with the Aegean island of the same name. (According to myth he rescued and married the Cretan princess Ariadne, who had been abandoned on Naxos by Theseus.) The conventions of his iconography—the ivy wreath, the long hair and beard—were established quite early in vase painting [3]. But the plastic treatment relates this work to severe style sculpture. The heavy-lidded profile eye in a large but delicately modeled socket; the high, rounded cheek; and the texture of hair and beard are all paralleled on famous masterpieces of this period, notably the figure of Zeus on the marriage metope of the Temple of Hera at Selinus and the bronze Zeus or Poseidon found off Cape Artemision. These sculptures belong to an artistic movement which sought to restore grandeur and moral significance to the depiction of the gods, and they share with the Naxian Dionysus an intensity of expression which is lacking from his portrayals on vases. It is heightened here by the lingering archaic smile. Its ambivalence is appropriate to the god's character, for Dionysus was not merely the god of wine but of the life force and of religious possession, mystic, amoral and sometimes violent. The superimposition of the beard over the dotted border enhances his numinous immediacy.

68 SILVER TETRADRACHM (continued)

The figure seated on the reverse is a silen, a wild woodland companion of Dionysus who embodied the animal aspect of human nature [16, 23, 29]. His awkward posture is typical of the challenging poses explored in the transitional period. The squat, not uncommon on vases, was restricted to lower orders of being, such as slaves, barbarians and subhumans. Nevertheless it called forth the artists' highest skill in anatomical observation and foreshortening, and here the result is an illusion of depth unsurpassed by any relief sculpture of the first half of the fifth century. The treatment of the abdominal muscles is also characteristic of this period, both on vases and in statuary. The hard modeling is expressive of the creature's toughness. The dreamy expression on the grotesque face is a reminder that in some versions of his legend Silenus was a master of music and the possessor of arcane knowledge. Here he represents the divine worshiper in communion with his god through holy drunkenness. This is an original approach to the subject, who was normally treated either as a violent being, as on [16] and on North Greek coins, or as a humorous and graceful reveler, as on [29] and on most red-figured vases.

69 SILVER TETRADRACHM OF LEONTINI

OBVERSE:
    Laureate head of Apollo right, hair rolled, dotted border.
REVERSE:
    [Λ]E—O—N—T—IN—[ON], lion's head right, four barley grains
    around.
Attic standard, weight 17.16 gm; diameter 27 mm. ←
Struck circa 460 B.C.
Same dies: Rizzo pl. 22, 26.
Rare dies.

After its tetradrachm issue of Demareteion style [65] Leontini
once again revised its coin types. The quadriga was dropped
from the obverse, a change perhaps to be associated with the fall
of the Deinomenid dynasty in 466 and the establishment of
democracies at Syracuse, Leontini and throughout Sicily. Apollo, who had appeared on the reverse of the previous issue, now
becomes the obverse type, wearing his appropriate crown of
laurel rather than the olive wreath of the Demareteion. The
reverse, still based upon Syracusan reverse designs [63], now
employs a lion's head surrounded by grains of barley. The lion,
as noted previously, was both an animal sacred to Apollo and a
punning type for Leontini, so that the whole complex may be
taken to symbolize the city surrounded by its fertile fields.

Leontini's Apollo heads do not develop in a linear fashion. One
group, of which this specimen is a typical example, exaggerates
features of the Demareteion-style Apollo but in a manner
which is light, even pert, rather than aloof. Another group,
which should be recognized as the mainstream of Leontini's
stylistic evolution, perhaps develops from the second Demareteion Apollo die [65], moving closer to the forms of severe
style sculpture with powerful parallels on the coinage of nearby
Catana.

The "mannered" Apollo heads of Leontini, such as this one,
show affinities to the finest known South Italian tomb paintings. The Paestan paintings use the same concave curve of the
upper eyelid with its long, drooping lashes, the same uplifted
chins and the same general proportions of the face. The tendency to depict hair by means of sharply cut parallel lines is widespread on Sicilian coins of transitional style [64, 68] including
the "severe" phase of Leontini's coinage. The rolled coiffure is
common in contemporary sculpture. Sculpture also provides
examples of spit curls framing the face, but the delicacy of their
execution here contributes much to the frivolous air of this
head. The same lightness and indeed similar facial features may
be observed on the red-figured pelike [13].

The lion's head of the reverse precisely resembles the stone or
terracotta temple ornaments used throughout the Greek world
in the archaic and transitional periods. Similar stylized lion
heads were also used as water spouts. The mane is characteristi-
cally reduced to a stiff fringe. The snarling expression is emphasized by the deep parallel wrinkles of the lion's upper lip and
nose, by the exposure of the scalloped lining of the mouth and
by the lolling tongue. This version is notably light and angular.
For a more harmonious treatment of the same motif which yet
retains all the typological features noted here, see [34].

70 SILVER TETRADRACHM OF AENUS

OBVERSE:
   Head of Hermes right in pilos with beaded rim, hair braided and wrapped around back of head.
REVERSE:
   AINI, goat standing right, before it cult image of Hermes Perpheraios, outline of square die visible around.

Persic standard, weight 16.24 gm; diameter 25 mm. ↘

Struck circa 455 B.C.

Published: Hess-Leu (16 April 1957), lot 152; Kraay-Hirmer 419.

Same dies: J.M.F. May, *Ainos, Its History and Coinage* (Oxford, 1950), 71; A.B. Brett, *Museum of Fine Arts, Catalogue of Greek Coins* (Boston, 1955), 770.

Ex M. Hirmer collection, Munich.

Aenus was a rather isolated trading city on the coast of Thrace. The types of its handsome tetradrachms derive from the cult of Hermes, chief god of the city. This specimen offers a rare illustration of the duality of ancient Greek religion, which embraced the familiar humanism of the Olympian gods but also an obscure yet potent substratum of prehellenic fetishism and nature worship.

The anthropomorphic Hermes of the obverse was the messenger of the gods and the patron of those who travel, including merchants, thieves and herdsmen. In archaic art he is usually depicted as long haired, bearded and virile, as on the black-figured amphora [4]. In the fifth century a beardless type appears very occasionally, perhaps in response to the Homeric description of Hermes as a youth whose beard was just beginning to sprout. On coins of Aenus he wears the pilos, a conical marine helmet of the Thracians. The Aenian Hermes is one of the most perfect examples of the sculptural severe style adapted to coinage. Canonical features of the style evident here include the heavy-lidded eye under a low, straight brow; thick lips; heavy chin; braided hair pinned up behind; simple modeling; restraint in the use of ornament; and of course the gravity and dignity which give the style its name. The three-quarter, nearly frontal eye seems distinctly old-fashioned compared with the preceding works and illustrates the strong conservative tendencies operant at many Greek mints.

The reverse offers another aspect of Hermes. Fundamentally he was the god of roads, and the primitive manner of portraying him was as a road marker, a carved plinth on which only the face and genitals were worked in detail. Such a *herm* appears here, seated on a high-backed throne. It represents a crude wooden idol worshiped at Aenus as Hermes Perpheraios. It was believed to have been carved by Epeios, the craftsman who fashioned the Trojan horse. Later it washed out to sea, where it was miraculously picked up in the nets of local fishermen. Here the small figure functions as a subsidiary symbol, that is, a variable element used to identify a specific issue.

The actual type of the reverse is a goat, a symbol of animal vitality and lust. These were major themes of the native religion of the Thraco-Macedonian region. Furthermore the goat was especially associated with Hermes who had yet another aspect as a phallic god, growing out of the form of the herm.

71 SILVER TETRADRACHM OF SELINUS

OBVERSE:
> ΣΕ—ΛΙΝΟ—ΝΤΙ—ΟΣ (retrograde), slow quadriga driven left by Artemis, in chariot beside her Apollo drawing bow, dotted border.

REVERSE:
> Σ—ΕΛ—Ι—ΝΟ—Σ, nude river god Selinus standing left, sacrificing from phiale over altar and holding lustral branch, sacrificial cock standing left on threshold of altar, in right field selinon leaf and votive statuette of bull.

Attic standard, weight 17.24 gm; diameter 29 mm. ↑

Struck circa 445 B.C.

Same dies: Schwabacher 4; *SNG Lloyd* 1222. Same obverse die: Rizzo pl. 31, 9; Gulbenkian 243.

Very rare variant.

Selinus was the westernmost Greek settlement in Sicily, far enough from Syracuse that its coinage preserved a local flavor. The obverse type of the Selinuntine tetradrachm is a quadriga, which spread from Syracuse to many Sicilian cities. But in the far west of the island it tended to take the form of a ceremonial car rather than a racing chariot. In this case the car bears two gods, Artemis and Apollo. They are also depicted together on metopes of the Selinuntine temples. They shared a joint cult in Selinus' mother city Megara and in other Megarian colonies as Apollo Agraios and Artemis Agrotera, the gods of the wilderness and of the hunt. The drawn bow here confirms their patronage of the chase. The horses of the quadriga have typical West Greek proportions, with large head and heavy neck atop a very slender body on long legs. This regional conception of equine proportions is perfectly exemplified by the Etruscan bronze [27] which closely resembles the lead horse here. The decidedly slender horse's body can be traced through Sicilian coinage even into the work of the signing artists at the turn of the century [63ff, 72, 75ff].

The complicated reverse type shows the local river god Selinus in his temple precincts, offering a libation for the welfare of his city. His pose derives from a major bronze statue of the second quarter of the fifth century, known today only from copies [47, 48]. This well-known statue type depicts a youth, probably an athlete, offering a gift in his extended right hand, standing with his weight on his right leg, his left leg flexed. His back is strongly curved, and his head turns toward his right. It is quite probable that the Selinuntine cult statue was of this type and that the coin type reproduces it. The exaggerated musculature, the manner of rendering torsion and the general stiffness of the figure on the tetradrachm seem a throwback to an earlier phase of figural art, recalling bas reliefs of the late sixth century. The hard modeling however is typical of the numismatic medium in this period.

The tiny horn over the forehead marks the god as a river deity. It derives from the strange western practice of depicting river gods as bulls with human faces—a convention still observed elsewhere in Sicily until the last years of the fifth century B.C. The small bull, identified as a statue by its base, represents a votive offering similar to [28]. The cock is a sacrificial animal especially associated with deities of the earth. The small leaf above the bull is a form of wild celery, called *selinon* in Greek, which gave its name to the city and served as a punning civic badge.

72 SILVER TETRADRACHM OF SYRACUSE

OBVERSE:
 Slow quadriga driven right by charioteer in long chiton, above
 Nike flying left to crown him, dotted border.

REVERSE:
 ΣΥΡΑΚΟΣΙΟΝ, head of Aphrodite-Arethusa right, wearing wire
 necklace and whorl-shaped earring, hair in sphendone fastened by
 band wound three times around head, four dolphins around.

Attic standard, weight 17.39 gm; diameter 27 mm. ←

Attributed to the Master of the Aphrodite Type. Struck circa 430 B.C.

Published: K. Schefold, *Meisterwerke griechische Kunst* (Basle, 1960),
 480; *Kunstfreund* lot 111.

Same dies: Boehringer 723 (V355/R493). Same reverse die: *Götter
 Griechenlands* pl. 63; Rizzo pl. 40, 15; Kraay-Hirmer 94.

After about 460 B.C. the Syracusan mint made a practice of
frequently revising its treatment of Arethusa. So varied are the
facial types, coiffures and details of the toilette that the authority on the Syracusan coinage, E. Boehringer, hypothesized the
use of live models. The truth however appears to be that the art-
loving Syracusans were extremely open to aesthetic influences
from outside. Contacts with Athens are well attested, and the
viewer is immediately struck by the resemblance of this head to
that of Artemis on the east frieze of the Parthenon. It has in fact
been identified as inspired by a different work of Phidias, a
statue of Aphrodite whose original is now lost but whose popularity is attested by the survival of many copies. The type, long
known as "Sappho" in sculptural scholarship, is characterized
by its hairdressing which involves a *sphendone* fastened by a
band wound several times around the head, with curly hair
escaping to frame the face. The best copies also show tender
young hairs below the sphendone on the back of the neck, as
here. Another distinctive feature of the Phidian Aphrodite is a
barely open mouth, again duplicated here. The narrow, slightly
squinting eye is a characteristic of the goddess's iconography
generally, although some of the other copies miss this important detail.

This Aphrodite-Arethusa embodies the Phidian ideal of lofty
serenity, combined with a sweet and modest expression which
is particular to that master's conception of the goddess of love.
But the Syracusan artist has gone beyond Phidias' restrained
prototype to create a more overtly sensuous type. Delicate features are combined with exquisitely nuanced modeling to create shadows which especially emphasize the soft skin around
the eye. This refined eroticism prefigures the mood of much
late fifth-century Sicilian coinage, especially the masterpieces of
Euainetus [75, 79, possibly 80]; and it also anticipates at least
part of the contribution of the fourth-century sculptor Praxiteles. The anonymous engraver of this die has been christened the
Master of the Aphrodite Type.

A minor novelty on the obverse is that the Nike figure now
crowns the charioteer rather than the horses. The change,
which is permanent, seems related to a quadriga votive relief
found at Athens, the only specimen known which features a
Nike as part of its design.

73 SILVER TETRADRACHM OF SICILIAN NAXOS

OBVERSE:
   Head of bearded Dionysus right, wearing diadem ornamented with ivy vine, dotted border.

REVERSE:
   ΝΑΞΙΟΝ, nude silen seated facing on rock, head turned left, lifting cantharus to lips and holding thyrsus, ivy vine in left field, linear border.

Attic standard, weight 17.19 gm; diameter 29 mm. ↖

Struck circa 425 B.C.

Published: F. Imhoof-Blumer and O. Keller, *Tier- und Pflanzenbilder auf Münzen des klassischen Altentums* (Leipzig, 1889), pl. 1, 22; Cahn 100, example 2; M&M 13 (1954), lot 1035.

Same dies: Rizzo pl. 28, 16; Gulbenkian 232. Same obverse die: Regling pl. 26, 562; *Götter Griechenlands* pl. 51; Kraay-Hirmer 8.

Ex Duke of Gotha collection.

Cahn lists 10 specimens from these dies.

This tetradrachm is only the second produced in Naxian history, and it repeats the types of the first [68]. This time they are presented in a manner which reflects the Olympianization of the barbarian god Dionysus and the domestication of his once orgiastic cult. The head of the god is executed in a high classical style which shows the influence of the master sculptor Phidias. The face with its straight nose, eye set high in the skull, small ear, simple modeling and impassive expression is closely related to the style of the Parthenon friezes, and especially to the well-known figure of Poseidon on the east frieze. The short hair and beard also relate to the Parthenon style. The profusion of corkscrew curls and the ornamented diadem seem to violate the self-conscious restraint of the Parthenon sculptures, but they are consistent with features of Phidias' nonarchitectural statues. The corkscrew curls are paralleled on an athlete's head of Phidian style in the Metropolitan Museum of Art, while the fancy diadem is a reminder that the subsidiary elements of Phidias' most celebrated cult statues were richly ornamented with symbolic motifs.

The silen on the reverse is as excessively soft as the earlier version was hard. The intention is perhaps to depict the elderly Silenus, tutor to the infant Dionysus, in contrast to the wiry young specimen on the earlier tetradrachm. The softness is also related to the pastel colors of polychrome painting and the loose draftmanship of late classical vase painting. Certainly an affinity to painting is suggested by the miniature landscape, consisting of rocky ground and a sinuous ivy vine. The whole design has a bucolic mood which seems slightly inappropriate to the public and patriotic nature of coinage and is in fact rarely encountered except at West Greek mints.

It is unclear what circumstances prompted Naxos to issue a major denomination after some thirty years during which the mint produced only small change. Perhaps the tetradrachms were needed to defray the costs of the war of 427 B.C., essentially a conflict between the Dorian and Chalcidian colonists of Sicily. What is certain is that the Naxian mint did not possess an employee of this level of artistry. The engraver of these dies had to be commissioned from elsewhere. Syracuse was the nearest source of talented glyptic artists, but the political circumstances of the day would scarcely have facilitated cooperation between the mints. On the other hand relations with Athens were close; and large numbers of artists working at Athens must have emigrated in search of work after the completion of the Parthenon in 432 B.C.

74 SILVER TETRADRACHM OF MENDE

OBVERSE:
  Mule walking right on which Dionysus reclines left, holding cantharus, dotted border.

REVERSE:
  MEN—ΔΑ—IO—N in shallow incuse square border around central square containing stylized grapevine with four clusters of fruit.

Attic standard, weight 16.97 gm; diameter 25 mm. ↑

Struck circa 415 B.C.

Same dies: S.P. Noe, *The Mende (Kaliandra) Hoard*, NNM 27 (New York, 1926), 85.

The Macedonian city of Mende was located close to Thrace where the Dionysiac religion originated or at least made its first contact with the rational Greeks. Many early coinages of the region feature Dionysiac types symbolizing the animal passions, executed in a rude but energetic style. This coin, like the preceding, illustrates the domestication and hellenization of the cult which was largely complete by the middle of the fifth century. The type of Dionysus riding on an ass—the so-called "drunken Dionysus"—is inherited from sixth-century Attic vase painting. It constitutes an embellishment of Mende's own archaic coin type, the ass alone. But the animal is now represented without the evidence of sexual excitement which characterized sixth-century versions on both coins and vases. Dionysus' reclining position is also a newer feature which contributes greatly to the grace and gentleness of the type. It allows the god a dignity which is lacking when, for example, he is depicted being helped onto his mount by his attendants.

The refined style of this coin matches the delicacy of its content. The modeling is both softer and simpler than on the figures of the transitional period [67, 68, 71]. Technical mastery is apparent in the foreshortening and in the torsion of the body, which is handled much more naturally than on the coins we have seen thus far. The slack muscles, curved back and loose grip on the cup combine to create a sense of repose. Both the concept and the means derive from the work of Phidias.

The reverse of this tetradrachm is built around the shallow square incuse type which developed early in the North Greek area [60, 62]. Even the grapevine in the center is conceived geometrically rather than realistically, forced into a symmetrical quadripartite form. The choice of type is surely related to the fact that Mende was one of the chief wine-producing centers of the ancient world. The conjunction of obverse and reverse types suggests that at Mende, at least, Dionysus was now viewed primarily as the god of wine.

75 SILVER TETRADRACHM OF CATANA

OBVERSE:
Fast quadriga left passing turning post, young driver crouching, above Nike flying right holding wreath and tablet with die engraver's signature ETAIN, crab beneath triple exergual line, dotted border.

REVERSE:
ΚΑΤΑΝΑΙΩΝ, laureate head of Apollo left with hair in krobylos, fillet in front, crayfish behind.

Attic standard, weight 16.94 gm; diameter 26 mm. ↗

Signed by Euainetus. Struck circa 415 B.C.

Published: Sotheby's (H.P. Smith collection, 5 June 1905), lot 64; Hirsch 20 (1907), lot 115; Jameson 1 (1913), 550; *Kunstfreund* lot 89.

Same dies: *Euainetos* pls. 11, 12; *Götter Griechenlands* pl. 7; Rizzo pl. 14, 6; Kraay-Hirmer 42; Gulbenkian 188, 189; *AGC* figs. 422, 423; G. Giacosa, *Uomo e cavallo sulla moneta greca* (Bellinzona, 1973), pls. 42, 43. Same reverse die: Pfeiff *Apollon* pl. 46.

Ex H.P. Smith collection, New York; R. Jameson collection, Paris.

Catana was located about thirty miles up the east coast of Sicily from Syracuse. It adopted the Syracusan quadriga obverse rather early, and it also participated prominently in the development of the numismatic rich style in the last years of the fifth century. Catana shared with Syracuse the services of Euainetus, the greatest numismatic artist of antiquity. This signed masterpiece is virtually contemporary with his first work at Syracuse, in which he introduced a mature treatment of the quadriga in high action. Euainetus' scheme, a popular one on contemporary works in other media, involves a three-quarter view of the chariot but overlapping horses in profile. It nevertheless achieves real pictorial depth, enhanced in this case by the device of superimposition. Realistic, individualized treatment of each horse contributes to a restless visual complexity. The sense of excitement is heightened by the crouching posture of the driver as he whips his horses on to victory. Yet the design is intentionally small in scale and engraved with consummate fluidity.

Apollo was the traditional reverse type at Catana, where he probably was worshiped as civic founder as at Leontini [65]. This version of his head, though unsigned, is universally accepted as the work of Euainetus. The identical face appears on Catanian drachms and a Syracusan tetradrachm signed by this artist. The Apollo head on this tetradrachm is characterized by small, rather precious features and delicate modeling used as an accent to create rather deep shadows around these features. Especially expressive is the shading under the eye which brings out the lower eyelid to enhance the seductive squint earlier associated with Aphrodite [72]. The lush hair revives a coiffure of the transitional period, frequently worn by Apollo in red-figured vase painting of around 500 B.C. Thereafter it appears sporadically down to the mid-fifth century, as on the beautiful white-ground cups at Delphi and in Boston. The krobylos was also the usual coiffure of Apollo on transitional tetradrachms of Catana, where however it is flat and restrained. Its writhing motion here serves to create a new tone of cultivated eroticism. There is a disquieting sexual ambiguity to this head of Apollo which can also be observed in the effeminate beauty of male figures in contemporary Attic vase painting. We shall have occasion to see that this dreamy languor is fundamental to Euainetus' work in this period, and his manner with it makes him one of the memorable stylists of all Greek art.

The subsidiary elements on the reverse are not intended to mark an issue. Instead they seem to complete the symbolism of the main type. The crayfish is a symbol of the local river Amenanus. The other object is a fillet or woollen skein, in this case knotted and terminating in a bell. The fillet is a token of religious consecration [78] which was, among other uses, bound around the head of a victorious athlete. A similar fillet appears carried by Nike on the earliest tetradrachms of Catana, circa 460 B.C. The crayfish and fillet on the tetradrachm of Euainetus may allude to local games in honor of the river Amenanus. Such games were a very typical expression of West Greek patriotism. In this agonistic context Apollo is to be viewed in his aspect as patron of the arts and of civilized institutions, more than as civic founder.

76 SILVER TETRADRACHM OF AGRIGENTUM

OBVERSE:

Fast quadriga driven right by charioteer in long chiton, above Nike flying left to crown him, beneath horses' feet a trailing rein and die engraver's signature MYP, Scylla right in exergue, dotted border.

REVERSE:

[AKP]—AΓANTINON, two eagles perched right on dead hare lying on rocks, the nearer bird with closed wings and head thrown back, the other with spread wings and head lowered.

Attic standard, weight 17.04 gm; diameter 28 mm. ↑

Signed by Myr . . . , reverse attributed to Polyc . . . . Struck circa 412 B.C.

Published: Hamburg auction (2 April 1894), lot 135; Sotheby's (Rothschild collection, 28 May 1900), lot 83; Rizzo pl. 2, 6 and pl. 4, 3; 'Akragantine Decadrachms'' p. 2, 3b and pl. 1, B/γ; *Kunstfreund* lot 80. Mentioned: ''Signatures de graveurs'' p. 299.

Same dies: *BMC Sicily* 53=''Akragantine Decadrachms'' 3a. Same obverse die: Kraay-Hirmer 177.

Ex Baron Rothschild collection, London; Mutiaux collection, Paris.

One of two specimens from these dies.

Agrigentum, located on the southern coast of Sicily, was the wealthiest and most powerful town on the island after Syracuse itself. Nevertheless toward the end of the fifth century it joined the general trend to conform local coinages to that of Syracuse. Thus Agrigentum adopted the Syracusan quadriga as its tetradrachm obverse and also adapted the prevailing ornate taste to its own formerly simple types.

This version of the racing scene is larger and bolder than the similar design by Euainetus on the preceding tetradrachm. The horses are under better control, running rather than rearing. But the detail of the broken rein, trailing under the horses' legs, still suggests the possibility of an accident. The positions of the horses' heads, the pattern of their legs and the broken rein have exact parallels at Syracuse, but reversed, as if one of the artists had deliberately copied his die from an existing coin. It is impossible to be sure which city was prior and which the imitator, for the other cities of Sicily were quickly able to innovate within

the rich style. At any rate the artist of this coin was proud enough to sign his work: MYP . . . , Myr(on?). Despite the larger scale of his work, he is unsurpassed even by Euainetus in his flair for minutely graceful engraving. This talent is evident in the well-drawn tendons of the horses' legs, the soft garment of the charioteer and the sinuous Scylla in the exergue.

The reverse type of this tetradrachm is a development of the traditional Akragantine obverse type, a standing eagle. The new design involves compositional complexity, emotional power and elements of landscape creating a degree of visual space. The animation of the scene relates it to the rich style of other Sicilian coinage, but its contents and mood could not be more opposite to the prevailing air of sensuous refinement. This powerful composition is unsigned but can be attributed to the hand of one Polyc(rates?), the inventor of this type. He may possibly be identical with an engraver Po . . . who worked at Olympia before 416 B.C. and later surfaced as the sculptor Polyclitus the Lesser. His pairing with Myr . . . is felicitous, for both artists have a bold style supported by careful detail. The masterpiece of their collaboration is the Akragantine decadrachm (see following).

77 SILVER DECADRACHM OF AGRIGENTUM

OBVERSE:
ΑΚΡΑΓΑΣ, fast quadriga driven left by Helios, above eagle flying
left with head thrown back and carrying snake, crab below, dotted
border.

REVERSE:
Two eagles perched left on dead hare lying on rocks, the nearer
bird with closed wings and head thrown back, the farther bird
with spread wings and head lowered, grasshopper symbol in right
field.

Attic standard, weight 42.18 gm; diameter 37 mm. ↘

Attributed to Myr . . . and Polyc . . . . Struck circa 411 B.C.

Same dies: *SNG Lloyd* 817; Rizzo pl. 2, 8; "Akragantine Decadrachms" 8 (F/θ).

The seventh specimen known.

The height of prestige for a fifth-century Greek lay in winning
an event at the Olympic games. In 412 B.C. this happiness befell
a certain Exainetus, a citizen of Agrigentum. The celebration of
his homecoming was magniloquent: he was accompanied into
the city by a procession of three hundred chariots drawn by
paired white horses. A small issue of decadrachms was struck
for the occasion as well.

The types of the Akragantine decadrachms are related to those
of contemporary tetradrachms (see preceding). But here they are
enormously enriched, both visually and symbolically. The obverse depicts the chariot of the sun at the noonday zenith of its
course. It is a flattering allusion to the success of Exainetus and

77 SILVER DECADRACHM (continued)

perhaps also a compliment to the island of Rhodes [88], which had sponsored the colonization of Agrigentum in the sixth century. The three-quarter angle of the quadriga is carried off more persuasively than on the numerous Sicilian tetradrachms which show the *chariot* at an angle but the *horses* in profile. Here the horses appear to veer toward the viewer in a grand and daring effect. The small eagle and crab are a gesture to the traditional types of Agrigentum's coinage, but here they fit symbolically into the whole scene, representing the heavens above and the sea below.

The reverse scene with two eagles exulting over a hare seems to be an illustration of the famous first chorus of Aeschylus' *Agamemnon* (114ff):

> The king of birds to the king of ships appearing,
>   one black and the other silver in the tail,
> Hard by the palace on the right hand, the spear-hand,
> On an all-conspicuous perch
> Devouring a hare, swollen with fruit, her young,
> Cruelly struck down from her last run.
>   (author's translation)

The eagles are an omen sent from Zeus to Agamemnon and Menelaus, commanding the sacrifice of Iphigenia before the Greek fleet might set sail for the Trojan War. Aeschylus was much appreciated in Sicily: he had visited the island twice and had written a play for the foundation of Aetna [64]. Most significantly, he had died in Sicily and was entombed at Gela, not far from Agrigentum.

It is clear that the Akragantine decadrachm was conceived as a work of exceptional artistry. Its compositions are forceful, yet the engraving is full of virtuosity and subtle effects. It was created in an era when Sicilian artists often signed their coins, yet this ambitious masterpiece oddly enough is unsigned. It can be attributed to the two artists who signed several magnificent contemporary tetradrachms at Agrigentum. The obverse is the

crowning achievement of Myr(on?), an engraver who devoted himself to racing scenes. The reverse comes from the hand of the mint's eagle specialist Polyc(rates?).

78 SILVER TETRADRACHM OF SELINUS

OBVERSE:
  Fast quadriga driven right by Apollo, Artemis beside him in chariot holding billowing veil, wreath above, in exergue ΣΕΛΙΝΟΝΤΙΟΝ and grain ear right.
REVERSE:
  Nude river god Selinus standing left, sacrificing from phiale over lighted altar and holding lustral branch, sacrificial cock left on threshold of altar, in right field selinon leaf and votive statuette of charging bull, linear border.

Attic standard, weight 17.08 gm; diameter 27 mm.↓

Attributed to Euth . . . (?) Struck circa 412 B.C.

Same dies: Schwabacher 45; Regling 572. Same obverse die: Rizzo pl. 33, 11; Gulbenkian 247; Kraay-Hirmer 189.

The finest of six known.

This tetradrachm represents the last issue of Selinus before the city was destroyed by the Carthaginian invasion of 409 B.C. Its types are updated versions of those we have already seen on [71]. The obverse is the only example of a galloping quadriga in the Selinuntine tetradrachm series. It is extremely close to an unusual quadriga die at Syracuse signed by the artist Euth . . . , otherwise unknown. The distinctive shared feature is the fan-like spread of the horses with their heads arranged like a row of cresting waves, a scheme which despite its formality comes close to a convincing three-quarter view of the team. The Selinuntine and Syracusan racing scenes differ in several respects. At Syracuse the charioteer is a winged Eros, a god not otherwise represented on the Syracusan coinage. At Selinus the occupants of the quadriga are the traditional divine twins Apollo and Artemis, but the manner of their depiction is new. Of particular interest is the use of the *velificatio* or billowing veil motif, which dramatizes the speed of the chariot but also introduces the language of erotic art for the first time to the Selinuntine coinage. The subsidiary symbols of the Syracusan die apparently allude to naval victory, for example the Nike who crowns the horses also holds an *aphlaston*, the stern ornament of a warship. There is no marine symbolism on the tetradrachm of Selinus, but the barley stalk in the exergue may suggest a link with the Syracusan tetradrachm series employing this same symbol.

The reverse type has all the same elements as on the earlier tetradrachm but the style is much advanced. The figure of Selinus epitomizes the developments in figure representation during the second half of the fifth century, developments associated with the name of Polyclitus. A harmonious, relaxed appearance is achieved by resting all the weight of the body on only one leg, throwing the hip out into a gentle median curve and tilting the axes of pelvis and shoulder in an alternating rhythm. The formerly excessive breadth of the shoulders is reduced, and modeling is softer.

The art of this tetradrachm is individualized by several exquisite details, such as the delicate foliage of the lustral branch, the unprecedented depiction of the sprinkled incense and the billowing veil of Artemis on the obverse. Such minute effects are unusual and argue that the same hand is responsible for both

dies of our coin. It is furthermore not improbable that the artist is the same who created the Syracusan prototype. Telling similarities are the scale and scheme of the quadriga, duplicated nowhere else in Sicily; the resort to erotic motifs; and the minute engraving.

The relationship between this pair of tetradrachms is uncertain, but it seems likely that we are dealing with a coordinated issue of Syracuse and Selinus, who were close political allies. The Syracusan tetradrachm has traditionally been associated with the repulse of the Athenian invasion of 415–413 B.C. However, coinage was far more often minted to finance military activities than to commemorate them. In 412 B.C. Syracuse and Selinus sent a combined war fleet—ten Syracusan ships, two Selinuntine—to the Aegean under the command of the Syracusan general Hermocrates to aid Sparta in its war against Athens. This endeavor, instigated and dominated by Syracuse, could well have been financed by a single issue of coinage produced at Syracuse in the name of the two participating cities.

79 SILVER TETRADRACHM OF CAMARINA

OBVERSE:
>Fast quadriga driven right by Athena, above Nike flying left to crown her, in exergue [KAM]AP—IN—AI[ΩN] and two amphorae.

REVERSE:
>Head of young Heracles right in lion skin headdress, bow in right field.

Attic standard, weight 17.38 gm; diameter 25 mm. ↘

Attributed to Euainetus. Struck circa 410 B.C.

Published: Sotheby, Wilkinson and Hodge (20 January 1898), lot 46; J. Ward, *Greek Coins and Their Parent Cities* (New York, 1902), 170; Sotheby's Zurich (Metropolitan Museum 2, 4 April 1973), lot 122; *Kamarina* 153, example 3 (O11/R20).

Same dies: Hess-Leu (16 April 1957), lot 68. Same obverse die: *SNG Lloyd* 870; Hess-Leu (27 March 1956), lot 74. Same reverse die: *SNG Oxford* 1698; *SNG ANS* 1207.

Exhibited: Burlington Fine Art Club, 1903.

Ex J. Ward collection, New York; Metropolitan Museum of Art.

Extremely rare variety: three specimens listed in *Kamarina*.

Camarina, a Syracusan colony on the south coast of Sicily, was several times destroyed and recolonized in the course of its early history. As a result it was slow to achieve either political or economic importance. Camarina produced a major coinage only in the last quarter of the fifth century, probably in connection with the Sicilian phase of the Peloponnesian War. The brilliant style of this coinage shows Syracusan influence, but there is much that is original at Camarina. Such independence reflects the political realities, for in these war-torn years Camarina either opposed its old mother city or held itself neutral.

The obverse type of this tetradrachm is yet another quadriga inspired by types of Syracuse. Stylistically it is very close to the Catanian racing scene signed by Euainetus [75]. The mirror image relationship raises the possibility of direct copying from the Catanian coin, especially since this is a new variant of the quadriga scene within the Camarinian series. The charioteer at Camarina is invariably Athena, chief goddess of the city. Her presence suggests a connection with a favorite design for hammered phialae or sacrificial dishes, featuring four galloping quadrigas carrying Heracles, Athena, Ares and Dionysus and interpreted as a depiction of the apotheosis of Heracles [4]. Such an allusion here is reinforced by the reverse type. On the other hand an agonistic or competitive interpretation is supported by the presence of the Nike and by the two jugs in the exergue, which are probably prize amphorae given to the victors at games. They are thus related to the major type in the same way as the exergual symbols of the Syracusan decadrachms of the following decade [84ff].

The reverse type is a head of Heracles, the national hero of the Dorian Greeks who colonized southern Sicily and a perennially popular subject of Greek art. His introduction to Camarina's coinage occurs puzzlingly during the years of Camarinian disaffection from Doric Sicily and sympathy for Athens. The beardless type was introduced at Camarina by a celebrated local engraver, Exakestidas. This head follows his prototype in some details, such as the fine, woolly texture of the lion's mane and the device of concealing the truncation of the neck beneath the tied paws of the lion. But the face of Heracles according to Exakestidas is impassive and idealized, a fleshier version of Polyclitan classicism. This head on the other hand has a scowling expression completely at odds with the classical ideal. Furthermore the delicate features seem a bit incongruous in a hero noted for his burly strength. The bow-shaped mouth, the fine pointed nose, the graceful lower eyelid, the use of modeling for emphasis, the rich side curls and even the shape of the ear recall the artistic language of the Catanian tetradrachm [75], already linked to this coin by obverse mirroring. This is surely another work of Euainetus, whose employment at Camarina is already established for the didrachm series where he also worked alongside or shortly after Exakestidas. It is proof of the artist's stature and originality that he succeeds in creating a lyric version of a quintessentially epic hero.

80 SILVER DIDRACHM OF CAMARINA

OBVERSE:

ΚΑΜΑΡΙΝΑΙΟ—Ν, diademed head of horned river god Hipparis left,
under neck truncation die engraver's signature ΥΛ?, dotted border.

REVERSE:

ΚΑΜΑΡΙΝΑ—[ΙΟΝ?] between double concentric circles of border,
nymph Camarina with billowing veil seated right on swan flying
left, waves below, fish swimming left below waves, double linear
border.

Attic standard, weight 8.30 gm; diameter 25 mm. ↓

Signed illegibly. Struck circa 410 B.C.

Published: *Euainetos* fig. 15; *Kamarina* 158, example 8 (01/R1), pls.
21, 23.

Same dies: Rizzo pl. 7, 3. Same obverse die: Regling 541.

Ex S. Schocken collection, Jerusalem.

Extremely rare: nine specimens listed in *Kamarina*.

This great rarity is one of the most stunning masterpieces of
Greek coinage, and the Hunt specimen is the finest example
known. The types exemplify a contemporary Sicilian fad for
depicting river gods on coinage, but the fad itself only reflects
the importance of local water spirits in an agricultural economy. Here the subject of the obverse is the river god Hipparis,
personified as a beautiful youth with a small horn above his
forehead; for the significance of the horn, see [71]. The river god
type bears a general relation to the Diadoumenos of Polyclitus
and the numerous derivative youthful athletes, but this example is decidedly sensuous and evocative where they are epitomes
of restraint. The full, arching upper lip may refer to a different
prototype, an Eros by Phidias known in various copies. However
this head certainly possesses an individual distinction. The unusual treatment of the hair, which is reduced to broad, flat
ribbons, may be intended to suggest the clinging smoothness of
wet hair or even to evoke water grasses. The delicate features,
the near-effeminacy and the mood of dreamy eroticism relate
the head to the contemporary rich style and above all to the
poetic works of Euainetus [75, 79]. Indeed the line of the profile,
the treatment of the eye and the atmospheric modeling could
come from the repertoire of that great stylist. The signature
below the neck is difficult to read and has been interpreted as
ΥΛ, assumed to be a retrograde abbreviation for a name beginning
Ly . . . . This splendid artist is otherwise unknown, and it is
tempting to hypothesize that we are dealing here with a semi-
legible signature of Euainetus.

The reverse offers a brilliant version of a motif popular on painted vases, gemstones, reliefs and mirrors—a graceful woman riding sidesaddle on a goose, swan or other animal. The subject is
generally but not invariably the epiphany of Aphrodite. The
billowing veil or *velificatio* is a salient detail of many of these
depictions, though it has an independent existence as a motif
with erotic overtones [78]. Here the subject is probably the
nymph Camarina, spirit of the local lake, who was invoked in
Pindar's Fifth Olympian Ode (1–14). This rendition is exceptionally delicate, with a tight composition built up of graceful curves
and virtuistic engraving of incredible minuteness. Its romantic
mood matches the charm of the obverse. The author of this *tour
de force* has sometimes been identified as Exakestidas on the basis

of a scarcely legible signature on the right side of the coin between the double lines of the border. But the reading is questionable. ΕΥΑ is at least equally possible, or the letters may not be an
artist's signature at all but rather the end of the ethnic inscription, ΚΑΜΑΡΙΝΑ—[ΙΟΝ?]. Furthermore the intimate and sensuous
appeal of the type finds no echo in the signed work of Exakestidas, a gifted but more straightforward classicist. Both technique
and content argue for a single artist for both dies of this coin,
either the unknown Ly . . . or Euainetus, whose participation
elsewhere in this didrachm series is unquestioned.

81 SILVER TETRADRACHM OF SYRACUSE

OBVERSE:
> Fast quadriga driven left by female charioteer holding torch (Demeter, Persephone or Hecate), above Nike flying right to crown her, grain ear left beneath double exergual line, dotted border.

REVERSE:
> [Σ]ΥΡ—ΑΚ—[Ο]ΣΙΟΣ, head of Athena inclined slightly to left, wearing triple-crested helmet ornamented with palmettes, whorl-shaped earring and necklace of pendant acorns, engraver's signature ΕΥ—ΛΕΙΔ/Α in tiny letters across helmet, four dolphins around, the lower pair emerging from behind the goddess's hair.

Attic standard, weight 16.48 gm; diameter 28 mm. ✓

Signed by Eucleidas. Struck circa 410 B.C.

Published: *Kunstfreund* lot 120.

Same dies: Tudeer 58 (V21/R36); Rizzo pl. 43, 22 and pl. 45, 4a and 5; *PCG* pl. 17, 69; Gulbenkian 282 and frontispiece. Same reverse die: Kraay-Hirmer color pl. 4, no. 111; *AGC* fig. 400.

Tudeer cites nine specimens from these dies.

In the last quarter of the fifth century Syracuse was the fountainhead of the rich style on Sicilian coinage. Among its most beautiful and celebrated products are two tetradrachm issues featuring three-quarter heads. The subject here is the warrior goddess Athena. This is her only appearance on the coinage of Syracuse, and at first blush it seems puzzling coming so soon after the unsuccessful Athenian invasion of Sicily of 415–413 B.C. But Athena was also one of the chief divinities of Syracuse. Her large temple was erected after the battle of Himera in 480 B.C. [64]. Thus she definitely had an aspect as patroness of the Greeks in their confrontations with barbarian peoples. Her depiction on the coinage is probably an appeal for her protection in the face of an even greater Carthaginian invasion, which was in fact to destroy the Greek settlements of western and southern Sicily by 405 B.C. The Temple of Athena, incidentally, was located on the island of Ortygia. Thus the dolphins could be carried over from the traditional Arethusa designs with exactly the same symbolic function [63].

Eucleidas' head of Athena is one of the most ornate works of this entire period. The triple-crested helmet is covered all over with exquisitely engraved palmettes, and the goddess's wavy tresses are rendered minutely, with individual hairs indicated within the locks. Their different texture makes it possible to recognize the double hoops of her earrings. The addition of the dolphins makes for a turbulent composition whose only resting place is Athena's calm, commanding face. This is strongly engraved, so that it holds its own against the ceaseless motion around it. The deep shadows of the face also create an illusion of depth far exceeding the actual relief of the design. This sense of receding space is further enhanced by imaginative arrangement of the dolphins, two of which emerge from behind the head.

The inspiration for this head was undoubtedly the celebrated statue of Athena Parthenos by Phidias which stood on the Athenian Acropolis. Her head alone, with the triple crest of the helmet lowered, became a popular subject for votive and toreutic art in the latter fifth century [35]. Eucleidas' head of Athena stands out from the mass of mediocre copies as an inspired

reinterpretation. The substitution of graceful palmettes for the bulky griffin and sphinx ornaments of the original Phidian helmet changes the character of the head from monumental to delicate. There is a sense of closeness to nature which is not normally counted among the attributes of Athena and suggests that we may be dealing with an assimilation of Athena to Arethusa. The famous Koul Oba medallions constitute a perfect foil to the genius of Eucleidas because their broad, heavy-featured faces demonstrate a common source even as the grotesque ornamentation of the helmet robs them of appeal. Eucleidas' simplified helmet is repeated in the many numismatic versions of the head of Athena Parthenos, demonstrating a probable derivation from his work.

82 SILVER TETRADRACHM OF SYRACUSE

OBVERSE:
    Head of Arethusa inclined slightly to left, wearing ampyx, pendant earring and wire choker, hair floating freely, four dolphins around, three of them emerging from hair, engraver's signature [ΚΙΜΩ]Ν across ampyx (mostly worn off on this specimen), dotted border, [ΑΡΕΘΟΣΑ] outside border.

REVERSE:
    Fast quadriga driven left by crouching charioteer, above Nike flying left to crown him, engraver's signature ΚΙΜΩΝ in tiny letters between double exergual line, in exergue ΣΥΡΑΚΟΣΙΩ[Ν] and ear of grain left, linear border.

Attic standard, weight 17.07 gm; diameter 25 mm. ↑

Signed by Cimon. Struck circa 410 B.C.

Published: Sotheby, Wilkinson and Hodge (Bunbury collection, 15–23 June 1896), lot 465; Comte A. du Chastel, *Syracuse, ses monnaies d'argent et d'or au point de vue artistique* (London, 1898), 89; Sotheby's (Benson collection, 8 February 1909), lot 347; Jameson 1 (1913), pl. 41, 822; Tudeer 80c (29/53).

Same dies: Rizzo pl. 48, 11 (obverse) and 10 (reverse).

Ex E. Bunbury collection, Cambridge; F. S. Benson collection; R. Jameson collection, Paris.

Very rare die combination: Tudeer lists five specimens.

Eucleidas' head of Athena (see preceding) was soon followed by a frontal head of rather different character, the work of Cimon, an artist previously unknown at the Syracusan mint. He was perhaps an émigré from Athens, for his name is typical of that city but rare elsewhere, and he was to become the leading exponent of Phidian style at Syracuse. His charming face of Arethusa eschews the high relief, deep shadows and violent contrasts which give Eucleidas' goddess her appropriate air of power. Its style owes much to the three-quarter heads of the Parthenon sculptures, with their thick-rimmed, almond-shaped eyes and full lips with downturned corners. Arethusa's head is even more directly related to the seductive facing female heads, usually identified as Aphrodite, which constituted a popular motif for the decoration of bronze mirror covers of Corinthian manufacture. Such articles would surely have been known in Syracuse, a wealthy city and a Corinthian colony besides. Because of the imprecision of their dating, it is impossible to be certain whether the mirrors are contemporary with Cimon's tetradrachm or slightly later, but they do constitute a vivid example of the cross fertilization among different branches of art.

Cimon has brilliantly emphasized the watery nature of his subject by loosening her hair so that it appears to float in a liquid medium. The position of the dolphins, though borrowed from Eucleidas, works to enhance the illusion. A unique feature of the design is that Cimon labeled his head as Arethusa in tiny letters outside the dotted border. (This legend is off the flan in the Hunt specimen.) Such labeling is unusual in Greek coinage generally, and this is the first such instance in the Syracusan tetradrachm series. It is probably no coincidence that a facing head of Apollo from Catana signed by Choirion, which bears an exact resemblance to another published mirror, also bears a legend identifying its subject. Such legends support the notion that the artists may have derived inspiration from an outside source and wished to dispel confusion as to the identity of their subjects. In Cimon's case the concern was misplaced, for his facing Arethusa head became one of the most widely imitated of coin types and was also used to make molds for the decoration of South Italian black-glazed pottery.

The pattern of similarities and contrasts between the two Syracusan facing heads indicates an intentional parallelism. Besides the position of the dolphins and the leftward orientation of both heads, the two artists adopted a similar method of concealing their signatures. It seems likely that Cimon's masterwork came later because of a technical adjustment. Throughout the Syracusan series the head of Arethusa normally occupied the reverse of the tetradrachms. But Eucleidas' facing head with its high relief resulted in a weak reverse die which broke in use. (The raised left edge of [81] is the result of that die break.) The obverse die however was much stronger because it was fixed into an anvil. Cimon's decision to place his facing head of Arethusa on the obverse was presumably motivated by this practical consideration.

Cimon also introduced his own version of the quadriga scene. It by no means lacks excitement, but in contrast to earlier treatments in the manner of Euainetus its movement is abstracted into a single compositional line quite similar to that in the votive stele of Echelos and Basile.

83 SILVER TETRADRACHM OF CATANA

OBVERSE:
> Laureate head of Apollo three-quarters left, in right field die engraver's signature HPAKΛEIΔAΣ.

REVERSE:
> Fast quadriga left, above Nike alighting from flight, holding kerykeion and wreath to crown charioteer, broken rein trailing from bridle of farthest horse, in exergue KATANAIΩN over tunny fish left.

Attic standard, weight 17.17 gm; diameter 30 mm. →

Signed by Heracleidas. Struck circa 410 B.C.

Same dies: Jameson 1 (1913), 546; *SNG Lloyd* 902; *SNG Lockett* 730; Rizzo pl. 14, 11; Gulbenkian 192.

Rare.

This small cluster of three-quarter heads illustrates a late fifth-century fad for frontality, not only on coinage but in associated arts such as bas relief, gemstones and decorative metalwork. The technical challenges of depicting the human face in low relief from these angles had already been overcome by the Parthenon sculptors. The sudden popularity of the motif in small scale art and more particularly its attraction for the finest die engravers may be related to two characteristics of the rich style which have already been commented upon: the striving for spatial depth which we have seen in the Sicilian quadriga scenes of this period; and the pursuit of emotional intensity. It is impossible to state for certain which city or which artist first sparked the enthusiasm for three-quarter heads on coinage. But the Catanian tetradrachms of Heracleidas seem to reflect a familiarity with experiments in frontality at Syracuse (see preceding) in their transfer of the divine head from its traditional position on the reverse to the obverse of the coin. A second interesting parallel is that Heracleidas' facing head issue, like Cimon's tetradrachm masterpieces, comprises just two pairs of dies. Each issue employs one reverse die on which Nike flies in her customary horizontal position and another on which she alights on the vertical, as here.

Apollo, together with his variant Helios, was to prove the most popular subject for frontal treatment on coinage. The conception of an Apollo with a laurel wreath and medium length, fluffy hair is common to the coins of Catana, Amphipolis and Clazomenae. Heracleidas' version seems to relate to a scarce statuary type which probably originated at Athens about this time and which is characterized by a midline part of the hair with flat waves forming a squarish hairline. Heracleidas' two dies are deliberately contrasted. This one adheres to the classical standard of beauty as defined by Phidias. The face is nobly masculine. The slightly drooping eyelids and the thick, barely parted lips create the gentle, abstracted expression of Apollo as the god of inspiration, but his dreaminess is not exaggerated as in so many fourth-century treatments [90]. Heracleidas' second die is both more original and less aesthetic: its incisive style, burning eyes, asymmetrical features and wispy hair seem to prefigure the expressionistic iconography of Helios, the god of the sun in its physical aspect [88]. Heracleidas was surely an artist of unusual breadth, showing in the space of one issue his mastery of two distinct and contrasted styles, one traditional and the other innovative. Indeed, it has been argued that the notion of style as something consciously chosen is a distinguishing characteristic of *hellenistic* art.

84 SILVER DECADRACHM OF SYRACUSE

OBVERSE:
Fast quadriga driven left by female charioteer, above Nike flying right to crown her, die engraver's signature ΚΙΜΩΝ in tiny letters on upper side of exergual line, in exergue panoply of arms labeled ΑΘΛΑ, dotted border.

REVERSE:
ΣΥΡΑΚΟΣΙΩΝ, head of Arethusa left, wearing ampyx and sphendone of heavy netting, triple-drop earring and bead necklace, die engraver's signature ΚΙ/Μ on ampyx, four dolphins around, one of them emerging from neck truncation, dotted border.

Attic standard, weight 42.55 gm; diameter 38 mm. ←

Signed by Cimon. Struck circa 405 B.C.

Same dies: K. Regling, "Dekadrachmen des Kimon," *ABKPM* (1914–15), 1; Jongkees 1 (Λ/α); Rizzo pl. 50, 1 and pl. 52, 1; Kraay-Hirmer 116–117; Gulbenkian 301.

Jongkees cites twenty-one specimens.

The decadrachm denomination was revived at Syracuse toward the end of the fifth century, probably to celebrate the city's deliverance from the Carthaginian siege of 405 B.C. The Carthaginian offensives of 409 and 406/5 B.C. destroyed the Greek cities of western and southern Sicily. The crisis also brought an end to democratic government at Syracuse. A new tyrant arose, Dionysius I, who negotiated the Carthaginian withdrawal. His decadrachm thus parallels the Demareteion [64] both in its commemorative function and in the climate of artistic patronage which produced it, though the underlying political facts are a trifle less heroic.

The artist commissioned to design the new decadrachm was Cimon, who had already produced the lovely facing head tetradrachm [82]. Cimon's new creation is notable for its Phidian serenity, so contrary to the turbulent excitement which characterizes the earlier phase of the rich style [75ff]. On the obverse Cimon has arranged his horses' legs in approximately parallel action, and all the heads face duly forward, with one just slightly lowered to create an accent. This disciplined team seems to glide forward effortlessly, whereas earlier versions churn about at the cost of their forward momentum. Cimon's conception of the racing scene is perhaps a subtle metaphor for the political climate, purged of the inefficient infighting which plagued ancient democracy.

The forward thrust of Cimon's quadriga requires generous horizontal space to achieve balance. The result is a smaller scale for the major type and a larger than usual exergue. This Cimon filled with a panoply of arms, labeled as prizes. This artist apparently had a fondness for explanatory legends [82], but in this case he failed to supply enough information. The arms are presumably the prizes offered to the winning charioteer depicted above them. But it is unclear whether the two types constitute a reference to specific games or merely to competitive sport in general.

The head of Arethusa on the reverse, despite its ornate accessories, is in the spiritual tradition of high classical art with its characteristic noble serenity. It bears a general resemblance to the famous Laborde head from the environs of the Parthenon. The Attic grave stele of Hegeso offers a parallel for the richly dressed hair which is nevertheless firmly controlled by its jeweled net, so that it contributes to the air of conscious restraint. But Cimon's proportions—small nose, compressed lips, heavy chin—are highly individual, and the realistic shape and modeling of the narrowed eye give the face a human quality which looks forward to fourth-century artistic concerns.

85 SILVER DECADRACHM OF SYRACUSE

OBVERSE:
Fast quadriga driven left by female charioteer, above Nike flying right to crown her, in exergue panoply of arms labeled AΘΛΑ, dotted border.

REVERSE:
ΣΥΡΑΚΟΣΙ—ΩΝ, head of Arethusa left, wearing ampyx and sphendone of heavy netting, pendant earring and bead necklace, die engraver's signature KI on ampyx, four dolphins around, dotted border.

Attic standard, weight 43.12 gm; diameter 36 mm. →

Signed by Cimon. Struck circa 400 B.C.

Published: Hirsch 32 (Virzi collection, 1912), lot 309; K. Regling, "Dekadrachmen des Kimon," *ABKPM* (1914–15), 7d; *BM Quarterly* 2, no. 3 (1927), p. 59; *NC* 1928, p. 4, no. 4; H. Boerger, "Von der Münzkunst der sizilischen Griechen," *Die Antike* 1931, pl. 30, 2; Jongkees 7h, pl. 2, B/ʒ; *PCG* pl. 17, 66.

Ex I. Virzi collection; R. Allatini collection, London; on loan to the British Museum; R. Lockett collection.

The most perfect of thirteen specimens cited by Jongkees.

Cimon's original decadrachm, struck from a single pair of dies (see preceding), was followed by subsequent issues involving an Arethusa head of slightly different style. The points of contrast are subtle but numerous. The eye and eyebrow are articulated by crisp lines rather than modeled. Their size and proportions derive from a mental scheme rather than from observation. The nose is heavier, the lips thick and rather pouting in expression. The face is relatively fleshless, and there are little creases on the neck known as "Venus rings." The lines of the hair are notably coarser, and the coiffure is far more turbulent as the loose curls burst forth around the ampyx, by the temple and across the crown of the head. Furthermore the psychological element is more prominent.

Although this sultry Arethusa head is signed by Cimon on the ampyx like the preceding, it seems to be the product of a different artistic personality. This was the conclusion of Jongkees, the authority on the Cimonian decadrachms. He marshaled evidence to show that the phenomenon of false signatures was common in various branches of Greek art and must have sprung from a different conception of authenticity from our own. Jongkees has not been generally followed. But the important question in any case is not the authorship of the die but its quality. The concern with individuality is a forward-looking trait. It brings the decadrachm into relation with contemporary literary trends, mirroring the fascination with personality in the history of Thucydides, in the dialogues of Plato and especially in the tragedies of Euripides with their passionate heroines. (Euripides, incidentally, was a favorite author at Syracuse: after the defeat of the Athenian invasion of 415–413 B.C. war prisoners who could recite choruses from Euripides were spared from slavery in the quarries.) The pursuit of individuality was to become a powerful theme in the visual arts of the fourth century, culminating on coinage in the medium of portraiture.

The obverse die of this decadrachm is a very close copy of the prototype and preserves its spirit faithfully.

86 SILVER DECADRACHM OF SYRACUSE

OBVERSE:
>Fast quadriga driven left by female charioteer, above Nike flying right to crown her, in exergue panoply of arms labeled [AΘ]ΛΑ, dotted border (mostly off flan).

REVERSE:
>[ΣΤΡΑΚΟΣΙΩΝ], head of Arethusa left crowned with leaves, wearing triple-drop earring and bead necklace, four dolphins around, die engraver's signature [ΕΥ—ΑΙΝΕ] beneath dolphin at neck truncation, dotted border (also off flan).

Attic standard, weight 41.95 gm; diameter 35 mm. ↗

Signed by Euainetus. Struck circa 390 B.C.

Same dies: *de Luynes* 1250; A. Gallatin, *Syracusan Dekadrachms of the Euainetos Type* (Cambridge, Mass., 1930), R.IV/C.XII.

Ex S. Schocken Collection, Jerusalem.

Ten specimens cited by Gallatin.

Only a few years after the creation of the Cimonian decadrachms [84, 85] Syracuse commissioned a new ten-drachma medallion from Euainetus, who had an even longer association with the Syracusan mint and a distinguished *oeuvre* at other Sicilian mints as well. The new decadrachms perhaps commemorated the victorious campaign of 397–396 B.C. in which the Syracusan tyrant Dionysius I virtually expelled the Carthaginians from Sicily. The types of this decadrachm and their significance are essentially similar to those of Cimon. Such imitative behavior is to say the least surprising in an artist of Euainetus' stature and originality, and it has been plausibly suggested that Dionysius himself may have imposed constraints on the creative process. Nevertheless Euainetus succeeded in placing his own distinctive stamp upon the Cimonian types.

Euainetus' racing scene shows some influence from Cimon in that the horses' heads all face forward, in opposition to his earlier practice [75, 79]. But the team is less disciplined than Cimon's. The thrashing legs create a restless eddy which opposes the forward movement, and the scale of the subject in relation to the flan also undercuts any sense of fleetness. This is a baroque sort of movement which calls attention to its own virtuosity.

The head of Arethusa offers a far stronger contrast with Cimon's work. In reaction to the civilized elegance of Cimon's nymph, Euainetus has sought to create a sense of communion with the powers of nature. His Arethusa has a spontaneous, unaffected beauty. Her curly hair is rather casually swept up, with many loose locks and a purling motion reminiscent of water. Its only adornment is a crown of leaves, sometimes described as grain leaves but more likely water grasses symbolic of Arethusa's identity as a fountain spirit. The face lacks the exquisite delicacy and sensuous finish of Euainetus' earlier masterpieces [75, 79, possibly 80]. Nevertheless it was Euainetus' head of Arethusa which became the most widely imitated coin type in the history of Greek numismatics. It was also used as a mold in toreutic metalwork and incorporated into the tondos of South Italian black-glazed cups.

Decadrachms in the style of Euainetus were produced in much larger numbers than those of Cimon. They must have been issued during much of Dionysius' long reign. It is virtually certain that Euainetus could not have engraved all the dies of the series, particularly the unsigned group at its end. Furthermore the pattern of the hoards, where these decadrachms typically are concentrated in large numbers, suggests that ultimately they circulated as currency, replacing the tetradrachms which had ceased to be minted shortly after 400 B.C. The puzzling phenomenon of the regular production of such a large denomination has been explained as the result of inflation in an economy dominated by military expenditures. However the decadrachms should also be viewed in the context of the courtly environment which produced them. Dionysius I lived in a fortified palace on the island of Ortygia, surrounded by his family and close associates, including a mercenary bodyguard, but isolated from the commoners of Syracuse. He affected the royal diadem half a century before Alexander, identifying himself with Zeus and inviting a form of worship. He was also a man of culture who wrote poetry and drama which he presented in international competitions, and he entertained Plato at his court. The decadrachms, both flamboyant and beautiful, had the quality of grandeur that Dionysius himself cultivated. It seems likely that he bestowed them personally on his honored guests and favored henchmen, whether as splendid gifts or as regular pay. More routine military expenses were probably met through payments in kind, bullion and land grants to mercenaries, while civilians were compelled to make do with bronze currency in their daily transactions.

87 GOLD 100 LITRAE OF SYRACUSE

OBVERSE:
  ΣΥΡΑΚΟΣΙΩΝ, head of Arethusa left, wearing sphendone ornamented with stars, triple-drop earring and wire necklace, barley
  grain and engraver's signature ΚΙ behind neck, linear border.

REVERSE:
  Heracles wrestling Nemean lion on rocky ground, stylized plant
  on right, ivy leaf above.

Sicilian standard, weight 5.76 gm; diameter 14.5 mm. ↑

Signed by Cimon. Struck circa 390 B.C.

Same dies: P. Orsi, "Di un insigne tesoretto di aurei persiani e
  siracusani rinvenuti ad Avola (Sicilia)," *AMIIN* 3 (1917), p. 12, D
  and pl. 1, 7; G. di Ciccio, *Gli aurei siracusani di Cimone e di
  Evaneto* (Rome, 1957), 3.

This 100-litra piece is an early example of the first regular gold
currency to be struck in the west; previously this metal was
used only for small and isolated emergency issues. The coin
belongs to a fairly extensive series which includes dies signed by
both Cimon and Euainetus. It is thus related to the Syracusan
decadrachms which were also issued in the form of imitative
series involving these same two great artists. The head on the
obverse of the 100-litra coin is modeled on Cimon's Arethusa
[84, 85], but the barley grain symbol which accompanies it
links the gold coin to the latter phase of the decadrachm coinage
in the style of Euainetus.

The head on this specimen is the prototype for the 100 litra
series. Not surprisingly it displays fine workmanship and a
more original conception than its copies. The slightly squinting
eye is modeled in the same convincing manner as on Cimon's
first decadrachm [84], but otherwise the face has rather different proportions. The hair is dressed in the same spirit as on the
decadrachm, confined and controlled in spite of its luxuriant
curls. The waves at the temple and over the ear are quite emphatic here and help to make the coiffure intelligible. The larger scale of the earring and the solid sphendone also aid in the
reading of this miniature type. The die bears the signature of
Cimon. On the face of it there is nothing dubious about the

signature of a major artist on the initial die of such a series. But
hoard evidence suggests a later date than that adopted here,
giving Cimon a rather long period of artistic activity in a medium which required excellent near vision. For this reason some
authorities question the authenticity of Cimon's signature or
suggest that by this time he may have been signing dies as a
mint magistrate rather than as artist.

The reverse type depicts the hero Heracles wrestling the Nemean lion. This is one of the most popular subjects of Greek art,
but it had not been treated previously on Sicilian coinage. Its
introduction now probably symbolizes the Greek struggle
against encroachment by barbarian peoples, with the lion a particularly apt reference to the African power of Carthage. The
fifth century witnessed an evolution in the treatment of the
Heracles and lion motif as the pyramidal composition of the
archaic period gained ever stronger curves and began to approach a circular format. This tight composition is the logical
end of the process. Its energy is so compressed that the scene
takes on a static, decorative aspect. Its formality contrasts oddly
with the miniature landscape in which the combat occurs. The
same schema was used frequently throughout the Greek world
in various media whenever the format was circular, its applica-
tions even including small gold ornaments in repoussé.

88 SILVER TETRADRACHM OF RHODES

OBVERSE:
    Head of Helios inclined slightly to right.
REVERSE:
    POΔION, rose, in right field eagle standing right, outline of square
    die visible around.
Rhodian (Chian) standard, weight 15.20 gm; diameter 24 mm. ↑
Struck circa 400 B.C.
Published: D. Bérend, "Les tétradrachmes de Rhodes de la première
    période," *SNR* 51 (1972), 14.
Same obverse die: Pozzi 2684.

The large island of Rhodes off the coast of Caria was one of the great maritime powers of the ancient world. Its three cities were commercial rivals which coined on incompatible weight standards. But about 407 B.C. they collaborated in the foundation of a new capital city, called Rhodes like the island itself. It became the mint for the entire island, producing a coinage which was to have enormous impact on fourth-century numismatics. Its types were much imitated locally, and its weight standard was adopted by many mints around the Aegean Sea [89, 91].

The obverse type of the Rhodian coinage is a head of Helios, the sun. The whole island was sacred to Helios, and its inhabitants claimed descent from him. The Rhodian reverse type is a rose, both a symbol of Helios and a visual pun on the name of the mint. The eagle on this tetradrachm is merely a magisterial symbol intended to distinguish this issue from others.

The face of Helios was not a common artistic subject when this coinage was inaugurated, but it did appear occasionally in Attic vase painting from about 420 B.C. Typologically it relates to the three-quarter Apollo heads at Catana and Amphipolis [83, 90]. But the style of the Rhodian heads is so different from the graceful work at other mints that we must suspect other influences, perhaps certain expressionistic sculptures attributed by Furtwängler to the circle of Phidias. This head is one of the earliest in the Rhodian series and also one of the finest artistically. It is highly expressionistic in conception, with deep-set, hypnotic eyes, fleshy lips slightly parted and a twisted neck. These features are all part of the Greek repertory for conveying emotion, a concern which gained importance in one line of fourth-century artistic development until it became a dominant theme of hellenistic art, especially in Asia Minor. The emphasis on the rounded lower lids gives the eyes an anguished expression and may derive from oriental sources; certainly it enhances the compelling numinous quality of the face.

The early Rhodian Helios heads display an extreme variability of form and workmanship which complicates and possibly invalidates the search for artistic sources. Nevertheless virtually all share the narrow face, burning eyes, ray-like hair and twisted neck in some combination. This expressionistic strain is characteristic of Rhodian art in the hellenistic era. Perhaps for once the coinage may have influenced the local school of sculpture. Rhodes was well known as the home of two famous statues of Helios, both probably commissioned soon after the failure of the siege of the city by Demetrius Poliorcetes in 304 B.C. Lysip-

pus depicted the god in his quadriga in a work that became his most celebrated, according to Pliny. His Rhodian pupil, Chares of Lindos, created the Colossus of Rhodes from bronze smelted from Demetrius' abandoned siege engines, and this gigantic statue was counted among the Seven Wonders of the World. Neither of these masterpieces survives, but the best efforts at reconstruction invariably endow them with heavy features, deep-set eyes, parted lips, twisted neck and abundant, wavy hair. Another Rhodian sculptor, Menecrates, was the chief artist of the Great Altar of Pergamum around 180–160 B.C., and thus the Rhodian style was transmitted to that important Asian capital [37].

89 SILVER "ALLIANCE" TRIDRACHM (?) OF SAMOS

OBVERSE:
  Σ—Υ—Ν, infant Heracles kneeling right and strangling snakes, linear border.
REVERSE:
  Σ—A, facing lion's scalp.
Rhodian (Chian) standard(?), weight 11.35 gm; diameter 23 mm. ↓
Struck circa 404 or 394 B.C.
Published: S. Karweise, "Lysander as Herakliskos Dragonopnignon," NC 1980, pl. 1, 6 (obverse).
Same dies: J.P. Barron, *The Silver Coins of Samos* (London, 1966), p. 210, 1; Kraay-Hirmer 616; *AGC* fig. 284.
Eight specimens known, all from the same obverse die.

This very rare tridrachm belongs to a curious issue of coins produced simultaneously by at least eight cities of Asia Minor. In each case the obverse type is the infant Heracles strangling snakes, while the reverse type is the civic badge of the minting city, here the lion's scalp of Samos. An inscription on the obverse clearly identifies the coins as the currency of an alliance.

The obverse type illustrates the myth of the infant Heracles, who successfully resisted the attack of the snakes sent against his cradle by the vindictive Hera because he was the offspring of one of Zeus' illicit amours. The motif is known from early fifth-century vases but was especially celebrated as the subject of a major painting by the great West Greek artist Zeuxis. It was also used on coins of Thebes in the fifth century and on coins of Croton in the fourth. There is considerable variation in the rendering of the motif. Early painted versions depict a miniaturized adult rather than a true child's body, but all the numismatic examples postdate this naive phase. The Asian coinage employs a pyramidal composition with the figure leaning to the right. Much is made of the decorative value of the coiling snakes. The string of amulets across the baby's chest also occurs at Croton. They probably should be understood to contain bits of amber, coral and a wolf's tooth, substances believed to protect a small child from the powers of evil.

Symbolically this type represents heroic resistance to injustice and oppression, thus characterizing the alliance which employed it as a defensive one. Unfortunately international politics after the Peloponnesian War were so unsettled that it is impossible to identify the alliance in question. Traditionally the favorite candidate has been the anti-Spartan coalition formed after 394 B.C. when the Persian fleet, led by the Athenian admiral Conon, destroyed the Spartan navy at the battle of Cnidus and liberated many Asian cities from oligarchies imposed by Sparta. In recent years persuasive arguments have been advanced in favor of a pro-Spartan alliance, either at the end of the Peloponnesian War or around 390 B.C. The date of issue and the nature of the alliance may eventually be illuminated by discovery of further specimens of the alliance coinage in hoard contexts.

The reverse type, as noted above, is the civic badge of Samos. Such heraldic emblems represent a survival from the archaic era, and their persistence on coinage, especially in Asia Minor, illustrates a conservative tendency within numismatic art.

The weight standard and denomination of the issue are ambiguous in another reflection of the instability of the times. Thus they also fail to provide clues as to the political orientation of the alliance.

90 SILVER TETRADRACHM OF AMPHIPOLIS

OBVERSE:
  Laureate head of Apollo inclined slightly to right, thick hair rolled, drapery(?) at neck.

REVERSE:
  AMΦ—ΙΠΟ—ΛΙΤ—ΩΝ on raised square border around race torch, Boeotian shield symbol in left field.

"Phoenician" standard, weight 14.03 gm; diameter 27 mm. →

Struck circa 375 B.C.

Published: *SNG Lockett* 1300; Glendining (Lockett collection 2, 12 February 1958), lot 1219; Glendining (December 1963), lot 205; Hess-Leu 45 (1970), lot 117.

Same dies: K. Regling, "Phygela, Klazomenai, Amphipolis," *ZfN* 33 (1922), p. 57, no. 15; *Traité* 4 (1932), 1102, pl. 321, 2.

Ex R. Lockett collection; R. Abecassis collection, Lisbon.

One of three specimens recorded by Regling.

Amphipolis produced the most artistic coinage of Macedon. This mintage seems to have originated in part out of revolutionary sentiment. Amphipolis was a colony of Athens, but it threw off its allegiance during the Peloponnesian War. Athens had not permitted its dependencies to issue coinage, so the very act of opening a mint was a symbol of defiance. Both the weight standard and the obverse type announce a reorientation away from Athens toward a local economy dominated by the Chalcidian League under the patronage of Apollo.

The obverse type of the Amphipolitan coinage is a facing head of Apollo. The type is on the one hand a gesture toward the Chalcidian League, but the god also appears as founder of the colony. His head is typically inclined to one side, lips slightly parted and eyes imbued with a gentle, dreamy expression indicating that the god is depicted in his aspect as patron of the arts and more specifically of the Pythian games celebrated in his honor at Amphipolis.

Many of the Amphipolitan heads may be plausibly compared with the delicate facing head of the Syracusan Arethusa by Cimon [82], though their underlying structure pays homage to famous sculptures of Apollo. At least one issue is directly copied from the Apollo of the east pediment of the Parthenon, whose laurel wreath is now missing. The Hunt specimen, which falls late in the series, introduces a new physical type with long, heavy-boned face, voluptuous features and dense hair rolled back from the face, the whole executed in extremely bold relief. The basic physiognomy and the inclination of the head to the right are inherited from a powerful sculpture of the second quarter of the fifth century, probably attributable to Phidias and known today as the Kassel Apollo after the location of the finest extant copy. The Kassel Apollo differs from the Amphipolitan head in that the hair around the face is luxuriantly curly rather than rolled; and more importantly it lacks the warmth which is the greatest attraction of the face on the tetradrachm. However both of these features soon emerge in the succession of Apollo statues made under the influence of the Kassel Apollo. A tender expression is already apparent in the slightly later Tiber Apollo. Even closer to the coin type is the Apollo Cithareodus (the Lyre-Player) with rolled hair and laurel wreath, of which the proto-

typical statue probably dates from the mid-fifth century. Later versions in statuary and vase painting become increasingly dreamy. This face, with its rapt, soulful expression, thus emphasizes a traditional characteristic of Apollo to suit the taste of an era which tended to humanize the Olympian gods by endowing them with human sensibilities.

The reverse type of the Amphipolitan tetradrachm is another of those North Greek elaborations of the quadripartite incuse [74]. The lighted torch symbolizes the torch races held at Amphipolis in honor of Apollo.

91 SILVER TETRADRACHM OF THASOS

OBVERSE:
 Head of bearded Dionysus left, crowned with ivy.

REVERSE:
 ΘΑΣΙΟΝ, Heracles kneeling right and drawing bow, wearing chiton and lion skin headdress, cantharus symbol in lower right field, linear square border.

Rhodian (Chian) standard, weight 15.40 gm; diameter 25 mm. ↘

Struck circa 360 B.C.

Published: G.F. Hill, *Select Greek Coins* (Paris-Brussels, 1927), pl. 40, 4; A.B. West, *Fifth and Fourth Century Gold Coins from the Thracian Coast*, NNM 40 (New York, 1929), p. 42, 32D; *SNG Spencer Churchill* 105; *Kunstfreund* lot 190.

Ex E.G. Spencer Churchill collection, Northfield Park; I. Vorres collection, Athens.

The island city of Thasos was another North Greek town which revolted against Athens in the course of the Peloponnesian War. As in the case of Amphipolis (see preceding) its disaffection was reflected in its coinage. The traditional stater denomination was replaced by a tetradrachm on the Rhodian weight standard, designed to fit into the currency system of western Asia Minor [88, 89].

The types of these tetradrachms honor the two chief gods of Thasos, Dionysus and Heracles. Dionysus had his great sanctuary atop Mt. Pangaeus, not far from Thasos, and his worship dominated Thraco-Macedonian religion. The earlier coinage of Thasos bears types relating to his cult but does not represent the god directly. As at Mende the shift of focus to the god himself is associated with the purification of the more uncouth manifestations of the cult and with the interpretation of Dionysus as the god of wine. For Thasos, like Mende, was a famous wine-producing center.

Thus we have here essentially the same civilized god as on the classical coins of Naxos and Mende [73, 74]. Fourth-century taste may be observed in the soft, realistic eye; in the rounded rather than chiseled orbital bone; in the wrinkled brow; and in

the emphatic yet smooth modeling. Indeed a supernatural smoothness is the unifying trait of this head, from its schematized hair to the geometrically conceived furrows of the brow to the large, waxy ivy leaves. The bulky Dionysiac crown may derive from a fifth-century prototype.

The figure of Heracles on the reverse is depicted in an anachronistic style. The exaggerated, bulging muscles, the hero's long garments and the strict profile without torsion belong to the archaic era. The model for the coin type was actually unearthed by archaeologists in 1866. It is a relief which decorated the Thasian city gates and was supposed to ward off evil. This Heracles figure was also used by Thasian potters of the fourth and third centuries as a hallmark.

92 ELECTRUM STATER OF CYZICUS

OBVERSE:
　　Gambling youth crouching facing, head right, on tunny fish right.
REVERSE:
　　Mill sail incuse.
Phocaic standard, weight 15.90 gm; diameter 21 mm.
Struck circa 350 B.C.
Published: *Kunstfreund* lot 214.
Equivalent coins, various dies: K. Regling, "Der griechische Gold-
　　schatz von Prinkipo," *ZfN* 41 (1931), p. 20, 127, pl. 3; M. Comstock
　　and C.C. Vermeule, *Greek Coins 1950 to 1963* (Boston, 1964), 150.
One of three specimens recorded.

Cyzicus was one of three Asian mints which continued to produce coinage in electrum long after the gold-silver alloy had been generally displaced by pure silver. The Cyzicene electrum retains several features of the early Ionian electrum coinage [55, 56]: frequent variation of type, apparently on an annual basis; the anachronistic incuse reverse; and the lumpy fabric of the earliest coinage. There is also a relative unconcern with identifying the issuing mint, which is indicated only by inclusion of the Cyzicene civic badge, a tunny fish, in each design of the series.

This electrum coinage was not the official legal tender of Cyzicus, for the city additionally produced a silver currency which conformed to the usage of other towns. Instead this electrum coinage existed to meet the need for a high-value international trade currency. Specifically, the Cyzicene electrum was the medium of exchange for the grain trade between the Black Sea breadbasket and the food-importing cities which ringed the Aegean.

Cyzicus coped with its need for ever fresh types by borrowing from foreign coinages and other artistic media. The subject here is a youth casting knucklebones, an ancient equivalent of dice. The gambling motif is quite rare as a numismatic subject but was popular in the late classical period for terracotta statuettes

and in the decoration of objects intended for domestic use. There does not seem to have been a fixed scheme for representing the game of knucklebones. Sometimes several players are shown, sometimes only one as here. They may be of either sex. Most but not all of the gamesters squat on the ground, and they are depicted from various angles. The Cyzicene stater offers an individual treatment employing carefully controlled rhythms. It is especially notable for its success in freezing motion. The youth is physically out of balance, but the imagined impetus of his throw restores the equilibrium. The infusion of motion into so essentially quiet a subject is a display of virtuosity which reflects a major concern of fourth-century art.

93. SILVER DIDRACHM OF THESSALIAN LARISSA

OBVERSE:
> Head of nymph Larissa inclined slightly to left, wearing necklace, pendant earring and ampyx, hair floating freely, dotted border.

REVERSE:
> ΛΑΡΙ—Σ—ΑΙΩΝ, bridled horse prancing right on ground line.

Aeginetic standard, weight 12.27 gm; diameter 26 mm. ↘

Struck circa 340 B.C.

Same dies: Numismatic Fine Arts 8 (1980), lot 133. Equivalent coins, various dies: F. Herrmann, "Die Silbermünzen von Larissa in Thessalien," *ZfN* 35 (1925), pl. 5, 2; *Traité* 4 (1932), 700, pl. 298, 12.

Larissa was the leading city of Thessaly, a large, mountain-ringed plain which specialized in the breeding of livestock. In 354 B.C. Larissa invited Philip of Macedon to intervene in Thessalian politics, resulting in the absorption of Thessaly into the Macedonian kingdom in 344 B.C. The pattern of Larissa's coinage indicates that it was rewarded for its services to Philip by a commission to mint currency for the whole of Thessaly, using silver supplied from the rich mines of Macedon.

The types of Larissa's coinage derive from the mythology of Poseidon, the god of the sea and of rivers, of earthquakes, of horses and bulls, and the chief god of Thessaly. When Athena and Poseidon competed to see which could provide the greatest gift for his people, Athena created the olive tree. Poseidon struck the ground with his trident, and simultaneously there burst forth a gushing spring and the first magnificent horse. The spirit of the spring was the nymph Larissa, foundress of the city and a consort of Poseidon. The horse was tamed by the national hero Thessalus and became the ancestress of the famous Thessalian horses, just as Thessalus fathered the Thessalian people.

The nymph Larissa as she appears on this didrachm is clearly inspired by Cimon's facing head of Arethusa at Syracuse [82]. The floating hair has the same symbolic function, but the nymph's features are much heavier than on the prototype. We have already seen evidence of a new appreciation for fleshiness on the coinage of Amphipolis which was located in the same northerly region [90]. Larissa also differs from Arethusa in the modeling of her eyes, which is both more realistic and more expressive. Such a melting gaze was the invention of Praxiteles and became the very soul of fourth-century faces. The head of Larissa thus exemplifies the tendency of fourth-century art to move away from ideal types toward warmer and more individual representations.

The horse was a traditional type of Larissa's coinage. The animal depicted here is a typical fourth-century specimen, excessively muscular and charged with a nervous energy. Comparison with some earlier horses [76, 77, 84ff] illustrates both the heavier proportions and the theatricality achieved by the use of tighter curves. The presence of a bridle on a riderless horse reinforces the suggestion of indomitable temperament. The pose of this horse is so similar to that of the victorious race horse on the tetradrachms of Philip of Macedon (see following) that an intentional parallelism must be intended. The Macedonian horse, however, is not nearly so dynamic and in fact seems merely stately by comparison.

94 SILVER TETRADRACHM OF PHILIP II OF MACEDON

Regnal dates: 359–336 B.C.

OBVERSE:
  Laureate head of Zeus right.

REVERSE:
  ΦΙΛΙΠ—ΠΟΥ, nude jockey on horseback right, carrying palm branch, thunderbolt beneath horse, tiny N in exergue, linear border.

"Phoenician" standard, weight 14.43 gm; diameter 26 mm. ↗

Struck at Pella, circa 342/1–337/6 B.C.

Same dies: G. le Rider, *Le monnayage d'argent et d'or de Philippe II* (Paris, 1977), 199 (D116/R163).

Philip of Macedon was a *bona fide* political genius who in little more than twenty years succeeded in unifying the intensely particularistic city-states of Greece under his sole rule. He was also treacherous and violent, and his imperialism ultimately required a strong financial underpinning. Thus his first expansion was into the mining region of eastern Macedon. Having acquired an almost inexhaustible supply of bullion he converted it to coin at a rate which made his staters and tetradrachms the most familiar currency of the day.

Philip chose his coin types with great subtlety, simultaneously flattering his own ego and advertising his philhellenism among the Greeks who generally regarded the Macedonians as barbarians. Zeus appears on the tetradrachms as the ancestor of the Macedonian royal house and as the patron of monarchy. He was honored by the institution of the Olympia at Dion, a competition held under the auspices of the Macedonian royal house. He was also the patron of the original Olympic games at Elis, the great panhellenic festival where Philip had won victories both at horse racing and at chariot racing. The mounted jockey on the reverse clearly symbolizes the former of these successes, for he holds the palm of victory.

Philip's tetradrachms are not on the whole of great artistic value, but this is a splendid exception. The quality of the head of Zeus allows us to classify it as inspired by the famous chryselephantine statue of Zeus by Phidias. As the cult statue at Olympia, it underscores the Olympic theme of the reverse type. The original statue is unfortunately lost, and evidence as to its appearance comes mainly from coins and literary sources. Features of the Phidian style apparent here are the smooth forehead and clean arch of the eyebrow, the finely chiseled nose, the protruding lower lip, the short beard and the noble serenity. But again we meet the gentle eye of the fourth century which gives the head a new air of sensitivity. The Olympian Zeus is thus reinterpreted as a god of compassion in much the same manner as the admirable Zeus of Mylasa in Boston. This vision, incidentally, is contrary to the main trend of contemporary coinage which largely adopted a jovial conception of the god with leonine hair and knotty modeling of the face, a type perhaps based on the statue of Zeus the Thunderer by Leochares.

95 SILVER NOMMOS OF METAPONTUM

OBVERSE:
Head of young Dionysus crowned with ivy and angled sharply to left, artist's(?) signature ΚΑΛ behind neck in tiny letters, dotted border.

REVERSE:
META, ear of barley with leaf on left, coiled serpent on leaf, magistrate's signature ΦΙ[ΛΟ] below.

Italic-Tarentine standard, weight 7.96 gm; diameter 20.5 mm. ↘

Obverse a signed work of Cal . . . . Struck circa 340 B.C.

Published: G. Fiorelli, *Catalogo del Museo Nazionale di Napoli, Collezione Santangelo, Monete greche* (Naples, 1866), 4108 or 4109; R. Garrucci, *Monete dell'Italia antica* (Rome, 1885), pl. 104, 3; M.P. Vlasto, "Les monnaies d'or de Tarente," *JIAN* 4 (1901), p. 107, nos. 4, 5, pl. ς′, 16; "Signatures de graveurs" p. 10, 7; L. Forrer, *Biographical Dictionary of Medallists* 3 (London, 1907), p. 108, 8; *ACMG* p. 15, no. 5 and p. 148; *Kunstfreund* lot 180.

Same dies: A.J. Evans, "The 'Horsemen' of Tarentum," *NC* 1889, p. 72, note 93; Jameson 1 (1913), 290 = Gulbenkian 70.

Ex Santangelo collection, Naples; Museo Nazionale, Naples.

Probably the third specimen known.

From about the middle of the fifth century the South Italian city of Metapontum had an unusual scheme governing its coin types. A different deity appears on the obverse of each issue, while the reverse remains a barley ear, the city's civic badge.

This extremely rare nommos is the masterpiece of the Metapontine series. Its subject is Dionysus, as evidenced by the ivy wreath almost camouflaged by his thick crop of curls. Such effeminate hairstyles are well attested on South Italian painted vases. The most striking feature of the head is the extreme angle at which it is viewed. Greek coinage had already achieved a complete mastery of the facing or near-facing head. But this new orientation posed challenging problems of modeling and foreshortening. The modeling is too flat for a realistic illusion, but as in the case of the early works of Euainetus [75, 79, possibly 80] its purpose is more expressive than structural. The bland flesh contrasts with the sharp and shadowy features, whose slight asymmetry has much to do with the fascination of the work. Such asymmetry is typical of the rare South Italian stone sculpture of the fourth century and is believed to result from the conception of a "correct" vantage point from which the statues were expected to be viewed. Another feature which links this head to regional sculpture is the shallow, linear treatment of the eyes and eyebrows. Characteristic also is the lingering influence of Euainetus, especially of the ideal of beauty expressed in his Syracusan decadrachms [86]. It is evident here in the Cupid's bow mouth, fine pointed nose and low eyebrows, and to a lesser degree in the fleshy chin. Also akin to the art of the decadrachms is the sombre expression, so opposite to the graceful and frivolous qualities of the earlier phase of the rich style.

The sobriety of the head suggests that Dionysus may be presented here in yet a different aspect from those we have already encountered on coins [68, 73, 74, 91]. For by extension of his chthonic associations as a vegetation god, Dionysus was transformed by some mystic cults into the Lord of Souls, king of the underworld. As time went on this became an increasingly prominent aspect of his worship. Dionysus was thus a common subject of South Italian funerary art; see for example the Apulian crater [15]. The orgiastic revels of Dionysus' followers originally symbolized his power over the human psyche, exercised through wine and religious possession. In a funerary context the same revels acquire an allegorical meaning, referring to the mysteries by which the god conferred the promise of an afterlife on his devotees or perhaps even to the altered spiritual state of the disembodied soul. Dionysus is frequently depicted as detached and impassive amidst the thiasos, emanating his power without direct contact with his votaries. Thus the fifth-century ideal of majestic serenity survives in his iconography into the fourth century and later, although other benevolent gods began to be portrayed with a compassionate expression [42, 94].

This head of Dionysus bears the signature Cal . . . , which occurs at several South Italian cities on dies of particular virtuosity. These signatures were long regarded as evidence for the regional activity of a major artist. But recent scholarship has tended to dismiss them as the marks of magistrates with coincidentally similar names.

96 SILVER TETRADRACHM OF PUNIC SICILY

OBVERSE:
  Female head left, wearing necklace and Phrygian cap bound with ribbon ornamented with palmettes, hair dressed in Libyan fashion, dotted border.

REVERSE:
  Lion walking left, head facing, superimposed on palm tree, in exergue Punic inscription ϟ ⟨ ⊟ ⌐ ⌐ ⌐ ⊬ (Š 'MMHNT = "people of the camp"), dotted border.

Attic standard, weight 16.73 gm; diameter 27 mm. ↖

Struck at a military mint, perhaps located at Lilybaeum, circa 320 B.C. or later.

Same dies: Rizzo pl. 66, 7; PCG pl. 26, 41; Kraay-Hirmer 207; G.K. Jenkins, "Coins of Punic Sicily, Part 3," SNR 56 (1977), p. 62, 271 and pl. 22, 271N and 271L.

Five specimens known to Jenkins.

Carthage, though the head of a great commercial empire, did not adopt the use of coinage until her presence in Sicily took on the character of a military occupation late in the fifth century B.C. The bulk of the Carthaginian coinage was struck in Sicily for military purposes. Many varieties use types borrowed from other Sicilian coinages, sometimes well executed, presumably by Greek artists, sometimes rather barbarized.

This great rarity belongs to an extremely small and isolated issue comprising just three pairs of dies. The undisputed master-pieces of the Siculo-Punic coinage, they must be the creations of Greek die engravers. The obverse type is a female head wearing a Phrygian cap. In Greek art this headdress is associated with persons of oriental origin [15], especially the Amazons, the great Anatolian mother-goddess Cybele and her youthful lover Attis. The head on this tetradrachm has traditionally been described as that of Dido, a Tyrian princess who fled her Phoenician homeland to found Carthage in 814 B.C. However it should probably be identified instead as the goddess represented in certain terracotta figurines of the latter fourth century found at the west Sicilian cities of Selinus and Gela, which lay within the Punic sphere of influence. These terracottas depict a female in Phrygian cap, sometimes accompanied by a lion and a palm tree. She has been called Artemis by some authorities and Cybele by others, but the only certainty is that she is one of the great Asian nature-goddesses who at any rate were subject to syncretic identifications. The reverse type combines two of her symbolic attributes. The palm tree is an ancient Semitic fertility symbol, perhaps recalling the Carthaginian homeland in Phoenicia. The lion is associated with several of the Asian mother-goddesses in their aspect as mistress of wild beasts. It is also a solar animal, and in this small issue it replaces the horse who appears regularly on Carthaginian coinage as a symbol of the sun. Thus the lion complements the symbolism of the palm tree, and both reflect the dominance of the theme of agricultural and pastoral fertility in ancient Semitic religion.

In this small series the head of "Dido" occurs in three distinct variants, each wearing a cap of slightly different cut and a different hairstyle, and each exemplifying a different facial type.

This is the most purely Greek of the trio, with luxuriant hair and heavy, chiseled features which conform to the classical standard inherited from the mid-fifth century. The modeling is simple except around the narrowed eye, creating a typical fourth-century emphasis on this feature. The great beauty of this type lies in its unusually restrained use of rich textures. The headdress is given a convincingly soft feel which demonstrates the virtuosity that Greek artists had achieved over the years in the rendering of drapery. This is an extremely important aspect of major sculpture which rarely finds expression on coinage.

On all reverses of this small series the lion shows strong Greek influence. The theatrical approach is characteristic of Attic funerary lions of the later fourth century, with muscular body, protruding veins, luxuriant mane and an emphasis on the power of the animal.

This coin belongs to a period in which Carthage was confronting Agathocles of Syracuse for control of Sicily. The Punic legend *Sham Machanat,* meaning "people of the camp," marks the tetradrachm as the product of a military mint. But the precise circumstances surrounding the extraordinary issue of "Dido" tetradrachms remain obscure.

97 GOLD STATER OF TARENTUM

OBVERSE:
> TAPA, female head right, wearing bead necklace, triple-drop earring, stephane ornamented with pellets and palmette, and a diaphanous veil, dolphin leaping downwards in front of chin, magistrate's signature KON under neck truncation, dotted border.

REVERSE:
> ΠΙΟΣΚΟΡ[OI], the Dioscuri on horseback left, the farther crowning his mount, the nearer holding palm hung with wreath and garland, magistrate's signature ΣΑ in exergue, dotted border.

Attic standard, weight 8.56 gm; diameter 18 mm. ✓

Struck circa 304 B.C.

Same dies: *de Luynes* 240; *SNG Lloyd* 182 = C. Seltman, *Greek Coins* (second edition, Cambridge, 1965), pl. 45, 15; Gulbenkian 37; *ACGC* 681. Same reverse die: *AGC* fig. 444. Equivalent coins, various dies: M.P. Vlasto, "Les monnaies d'or de Tarente," *JIAN* 2 (1889), p. 320, Type K, no. 1 and the continuation of the article in *JIAN* 4 (1901), p. 96; O.E. Ravel, *The Collection of Tarentine Coins formed by M.P. Vlasto* (London, 1947), 21.

A great rarity: ten specimens cited by Vlasto.

In Greek Italy, gold coinage was not produced routinely and was usually associated with military emergency. The prolonged threat from Italian tribal migrations in the later fourth and early third centuries created many such crises. Tarentum, the leading city of southern Italy in this period, regularly responded by hiring a famous foreign general and his army to provide protection. Gold coins were minted to pay the mercenaries.

This very rare stater bears on its obverse a female who had already appeared on several previous emergency issues and must therefore represent one of the very greatest divinities of Tarentum. The facial type and hairstyle are inherited from the Arethusa head of Euainetus' famous decadrachms [86]. Euainetus' influence was perhaps mediated by local copies of his work, such as the marble head of a goddess in the Museo Archeologico di Taranto; but the decadrachms themselves were probably known as well. The wild freedom of Arethusa's coiffure is restrained here, and the diaphanous veil and stephane contribute to an air of civilized artificiality familiar from South Italian vases [15]. The veil may represent a delicate garment manufactured locally and known as a *tarantion* or *tarantidion*, "little Tarentine." Similar veils are found in Orphic and Dionysiac art and may have a special association with the mysteries. The combination of stephane and veil is a part of the iconography of Persephone in her aspect as consort of Hades and queen of the underworld. The cult of the chthonic Persephone was one of the greatest at Tarentum and indeed throughout southern Italy. However the identification of this head as Persephone Gaia has never been universally accepted, with some authorities preferring to see it as Hera, another major goddess in Magna Graecia, or even Amphitrite, consort of Poseidon.

The reverse of this stater depicts the divine twins Castor and Polydeuces, known collectively as the Dioscuri, "sons of Zeus." They were the patrons of Tarentum as of its mother-city Sparta. As a coin type they possess multiple layers of significance. One of the brothers holds the *palma lemniscata*, a palm branch with pendant ribbon which was awarded to the highest victor in athletic contests, while the other crowns his mount. These attributes and gestures clearly relate the Dioscuri to the agonistic types which regularly appeared on the reverses of Tarentum's silver nommoi from the last third of the fifth century B.C. The Dioscuri also had a confused myth according to which they shared one immortality, so that one or the other was in the underworld at a given time—perhaps a thematic link with the obverse type. A different myth, highly relevant here, had them sent from Sparta to aid the Locrians in battle against neighboring Croton in the sixth century. Tarentum appealed for help from Sparta on several occasions during the Italian migrations. This stater was probably struck to finance the activities of one of the Spartan princes who answered those appeals—Acrotatus (315 B.C.) or his brother Cleonymus (302 B.C.).

98 GOLD STATER OF PANTICAPAEUM

OBVERSE:
  Head of silen left with goat's ear, crowned with ivy.
REVERSE:
  Π—A—N, horned lion-griffin standing left on barley stalk, head facing, holding spear in mouth.
Local standard, weight 9.03 gm; diameter 22 mm. ⟍
Struck circa 320–300 B.C.
Published: M&M 11 (1953), lot 44; M&M 25 (1962), lot 425.
Same obverse die: Naville-Ars Classica 18 (1934), lot 398. Variants: *Götter Griechenlands* pl. 47; Kraay-Hirmer 440; *AGC* figs. 231, 243.
Rare.

This splendid stater comes from Panticapaeum, a Greek colony on the north shore of the Black Sea which acted as a depot for the grain produced abundantly in southern Russia. Another allure of this region was its wealth of gold, which was mined in the Altai and Ural mountains and utilized by the Scythian nobility in the form of jewelry and gold vessels. In fact Panticapaeum was located not far from Kertch, the site of the Scythian tumuli which yielded the fabulous treasures now in the Hermitage Museum. Conceivably local craftsmen of Panticapaeum were responsible for much of the Graeco-Scythian metalwork, though there seems to be influence from Tarentum, a great center of the toreutic arts.

For a few years in the second half of the fourth century, Panticapaeum was able to convert a portion of the Crimean gold into coin. The obverse type of Panticapaeum's staters is generally identified as a head of the shepherd-god Pan, comprising a pun on the name of the mint city. But the god depicted here shows more affinity to the iconography of Silenus [23, 68, 73] than to that of Pan, who in the fifth and fourth centuries is always shown with goat's horns. There are also connections to the colorful local style used by Greek craftsmen to depict Scythian subjects for the Scythian market. Characteristics of the style include rough features; coarse, straight shoulder-length hair;

and long beards. Some commentators have also suggested that the peculiar modeling of his head, composed of many discrete lumps instead of smooth surfaces, owes something to the decorative ''commas'' of Central Asian art.

Panticapaeum's reverse type is a griffin, mythical guardian of the secret sources of the Crimean gold. Already familiar from the orientalizing period [21, 55, 60], it remained a popular subject for decorative metalwork and gilded terracotta imitations. The beast presented here is a lion-griffin, a variant with a lion's instead of an eagle's head, spiral goat's horns and anachronistic curled wings. The spear in the griffin's mouth suggests that it has successfully confronted human predators and places it in relation to a class of lions similarly depicted. The barley stalk on which it stands symbolizes the rich grain of southern Russia which was transported across the Black Sea and through the Dardanelles to the Greek mainland, constituting the basis of Panticapaeum's prosperity.

99 SILVER STATER OF SYBRITA

OBVERSE:
> Young Dionysus seated sidesaddle on back of panther running left, wearing long chiton and holding filleted thrysus.

REVERSE:
> ΣΙΒΡΥΤ[ΙΩΙ], Hermes left, nude except for chlamys over shoulders, resting right foot on rock to tie sandal, kerykeion in left field.

Aeginetic standard, weight 11.41 gm; diameter 27 mm. ↖

Struck circa 300 B.C.

Published: Hess-Leu (2 April 1958), lot 191; Kraay-Hirmer 553.

Same dies: *Traité* 3 (1914), 1715, pl. 259, 10; G. le Rider, *Monnaies crétoises du Ve au Ier siècle av. J.-C.* (Paris, 1966), pl. 9, 11. Cf. *Pozzi* 2010 for the complete reverse legend.

Ex Phaestos hoard, 1953 (*ICGH* 152); M. Hirmer collection, Munich.

Extremely rare.

Cretan coinage is on the whole provincial and technically unpolished. It is thus extremely difficult to account for the production of a consummately artistic coinage by the obscure city of Sybrita in central Crete. Little is known of the city's history or culture, and it is only from the coins that we can deduce that its major cults were dedicated to Dionysus and Hermes.

Dionysus is depicted here in yet a different guise from those we have seen on other coinages [68, 73, 74, 91, 95]. The long chiton which he wears and the panther on which he rides strike an exotic note. The one alludes to the god's eastern origin, the other to the myth of his invasion and conquest of the orient. The motif of Dionysus on a panther may derive from a major painting from the end of the fifth century, perhaps in the Temple of Dionysus below the Athenian Acropolis. The motif enjoyed a modest popularity in the hellenistic and Roman periods, when Dionysus' Indian triumph came to be understood as a metaphor for the soul's escape from mortality. Here the pairing with Hermes, the guide of dead souls, reinforces the suggestion that Dionysus appears as the lord of the afterlife. This version of the motif is most closely related to the well-known Pella mosaic, with which it shares graceful lines, small-headed Lysippean proportions and an absence of distracting detail. Very unusual, perhaps even unique, is the god's forward orientation here, which minimizes the implications of intoxication normally carried by the sidesaddle posture.

The figure of Hermes on the reverse is engaged in an action which recalls the fact that he is often depicted wearing only one sandal. The wearing of one sandal, usually leaving the right foot bare, seems to have had ritual significance and is particularly associated with prayerful approach to a divinity, especially in the underworld cults. This Hermes has traditionally but wrongly been described as based upon a famous statue by Lysippus or a follower, of which the best-known copy is the so-called Jason in Copenhagen. But this prototype virtually bristles with contrived directionality: the head is turned to face the viewer, and the left arm rests perpendicularly across the thigh. The pose on the coin is far more natural, deriving from a long tradition which perhaps originates in transitional representations of warriors donning their greaves; see for example the figure on the exterior of

the Proto-Panaitian cup [8]. The sandal-tying motif may be observed earlier in the west frieze of the Parthenon, and later on a gold finger ring from Tarentum. Lysippean influence may however be detected in the proportions of the body, tall and slender with a small head. A most striking feature of the Sybrita Hermes is the detailed depiction of the powerfully knotted muscles, giving the figure a "flayed" appearance. In this respect it strongly resembles the expressionistic style of slabs 1020 and 1021 of the Amazonomachy frieze of the Mausoleum at Halicarnassus, variously attributed to Scopas or Leochares.

100 SILVER DECADRACHM OF ALEXANDER THE GREAT

Regnal dates: 336–323 B.C.
OBVERSE:
    Head of young Heracles right in lion skin headdress, dotted border.
REVERSE:
    ΑΛΕΞΑΝΔΡΟΥ, Zeus enthroned left, holding eagle and sceptre,
    monogram ⋈ and Μ under throne, border of dots.
Attic standard, weight 41.54 gm; diameter 36 mm. ↙
Struck at Babylon, 327–326 B.C.
Published: Mitchiner 1, p. 11; *Coin Hoards* 1 (1975), 10, 1–3.
Same obverse die: Bellinger *Essays* pl. 1, 10.
Ex Mesopotamia hoard, 1973 (*Coin Hoards* 1 [1975], 10).
A great rarity: one of twelve specimens known.

The coinage of Alexander the Great includes one small issue of decadrachms employing the types of his regular silver coinage. The head of Heracles was a traditional type for the Macedonian royal coinage, where he appeared as ancestor of the royal house. He was also an apt symbol for Alexander himself, who like Heracles undertook superhuman labors. Alexander often made the comparison explicitly, and the two were later assimilated into a single artistic type, exemplified by the bronze statuette [38]. The reverse type of the Alexandrine silver alludes to Philip's cult of Zeus [94]. However this figure does not represent the Olympian cult statue by Phidias, but the even older Zeus Lycaeus of the Arcadians.

The monograms of this decadrachm and the style of the familiar types link it to the tetradrachm issues of the Babylon mint around 327–326 B.C. However there are also telling details which elevate the decadrachm above the artistic level of contemporary tetradrachms. The face of Heracles is heavy-featured and organically modeled with an intense and commanding expression. The three curls above the forehead, which tend to appear schematized on the tetradrachms, are here freer and more realistic. The lion skin headdress also receives special attention. The sparse locks of the mane are handled with deliberate asymmetry, while the deep wrinkles along the jaw create a soft, leathery texture which makes this iconographical convention for once believable as an object [79]. Despite the majesty of its expression this face of Heracles is almost certainly not a portrait of Alexander: it lacks the identifying cowlick above the forehead, the deep-set eye and Alexander's straight or slightly aquiline nose [102].

The figure of Zeus is the work of one of two artists whose hands can be recognized in the reverses of contemporary tetradrachms. He was either a Greek or an oriental fully steeped in the Greek artistic tradition. His depiction of Zeus follows the general schema of his tetradrachm reverses, with legs parted, torso curved and head thrust forward eagerly. But again there is evidence of greater care and finesse lavished on the important decadrachm issue. Zeus has the tall, slender proportions made fashionable by

100 SILVER DECADRACHM (continued)

Alexander's favorite sculptor Lysippus. The relaxed torsion of the body and the independent directionality of the limbs give the figure a lifelike quality, again in accordance with the Lysippean style. The expressive inclination of the god's head, slightly to the side as well as forward, and his affectionate gaze toward his familiar animal supply the emotional dimension found in the best of fourth-century art.

The royal Alexandrine coinage of the Babylon mint was produced to facilitate commercial transactions with the Levant. However the restricted size of the decadrachm issue and the Mesopotamian find sites of most recorded specimens point to a different function for the decadrachms. Seemingly they were struck for distribution to Alexander's intimates and held at Babylon pending the army's return from its eastern campaign. The occasion which sparked their production was perhaps the news of Alexander's penetration into India. From 330 B.C., when he acquired the vast treasure of the Persian empire, Alexander cultivated the kingly trait of prodigality toward his friends and followers. Compared with the scale of his donatives or military bonuses, the decadrachms were small change indeed. We must therefore imagine that it was the circumstance and manner of their presentation which was exceptional. A probable occasion was the lavish mass wedding at Susa in 325 B.C., in which Alexander, eighty of his officers and ten thousand enlisted men espoused Persian wives in a gesture symbolizing Alexander's new policy of a permanent Macedonian presence in the orient.

101 SILVER DECADRACHM OF ALEXANDER THE GREAT

Regnal dates: 336–323 B.C.

OBVERSE:
Macedonian cavalryman right lancing at retreating war elephant bearing Indian warrior who leans back to seize the sarissa and a mahout (obliterated on this specimen) who threatens with a raised lance and holds two spares; Ξ above.

REVERSE:
Alexander in battle attire standing left, holding thunderbolt and sceptre (or sarissa), crowned by Nike flying right; monogram ⚹ in lower left field.

Attic or Babylonic(?) standard, weight 40.70 gm; diameter 31 mm. ↘

Struck at a Bactrian or Indian mint(?), circa 327 B.C. or shortly after.

Published: *Coin World* (19 November 1980), p. 3; M.J. Price, "The 'Porus' Coinage of Alexander the Great: A Symbol of Concord and Community," *Essays in Honor of P. Naster* (forthcoming), p. 76, A/c (2) and pl. 9, 3.

Equivalent coins, various dies: Mitchiner 1, p. 20, series H; Bellinger *Essays* pl. 1, 13=*PCG* pl. 27, 4.

Ex Mesopotamia hoard, 1973 (*Coin Hoards* 1 [1975], 10).

Of the highest rarity: perhaps the seventh specimen known.

This medallion, though far from beautiful, is one of the most fascinating and controversial of all ancient coins. Traditionally it has been associated with Alexander's defeat of King Poros of the Punjab in the battle of the Hydaspes in 326 B.C. The obverse has been understood as a symbolic portrayal of the battle, which hinged in part upon Alexander's ability to neutralize his enemy's large squadron of war elephants. But the type is in fact ill suited to the circumstances of the actual historical encounter, for Alexander was so impressed by Poros' courage and kingly demeanor that he restored and later enlarged his kingdom. It is probably more accurate to say that the decadrachm type symbolizes Alexander's Indian campaign in a general sense. The reverse depicts Alexander as a military victor, crowned by Nike and wearing Macedonian battle dress including a crested Phrygian helmet [35] adorned with the conspicuous plumes of command. He holds the thunderbolt, an attribute of Zeus which was part of the iconography of apotheosis developed by Alexander's court painter Apelles.

The interpretation of the "Poros" decadrachms is complicated by the recent discovery of tetradrachms belonging to the same issue. Their types are manifestly both Indian and military: an Indian archer occupies the obverse and an elephant the reverse. A unique but related variety features an Indian archer in galloping quadriga on the obverse, and on the reverse a war elephant carrying mahout and standard bearer. On the surface these tetradrachms appear to be a military coinage for the payment of Indian troops, either the Indian auxiliaries in Alexander's own service or the troops of an allied or vassal Indian rajah. Yet this in itself is a perplexing conclusion, for Alexander's own Macedonians were to the best of our knowledge compensated with bullion or war booty, not coined money. There was however a coinage of sorts in northeast India as early as the fifth century

101 SILVER DECADRACHM (continued)

B.C., and perhaps the military coinage for the Indians should be considered in that context.

The mint of the "Poros" coinage remains uncertain. The Babylonian find site for the tetradrachms and their resemblance in fabric to the satrapal coinage of Mazaeus has led prominent numismatists to the conclusion that the mint must have been in Mesopotamia. However there is no evidence that coinage was forwarded from Mesopotamia to Alexander in the field, and the relevance of these Indian military types to Mesopotamian needs has yet to be explained. Recorded find spots for the "Poros" decadrachms include Iran and Bokhara as well as Mesopotamia. Thus it has also been suggested that the issue could have been struck at a Bactrian or Indian mint, whence some specimens would naturally find their way back to the capital of Alexander's empire in Mesopotamia with returning veterans. The hypothesis of a campaign issue is most compatible with the workmanship of the decadrachms. All known specimens are marred by shallow engraving, weak striking and areas of flatness on the flan, all evidence of incompetent minting technique. It is difficult to imagine that Alexander or any of his vicegerents could have commissioned a commemorative coinage introducing important new types which bore directly on the conqueror's iconography and then entrusted its execution to any but the most accomplished craftsmen available. Mesopotamia was capable of better work than this.

If the Indian coinage is a campaign issue, then the occasion for the decadrachms was most likely either Alexander's announcement of his decision to invade India or the formal opening of the campaign in early October 327, celebrated with sacrifices to Athena Nike. This represented a whole new phase in Alexander's career of conquest, for thus far his eastern campaign had had as its purpose the pacification of rebellious provinces of the Persian empire. The decadrachms, a small issue, would have been distributed among Alexander's chief lieutenants, while the tetradrachms probably can be associated with the surrender and cooperation of the Indus valley rajahs who provided Alexander with twenty-five war elephants, and especially with Āmbhi of Taxila who served as guide to a large detachment under the command of Craterus.

102 GOLD STATER OF LYSIMACHUS OF THRACE

Regnal dates: 323–281 B.C.

OBVERSE:
Diademed head of the deified Alexander right with horn of Ammon.

REVERSE:
ΛΥΣΙΜΑΧΟΥ— ΒΑΣΙΛΕΩΣ, Athena enthroned left, holding Nike who crowns royal name, BI in left field, ⅀ under throne.

Attic standard, weight 8.44 gm; diameter 19 mm. ↘

Struck at Alexandria Troas, 297/6—282/1 B.C.

Unrecorded variety. Variants: M. Thompson, "The Mints of Lysimachus," *Essays Robinson*, 139, 152.

Very rare.

Lysimachus was a close companion of Alexander the Great and a member of his bodyguard. In the division of Alexander's empire after his death Lysimachus was given control of Thrace. He usurped the royal title in 306–305 B.C. along with the other Successors. In 301 B.C. he expanded his holdings into Asia Minor at the expense of Antigonus the One-Eyed, and thereafter he was perpetually at war in the effort to increase his kingdom. His downfall in 281 B.C. was triggered by a sordid dynastic intrigue within his own family. Lysimachus' kingdom was promptly dismembered by his rivals and never reconstituted.

Like all of the Successors Lysimachus at first was legally only a governor for the titular king of Macedon. Consistent with this position he issued coinage which continued Alexander's types and was struck in Alexander's name or that of his heirs. After assuming the royal title Lysimachus substituted his own name as issuing authority but still retained the Alexandrine types. About 297 B.C. he finally inaugurated types of his own, but types which still emphasized his connection with Alexander. Lysimachus' obverse type is one of the earliest indisputable portraits of Alexander on coinage. He is depicted as deified, with attributes derived from his portraits on Ptolemaic coinage: the diadem, symbol of divine kingship, and a ram's horn denoting his purported descent from the Libyan desert god Zeus Ammon.

The raised chin and upward gaze, suggesting heavenly inspiration, may have entered his iconography during his lifetime. The chiseled features of this portrait seem closest to those of the marble head of Alexander at Geneva, which is regarded as the best extant copy of an original portrait by Lysippus. The idealized beauty of the stater portrait also relates it to the Rondanini Alexander, a romanticized likeness from Alexander's teenage years which is variously attributed to Leochares or Euphranor. Notably lacking from this godlike head is the obvious masculinity of most Alexander portraits, also their air of humanity.

Lysimachus' reverse design conflates the obverse and reverse types of Alexander's gold staters into a single composition [105]. The majestic Athena strikes the same monumental note as several well-known contemporary sculptures of enthroned goddesses, notably the Cnidian Demeter and the Tyche of Antioch by Eucharides. However high magnification reveals an admirable attention to detail, as in the graceful palmette ornament on the throne and the ecstatic expression on Athena's lovely face. The fine detail of Nike crowning the name of Lysimachus is an imaginative visual expression of the relationship between the king and his tutelary goddess.

103 SILVER OCTODRACHM OF PTOLEMY I SOTER OF EGYPT

Regnal dates as king: circa 305–283 B.C.

OBVERSE:
   Diademed head of Ptolemy right with aegis at shoulder, tiny Δ behind ear, dotted border.

REVERSE:
   [ΠΤΟΛΕΜΑΙΟΥ] ΒΑΣΙΛΕΩΣ, eagle standing left on thunderbolt, Λ in left field, dotted border.

Ptolemaic ("Phoenician") standard, weight 28.33 gm; diameter 34 mm. ↗

Struck at Alexandria after circa 300 B.C.

Published: G.K. Jenkins, "An Early Ptolemaic Hoard from Phacous," *ANSMusN* 9 (1960), pl. 5, 1.

Variants: Svoronos pl. 7, 14–17.

Ex Phacous hoard, 1956 (*IGCH* 1678).

Unique.

Ptolemy was an intimate companion of Alexander the Great from childhood and was rumored to be his half-brother. He accompanied Alexander on his campaigns, and after the conqueror's death he received Egypt as his province. The ancient kingdom was enviably rich and naturally defensible, and Ptolemy wisely restricted himself to a basically defensive role in the endless Wars of the Successors. An important historian himself, he was the founder of the university and library of Alexandria, the greatest academic center of the ancient world.

Ptolemy's coinage evolved much like that of Lysimachus (see preceding): first Alexandrine issues; then variations on these types including a portrait of Alexander in apotheosis. But after his assumption of the royal title Ptolemy became the first of the Successors to introduce his own portrait to his coinage. It is customary to relate his innovation to the Egyptian ethos of Pharaoh worship. But in reality it was the logical extension of Alexander's own enthusiasm for portraiture which had included commissioning sculptures of his companions.

Ptolemy's portrait is a landmark of Greek art, for it is the first portrait of a living subject to break with the structural concepts and idealizing tradition of classical art. The architecture of the face and indeed a sense of its solidity is eclipsed by an exaggerated emphasis on individual features—the bulging forehead, blunt nose, grimacing mouth and protruding chin. The wide, staring eye under its massive orbital ridge almost caricatures a feature of Alexander's iconography (see preceding). The ungainly features are articulated beneath a smooth surface which disguises the age of the subject, who was at the time of this portrait at least in his middle sixties. The hair is artificial yet minutely engraved. The net effect of the portrait is a magnificent statement of character in which it is easy to read Ptolemy's shrewd, practical intelligence, bluff good nature and rejection of pretense. The author of this powerful new portrait type, surely an important artist, has initialed his work with a tiny letter delta (Δ) behind the ear.

Despite its earthy quality Ptolemy's likeness is a portrait in apotheosis. It is divinized by the heavenward gaze, royal diadem and the aegis around the neck. The last was an attribute of Zeus which conferred invulnerability in battle and which he might loan to Athena or other favored gods as needed. The eagle and thunderbolt of the reverse are further symbols of Zeus. According to legend, at birth Ptolemy was exposed upon a shield by his father Lagus, who doubted his paternity, but Zeus sent his eagle to feed and protect the child. The clear implication of the myth is that Ptolemy was the son of Zeus. The coins perhaps go even farther, suggesting an identification between the two. In fact, Ptolemy was depicted in the guise of various gods on utilitarian and decorative objects as early as the close of the fourth century.

The silver octodrachm was not a usual denomination. All known specimens belong to a small, die-linked issue, connected by shared monograms to Ptolemy's tetradrachm coinage. Their size, artistry and rarity suggest that their purpose was festive. The silver octodrachm may be regarded as the first manifestation of the Ptolemaic penchant for large and showy denominations, though in succeeding reigns these came to be associated with the cults of deceased and deified family members [106ff].

104 SILVER TETRADRACHM OF PHILETAERUS OF PERGAMUM

Regnal dates: 282–263 B.C.

OBVERSE:
Head of the deified Seleucus right, wearing taenia, dotted border.

REVERSE:
ΦΙΛΕΤΑΙΡΟΥ, Athena enthroned left, resting right hand on round shield with gorgoneion boss, holding spear in left hand and resting left elbow on sphinx support, ivy leaf symbol in left field, bow symbol in right field.

Attic standard, weight 16.97 gm; diameter 28 mm. ↑

Struck at Pergamum, probably circa 270 B.C.

Same obverse die: E.T. Newell, *The Pergamene Mint under Philetaerus*, NNM 70 (New York, 1936), die XVIII, pl. 10, 1 but reverse type as no. 14.

Very rare: Newell cites twenty-seven specimens.

The Thracian king Lysimachus kept his treasury at the city of Pergamum in Asia Minor under the care of the faithful eunuch Philetaerus. But Lysimachus' execution of his son Agathocles in 283 B.C. put all the young man's friends in a false position. When Seleucus of Syria declared war on Lysimachus on behalf of the dead man's children, Philetaerus switched his allegiance. Within a few months both Lysimachus and Seleucus were dead. Philetaerus was left in legal possession of the 9000 talents of silver in the Pergamene treasury.

Pergamum under Philetaerus had already served as a mint for Lysimachus. But the eunuch probably did not begin coining in his own name until 274 B.C., when he received a grant of autonomy from Seleucus' successor Antiochus, who wished to secure his rear while campaigning in Egypt. Philetaerus' coin types constitute both a formal admission of Seleucid suzerainty and a reminiscence of his former service of Lysimachus. His obverse type is a portrait of the deified Seleucus, whom he had genuinely revered, replete with the taenia of victory and the elevated gaze of divine inspiration. The enthroned figure of Athena on the reverse is retained from the coinage of Lysimachus with minor alterations [102]. Philetaerus' name appears as issuing authority, but significantly there is no attempt to claim the royal title.

The rare Pergamene portraits of Seleucus share the same fascination with character as the portraits of Ptolemy (see preceding), exaggerating certain features to achieve a rugged vitality which conveys the magnetism of a leader. In this case however theatricality does not involve rejection of the inherited sense of the structure of the face. Indeed the modeling here is more sensitive to the underlying bone structure than anything we have seen since the archaic tetradrachm of Athens [58]. At the same time it brilliantly suggests the loss of tone of the facial muscles and the beginnings of sagging flesh, without however vitiating the force of the image. An expressionistic strain remains typical of Pergamene art, finding its full flowering in the Great Altar of Pergamum [37].

105 GOLD STATER OF PYRRHUS OF EPIRUS

Regnal dates: 295–272 B.C.

OBVERSE:
> Helmeted head of Athena right, wearing triple-drop earring, bead necklace and crested Corinthian helmet with griffin on bowl, flying owl symbol behind head, small Λ under neck truncation, dotted border.

REVERSE:
> ΠΥΡΡΟΥ—ΒΑΣΙΛΕΩΣ, Nike walking left, carrying oak wreath and trophy, thunderbolt symbol in inner left field, dotted border.

Attic standard, weight 8.49 gm; diameter 21 mm. ↘

Struck at Syracuse, 278 B.C.

Published: *Kunstfreund* lot 240.

Same dies: *de Luynes* 1894 = P. Lévêque, *Pyrrhos* (1957), p. 692, 1 and pl. 6 = W. Giesecke, *Sicilia numismatica* (Leipzig, 1925), pl. 23, 1 = Hirsch 20 (1907), lot 281.

Extremely rare.

———

Pyrrhus of Epirus, hereditary king of the Molossian tribe, was a cousin of Alexander the Great and his only surviving kinsman. Among his contemporaries he enjoyed a reputation as a brilliant general, but he was nevertheless unable to expand the impoverished kingdom of Epirus into a world power. Eventually Pyrrhus hired himself out as a mercenary. In 281 B.C. he was commissioned by the South Italian city of Tarentum [97] to prosecute its war against Rome. He won a pair of major victories but his heavy losses gave rise to the expression "Pyrrhic victory." Realizing that he was trapped in a war of attrition against a power with enormous reserves of manpower, Pyrrhus crossed over to Sicily in 278 B.C. and was enthusiastically acclaimed as a liberator. Yet after only two years' campaigning on the island he was feared and hated more than the Carthaginian enemy. He returned to Italy but found the situation there irretrievable. Ultimately the result of his intervention in the west was that Rome won control of all of southern Italy.

This extraordinary stater was struck at Syracuse in 278 B.C., shortly after Pyrrhus' triumphant arrival. Its types are those of the gold staters of Alexander the Great, implying an extremely flattering comparison between the two kings. The style of these staters however is far more refined than that of genuine Alexandrine gold and demonstrates the irrepressible eroticism of West Greek art in the early hellenistic period. In contrast to the pudgy, asexual Athena of the Alexandrine staters, Pyrrhus' coin presents an extremely elegant and beautiful woman who almost looks out of place in a helmet. The curly hair tied in a queue derives from representations of Athena on the gold staters of Agathocles struck at Syracuse only a few years earlier, but here the hair is thicker and more sensual. The heavy-lidded eye and full, slightly parted lips belong more to the iconography of Aphrodite than to the war goddess Athena.

The Nike figure on the reverse is even farther removed from the Alexandrine prototype. This Nike literally dances where the other stands still, her whole body animated by a circular movement. This spiral motion was perhaps influenced by a sculpture of a dancing female by Lysippus, which has been described as a maenad and as a flute girl; identification remains uncertain as her head and attributes are broken off. There is

certainly evidence for a dancing Nike motif in the contemporary toreutic art of Tarentum, whence Pyrrhus had so recently arrived. The dancing Nike carries a trophy, as here, on a silver horse phalera evidently crafted for a victory festival during the very years of Pyrrhus' activity in the west. The motif appears without the trophy on gold earrings from a tomb near Bolsena. Each of these figures wears transparent drapery whose expressive swirls emphasize the motion of the dance, a conceit developed in the rich style sculpture of late fifth-century Greece. The dance also permits a pretense of spontaneity in the baring of Nike's bosom. Of the dancing Nikes cited here, this figure on the stater is the most mannered, with slender Lysippean proportions, an exaggerated delicacy to the curve of the wing feathers and a dainty but idiosyncratic bone at the wing tip. The oak wreath which she carries constitutes a symbolic link to Pyrrhus: it was an attribute of Zeus of Dodona whom Pyrrhus had recognized as the Epirote national god in an effort to unify his kingdom through religious sentiment.

106 SILVER DECADRACHM OF ARSINOE II OF EGYPT

Regnal dates in Egypt: 276–270 B.C.

OBVERSE:
Head of the deified Arsinoe right with ram's horn, wearing stephane and veil, lotus-tipped sceptre over far shoulder, behind head date ΕΕ (year 29 of the era of Arsinoe), dotted border.

REVERSE:
ΑΡΣΙΝΟΗΣ—ΦΙΛΑΔΕΛΦΟΥ, filleted double cornucopia with grape clusters, dotted border.

Ptolemaic ("Phoenician") standard, weight 35.42 gm; diameter 35 mm. ↑

Posthumous issue, struck at Alexandria, 242 B.C.

Published: Sotheby's (H.P. Smith collection, 5 June 1905), lot 356; Jameson 1 (1913), 1812; Hess-Leu (16 April 1957), lot 322.

Equivalent coins, various dies: Svoronos 940; *BMC The Ptolemies* p. 44, 21.

Ex H.P. Smith collection, New York; R. Jameson collection, Paris.

Rare.

Arsinoe II, daughter of Ptolemy I of Egypt, was a woman of powerful character and few scruples. Her first two marriages, to Lysimachus of Thrace and to her half-brother Ptolemy Ceraunus, ended in bloodshed motivated by dynastic machinations. In 276 B.C. she returned to Alexandria a widow. She intrigued against the current queen, also named Arsinoe, and somehow persuaded King Ptolemy II to marry her. This union was a great success politically, for Ptolemy Philadelphus was a passive character, primarily interested in cultural pursuits, and Arsinoe's conduct of foreign affairs constituted a distinct improvement. Under her direction Egypt recovered lost territories in Phoenicia and southern Asia Minor. The fact that Ptolemy and Arsinoe were brother and sister was not a sticking point, for the Pharaonic tradition had already legitimized incest and Ptolemy I had set an even closer example by marrying his half sister. Even before Arsinoe's death in 270 B.C. the pair were deified as *philadelphoi*, "loving siblings," and shared a cult.

After her death, on the orders of her widower, temples to Arsinoe were constructed at Zephyrium and Alexandria, where the deceased queen was worshipped as Aphrodite. Curious features of the Alexandrian Arsinoeium illustrate the scientific ingenuity of Ptolemy Philadelphus' circle: he planned to install a magnetized chapel in which an iron cult figure would hover. This vision was not realized, but there was in fact a six-foot cult statue carved in topaz. Philadelphus also founded the Ptolemaia, a festival modeled on the great panhellenic games, at which Arsinoe's cult statue was paraded and public sacrifices made to her memory. Her cult was voluntarily adopted by various cities of Asia Minor. Coinage was issued in Arsinoe's name, including several series of gold octodrachms and annual issues of silver decadrachms over a fifty-year period.

Arsinoe's portrait is perhaps the first portrayal on coins of a mortal, historical woman, certainly the first on a major coinage. It presents her veiled, indicating that she is deceased. The horn which peeps out underneath her ear is a divine attribute associating her with the Egyptian ram or goat god Mendes, a spirit of fertility. The connection is slightly puzzling in view of the fact that Arsinoe bore no children to Ptolemy, but it may reflect her personal devotions during her lifetime. A smooth, post-Praxitelean modeling is combined with a long, pointed nose and pursed lips. These features effectively suggest Arsinoe's tough, shrewish character and seem to be survivals from the expressionistic portrait style of Ptolemy I [103], as is the oversized eye. This feature displays an Alexandrian mannerism in the extension of the upper eyelid over the lower. The hairstyle is the so-called melon coiffure well attested on fourth-century Tanagra figurines.

The double cornucopia of the reverse is a new device prescribed by Ptolemy II for representations of his desceased and deified queen. The letters ΕΕ behind the head express the date (year 29) in a slightly unusual, non-decimal numbering system. Oddly enough the same series of numbers appears on a group of Roman Republican didrachms which apparently constitute a parallel series enjoined by treaty.

107 GOLD OCTODRACHM OF PTOLEMY III EUERGETES OF EGYPT

Regnal dates: 246–221 B.C.

OBVERSE:
  Radiate bust of the deified Ptolemy III right, wearing aegis and holding trident over far shoulder, dotted border.

REVERSE
  ΠΤΟΛΕΜΑΙΟΤ ΒΑΣΙΛΕΩΣ, radiate and filleted cornucopia, ΔΙ below, dotted border.

Ptolemaic ("Phoenician") standard, weight 27.63 gm; diameter 27 mm. ↑

Posthumous issue struck at Alexandria under Ptolemy IV Philopator, 221–204 B.C.

Same obverse die: Svoronos 1117, pl. 36, 6; *AGC* fig. 566.

Rare.

Ptolemy III Euergetes was a vigorous man who loved hunting and warfare. As a young man he was sent to Cyrenaica (Libya) to marry its queen Berenice (see following) and restore order after the murder of her husband Demetrius the Fair. Ptolemy was recalled to Egypt at his father's death, but in less than a year he became involved in the affairs of Syria on behalf of his sister Berenice, wife of Antiochus II. He campaigned for five years in the eastern reaches of the Seleucid kingdom. Eventually unrest at home forced him to abandon his eastern conquests. But from Egypt Ptolemy III continued an aggressive foreign policy which won him control of the Aegean and of many cities along its coasts.

This gold octodrachm with the portrait of Ptolemy Euergetes was actually issued by his son Ptolemy IV Philopator. It illustrates the cult of ancestor worship which the Ptolemies adopted from the Egyptian Pharaohs and which found expression in the construction of temples, in the maintenance of cult in both Greek and Egyptian forms and in the issue of commemorative coinage of high value. Euergetes is depicted here with the attributes of three great Greek gods, the aegis of Zeus, the radiate crown of Helios and the trident of Poseidon. There is some evidence that all these gods were assimilated to Sarapis, a religious creation of the Ptolemies with whom Euergetes may be identified here. However this melange of attributes need not imply identification with any particular god or gods so much as it symbolizes aspects of Euergetes' own royal divinity. The trident, for example, must surely allude to his role in building Ptolemaic sea power, which was at its height in his reign; while the radiate crown, repeated on the reverse, symbolizes his beneficent effect on the productivity and hence the welfare of the kingdom.

The cornucopia or horn of plenty is a reverse type strongly associated with the posthumous Ptolemaic coinage. It symbolizes the fertility of the Nile which was believed to depend upon the proper maintenance of the ruler and ancestral cults. These cults under the Ptolemies are superficially hellenized versions of the Egyptian state religion which taught that each Pharaoh was a divine incarnation who took his place among Egypt's protective gods upon his death.

The style of Euergetes' portrait illustrates a reaction against the expressionistic portraiture of the dynastic founder [103]. His mild, impersonal expression suggests a renewed contact with the classical tradition, which was mediated at least in part by the emigration of Tarentine metalworkers to Alexandria after the fall of their city to Rome in 272 B.C. There are reminiscences of the refined eroticism of Tarentum [97] in Euergetes' dainty features and soft, rounded face. This sensual manner is typical of Alexandrian art and reflects the influence of the school of Praxiteles as well as West Greek taste.

The octodrachm or *mnaieion* was the largest gold coin produced regularly in the ancient world. It was minted principally under the Ptolemies and is mostly associated with commemorative coinage, attesting simultaneously to the wealth of the Ptolemaic kingdom and to the great emphasis laid on the ancestor cult. Its weight, incidentally, is incompatible with the Attic standard used by most other hellenistic states. The adoption of a unique Ptolemaic weight standard was only one of several measures designed to prevent coin from leaving the kingdom.

108 SILVER DECADRACHM OF BERENICE II OF EGYPT

Regnal dates: in Cyrene, 253–221 B.C.; in Egypt, 247–221 B.C.

OBVERSE:
 Veiled bust of Berenice II right, dotted border (mostly off flan).

REVERSE:
 ΒΕΡΕΝΙΚΗΣ—ΒΑΣΙΛΙΣΣΗΣ, filleted cornucopia, dotted border.

Ptolemaic ("Phoenician") standard, weight 35.43 gm; diameter 35 mm. ↘

Probably a posthumous issue, struck at Alexandria after 221 B.C.

Published: Bourgey sale (Castro Maya collection, 1957), lot 157.

Equivalent coins, various dies: Svoronos 1114; *BMC The Ptolemies* p. 59, 2.

Ex Castro Maya collection.

Five specimens known to Svoronos.

Berenice II was a granddaughter of Ptolemy I Soter in a collateral line of the family which ruled the subject kingdom of Cyrenaica. The two kingdoms were reunited when she was married to her cousin Ptolemy III Euergetes. Her early married years were spent administering Egypt and commanding the operations of its fleet while Ptolemy campaigned in the east. After five years famine in Egypt provoked civil disturbances which compelled Ptolemy's return.

Rather little is known of the rest of Ptolemy's reign, but its artistic and intellectual climate can be appreciated from the episode of the Lock of Berenice. On Ptolemy's departure eastward Berenice dedicated a ringlet of her hair in the Temple of Arsinoe at Zephyrium as a votive offering to insure his safe return. This token later mysteriously disappeared. But the evil omen was gracefully averted by the court astronomer Conon, who "found" the tress in a new constellation, the *Coma Berenices*. The apotheosis of the Lock of Berenice was celebrated in a famous poem by the court poet Callimachus, which was translated into bantering Latin by Catullus some two centuries later and finally inspired the mock-epic conceit of Alexander Pope's "Rape of the Lock." Through the efforts of Callimachus Berenice entered the literary tradition as a romantic symbol of wifely devotion and the personification of the lonely longing of unconsummated marriage.

Berenice was possibly the first Ptolemaic queen to be honored on coinage during her own lifetime. However the bulk of her coinage must surely be posthumous, constituting a parallel to the commemorative portrait coinage of her husband Euergetes. Berenice's portrait is obviously modeled on that of Arsinoe II [106] and projects a similar concept of matronly divinity. The classicizing style shows even closer affinities to the portrait of Euergetes (see preceding), with the same general profile and similar rounded forms. The eye is drawn in profile like that of Euergetes and in contrast to that of Arsinoe, though in the case of both ladies the feature is extravagantly enlarged. The divine attributes are conspicuously reduced for Berenice, who wears only the royal diadem. But she is permitted a deep decolletage which displays a long necklace, an erotic touch which reflects Alexandrian taste. The details of her cult are unfortunately obscure, so that it is impossible to comment on the symbolism of her iconography.

The reverse inscription names Berenice as queen. This usage is unique among the Ptolemaic royal consorts, who are normally referred to by honorary epithets such as Philadelphus or Philopator. The legend presumably alludes to Berenice's possession in her own right of the throne of Cyrenaica.

109 GOLD STATER OF T. QUINCTIUS FLAMININUS

OBVERSE:
Bare head of Flamininus right.

REVERSE:
T. QVINCTI, Nike advancing left to crown name, holding palm branch in left hand.

Attic standard, weight 8.47 gm; diameter 20 mm. ↗

Struck in Greece, perhaps in Chalcis, circa 196–194 B.C.

Same dies: Leu 20 (1978), lot 79. Equivalent coins, various dies: Bahrfeldt 9, pl. 2, 23–25; H. Gaebler, *Die antiken Münzen Nordgriechenlandes*, 3, part 2 (Berlin, 1935), p. 197f, 1–2; Crawford p. 544, no. 548; R.A.G. Carson, "The Gold Stater of Flamininus," *BM Quarterly* 1955, pp. 11ff, pl. 6, 2 = Kraay-Hirmer 579 = Kent-Hirmer 23.

Found in Sicily.

Perhaps the seventh specimen known.

This excessively rare gold stater is one of the most provocative of ancient coins, because it defies classification as either Greek or Roman and illustrates the early fertilization of Roman culture by the hellenistic Greeks. The subject of the portrait is T. Quinctius Flamininus, the Roman warrior-politician who finally broke the myth of Macedonian military invincibility by defeating King Philip V of Macedon at the battle of Cynoscephalae in 197 B.C. Although the victory left Rome in control of Macedon and Greece, Flamininus persuaded the Senate not to garrison any Greek city. He was present at the Isthmian Games of 196 B.C., at which the restoration of civic autonomy was proclaimed. The herald's announcement was greeted by a shout of joy so explosive that it was said to have caused the crows to drop dead out of the sky. Flamininus was invited to preside over the Nemean Games at Argos, and the proclamation was repeated there. He spent the next two years traveling from city to city, establishing constitutions and organizing regional leagues. In the process he adopted the divine pretensions which were usual among the great men of the hellenistic era, at least in the Greek-speaking world. About 190 B.C. he was made the object of a cult at Chalcis in gratitude for his intercession on the city's behalf after it had supported the invasion of Antiochus III of Syria. Such divine honors were a common form of compliment, but they had never before been paid to a Roman.

Flamininus' stater was minted in Greece during his proconsular assignment there. It is related by types, style and metrology to the royal Macedonian coinage. His portrait has the disheveled hair and upward gaze in vogue since Alexander and has been shown to be closely modeled on the coin portraits of Flamininus' erstwhile enemy Philip V. Its baroque style belongs to the Asian rather than the Alexandrian school. It features rugged, expressive modeling, softened a bit since the days of the Diadochi [104]. It also displays a sympathy for lean, aquiline features which is evident in contemporary Seleucid as well as Macedonian portraiture.

The reverse type is derived from the gold staters of Alexander the Great, even to the stiffness of the Nike figure; contrast [105]. The coronation of Flamininus' name is a detail used previously by Lysimachus among others [102]. The Roman character of Flamininus' staters lies in their Latin legend, which identifies him as the issuing authority. These staters thus prefigure the Roman military issues in gold, struck by field commanders on their own authority to meet military needs [118, 120]. However the circumstances and purpose of Flamininus' coinage remain elusive. The lack of associated silver suggests its purpose was honorary or commemorative rather than practical; in this regard see also [113].

110 SILVER TETRADRACHM OF LEBEDUS

OBVERSE:
   Helmeted head of Athena right, wearing thunderbolt earring.
REVERSE:
   ΛΕΒΕΔΙΩΝ, owl standing right on club between the horns of a
   filleted double cornucopia, across lower field magistrate's name or
   title ΠΡΥΤ—ΑΝΙΣ, all within laurel wreath.

Attic standard, weight 17.02 gm; diameter 34 mm. ↑

Struck circa 160 B.C.

Same dies: Kastner 4 (1973), lot 117 = Leu 28 (1981), lot 152; Leu 13
   (1975), lot 234. This magistrate not represented in major collections.

Ex Kirikhan hoard, Cilicia 1972 (*Coin Hoards* 1 [1975], p. 26, 87a).

Very rare variant of a rare coinage.

The second century B.C. saw a tendency among autonomous cities to abandon the old principle of particular civic coinage in favor of larger currency systems. In this they were of course only following the example of the hellenistic kingdoms which had produced essentially uniform coinages from multiple mints. The development of such broad currency systems entailed a loss of typological diversity in the major denominations and often of a weakening of aesthetic standards as well.

A happy exception to these bleak generalizations is the body of tetradrachms to which this coin belongs. Such broad-flanned tetradrachms were issued by a number of coastal Asian cities which retained local types even as they adopted a common style and fabric along with the unifying device of a wreath on every reverse. The ubiquitous wreath inspired the nickname *stephanephori*, "wreath-bearers," for this class of tetradrachms. It has been hypothesized that the coins were issued from a single mint. But if this was the case, magistrates from each participating city must have supervised the coining of their own consignment of silver.

The head of Athena appears on the tetradrachms of several of the participating cities, reflecting the widespread popularity of her worship. The version produced for the town of Lebedus stands apart because it is *not* based on the Athenian cult statue of Athena Parthenos as popularized on Athenian tetradrachms of the middle hellenistic period. The principal difference lies in the pleasing simplicity of the helmet, whose decoration is reduced to its triple crest, an olive wreath over the visor and a double rim which curves gracefully at the neck and forms a restrained spiral over the ear. The features of Athena's face are extremely delicate, even the distorted eye. Its huge size, semi-frontal shape and rigid stare may reflect the influence of Ptolemaic coinage [106], for Lebedus had been a Ptolemaic dependency in the preceding century. The ultra-refined modeling too has a perfumed quality deriving from the Alexandrian school. The engraving is minutely graceful, far surpassing the delicacy of most stephanephori from other cities.

The reverse type of this tetradrachm, as of most stephanephori, is not so much a subject as a conglomeration of symbols. This in fact is characteristic of much middle hellenistic coinage [112]. The owl is associated with Athena [58, 66] and is depicted much as on contemporary Athenian tetradrachms. The double

cornucopia may be a survival from Ptolemaic days [106ff] or it may symbolize the cult of Dionysus which inspired the types of the city's bronze coinage.

The magistrate's name on the reverse fulfills the same function as the symbols and/or monograms on earlier coins; it serves to distinguish an issue and identify the responsible magistrate. The appearance of full names in hellenistic times has been connected with widespread economic stagnation which made citizens reluctant to assume the burdens of local public office. The small celebrity of having one's name inscribed on coins or public works was intended as an inducement to public service.

111 SILVER TETRADRACHM OF COS

OBVERSE:
  Draped bust of Aphrodite right, crowned with myrtle, wearing bead necklace.
REVERSE:
  ΚΩΙΩΝ, Asclepius standing right, resting weight on staff entwined by serpent, in left field magistrate's name ΝΙΚΟΣΤΡΑΤΟΣ.

Attic standard, weight 16.96 gm; diameter 37 mm. ↑

Struck circa 150 B.C.

Same obverse die: *Hunter* p. 432, 10 and pl. 54, 18; *Pozzi* 2660;
  K. Regling, "Hellenistischer Münzschatz aus Babylon," *ZfN* 38 (1928), 124ff.

The seventh specimen published, the fifth with this magistrate.

The island of Cos in the Sporades was one of the great hellenistic centers of the healing arts. In the fifth century it was the home of Hippocrates, the founder of scientific medicine. The cult of Asclepius, the god of healing, was introduced in the middle of the fourth century. The sanctuary was not unlike a modern spa or sanatorium with associated baths, gymnasia and entertainment facilities. The medicine practiced by the Coan physicians depended heavily on lifestyle prescriptions such as diet, bathing and regimens of exercise. These wholesome practices were only secondary to the religious experience of *incubation*, in which the patient spent the night in the holy precincts and received a visitation from the god, who either healed him directly or recommended a course of treatment. The intense, personal relationship between the god and his worshiper represents a new phase of Greek religion. It testifies to a spiritual hunger which persisted from hellenistic into Roman times and eventually contributed to the rise of Christianity.

Though Cos had had a coinage since the seventh century B.C., Asclepius did not figure on it until the time of this tetradrachm. He appears with his usual attributes, a staff and a sacred snake, symbolic of his ancient connection with the earth. The snake was in fact Asclepius' alter ego, whose presence was required whenever a new temple was dedicated. It would seem a natural supposition that the figure on the tetradrachm duplicates the Coan cult statue, but this cannot be proved. It does replicate a series of statuettes found in the sanctuary of Asclepius at Epidaurus, which definitely do not resemble the seated cult statue there. It has been suggested that the statuettes and the Coan tetradrachm reverse reflect a lost masterpiece of Bryaxis, perhaps located at Alexandria if not at Cos.

Cos was described by Pliny (*N.H.* 36.5.4) as the home of two brilliant art works which had Aphrodite as their subject. One was a draped statue of the goddess by Praxiteles which the Coans had acquired in preference to the celebrated nude at nearby Cnidus, and which seems to have disappeared without leaving identifiable copies. Far more influential was the painting of Apelles, Aphrodite *Anadyomene*, which depicted the goddess rising from the sea and wringing the water out of her hair. The theme was widely adapted by hellenistic sculptors, while the motif of holding her tresses away from her head in two thick bunches was applied to other poses as well. The head of Aphrodite on this tetradrachm cannot be securely connected with either of these masterpieces. The drapery at her neck indicates that she is conceived as modestly clothed, perhaps like the statue. But the rolled hair, loosely knotted with wavy locks falling at the back of the neck, creates at least a vague relation to the many depictions of Aphrodite Anadyomene and Aphrodite bathing. The goddess's features are rather contemporary, with a pointed and slightly upturned nose, protruding eye and small mouth which would not have been found beautiful in the fourth century. The same delicacy of feature may be observed in other middle hellenistic works [39], all of which seem to reflect a diffusion of the erotic style of Alexandria.

112 SILVER TETRADRACHM OF ALEXANDER I BALAS OF SYRIA

Regnal dates: 150–145 B.C.

OBVERSE:
Laureate head of Zeus right.

REVERSE:
ΒΑΣΙΛΕΩΣ ΑΛΕΞΑΝΔΡΟΥ above and below horizontal winged thunderbolt, above date ϹΞΡ (year 166 of the Seleucid era) and monogram ⊠, below monograms ⊟Υ and Ҳ, all within laurel wreath.

Attic standard, weight 16.06 gm; diameter 31 mm. →

Attributed to the Zeus Master of Seleucia Pieria. Struck at Seleucia Pieria, 147/146 B.C.

Published: A. Houghton, "A Tetradrachm of Seleucia Pieria at the Getty Museum," *JPGM* 10 (1982), p. 155, F.

Equivalent coin, various dies: E. Babelon, *Les rois de Syrie* (Paris, 1890), 885. Variant: *BMC Seleucid Kings of Syria* 16.

Of the highest rarity: one of ten specimens known to Houghton, and the only one from these dies.

Alexander Balas was a pretender to the Syrian throne who claimed to be a younger son of Antiochus IV. Supported by Ptolemy VI of Egypt, who gave him his daughter to wife, Alexander possessed himself of the Phoenician coastal town of Ake in 150 B.C. Ake was the base from which he extended his rule over the rest of Syria. There is numismatic evidence which suggests that Seleucia Pieria was the first city of northern Syria to recognize Alexander, and as such it was surely of the utmost strategic importance to him. The special ties between Alexander and Seleucia Pieria probably account for the small and exceptional issue of royal tetradrachms struck at the port city in 147/146 B.C. These stand apart from the main royal series of the Seleucids because they employ the municipal types of Seleucia Pieria itself, although Alexander is plainly named as the issuing authority. Zeus and the thunderbolt both recall the foundation of Seleucia Pieria in 300 B.C. by Seleucus I Nicator, who chose the site after a thunderclap which he interpreted as an omen from Zeus. In fact, thunder enjoyed an ancient cult in northern Syria, so that Seleucus was blending native and Olympian religion in the service of his political aims.

Alexander's tetradrachm issue from Seleucia Pieria comprises only three obverse dies of contrasting style. This one combines certain revivals of the Phidian manner—chiseled features, straight forehead, protruding lower lip and smooth modeling—with others which derive from more expressive contemporary models, notably the sunken cheek. The head generally exemplifies an archaizing tendency which exists alongside contemporary style in hellenistic coinage and which, on Seleucid coins of the mid-second century, reflects a special interest in fifth-century classicism. This tetradrachm also offers a rare glimpse of an artist struggling to find his own language, an artist important enough to risk working independently of the stylistic canons of Greek art. His line is exceptionally delicate, his modeling subtle yet expressive. The Zeus Master of Seleucia Pieria is certainly a major figure, and his hand can be detected at several Seleucid mints in succeeding reigns.

The unusual hairstyle, involving tight corkscrew curls all around the face, perhaps reflects Ptolemaic influence. A Libyan coiffure, it was associated with the Egyptian goddess Isis and became popular with the Ptolemaic queens in the second century B.C. In fact, Alexander Balas' Egyptian wife Cleopatra Thea affected such a coiffure. It is difficult to explain its transfer to a male, however it is the usual coiffure for the kings of several Semitic kingdoms in the first century. Perhaps, then, the coiffure is a reference to the Semitic roots of the thunder cult at Seleucia Pieria. There may be a common origin for both the Libyan and Semitic corkscrew coiffures. There is also evidence for an important statue of Zeus the Thunderer with classical features and corkscrew curls at the back of the head, but its relation to the coin type is obscure.

113 GOLD STATER OF PHARNACES II OF THE CIMMERIAN BOSPORUS

Regnal dates: 63–47 B.C.

OBVERSE:

Diademed head of Pharnaces right with flowing locks, wearing earring.

REVERSE:

ΒΑΣΙΛΕΩΣ ΒΑΣΙΛΕ—ΩΝ above, ΜΕΓΑΛΟΥ ΦΑΡΝΑΚΟΥ below, Apollo seated left on omphalos, holding laurel branch and resting left elbow on lyre, tripod in front, three pellets in left field, in right field date ϹΜϹ (year 246 of the Pontic era).

Attic standard, weight 8.19 gm; diameter 20.5 mm. ↑

Struck at Panticapaeum, 52/51 B.C.

Published: K.C. Golenko and P.J. Karyszowski, "The Gold Coinage of King Pharnaces of the Bosporus," *NC* 1972, p. 38, fig. 3; M&M 47 (1972), lot 478.

Found near Trebizond.

Approximately fifteen specimens known, ranging in date from 55/54 to 51/50 B.C.

Pharnaces II was the unfilial son of Mithradates VI of Pontus. Mithradates' attempt to drive Rome out of Asia was the dominant problem in foreign affairs for the Roman Republic during the first half of the first century B.C. Neither Lucullus nor Pompey the Great could break Mithradates, but the treacherous Pharnaces drove him to suicide by fomenting a revolt among his own men. Pompey rewarded Pharnaces somewhat stingily, granting him only the European portions of his father's kingdom. In 48 B.C., when Rome was incapacitated by the civil war between Pompey and Caesar, Pharnaces reappropriated his father's lands in Asia. The following year the victorious Caesar defeated him in a lightning five-day campaign. This was the victory which Caesar commemorated in his Roman triumph with the famous motto *Veni, vidi, vici*—"I came, I saw, I conquered." Pharnaces nonetheless retained possession of his European kingdom until his death in 45 B.C.

The portrait on Pharnaces' extremely rare gold staters adopts the divine pretensions introduced on the coinage of his father, who had claimed to be a new incarnation of Dionysus. The signs of this apotheosis are the flowing leonine locks and inspired upward gaze, both deriving ultimately from the iconography of Alexander the Great. Pharnaces also bears a certain physical resemblance to Mithradates, but the bolder plasticity of his coinage emphasizes the ungainliness of his features. The resulting grandiose awkwardness is reminiscent of the portraits of Ptolemy I [103].

Apollo is a new reverse type for the Pontic and Bosporan royal coinage. He is particularly associated with the Seleucid dynasty and perhaps appears here as a claim to the Seleucid heritage. The Seleucid throne in fact fell vacant in the year these staters were first struck. Pharnaces, the son of a Seleucid princess, might well consider himself the logical heir to the Seleucid realm despite the inconvenient fact that Rome had recently converted Syria into a province.

The titulature of Pharnaces' coinage bespeaks great ambitions. The imperial title King of Kings was particular to the Persian ruler, but it had been successfully usurped by the Armenian king Tigranes the Great, last ruler of the Seleucid kingdom. On his death several eastern potentates adopted the evocative formula, but none was universally recognized as entitled to its use. Indeed Pharnaces dropped it when he allied with Orodes of Parthia, also a King of Kings, prior to his invasion of Asia Minor.

Pharnaces' gold staters are dated according to the Pontic era, a calendar based on the foundation of the kingdom of Pontus in 297 B.C. It is surprising to find them unconnected with the finances of Pharnaces' Asian campaign. It has been suggested that the sole purpose of this small series was to lay formal claim to the title King of Kings.

114 GOLD STATER OF PHARAONIC EGYPT

OBVERSE:
  Horse rearing right, dotted border.

REVERSE:
  Hieroglyph beaded necklace (*nub*, "gold") across hieroglyph heart and windpipe (*nefer*, "good").

Persic standard(?), weight 8.25 gm; diameter 19 mm. ↑

Struck by Nektanebo II, circa 350 B.C.

Same obverse die: *ACGC* 1064. Same reverse die: J.W. Curtis, "Coinage of Pharaonic Egypt," *JEA* 43 (1957), pl. 10, 5. Equivalent coins, various dies: E. Chassinet, "Une monnaie d'or à légendes hiéroglyphes trouvée en Egypte," *BIAO* 1 (1901), pp. 78ff = Svoronos 9; G.K. Jenkins, "Greek Coins Recently Acquired by the British Museum," *NC* 1955, p. 145, no. 24 = *PCG* pl. 51, 12.

Rare: about two dozen specimens known to Curtis, from three obverse and two reverse dies.

A mere handful of coins is known from Pharaonic Egypt. This very rare stater belongs to the only issue with original and distinctly Egyptian types. It dates from Egypt's last independent dynasty, the thirtieth, and probably from the reign of its last king, Nekht-har-hebi, known to the Greeks as Nektanebo II (359–340 B.C.). The nephew of Pharaoh Tachos, he was commander of the Egyptian troops in Syria during the Satrapal Revolt against Persia but rebelled against his king and returned to take Egypt by force. In 351–350 B.C. he foiled a long-planned Persian attempt to restore Egypt to its empire. A second Persian invasion in 344–343 was successful, but Nektanebo found refuge in Ethiopia and retained control of Upper Egypt for another few years. Normally we would expect to connect the issue of currency with one of these military adventures. But the types of Nektanebo's gold staters strongly suggest that they were intended for educated native recipients rather than Greek mercenaries.

The staters of Nektanebo have the unique distinction of bearing a double hieroglyphic inscription. The running horse, seemingly a type drawn from the Greek repertory, in fact represents the word *nefer*, "good," in the Saite dialect. On one specimen of the stater it is accompanied by the symbol for gold. The same sym-

bol, a beaded necklace (*nub* or *nebou*), appears on the reverse of these staters. The heart and windpipe is the more usual hieroglyph for *nefer*, "good," and was occasionally used as a countermark on silver coins. Thus both sides of the stater proclaim its pure metal content, a precaution perhaps inspired by the memory of the days when coins were commonly defaced or chisel-cut to test their purity.

The archaistic stallion with its long trunk is stylistically comparable to the horses on contemporary Siculo-Punic and later Carthaginian coinage; Greek horses at this period tend toward a theatrical style, featuring rounded forms and high action [93, 94]. The hieroglyph of the reverse is far more solid than normal for hieroglyphs and lacks their decorative elegance.

The inexperience of the moneyers is manifest in the fluctuating weight of these staters, which are described only conjecturally as conforming to the Persic standard. There is no inconsistency in the use of this standard by enemies of Persia, for until the conquest of Alexander the Great the Persian daric was the accepted gold coin of the eastern Mediterranean world.

115 SILVER DECADRACHM OF CARTHAGE

OBVERSE:
   Head of Tanit left, wearing crown of grain and droplet earring, dotted border.

REVERSE:
   𐤟𐤟𐤟𐤟𐤟 (B'RST, "in the land"), Pegasus flying right, dotted border.

Uncertain standard, weight 37.74 gm; diameter 42 mm. ↑

Struck probably in Sicily, circa 260 B.C.

Same dies: G.K. Jenkins and R.B. Lewis, *Carthaginian Gold and Electrum Coins*, RNS Special Publication no. 2 (London, 1963), pl. 27, 2; G.K. Jenkins, "Coins of Punic Sicily, Part 4," *SNR* 57 (1978), pl. 18, 440 (2"/9).

This decadrachm is an issue of Carthage, the great Phoenician colony in North Africa which dominated the far western Mediterranean. It dates from the early years of the First Punic War, when Carthage matched its strength against Rome. Sicily was the main theatre of the war around 260 B.C., and that is where these decadrachms have been unearthed. Possibly they were minted on the island, possibly at Carthage and then transported to Sicily. The issue of decadrachms must have some connection with war finances. However this is the only decadrachm group which does not seem to have been intentionally elevated above ordinary coinage, and no commemorative function has ever been suggested for it. Indeed there is scant reason to think that the Carthaginians regarded these coins as ten-drachma pieces, for their monetary system was in a state of rapid flux in this period and the drachma was no longer their unit of weight. Furthermore Carthage produced an even larger silver denomination at approximately the same time, though with simpler types.

The earliest Carthaginian coins were inspired by Sicilian models, and this head can still be recognized as a descendant of the Arethusa head on decadrachms of Euainetus [86]. The goddess represented here is Tanit, chief divinity of Carthage. She was particular to that city but was recognized as equivalent to Greek Hera and Phoenician Astarte. Just as Arethusa underwent a transformation on coinage into the grain goddess Persephone, Tanit seems to have become assimilated to Demeter, goddess of the fertile earth. This is the significance of the grain ears woven into her hair.

The reverse type of Pegasus may have been inspired by the Corinthian staters which circulated widely in Sicily in the second half of the fourth century B.C. The winged horse might also have been familiar as a popular subject of South Italian vase painting [15]. Pegasus is not known to have played a role in Carthaginian mythology, but our knowledge is distressingly scanty as a result of Rome's vindictive destruction of all Punic records. It is possible that he is merely an elaboration on the wingless horse which constitutes the regular reverse type of Carthaginian coins and which has been clearly identified as a solar symbol.

The Carthaginian decadrachms display a distinct Punic style which is something more than mere barbarization of Greek models. Fourth-century Greek numismatic art evolved in the direction of greater realism, including the ability to portray soft textures. The style of the Siculo-Punic decadrachms on the other hand immediately impresses with its flat, hard and slightly abstract aesthetic. Tanit's hair is schematized along geometric lines, with little to suggest that the neat rows of curls are of the same substance as the gently waving hairs on the crown of the head. Her nose is harsh, and the elongated profile eye is sharply cut to create strong shadows in alternating bands. The Pegasus is related to the muscular, theatrical type of horse favored by the Greeks since the fourth century, but his anatomy contains many impossibilities. The excessively long body is a West Greek mannerism. The swayed back and strangely misshapen wing occur consistently on other Punic coins of this period, while the too-short forelegs characterized even the fourth-century Punic coinage of the Panormus and Rash Melqart mints.

116 SILVER SHEKEL OF THE JEWISH WAR

OBVERSE:
[לF]٩W⅄ לᵖW (shekel yisrael, "shekel of Israel"), chalice, above ⅄W (sh[nat] ⅄, "year five"), dotted border.

REVERSE:
⅄Wᶠ٩ᵖ⅄ ⅄⅄⅃Wᶠ٩⅄ (Yerushalayim hak'dosha, "Jerusalem the holy"), stem with three fruit, dotted border.

Phoenician standard, weight 13.86 gm; diameter 22 mm. ↖

Struck in Jerusalem, 70 A.D.

Equivalent coins, various dies: J. Baramki, "Coins in the Palestine Archeological Museum, Part 3," *QDAP* 8 (1939), p. 77, pl. 41, 2 = Y. Meshorer, *Jewish Coins of the Second Temple Period* (Tel Aviv, 1967), 164; A. Spijkerman, "Trésor de sicles juifs trouvé au Mont des Oliviers à Jerusalem," *SM* 11, No. 42, p. 32, no. 14; L. Kadman, *Corpus Nummorum Palaestinensium, 3. The Coins of the Jewish War of 66–73 C.E.* (Jerusalem, 1960), 44, 45; *Israel Numismatic Bulletin* 1 (January–March 1962), p. 18.

Found at Masada prior to 1965.

One of nine specimens known, the only one in private hands.

The first Jewish revolt against Rome erupted in 66 A.D. in protest over the effort of the Roman procurator Gessius Florus to requisition seventeen talents from the Temple treasury. This was only the last in a series of affronts to Jewish religious sensibilities, and the revolt was fueled in addition by the economic grievances of the lower classes. Initial success in deposing collaborationist politicians and in driving the Romans from Judaea, Samaria and Idumaea left the rebels free to organize a provisional national government. They gave high priority to the design and production of an autonomous coinage of specifically Jewish character. Their silver shekels are of particular importance because the issue of precious metal coinage was a prerogative of sovereign governments only. This was in fact the first such coinage in Jewish history.

The obverse type of the Jewish War shekels is a chalice. It represents a ritual vessel pertaining to the Temple, probably one of the two mixing bowls for the libation service which flanked the menorah. Similar chalices are associated with the menorah in contemporary folk art. The reverse depicts three budding pomegranates, a motif used repeatedly in the decoration of the Temple, its vessels and the priestly garb. A specific allusion may be intended to the mantle of the high priest, whose custody by the Romans had been a sore point.

A very prominent feature of the Jewish War coinage is its handsome calligraphy. The legends are expressed in an archaic Hebrew script revived for symbolic purposes, although the daily language of Judaea was now Aramaic. Also prominent is a series of dates, "Year One" through "Year Five." Traditionally it has been assumed that the basis for these dates was the Jewish liturgical calendar, which probably began its year in autumn in the month of Nisan. According to this hypothesis, Years One and Five were partial years—a supposition supported by the rarity of coins bearing these dates. However it has also been argued that the rebels may have conceived their national rebirth as the beginning of a new era and made it the basis of a new calendar after the fashion of the hellenistic monarchies [112, 113]. The era of freedom was probably reckoned from the repudiation of

sacrifice to the Roman emperor in late spring of 66 A.D., probably in the month of Iyyar. This hypothesis accords even better with the frequencies of the Jewish War shekels. The relative rarity of the Year One coinage can be explained by a slow start-up and lack of bullion in the early days of the fighting, while the extreme rarity of Year Five coins results from the fact that the Temple, probable location of the mint, was captured by Titus only a few months into the fifth year of the new era.

This shekel is one of only nine specimens known bearing the date Year Five. All were found either in Jerusalem or at the fortress of Masada, where the last small band of some 900 fanatics chose mass suicide rather than succumb to Roman siegecraft. This shekel is blackened from burning, quite probably in the holocaust which destroyed the Temple.

117 BRONZE DECUSSIS

OBVERSE:
    Head of Roma right, wearing Phrygian helmet with crest ending in griffin's head, mark of value X behind neck, all on raised disc.

REVERSE:
    Prow left, mark of value X above, all on raised disc.

Post semilibral standard, weight 708 gm; diameter 115 mm. ↑

Rome mint, struck 215–212 B.C.

Published: M&M 52 (1975), lot 296.

Equivalent coins, various dies: E. Haeberlin, *Aes Grave, das Schwergeld Roms und Mittelitaliens* (Frankfurt, 1910), pl. 46, 1–3; R. Thomsen, *Early Roman Coinage* 1 (Copenhagen, 1957), fig. 103; Crawford 41/1.

Thomsen cites two specimens.

While the Greeks had made use of precious metal coinage from the very beginning and only came late to the use of bronze, the original native currency of Italy was bronze. The reason for this was probably supply: silver was scarce in the Italian peninsula, whereas the ores for smelting bronze were plentiful in northern and central Italy. The earliest pieces for exchange were simply large, rough bars of bronze of varying weight (*aes rude*), later superseded by flat rectangular plates bearing various designs (*aes signatum*).

Actual coinage, in the sense of round tokens of prescribed weight, was first attempted in the last quarter of the fourth century B.C., apparently inspired by contact with the Greek city of Neapolis in southern Italy. Around 289 B.C. a true monetary system was at last established, based on a bronze *as* with several fractional denominations, each identified by a mark of value and relatively constant types. This cast bronze coinage (*aes grave*) remained the basis of Roman exchange throughout the third century. Though silver didrachms were occasionally struck in Rome's name in southern Italy, they bore no marks of value and seem to have circulated as bullion, not as an intrinsic part of the currency system.

For Rome, the third century was a period of territorial expansion and nearly constant warfare, with significant consequences for her coinage. The enormous expenses involved in building fleets and equipping and maintaining armies produced a steady inflation, and the demand for bronze for weapons caused its value to rise. Thus every successive issue of coinage was struck with reduced weights reflecting the diversion of the metal to other uses. But by the time of the Second Punic War the as, which had begun with a weight of around 322 gm, had been reduced to a mere eighty-eight gm.

This coin dates from that black hour of crisis, in which Hannibal ravaged Italy at will, and Rome sent out army after army to be destroyed. The decussis is in fact a ten-as multiple, as the mark of value X (Roman numeral ten) indicates. It belongs to the last issue struck on the bronze standard. Efforts to rehabilitate the standard were vain, and in 211 B.C. or thereabouts Rome was forced to convert to a monetary system based on silver, whose standard denomination, the denarius, was equivalent to ten asses or one decussis.

The head of Roma on the obverse of the decussis shows the influence of hellenistic royal portraiture in her elevated gaze and noble, commanding expression [102, 104, 109, 113]. The winged Phrygian helmet is a symbol of victory and of godly power with strong oriental associations, perhaps alluding to the supposed Trojan roots of the city. Interestingly, the helmet with its griffin ornament is paralleled on contemporary silver coins of Philip V of Macedon, an ally of Hannibal with whom Rome skirmished about this time. On both coinages the winged helmet may signify imperial ambitions.

The prow is the regular reverse type of all Republican bronze coinage produced after about 225 B.C. Ancient commentators relate the type to the mythology of Saturn or to Janus, patron of shipbuilding. This type too has a parallel on the royal Macedonian coinage, in this case the tetradrachms of Antigonus III Doson.

50% of actual size

118 AUREUS OF BRUTUS

† 42 B.C.

OBVERSE:
  IMP BRVTVS, bare head of Brutus right, laurel wreath around.

REVERSE:
  CASCA LONGVS, combined military and naval trophy, L in left field, dotted border.

Weight 8.04 gm; diameter 20 mm. ↓

Moneyer Casca Longus, mint moving with Brutus, struck 43–42 B.C.

Same dies: *BMCRR* 2, p. 478, 62 and pl. 111, 14; Bahrfeldt 65, pl. 7, 16; Sydenham 1297; Crawford 507/1b.

Of the highest rarity.

The history of the late Roman Republic is a tale of the collapse of institutions when confronted by ruthless individualism. Legitimate possessions of the state—its armies, treasure and even provinces—were somehow appropriated by a series of warlords whose rivalries unleashed cataclysmic civil wars. Coinage was one of several government functions transformed in this process. Official state currency was virtually superseded by emergency military issues, the so-called imperatorial coinage. This coinage was minted by the leading contenders for power, in their own names, in order to maintain their private armies. Its types are aggressively propagandistic, celebrating the personality and achievements of the commander or pressing his political claims.

This extremely rare aureus is such an issue of Caesar's assassin Brutus. Shakespeare has taught us to regard him as "the noblest Roman of them all," a patriot and a defender of liberty. But in reality he was a mirror image of the man he murdered, a keenly ambitious and opportunistic Roman aristocrat—but without Caesar's redeeming features of generosity and genius. The aureus was struck after Brutus and his fellow assassin Cassius spurned their legally assigned commands, fled Italy in the summer of 44 B.C. and seized the empire's eastern provinces. The Senate eventually legalized these actions *ex post facto*, but only because the extraconstitutional alliance of the Second Triumvirate threatened closer to home.

The appearance of Brutus' portrait on his coins is extremely significant. Julius Caesar had been the first living Roman to place his portrait on the Republican coinage, and though he had done so by special dispensation of the Senate, the action was bitterly criticized as "monarchical" by his opponents. After his death the Caesarian party eagerly embraced the notion of portraiture. Thus Brutus' own portraits represent both a betrayal of the stated position of his own party and a contradiction of his own alleged devotion to the old mores.

The style of this portrait owes little to hellenistic royal coinage, which maintained a monumental quality and elevated tone even when relatively small in scale. It shows some affinity to the native Italic portrait tradition, dry, incisive, often with prominent bone structure [43, 44]. However most numismatic portraits of the imperatorial age display an idiosyncratic style, rougher than Italic sculpture and conceptually closer to caricature than to any shade of naturalism. This crude, impressionis-

tic treatment may reflect the personal and informal nature of the bond between these commanders and their men. In this case the exaggerations are certainly vividly expressive of the intangible called character, the true subject of most Roman portraiture. Brutus' intense eye and knotted facial muscles communicate a grim fanaticism which was borne out by all his actions.

The remaining features of the aureus require little elaboration. The wreath and title IMP allude to the acclamation of Brutus and Cassius as *imperatores* ("supreme commanders") by their troops at Sardes in 42 B.C., actually the second acclamation for each. The reverse depicts a battlefield monument composed of the arms of the vanquished, symbolizing actual and anticipated victories. The reverse inscription names the officer entrusted with the supervision of the camp mint, Brutus' fellow conspirator Casca.

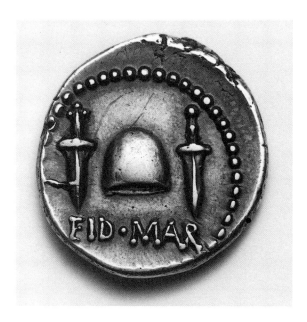

119 SILVER DENARIUS OF BRUTUS

† 42 B.C.

OBVERSE:
BRVT • —IMP—L • PLAET • CEST, bare head of Brutus right, dotted border.

REVERSE:
EID • MAR, pileus between two daggers, dotted border.

Weight 3.73 gm; diameter 19 mm. ↑

Moneyer L. Plaetorius Cestianus, mint moving with Brutus, struck 43–42 B.C.

Published: Naville-Ars Classica 15 (1930), lot 1315.

Same obverse die: H.A. Cahn, "L'aureus de Brutus avec EID.MAR," *Actes*, CIN 1953 (Paris, 1957), obverse die B. Equivalent coins, various dies: E. Babelon, *Monnaies de la republique romaine* (Paris, 1885–86), Junia 52; Cohen 15; Sydenham 1301.

Twenty-three specimens known to Cahn.

The greatest interest of this rare denarius of Brutus lies in its extraordinary reverse type, which celebrates the assassination of Julius Caesar on the Ides of March of 44 B.C. The two daggers represent the weapons of the assassins. Between them is a *pileus*, the cap of liberty. This was the particular headgear of the divine twins Castor and Pollux, patrons of Rome who were believed to have taken the battlefield at the blackest crises of Roman history. Thus the pileus serves to characterize the assassination of Caesar as a profoundly patriotic act, perhaps even divinely authorized. The symbolism of the design is doubly rich because all Romans knew that Brutus was a descendant of Lucius Brutus, the founder of the Roman Republic, who in 509 B.C. swore *on a bloody dagger* to expel the Tarquin kings from Rome. The implied parallel is not merely legendary window-dressing but an essential part of Brutus' justification for his act: violence against a fellow citizen was a capital crime, but the right of regicide might cancel the offense. Still, so direct an allusion to an act of questionable morality was probably imprudent, and it is virtually unique in Roman coinage. Elsewhere Roman numismatic propaganda cloaks the tragedy of civil war in generalized references to the concepts of patriotism and victory.

The portrait of Brutus on the obverse offers a most interesting contrast to the likeness on the aureus preceding. It is just possible to recognize that the same man is depicted from the hollow cheek and lantern jaw. But this portrait is at the same time more realistic and less vivid than the aureus portrait. The wide eye and raised eyebrow give the face a noble and sympathetic expression but do not hint at the intensity so brilliantly portrayed on the aureus. The denarius portrait in fact shows affinities to a different tradition, the hellenizing classicism which was perhaps the dominant style of late Republican portrait sculpture. It aimed for refinement, exquisitely modeled and finished surfaces and psychological subtlety. The history of Roman imperial portraiture can be written largely in terms of alternation between these two poles: the vigorous and unaffected Italic style and the elevated and cultivated hellenistic style.

120 AUREUS OF MARC ANTONY AND ANTYLLUS

† 30 B.C.

OBVERSE:
ANTON • AVG • IMP III • COS • DES • III • III • V R P • C, bare head of Antony right, dotted border.

REVERSE:
M • ANTONIVS M • F • F, bare head of Antyllus right, dotted border.

Weight 8.06 gm; diameter 19 mm. ↗

Mint moving with Antony, struck 34 B.C.

Published: Kastner 4 (1973), lot 212.

Equivalent coins, different dies: *BMCRR* 2, p. 521, 174; Bahrfeldt 93; Crawford 541/2, pl. 44.

Nine examples known to Bahrfeldt, none sharing dies with the Hunt specimen.

Although coin portraiture of living Romans was shocking at its introduction, it became a commonplace virtually overnight. The members of the Second Triumvirate—Marc Antony, Octavian and Lepidus—made extensive use of double portraits to advertise their political alliance. But the exuberant Antony went beyond the practice of his colleagues to honor members of his own family. These included his brother Lucius Antony in the year of his consulship (41 B.C.); Antony's fourth wife Octavia, sister of Octavian (39 B.C.); his eldest son Marc Antony Junior (34 B.C.); and his fifth wife Cleopatra, queen of Egypt (32 B.C.). This series of portraits moves from innovation within the Roman tradition to complete estrangement from Roman values, paralleling Antony's own personal development.

Of these portrait coins, the aurei featuring Marc Antony Junior are by far the rarest. The boy, nicknamed Antyllus by the Greek historians, was born of Antony's third marriage to Fulvia. In 44 B.C. he was left in Rome as a pledge of his father's good conduct. In 36 B.C. he was betrothed to Octavian's daughter Julia and then joined Antony in Asia Minor. Antyllus was only eleven years old when coinage was issued in his honor. Its purpose must have been to publicize the boy and to promote his career, presumably among a select group of high-ranking officers. This paternal concern for Antyllus' future fits well with Antony's other actions in 34 B.C., for this was the year of the "Donations of Alexandria" in which Antony and Cleopatra unveiled their dynastic settlement and parceled out the orient among the queen and her four children. Antyllus was excluded from these arrangements and was deliberately raised as a Roman. The defeat at Actium in September of 31 B.C. provoked a reassessment: after Antyllus as intermediary failed to effect a reconciliation between Octavian and his father, he assumed the *toga virilis* in Roman ceremonies along with Caesarion, Cleopatra's son by Julius Caesar. This ceremony fatally marked the two young men as joint heirs to Cleopatra's kingdom. When the victorious Octavian entered Alexandria, Antyllus claimed sanctuary in the temple of Divus Julius but was nevertheless seized and put to death.

In Antony's portrait we are faced with the rather incongruous combination of an elegant finish applied to grotesque and exag-

gerated features, perhaps the result of exposure to Ptolemaic portraiture. The general outlines of Antony's countenance are not unlike those of Ptolemy I [103], whose portrait, considerably vitiated, remained the obverse type of Ptolemaic tetradrachms almost to the end of the dynasty. Antony's portrait, like Ptolemy's, is extremely expressive in terms of character, communicating physical vitality, bluff sociability and a guileless nature. The eye is one of the finest details in all of Republican coinage. It sparkles with animation and love of pleasure, but the loose flap of skin below it hints at excess and dissipation.

The portrait of Antyllus is the first likeness of a child in a medium specialized in suggesting the qualities of successful politicians. Thus it is hardly surprising that the artist was incapable of finding depth in his subject. The lack of a conscious approach becomes even more apparent upon comparison of the different versions of this portrait, for there is little similarity among the dies. Here the artist has emphasized Antyllus' resemblance to his father through the modeling of the cheek and of the deepset eye and also through the open, smiling expression with its suggestion of social rather than intellectual virtues.

121 AUREUS OF OCTAVIAN

Dates as Octavian: 44–27 B.C.

OBVERSE:
CAESAR DIVI F—COS • VII, bare head of Octavian right, small capricorn under neck truncation, dotted border.

REVERSE:
AEGVPT—CAPTA above and below crocodile right, dotted border.

Weight 8.12 gm; diameter 21 mm. ↑

Pergamum(?) mint, struck in the first two weeks of 27 B.C.

Published: Leu 10 (1974), lot 14.

Same dies: *BMCRE* 1 (1923), p. 106, 655 = Bahrfeldt 112, 1 = Kent-Hirmer 124.

One of three specimens known.

This excessively rare aureus belongs to a short-lived issue released in the first two weeks of 27 B.C. The obverse legend identifies Octavian only as the son of the deified Julius Caesar and records his seventh consulship, which began on 1 January. Yet on 16 January the Senate awarded him the extremely flattering title Augustus ("Revered One") along with other extraordinary honors. These were promptly publicized on the coinage, and the old nomenclature was never revived.

The portrait is a magnificent early example of official Augustan art. The style and expressive content of the emperor's portrait was a matter of some importance, for in the absence of news media statuary and coin portraits were the primary means of giving the average citizen some sense of familiarity with his ruler. These portraits were officially controlled, with the coin images based on three-dimensional portraits (*imagines*) provided by the central government to each mint. Here Octavian, soon to be Augustus, is rendered in an idealizing Greek style following a sculptural variety developed soon after the battle of Actium (Brendel Type C). This particular die far surpasses others of the same issue in delicacy of conception and execution, and indeed the portrait is one of the greatest of the entire Augustan coinage. The modeling is exquisite, and the dreamy expression suggests

an assimilation to the god Apollo whom Octavian adopted as his patron in the tasks of rebuilding civilized institutions, beautifying Rome and fostering an art and literature worthy of a great culture.

The reverse type celebrates the conquest of Egypt in 30 B.C. which provoked the suicides of Antony and Cleopatra. The crocodile symbolizes the exotic land of the Nile, the newest and richest province of the empire. It is significant that this type, like all of Octavian's extensive victory coinage, makes no direct allusion to the potentially divisive fact that his real antagonist had been another Roman, and a great one. Such choice of types may seem simple and obvious, but comparison with Brutus' passionate EID • MAR reverse [119] shows it was by no means inevitable. Indeed, discreetly jubilant coin types of this sort should probably be counted among the many proofs of Octavian's political genius.

A suitably veiled reference to Antony may be implied by the small capricorn under the neck truncation of the obverse. The capricorn was Octavian's astrological sign. It first appeared on his coinage in 28 B.C., also on an AEGVPTA CAPTA issue, probably in response to a decree of the Senate which declared Octavian's birthday a lucky day and Antony's a day of ill omen.

122 COPPER MEDALLIC AS OF AUGUSTUS

Regnal dates: 27 B.C.–14 A.D.

OBVERSE:
   CAESAR AVGVST • PONT • MAX • TRI—BVNIC • POT, laureate head of Augustus left, crowned from behind by Victory standing left and holding cornucopiae, dotted border.

REVERSE:
   M • SALVIVS • OTHO • III • VIR • A • A • A • F • F • around large S • C, dotted border.

"Triumphal" issue, weight 19.44 gm; diameter 34 mm. ↑

Moneyer M. Salvius Otho, Rome mint, struck 7 B.C.

Published: Naville-Ars Classica 2 (Vautier-Collignon collections, 1922), lot 176; Naville-Ars Classica 11 (Lévis collection, 1925), lot 224; Leu 10 (1974), lot 25.

Same dies: H.A. Grueber, "Roman Bronze Coinage from BC 45–3," NC 1904, p. 232, 56 and pl. 14, 9 = BMCRE 1 (1923), p. 43, 224 = Kent-Hirmer 140. Same obverse die: BN 1 (1976), p. 125, 686 with bibliography for further die mates, pl. 29, 686. Equivalent coins, various dies: Cohen 518, 519; H. Dressel, Die römischen Medaillone des Münzkabinetts der staatlichen Museen zu Berlin (Dublin-Zurich, 1973), 285.

Ex M.P. Vautier or M. Collignon collection, Paris; H.C. Lévis collection, London.

Very rare.

Bronze coinage was of slight importance during the late Republic but was revived by Augustus around 23 B.C. in an attempt to build a monetary system responsive to peacetime needs. Bronze coinage was produced for use in the routine economic transactions of the population at large, whereas precious metal coinage was minted to cover government expenses, such as military payrolls, public works and the like. The two species of coinage display different artistic conceptions which seem to imply different propaganda functions. The precious metal coinage is pictorial in design, and its frequently changing reverse types reiterate Augustus' accomplishments. The bronze by comparison is very dull, its unchanging types relying more on legends than on images; and curiously, the emperor's portrait appears only on the as denomination. The most prominent feature of the bronze coinage is the conspicuous inscription S C on the reverse of every denomination. These letters have long been recognized as an abbreviation for Senatus consulto, "by order of the Senate." The traditional and obvious conclusion, that Augustus authorized the issue of precious metal coinage but left control of bronze coinage with the Senate, is no longer seriously entertained. However it has proved impossible to determine the true relationship of the Senate to bronze coinage despite profound study and ingenious arguments. Augustus' Roman bronze additionally bears the name of a monetary triumvir, in this case M. Salvius Otho, in a survival of a Republican magistracy which was however discontinued within a few years after the issue represented here.

This issue comprises the only conspicuous variation within the otherwise highly standardized Augustan bronze. The most obvious anomaly is the addition of the figure of Victory behind the portrait head. Her presence gives special emphasis to the laurel wreath, the emblem of an imperator or victorious commander, so that the issue is traditionally referred to as triumphal. The medallic flan suggests it may be a special commemorative issue rather than regular currency. The date of issue corresponds to Tiberius' triumph of 7 B.C., celebrating his victories over the Germans. More importantly it also coincides with the vicennalia or twentieth anniversary of the constitutional settlement of 27 B.C. by which the Senate formally recognized Octavian as indispensible to the state. The name Augustus and other honors were conferred on him as perpetual victor and savior of the citizens, thus creating a conceptual link between Victory and Peace as coordinate virtues inherent in the emperor. This commemorative issue extends the symbolism of the triumphal types of Victory and the laurel wreath to imperial anniversaries, an association which persists to the end of Roman coinage [148, 159, 160].

The portrait, though somewhat hard in comparison with the preceding, represents by far the finest style for the Augustan bronze coinage. The raised chin echoes the theme of apotheosis which informs so much of hellenistic royal portraiture. The troubled expression may be intended to convey the emperor's concern for the state and the people. The prototype of the "compassionate victor" portrait variety is the famous Primaporta statue of Augustus, the most influential of his many sculpted portraits.

123 COPPER AS OF GAIUS

Regnal dates: 37–41 A.D.

OBVERSE:
C • CAESAR • AVG • GERMANICVS • PON • M • TR • POT •
bare head of Gaius left, dotted border.

REVERSE:
VESTA S—C, Vesta enthroned left, holding patera and long
sceptre, dotted border.

Weight 11.63 gm; diameter 35 mm. ╱

Rome mint, struck 37–38 A.D.

Published: M&M-Leu (Niggeler collection 3, 1967), lot 1088; Leu 10
(1974), lot 50.

Equivalent coins, various dies: Cohen 27; *RIC* 1 (1923), p. 117, 30;
BMCRE 1 (1923), p. 154, 45.

Ex W. Niggeler collection.

Gaius, nicknamed Caligula ("Little Boots"), was a great-grand-son of Augustus through his mother Agrippina and a great-grandson of the empress Livia through his father Germanicus. The mysterious early death of Germanicus unleashed a titanic feud between Agrippina and the emperor Tiberius. Gaius, trapped in the middle, was raised in obscurity without the special education and early responsibilities of a young man being groomed for the succession. He also suffered immeasurable psychological harm as he witnessed the extermination of his family, while he in residence at the imperial court was forced to dissimulate his feelings. When he inherited the throne at the age of twenty-five he was thus peculiarly unsuited to rule, with nothing to recommend him but his distinguished ancestry.

This as dates from early in Gaius' reign, when he presented himself as the pliant and respectful ward of the Senate. The absence of a laurel wreath emphasizes his civilian aspect, although Gaius also avidly courted the support of the military. The portrait is among the finest of his coinage, which is in fact quite uneven artistically and sometimes even revives the pre-Augustan caricature style. This likeness basically belongs to the classicizing tradition. But the combination of pinched features with an elaborate modeling almost excessive in so young a subject creates a slightly nervous quality which prefigures the young emperor's mental breakdown. Otherwise the portrait is not especially strong in terms of character. In this respect it corresponds to early sculptures of Gaius, presumably accession pieces, which represent the young man as sensitive but bland.

It will be seen that the dull, epigraphical reverses of the Augustan bronze have by this time been replaced by pictorial types similar to those used on precious metal coinage. The figure enthroned here is Vesta, Roman goddess of hearth and home. She was the chief deity of Rome and the object of the cult which was headed by the emperor himself as Pontifex Maximus. For Gaius she had an intense personal significance, for she embodied his reverence for his immediate family, which he took pains to rehabilitate. He even had his mother Agrippina sculpted with attributes of Vesta (see [124] notes). As a figure of propaganda Vesta helped to focus attention on his genuine piety and on the dynastic basis of his succession. The treatment here

displays a visual richness associated with the finest Roman sestertii but rarely found on the small compass of an as. The throne is corniced and heavily ornamented with volutes or rings. The goddess wears transparent garments of great elegance, including a tasseled veil or stole, under which her body assumes a pose of graceful relaxation; this is a Greek conceit dating back to the rich style in sculpture. Vesta's tiny face resembles that of Gaius himself—a detail not without parallel on sestertius reverses of this reign. Perhaps contemporaries recognized one of the emperor's sisters, who enjoyed the social privileges of Vestal Virgins.

124 ORICHALCUM SESTERTIUS OF AGRIPPINA

† 33 A.D.

OBVERSE:

AGRIPPINA • M • F • MAT • C • CAESARIS • AVGVSTI • draped bust of Agrippina right, dotted border.

REVERSE:

S • P • Q • R MEMORIAE AGRIPPINAE, carpentum drawn left by two mules, dotted border.

Weight 30.43 gm; diameter 31 mm. ↓

Rome mint, struck under Gaius, 37 A.D. and later.

Same dies: W. Trillmich, *Familienpropaganda der Kaiser Caligula und Claudius—Agrippina Maior und Antonia Augusta auf Münzen*, AMuGS 8 (Berlin, 1978), obverse die as pl. 2, 6–7, reverse die as pl. 2, 8–9. Equivalent coins, various dies: Cohen 1; *RIC* 1 (1923), p. 118, 42; *BMCRE* 1 (1923), p. 159, 86.

Agrippina the elder was a granddaughter of Augustus, born in 15 B.C. to the emperor's daughter Julia and his co-regent Agrippa. Agrippina's character was unfortunate, for she inherited her father's energy and toughness and her mother's rashness and defiance. She seemed destined for a brilliant future as her charismatic husband Germanicus was next in the line of succession after Tiberius. Germanicus' sudden death perhaps unhinged her. Agrippina attempted to place the blame on Tiberius, by now emperor, and she was so indiscreet in her efforts to organize a dissident party that she brought ruin upon herself and her two older sons. Agrippina committed suicide by voluntary starvation in 33 A.D.

Rather surprisingly Tiberius' heir ultimately was the youngest son of Agrippina and Germanicus (see preceding). Gaius not unnaturally took energetic steps to rehabilitate his mother's reputation. One of the first acts of his reign was the transfer of Agrippina's remains to the mausoleum of Augustus, and the Senate authorized annual games in honor of her memory. Both of the emperor's parents were also commemorated on coinage. That dedicated to Agrippina was particularly epoch-making because no Roman woman had ever before had a coinage issued solely in her name.

The likeness of Agrippina on this sestertius illustrates the power of characterization achieved on the best coin portraits of Gaius' reign. This toughly handsome woman bears a decided resemblance both to her father Agrippa, whose portrait appears on the most common of Gaian bronzes, and to her son the emperor (see preceding), providing a clear link between him and his distinguished grandfather. Yet her domineering personality is given individual expression in her tight lips and shrewish glare. The modeling of the face is somewhat dry and very simple. The hair, with its frizzy texture and real substance, is more lifelike than any we have yet seen on either Greek or Roman coinage.

The reverse of this sestertius is one of the earliest to exploit the elaborate pictorial possibilities offered by the broad flan of this denomination. It depicts a *carpentum*, the ornate mule car used exclusively in Rome by the ladies of the imperial household. It appears here for its role in the annual funeral games in honor of Agrippina: her portrait was affixed to the carpentum and carried in state through the streets of Rome to the circus, where its arrival signaled the start of the celebration. A similar type was used by Tiberius to honor his mother Livia in 22–23 A.D. But the fact that the type is a revival only increases the compliment to Agrippina by implying her equality with the great matriarch of the Julio-Claudian family.

125 ORICHALCUM SESTERTIUS OF NERO

Regnal dates: 54–68 A.D.

OBVERSE:
NERO CLAVD • CAESAR • AVG • GER • P M TR P IMP P P,
laureate head of Nero right with aegis on left shoulder, dotted
border.

REVERSE:
AVG$\bar{\text{V}}$STI—POR—OST • S—C, Port of Ostia flanked by colonnade and breakwater, lighthouse surmounted by statue of
Neptune at top, reclining statue of harbor god below, eight ships in
harbor, dotted border.

Weight 26.93 gm; diameter 36 mm. ↙

Rome mint, struck 64–66 A.D.

Published: Naville-Ars Classica 6 (Bement collection 1, 1924), lot 642.

Equivalent coins, various dies: Cohen 38; *BMCRE* 1 (1923), p. 222,
131f; *RIC* 1 (1923), p. 151, 91; D.W. MacDowall, *The Western
Coinages of Nero*, NNM 161 (New York, 1979), p. 167, 120.

Ex C.S. Bement collection, Philadelphia.

Among the dominant traits of Nero's personality were philhellenism and a comprehensive aestheticism. These far out-
weighed his interest in government, with the absurd result that
he tried to develop two outside careers as a professional stage
actor and as a charioteer. Eventually Nero abandoned Rome for
nearly two years to make an artistic tour of Greece. The four
great panhellenic festivals—the Olympian, Pythian, Isthmian
and Nemean games—were compressed into a single year so that
he could compete in them all, and their traditional programs
were altered so that the emperor could display all of his talents.

Naturally Nero won every contest he entered, and he returned
to Rome to exhibit his more than 1800 prizes in a parody of a
military triumph.

The magnificent corpus of Neronian bronze mostly dates from
the tenth year of his reign or later. It introduces Nero's unforget-
table mature portrait, which reflects his genuine sophistication
and his vulgarity in an incongruous blend. It revives the imagery of divine kingship which colors much hellenistic royal portraiture but which must have been profoundly offensive to a
Rome not yet a century removed from its Republican past. Hellenistic Greek practice accounts for the extremely bold relief;
for the adoption of the aegis, an attribute of Zeus; and above all
for the heroic tone of the portrait despite the undisguised gross-
ness of Nero's features. The octodrachm of Ptolemy III [107] is a
rather good example for all these features and indeed could have
served as Nero's model. The laurel wreath of course belongs to
the Roman tradition, though by this time it had been transformed from a symbol of military victory into an insignia of
imperial rank. The elevated tone of both Greek and Roman
traditions is mocked by the emperor's affected pompadour hairstyle, which he adopted from the lower-class actors and chario-
teers with whom he loved to associate.

More than any previous emperor Nero employed his reverse
types to publicize his specific services to the Roman people,
seemingly in a propaganda offensive following the politically
damaging Great Fire of 64 A.D. Several of his types refer to his

careful supervision of Rome's largely imported and therefore precarious food supply. The most interesting of these celebrates the Port of Ostia, a facility of vital importance to Rome's provisioning. The port was planned and built under Nero's predecessor and adoptive father Claudius and probably dedicated before Nero's accession. Nevertheless as one of the greatest public benefactions of the Julio-Claudian dynasty, it was certainly worthy of a place on Nero's coinage.

Nero also greatly expanded the visual language of the Roman reverse type. This one derives from the hitherto untapped genre of landscape painting. The design offers an aerial view of the artificial harbor, embraced by an arcaded breakwater on the right and a colonnade on the left. The latter presumably represents the offices and warehouses on the docks. These architectural boundaries are balanced by a pair of statues: at the top the sea god Neptune atop the four-storied lighthouse which marked the entrance to the harbor, and at the bottom an artier sculpture of the spirit of the harbor, Deus Ostiensis. Within the frame of these formal elements is a scene of great liveliness, illustrating the workings of the port. The eight vessels are arranged in three tiers in approximate narrative order: those at the top enter the harbor under full sail or oar; those in the middle tier are furling their sails; and those at the bottom are met by guide boats, dock and unload. The degree of detail is remarkable. Tiny human figures can be discerned at their work on most of the vessels, unloading cargo from the docked ship at lower left, climbing

the rigging of the central ship, rowing and catching a line in the skiff at lower center. The composition has sometimes been criticized as cluttered, and indeed it is when compared with the programmatic simplicity of most Roman reverse types. But the animation and spontaneity of the picture are quite germane to its propaganda purpose.

126 ORICHALCUM SESTERTIUS OF GALBA

Regnal dates: April 68–15 January 69 A.D.

OBVERSE:

SER • GALBA • IMP— • —CAES • AVG • TR P, laureate head of Galba right, dotted border.

REVERSE:

ROMA—R XL around, S—C across, statue of Roma in military attire standing left, holding Pax on globe and legionary standard (*aquila*) and resting left elbow on trophy, shield at feet, dotted border.

Weight 28.69 gm; diameter 36 mm. ↓

Gallic mint (Narbonne?), struck toward December of 68 A.D.

Published: Leu 10 (1974), lot 84.

Same dies: C.M. Kraay, *The Aes Coinage of Galba*, NNM 133 (New York, 1956), A81/P22. Equivalent coins, various dies: Cohen 192; *RIC* 1 (1923), p. 203, 41; *BMCRE* 1 (1923), p. 322, 84.

Very rare.

In the general revolt which erupted against Nero in 68 A.D. the first pretender to reach the throne was Galba, an elderly and old-fashioned aristocrat. He was backed by the armies of Spain and Gaul. His political program was based upon a restoration of constitutional government, and he personally embodied the ancient Republican virtues of courage, austerity and discipline which would have to be revived to make it work. Galba's coinage was naturally designed to promote these ideals. At Rome he inherited Nero's mint with its splendid bronze technique, but the Neronian style was burdened with noxious connotations and was largely discarded. Instead Galba reverted to the Italian tradition of naturalism which was associated with the Republic and which had always excelled at depicting tough old men. To this tradition we may trace the honest depiction of Galba's craggy features; his short military haircut; the use of deep cutting rather than subtle modeling; the direct, unpretentious quality; the serious tone; and the dour expression. The style is simultaneously aggressive and polished. The high relief is a holdover from Nero and makes no small contribution to the effect of the work.

This sestertius is in fact a product of an unidentified Gallic mint rather than of Rome, but die linkages and the superb style of its output demonstrate that the mint comprises a workshop of the Roman mint transplanted to the west. This coin is one of the last in the series, and the attenuation of Roman influence may perhaps be perceived in the slight tendency toward idealization. Galba's advanced years are belied by his firm, almost unlined flesh, by his muscular neck and by the military set of his head, implying physical vigor. To be sure there are hints of aging, such as the haggard concavity beneath the fierce, commanding eye and the deep frown line, but these features function equally as expressions of Galba's severe character. Its force is such, in fact, that his portrait seems fully as heroic as Nero's, though the heroism here bears a human, self-achieved stamp in place of pretensions to divinity.

The reverse type of this sestertius is one used exclusively in the western provinces. It celebrates a tax reform designed to reward them for their support of Galba's candidacy—the remission of the *quadragesima Galliarum*, a two and a half percent customs duty levied on all goods transported across the borders of Gaul. (The letter R stands for *remissa*, and the XL is the numeral 40, two and a half being equivalent to one fortieth.)

The visual symbol for the reform is a personification of Rome. Her cult, curiously enough, originated not at Rome but among the hellenistic Greeks, who divinized the increasingly powerful Roman Republic just as they did their own kings and heroes. In Asia the cult of Roma was linked with the worship of the powerful proconsuls of the late Republic, culminating in the cult of Roma and Augustus first recorded at Pergamum in 29 B.C. In this form it was introduced to the western provinces of the empire. Galba's sestertius type thus expresses the loyalty of western Europe to Roma, an attachment no doubt enhanced by the tax reform; but it also implies his own devotion to the Augustan tradition. Roma is more commonly depicted enthroned [137, 154, 165]. This standing version is quite obviously copied from statuary, for the trophy serves as a sculptural support; but the prototype has not been identified. Also exceptional is Roma's military attire with bared right breast, showing a relationship to Virtus, the spirit of martial valor. The iconography of both derives ultimately from that of the ancient Greek Amazons.

127 SILVER DENARIUS OF CLODIUS MACER

Dates of usurpation: April–October 68 A.D.

OBVERSE:
L • CLODI—VS MACER—S • C, bare head of Clodius Macer right, dotted border.

REVERSE:
PRO/PRAE—AFRICAE, galley right, dotted border.

Weight 3.63 gm; diameter 20 mm. ↖

Carthage mint, struck June–August 68 A.D.

Published: Sternberg sale (29 November 1974), lot 47.

Equivalent coins, various dies: Cohen 13; R. Mowat, "Le monnayage de Clodius Macer," *RIN* 15 (1902), 1–6; *RIC* 1 (1923), p. 195, 11; A. Gara, "La monetazione di Clodius Macer," *RIN* 1970, p. 67, 7 and pl. 1, 11 and 12. Variant: *BMCRE* 1 (1923), p. 285, 1.

Ex Tunis hoard, 1964.

Extremely rare: only six portrait dies known to Mowat.

When Galba was recognized by the Senate, several of the other commanders in revolt against Nero delayed swearing allegiance to the new emperor in order to preserve their own freedom of action in an uncertain situation. One of these was L. Clodius Macer, legate of Numidia. His campaign plan was to deprive Rome of African grain and then capture Sicily, the other great granary of the capital, thus starving the imperial city into submission. Clodius Macer's own propaganda represents him as a defender of the constitution and as Rome's liberator, but his contemporaries in Rome regarded him as an ordinary pirate and opportunist. Galba found it easy to remove him by assassination at the hands of an imperial agent, one Trebonius Garutianus. Macer's legions and civilian partisans remained disaffected, however, and threw their support to Vitellius [129], a popular former governor of Africa.

Macer's coinage, struck in silver only, is an eloquent illustration of his pose as a Republican. It actually revives the style of the imperatorial coinage [118] and follows the same principles of type choice. The significance of this revival was not lost upon his contemporaries, for Republican issues still circulated widely, most particularly the debased legionary coinage of Marc Antony. Macer's obverse types include personifications of Roma, Africa, Carthage (his headquarters) and Victory as well as his own much rarer portrait. His reverse types borrow conspicuously from Marc Antony's legionary issues of 32–31 B.C. This borrowing is in the first place a centenary revival. Furthermore Antony made an appropriate political hero, for he was the last significant opponent of Julio-Claudian rule.

The galley, an Antonian type, symbolizes Macer's control of the grain fleet or perhaps his aspirations against Sicily. The letters S C on the obverse legend suggest, falsely, that Macer was acting by decree of the Senate. The reverse legend magnifies his actual title, imperial legate with propraetorial powers, to the grander-sounding Propraetor of Africa, which implies a senatorial grant of *imperium*.

Macer's portrait is executed in the sketchy imperatorial style which approaches caricature. The long, scraggy neck with prominent larynx is a regular feature of portraits of Caesar and of early likenesses of Octavian. The widely spaced legends and uneven lettering also recall the epigraphy of Republican coins. Such observations should make it clear that the relative crudity of Macer's coinage does not result from a lack of adequate workmen in provincial Africa. On the contrary it is an intentional and rather sophisticated reaction against the polish of the Roman mint with all it implied of centralization and authoritarianism.

128 "CIVIL WARS" AUREUS

OBVERSE:
  I • O • M—CAPITOLINVS, diademed bust of Jupiter left, drapery over left shoulder, small palm branch in front, dotted border.
REVERSE:
  VESTA—P—R QVIRITIVM, Vesta enthroned left, holding patera and torch, dotted border.
Weight 7.47 gm; diameter 19 mm. ↓

Nemausus (?) (Nîmes) mint, struck 68 A.D.

Published: Santamaria sale (Bruno Liberati collection, 1924), lot 160; M&M 43 (1970), lot 314; P.-H. Martin, *Die anonymen Münzen des Jahres 68 nach Christus* (Mainz, 1974), p. 81, 95 and pl. 8, 95; recorded *BMCRE* 1 (1923), p. 307, note 72.

Same obverse die: Martin 96K, 96M. Same reverse die: Martin 96r.

Ex Marchese Bruto Liberati collection.

Unique.

Probably the most fascinating relic of the chaotic revolt against Nero is the so-called "Civil Wars" coinage. It is most notable for the absence of any reference to an issuing authority or even to the institution of the Principate. Many of the types would fit well into the repertory of Republican coinage, and the style too shows a loosening of the formality of official imperial art. The various types of this coinage constitute a carefully coordinated propaganda for revolt, with some coins emphasizing Roman patriotism, others honoring the revolted provinces and still others designed to woo and unify the various branches of the military.

This extremely rare aureus is a splendid example of the appeal to patriotism. The obverse shows Jupiter Capitolinus, also called Jupiter Optimus Maximus, whose great temple on the Capitoline Hill was one of the chief centers of Roman state religion. He himself personified the majesty and authority of the state. Thus as a coin type he fulfills at least part of the function of the customary imperial portrait. The style draws on the hellenizing fine arts tradition to which the cult image of Jupiter Capitolinus itself belonged [42]. Such forceful and exuberant treatment is

also found on some Republican coins of the early first century B.C., and it is possible that a Republican allusion is intended.

The figure on the reverse is Vesta, who had already appeared with some frequency on imperial coinage [123] and had been invoked specifically as the patroness of the imperial family. She is depicted here very much in the manner of the imperial coinage. However the legend P R QVIRITIVM is her formal state title and makes it clear that she appears in her aspect as guardian of the sacred relics of Rome's foundation and as protectress of the welfare of the state. She like Jupiter Capitolinus was a chief focus of the old state religion and thus a legitimate object of civic patriotism.

The "Civil Wars" coinage has for some decades been associated with the revolt of the Rhine army against Galba and conjecturally attributed to the fomenters of the revolt, Fabius Valens and A. Caecina. However a recent comprehensive study challenges these views and concludes that the entire coinage was issued by Galba in the course of his revolt against Nero.

129 ORICHALCUM SESTERTIUS OF VITELLIUS

Regnal dates: 19 April–21 December 69 A.D.

OBVERSE:
  A VITELLIVS GERMANICVS IMP AVG P M TR P, laureate and draped bust of Vitellius right, dotted border.

REVERSE:
  PAX—AVGVSTI around, S—C across field, Pax standing left, holding branch and cornucopiae, dotted border.

Weight 27.74 gm; diameter 36 mm. ↓

Rome mint, struck July–December 69 A.D.

Equivalent coins, various dies: Cohen 67; *RIC* 1 (1923), p. 226, 8.
  Same obverse die: NFA 12 (1983), lot 214.

Aulus Vitellius was the most unworthy and incompetent man to achieve imperial rank in the first century. He had been a companion in vice to the last four Julio-Claudian emperors. His appointment as commander of the Lower German legions in November of 68 was no doubt motivated by Galba's hope that his military inexperience and notable lack of character would tend to forestall further revolts like the one which had carried him to power. However, Vitellius' passivity made him an ideal front for two seditious legionary officers, who proclaimed Vitellius emperor and marched on Rome in his name. The invasion was successful, but the army pillaged as if in enemy territory. Its scandalous indiscipline was an omen for the behavior of the emperor himself. Vitellius' brief reign was characterized by extravagance, buffoonery and epicurean gluttony on a heroic scale. He is reported to have spent over 900 million sesterces on

dinners during his six months at Rome, though he usually dined at the homes of others who were often ruined by the expense of entertaining him.

Vitellius' portraits are often classed with those of Galba as splendid examples of naturalism. However there is a category of bronze coin portraits, to which this belongs, which adopts a more pretentious tone. Vitellius had been a close friend of Nero and as emperor made public display of his devotion to Nero's memory. Neronian portraiture must surely have suggested this apotheosis of obesity. In fact it offers a precedent for the arching eyebrow, intently focused eye, flaring nostril and sneering mouth [125]. The firm, virile quality of Vitellius' fat as depicted here must be counted as an effort to idealize without resorting to total falsification. The soft, sophisticated modeling is different from both Nero's simplicity and Galba's deep cutting. The application of such virtuistic modeling to a bust in extremely high relief yields results which are startlingly lifelike. The expression is animated, again in contrast to Nero's aloofness and Galba's simple dignity. The portrait expresses the keenness and confidence of the gods' favorite—propaganda well suited to Rome's current needs but alas quite unrelated to the real personality of Vitellius.

The reverse type of this sestertius is a personification of Peace with her traditional attributes, an olive branch and a horn of plenty symbolizing the prosperity of peaceful times. Like other personified virtues which appear on Roman coinage, she was a

129 ORICHALCUM SESTERTIUS (continued)

real deity and had a temple, begun by Claudius, in the Via Sacra. Theologically these virtues were conceived as expressing themselves through the acts of great men, eventually almost exclusively through the acts of the emperor. Thus the hellenistic practice of offering worship to a hero's virtues evolved into the cult of the imperial virtues, a form of indirect emperor worship. Peace was arguably the most prominent of these virtues under the early empire because the establishment of peace was the primary justification for the Principate. This is the propaganda message of the great Ara Pacis of Augustus and also of the many figures of Pax on imperial coinage. In this case the implicit promise was belied by actual events, both the behavior of the Vitellian troops in Italy and the torpid emperor's failure to quell yet another revolt in the eastern provinces, which in due order toppled him from his throne.

130 AUREUS OF TITUS

Regnal dates: Caesar 69–79 A.D.

OBVERSE:
    T CAESAR IMP—VESPASIANVS, laureate head of Titus right, dotted border.

REVERSE:
    COS V̄, cow standing right, dotted border.

Weight 7.29 gm; diameter 21 mm. ↓

Rome mint, struck under Vespasian, 76 A.D.

Published: Sotheby's Zurich (Metropolitan Museum 1, 10 November 1972), lot 64.

Equivalent coins, various dies: Cohen 53; *RIC* 2 (1926), p. 37, 188; *BMCRE* 2 (1930), p. 35, 187.

Ex Bosco Reale hoard; Metropolitan Museum of Art.

The designation of an heir was a tenuous and experimental matter for the Julio-Claudians, and it was not until 50 A.D. that Claudius hit on the notion of a separate coinage to publicize and popularize his choice. Vespasian, the ultimate victor in the civil war of 68–69 A.D., faced a slightly different problem. His son Titus was mature, already distinguished in warfare and diplomacy and in fact largely responsible for the success of his father's revolt. He was also intensely ambitious. Prudence dictated that he be rewarded by a virtual joint regency and by clear public recognition of his right to the succession. One obvious vehicle for dynastic propaganda was a coinage issued in Titus' own name. A similar coinage was also produced for the younger son Domitian.

Vespasian was of bourgeois background and encouraged an unpretentious, even unflattering naturalism in the portraiture of his reign. The precious metal coinage has a peculiar manner of its own, applied to all members of the Flavian family. Its characteristics, evident here, are an extremely broad head and neck with minute, pinched features almost overwhelmed by an expanse of puffy flesh. The likeness is not as realistic as the best contemporary bronze portraits, but it makes a more incisive statement of character. Titus' near smile conveys the amiability for which both he and Vespasian were noted. The heavy brow on the other hand hints at the ruthlessness with which Titus prosecuted the Jewish War and afterward served as his father's praetorian prefect or chief of security. The alertness and mobility of the small, intense features gives us the Caesar's exceptional intellect, vivid personality and manipulative gifts. However it is incongruous to find this same Titus described in literary sources as a paragon of manly beauty.

The reverse of this aureus records Titus' fifth consulship, held with Vespasian as his colleague. The consulship was the dual supreme magistracy of the Roman state, by now largely honorary. The pair's monopoly of this coveted office was one of the prime indications of Vespasian's dynastic intentions. The actual design of the reverse is a revival of a common reverse type of Augustus. The significance of the original is unclear. But the reissue of numerous Augustan types by Vespasian was probably suggested by the fact that he won the throne in the centenary year of the battle of Actium, by which Augustus obtained supreme and uncontested power over the Roman state. The Romans were keenly aware of such anniversaries and susceptible to the notion of historical cycles. Thus Vespasian might represent his reign as a revival of the Augustan age, an era of peace and political stability, of a constructive administration, of genuine reverence for the emperor. This complex of positive feelings, associated on coinage with the two Flavian sons, was presumably intended to recall public acceptance of Augustus' dynastic policy, which also tended to express itself in pairs of successors.

131 ORICHALCUM SESTERTIUS OF DIVUS TITUS

Regnal dates: 79–81 A.D.

OBVERSE:
  DIVO AVG T DIVI VESP F VESPASIAN—S C, Titus seated left on curule chair, holding branch, arms around, dotted border.

REVERSE:
  Colosseum between Meta Sudans on left and Macellum on right, dotted border.

Weight 26.70 gm; diameter 38 mm. ↙

Rome mint, struck under Domitian, 81 A.D.

Equivalent coins, various dies: Cohen 339 = *RIC* 2 (1926), p. 208 note = *BMCRE* 2 (1930), p. 262, note 191.

Extremely rare.

The Flavian amphitheatre, better known today as the Colosseum, was begun by Vespasian in 72 A.D. as a memorial to the Jewish War. The arena seated 45,000 to 50,000 spectators and was intended for the display of gladiatorial combats and wild beast hunts, but it could also be flooded for aquatic games. Its inauguration in 80 A.D. was the chief event of Titus's brief reign as sole emperor. The festivities lasted one hundred days and included such outlandish spectacles as a battle between cranes and a reenactment of the fifth-century naval war between Athens and Syracuse. In all some 2000 gladiators and 9000 animals perished for the amusement of the Roman people. Titus commemorated the opening of the Colosseum on a sestertius issue of the same year. This sestertius is an even rarer revival authorized by Domitian the following year in memory of Titus, now deceased and deified.

The Flavians' greatest gift to Rome is depicted on the reverse of the sestertius with charming naiveté. The modern viewer is apt to be struck first by the disjointed perspective. The distortion may be intentional, however, in order to permit good simultaneous views both of the facade, with its tiers of statuary, and of the interior, where the populace is seated according to social rank. A second obvious distortion is in the proportions of the amphitheater, which here appears taller than it is wide. This license enabled the artist to include two familiar local landmarks, a pyramidal fountain known as the Meta Sudans and the Macellum or produce market. Presumably these identified the Colosseum more precisely for contemporaries than would an absolutely faithful reproduction of the structure itself. It is also true that at close quarters the height of the facade is more immediately impressive than its circumference. No such justifications can be adduced for the license in the rendering of the upper tier of the Colosseum; it is in reality taller and flatter than the other tiers and functions visually as a sort of cornice. At the very top edge of the building we can discern a row of dots which represent the supports for the *velarium*, an enormous canopy which protected the spectators from the weather and which required a thousand experienced seamen to raise and lower it.

The obverse of the sestertius depicts Titus enthroned as the triumphator of the Jewish War, holding the branch of peace and surrounded by the arms of the vanquished. Such seated figures occasionally appear on Julio-Claudian coinage in lieu of

an imperial portrait and seem to be associated with the concept of the emperor as public benefactor. This particular version is closely copied from the reverse type of bronzes struck by Claudius (41–54 A.D.) in the name of his father Nero Claudius Drusus. The displacement of the letters S C from reverse to obverse is unusual but not unprecedented. The motive was perhaps to avoid the appearance of crediting the Senate with the construction of an immensely popular public facility.

132 ORICHALCUM SESTERTIUS OF TRAJAN

Regnal dates: 98–117 A.D.

OBVERSE:
IMP CAES NERVAE TRAIANO AVG GER DAC P M TR P COS V P P, laureate and draped bust of Trajan right, dotted border.

REVERSE:
S • P • Q • R. OP[TIMO PRIN]CIPI—S C, Circus Maximus, showing outer colonnade and partial view of interior with obelisk in center and *metae* or turning posts marking the ends of the track, dotted border.

Weight 26.87 gm; diameter 35 mm. ↓

Rome mint, struck 103 A.D.

Equivalent coins, various dies: Cohen 575; *RIC* 2 (1926), p. 284, 571; Strack 1 (1931), pl. 6, 391; Hill *Undated Coins* p. 134, 181.

Trajan's most interesting series of coinage illustrates a number of the public works which he undertook on behalf of the Roman people. The most famous of these is the sestertius depicting the Circus Maximus, oldest and largest of Rome's four racetracks. Its basic facilities dated back to 329 B.C. Trajan restored some damaged spots and increased the seating capacity to an incredible 250,000. This was the most popular of all his public works, for the track was in use some 240 days a year.

The track was an elongated U-shape, necessarily shortened to fit on a coin. Down the center ran a divider with double conical turning posts at each end. It was adorned with a large central obelisk and various shrines and statues. The flat side of the U, which appears on the right side of the coin, consisted of starting stalls flanked by two towers, the towers surmounted by sculptured racing chariots. At the opposite end was the entry, which passed through a triumphal arch dedicated to Titus by Domitian, again surmounted by a sculptured quadriga.

The artistry of this architectural reverse is of quite a different order from that of the Colosseum sestertius preceding. The technique appears rather more painterly than numismatic, though there are parallels in contemporary relief sculpture. Nearly correct perspective lends an illusion of considerable depth. The sense of space is heightened by subtle atmospheric effects, achieved by varying the strength of the engraving in a glyptic equivalent to the painter's use of dilute colors for his background. The absence of human activity is usual for Roman architectural types and places emphasis on the beauty of the building rather than its utility.

Trajan's portraiture in all media generally abandons the color and expressiveness achieved under his predecessors in favor of a hard, flat style. The effect is particularly pronounced in his coin portraits. The rather low relief is perhaps a concession to the practical problems of die strength and wear in circulation. But the combination of sharply drawn features and dry modeling makes a frigid impression, heightened by a stern, even grim countenance. These qualities are not inappropriate to Trajan the professional soldier, and indeed at the time of this issue Trajan was freshly returned to Rome from his victory in the First Dacian War. However the representation of Trajan as imperator scarcely compliments the civilian, public service theme of the reverse. Furthermore this portrait fails to do justice to a complex

personality who was universally adored for his high-mindedness, generosity and conviviality. Trajan's popularity received formal recognition in the title *Optimus Princeps*, "most beneficent first citizen," conferred by the Senate in 103 A.D. and featured extensively on Trajan's coinage, as here. Trajan's best portrait sculptures suggest that he wished to be depicted on the model of Augustus' Primaporta statue, as the military triumphator who is nevertheless moved by deep compassion and concern for the welfare of his subjects.

133 AUREUS OF PLOTINA

Regnal dates: wife of Trajan, 98–117 A.D., † 122 A.D.

OBVERSE:
   PLOTINA • AVG—IMP TRAIANI, diademed and draped bust of Plotina right, wearing necklace, dotted border.

REVERSE:
   CAES AVG GERMA DAC • COS VI P P, Vesta enthroned left, holding Palladium and sceptre, dotted border.

Weight 7.27 gm; diameter 19 mm. ↓

Rome mint, struck 112 A.D., issue for consecration of Marciana.

Equivalent coins, various dies: Cohen 2; Strack 1 (1931), 261; *BMCRE* 3 (1936), p. 106, 525; Hill *Undated Coins* p. 142, 546.

Very rare.

Trajan's wife Plotina was the first Roman empress since Livia to play a constructive role as a partner in her husband's administration and as a model of virtue. She lived affectionately with Trajan's female relations, and together they turned the court into a sort of philosophical salon.

Trajan issued coinage in Plotina's name during the final years of his reign. Apparently it was occasioned by the death of Trajan's sister Marciana in 112 A.D. Her consecration and commemoration on coinage necessitated suitable honors for the other imperial ladies. Plotina's portrait as it appears on this aureus is much finer than her husband's (see preceding); its hellenizing-classicizing quality suggests that Plotina must have been assigned a separate workshop at the mint. Plotina's years are indicated gently through nuanced modeling rather than through the callous depiction of wrinkles. The small, slightly fuzzy eye and soft brow line brilliantly capture the watery gaze of old age. As usual with this style there is a profound sense of psychological life and inner beauty, and for once they match the actual qualities of the subject. The pompadour coiffure and high diadem may seem incongruous on an older lady noted for her lack of pretension, but they are in fact the least artificial adornments of the period. The queue on the back of the neck is probably intended to recall the extremely simple hairdressing of the Republic and Julio-Claudian era [124].

The reverse type of this aureus is a figure of Vesta. She appears here as on the Gaian bronze [123], as a symbol of family piety. She encompasses both the happy relations between Trajan and Plotina and also the empress's well-known devotion to her husband's female kin. Vesta's attributes are slightly different from those on the Gaian as. Instead of a patera or sacrificial dish she holds the Palladium, a small statue of Athena supposedly brought from Troy by Aeneas. Vesta was the guardian of this relic from Rome's foundation, and this aspect of Vesta highlights Plotina's role as caretaker of the traditional Roman virtues.

134 ORICHALCUM SESTERTIUS OF HADRIAN

Regnal dates: 117–138 A.D.

OBVERSE:
    HADRIANVS AVG COS III P P, bare-headed and draped bust of
    Hadrian right, dotted border.

REVERSE:
    PAX AVG around, S—C across field, Pax standing left, holding
    branch and cornucopiae, dotted border.

Weight 25.40 gm; diameter 34 mm. ↘

Attributed to the Alphaeus Master. Rome mint, struck 135 A.D.,
    vicennalian issue.

Published: M&M 52 (1975), lot 617.

Same dies: *Trau* lot 1267 = C.C. Vermeule, *Roman Medallions*
    (second edition, Boston, 1975), 24; Hirsch 31 (1912), lot 1325;
    M&M 43 (1970), lot 343. Equivalent coins, various dies: Cohen
    1016; *RIN* 1914, p. 182; *RIC* 2 (1926), p. 438, 769; Strack 2 (1933),
    678; *BMCRE* 3 (1966), p. 472, 1528; Hill *Undated Coins* p. 167, 568.

The fourth specimen known from these dies.

Hadrian was perhaps the most versatile of the Roman emperors, respected by the military but primarily devoted to the promotion of peacetime pursuits. He spent much of his reign on extended tours of the provinces, where trade and industry were expanding with a resultant growth of city life. Hadrian was also profoundly interested in the arts, but his aestheticism in contrast to Nero's had an antiquarian cast: he collected Greek sculpture and encouraged the production of copies; presided over the revival of Greek as a literary language; and in general earned his nickname *Graeculus*, "Greekling." His taste naturally stimulated a resurgence of classicizing hellenism within Roman official art, which is to to say that an idealizing tendency came to predominate. Hadrian's long reign produced various interpretations of the imperial portrait: the emperor as god-like military man; the emperor in heroic nudity; and finally the emperor as a dignified human being, rich in psychological complexity and needless of external marks of rank or divinity.

The present portrait is a superlative example of the last type, struck from a medallion rather than a sestertius die. The portrayal is distinguished by great technical finesse which can bear any degree of magnification; by coloristic treatment of the gently curled hair and short Greek beard; and by sensitive rendering of the nose, mouth and chin. Only the wide, staring eye fails to convey the quality of intense humanity which is the theme of late Hadrianic portraiture.

This portrait is probably the work of the Alphaeus Master, a Greek artist of Hadrian's circle whose hand has been recognized in Peloponnesian coin dies produced for the first quadrennial games in honor of Hadrian's deified favorite Antinous and also in medallion dies employed by the Rome mint. The Alphaeus Master has been conjecturally identified with the sculptor Antoninianus of Aphrodisias, the last great exponent of Greek classicism.

This medallic sestertius with its exceptional artistry was part of an issue which commemorated Hadrian's vicennalia, the twentieth anniversary of his succession. The actual anniversary did not fall until 137 A.D., but it was not unusual for such major celebrations to be anticipated on coinage by one or two years or to be recalled for some time afterward. The reverse type of Peace was one of the most richly symbolic of the imperial virtues, as explained in connection with [129]. She had been employed on the coinage of Hadrian's very first year to advertise one of the ideals of his reign. Her revival is an allusion to that early promise, so abundantly fulfilled; but she also celebrates the final pacification of Judaea after the Bar Cochba revolt of 132–135 A.D., which Hadrian rather uncharacteristically provoked through anti-Semitic legislation.

135 AUREUS OF AELIUS

Regnal dates: Caesar 136–138 A.D.

OBVERSE:
 L • AELIVS—CAESAR, bare head of Aelius left, dotted border.

REVERSE:
 TRIB POT—COS II around, CONCORD in exergue, Concordia enthroned left, holding patera and resting left elbow on cornucopiae, dotted border.

Weight 7.46 gm; diameter 20 mm.↓

Rome mint, struck 137 A.D., adoption issue.

Published: Leu 10 (1974), lot 157.

Equivalent coins, various dies: Cohen 12; Strack 2 (1933), 398; *BMCRE* 3 (1966), p. 368, 999; Hill *Undated Coins* p. 171, 772.

Very rare.

The childless Hadrian waited until the age of sixty before designating an heir. His choice fell upon Aelius, a noble of great physical beauty but unproven abilities and precarious health. Hadrian adopted Aelius in 136 A.D. and spent over 300 million sesterces on the celebrations which followed. He appointed two of the six workshops of the Roman mint, formerly assigned to his wife Sabina, to produce coinage exclusively in Aelius' name. Then he had the disappointment of watching the younger man's health decline under the burdens of office. Aelius died of tuberculosis on the first of January, 138 A.D., only six months before Hadrian himself expired.

This very rare aureus belongs to the issue struck to celebrate the adoption, the first coinage in Aelius' name. Though the adoption occurred in 136, Aelius' coinage was not inaugurated until 137 when he assumed his second consulship. Aelius' portrait is a particularly successful adaptation of the official sculptured portrait type commemorating the adoption, a magnificent example of the mature Hadrianic style. The features are refined, the modeling subtle and expressive, a little softer even than on the ambitious sestertius of Hadrian preceding. This is the variety of hellenizing classicism which Schweitzer called "pathetic," meaning that the style *per se* tends to imbue the subject with psychological depth. In this case the contemplative and slightly melancholy expression was probably an authentic attribute of the Caesar. The eye is the finest of these beautiful features, admirable both for its rare anatomical accuracy and for its intimate revelations. The viewpoint, behind and slightly below the subject, is typical of Hadrianic portraiture. It provides a distance which balances the psychological immediacy of the portrait and so preserves the classical quality of restraint.

The reverse type of this aureus depicts Concord or Harmony, an ancient object of worship at Rome. Her oldest temple was constructed in 367 B.C. In 10 A.D. it was restored by Tiberius and rededicated to the memory of the deified Augustus. Thus Concord was specifically characterized as an imperial virtue, the power of the emperor to inspire a happy spirit of cooperation all around him. She was frequently honored on coins, often with the connotation of harmony within the imperial family. Here she symbolizes the affectionate relations between Hadrian and his adoptive son and perhaps implies a comparison with the filial bond between Augustus and his heir Tiberius, also adopted.

136 AUREUS OF PERTINAX

Regnal dates: 1 January–28 March 193 A.D.

OBVERSE:
  IMP CAES P HELV—PERTIN • AVG, laureate, draped and cuirassed bust of Pertinax right, dotted border.

REVERSE:
  OPI DIVIN • —TR P COS II, Ops enthroned left, holding two ears of grain, dotted border.

Weight 7.28 gm; diameter 21 mm.↑

Rome mint.

Same dies: Kent-Hirmer 369. Equivalent coins, various dies: Cohen 36; *RIC* 4, part 1 (1936), p. 8, 8(a), pl. 1, 6.

Very rare.

Pertinax was the son of a freedman timber merchant. He nevertheless enjoyed a distinguished military and political career and acquired a fortune. As prefect of Rome he was one of the co-conspirators in the assassination of Commodus. To his surprise the praetorian prefect offered him the crown, and Pertinax accepted reluctantly. His program showed him a sincere administrator rather than an astute politician: his primary concern was to reverse the near bankruptcy of the state treasury. To this end he formulated policies to restore abandoned land to cultivation, reduced the costly ostentation of court life and withheld part of his promised accession donative as an inducement to better discipline in the Praetorian Guard. This last measure led to Pertinax's own assassination after a reign of only eighty-six days.

The portraits of Pertinax on his coinage are quite variable in appearance, even within die-linked issues. It almost appears that the engravers at the mint were not supplied with an *imagen* or official portrait in the round on which to base their work. The likeness on this aureus represents a continuation of the style of the preceding reign, with a long, flat profile, tightly curled hair and full curly beard. Such adaptation of a predecessor's portrait sometimes occurred when the succession was sudden and unforeseen. But it must be emphasized that this is not the usual approach on Pertinax's coinage.

Pertinax had a propensity for recondite reverse types. The goddess Ops is not only a rarity as a coin type, but her very function in Roman religious life is obscure, despite the fact that she was honored in several annual festivals. Some of the evidence points toward her being an agricultural divinity, while some suggests she was the equivalent of Rhea, mother of the gods. The type of Ops had appeared only once previously on coinage, on an early series of Antoninus Pius, circa 143–144 A.D. The type thus represents a fiftieth-anniversary revival, an allusion to the emperor who had first promoted Pertinax's political career. The revival also implies a restoration of the golden age of peace and prosperity enjoyed under Pius. The image of Ops under Pertinax differs from that used by Pius in that she holds grain ears. Thus she probably also functions as a topical reference to Pertinax's agricultural reforms.

The obscurity of this reverse type demonstrates an ineptitude for public relations. Indeed, Pertinax and his goals were generally misunderstood by his contemporaries. So deeply rooted was the ancient admiration for prodigality and so strong the contempt for productive work that they could not comprehend the notion of fiscal prudence. Pertinax's pseudonymous biographer Julius Capitolinus excoriates him as both avaricious and mean for not eating pheasant and for serving small portions or leftovers to dinner guests. But unlike certain more lavish emperors Pertinax did not have to resort to extortion, confiscation, abusive taxation or legacy hunting in order to sustain his expenditures.

137 AUREUS OF PESCENNIUS NIGER

Regnal dates: 193–194 A.D.

OBVERSE:
IMP CAES C • PESC—NIGER IVSTVS AVC, laureate, draped and cuirassed bust of Niger right, dotted border.

REVERSE:
ROMAE— • ΛE—[T]ERNAE, Roma enthroned left, holding Victory with wreath and sceptre, • P • P in exergue, dotted border.

Reduced standard, weight 6.80 gm; diameter 20 mm. ↑

Uncertain eastern mint (Alexandria?), struck April–May 193 A.D., accession issue.

Unrecorded variety. Variant: Cohen 59 = *RIC* 4, part 1 (1936), p. 34, 71 (IVST AVG, PP lacking).

Ex Turkey hoard, 1972 (*Coin Hoards* 2 [1976], 236 = *Coin Hoards* 3 [1977], 156).

Apparently unique.

Despite his suggestive surname, Pescennius Niger ("the Black") was an Italian of knightly origin. As legate of Syria he was one of three military commanders who revolted in the spring of 193 at the news of the murder of Pertinax and of Didius Julianus' disgraceful purchase of imperial rank. At first Niger appeared the most legitimate of the three pretenders, because the rioting population of Rome had called on him to deliver the city from Julianus. His control of Asia Minor, Syria and Egypt gave him an especially strong base. But Niger was more notable for his rectitude than for imagination or intellect, and he simply allowed himself to be outmaneuvered by the governor of Pannonia, Septimius Severus. He was captured and beheaded in 194 A.D.

Pescennius Niger struck coins only in gold and silver, the latter generally of low technical and aesthetic quality which suggests it was produced as emergency currency. Antioch and Caesareia in Cappadocia have been securely identified as his major mints. However the exotic style of this aureus must emanate from a different source. The portrait is crisp and sturdy in contrast to the droopy likeness from Niger's major mints, which resembles a wax figurine beginning to melt. The enormous frontal eye with thickened lower lid, the exaggerated S-curve of the brow and the blissful disregard for Niger's sixty years all seem to derive from oriental art rather than from the Graeco-Roman tradition. The hard, assertive treatment of the reverse is equally un-Roman. Yet another anomaly is the inscription P P, of uncertain significance, in the exergue of the reverse. All of these peculiarities would seem to point to a different mint where Roman artistic practice had not struck deep roots. The closest stylistic parallel occurs, surprisingly, at Alexandria, and the letters P P perhaps also point to that mint. However the military functions of gold coinage would seem to argue for a mint in Syria or central Anatolia, near the scene of Niger's military operations.

The type of Roma Aeterna or Eternal Rome is based upon the first cult statue of the goddess ever consecrated at Rome. It was installed in Hadrian's Temple of Venus Felix and Roma Aeterna, personally designed by the dilettante emperor and dedicated circa 135–136 A.D. This statue, which took account of previous numismatic tradition, depicted Roma with attire and attributes suggesting an ultimate derivation from the Greek war goddess Athena; compare [102, 104], and contrast [126]. The statue was widely copied. In the coinage of Pescennius Niger the Roma Aeterna type is closely associated with Jupiter and has been identified as an accession type. Both types are intended to reinforce the patriotism of Niger's accession ceremony, in which he attempted to duplicate Roman ritual by offering sacrifice in the Temple of Jupiter Optimus Maximus at Antioch. Furthermore, like the type of Ops on the preceding aureus, Roma Aeterna is a revival from the coinage of Antoninus Pius of the years 140–141 A.D., where it commemorated the final consecration of Hadrian's temple and also perhaps anticipated Rome's 900th anniversary to be celebrated in 148. Even more than Pertinax, Pescennius Niger had reason to imply a comparison with the happy reign of Antoninus Pius, for his personal motto was *Aurea saecla volens*, "desiring the golden age."

This aureus like all in the accession issue was struck on a reduced weight standard introduced by Didius Julianus at Rome. Niger restored the traditional heavier standard for a subsequent issue of aurei.

138 AUREUS OF CLODIUS ALBINUS

Regnal dates: Caesar 193–195 A.D.

OBVERSE:
D • CL • SEPT AL—BIN • CAES, bare head of Clodius Albinus right, dotted border.

REVERSE:
SAECVLO FRVG—IF—ERO COS II, African god standing left, wearing radiate crown, holding caduceus and trident, dotted border.

Weight 7.28 gm; diameter 20 mm. ↑

Rome mint.

Same obverse die: V. Zedelius, *Untersuchungen zur Münzprägung von Pertinax bis Clodius Albinus* (1977), pl. 6, 2. Variant: Cohen 70 = *BMCRE* 5 (1975), pl. 8, 7 (same obverse die but different reverse type).

Ex Turkey hoard, 1972 (*Coin Hoards* 2 [1976], 236 = *Coin Hoards* 3 [1977], 156).

The third specimen known.

Clodius Albinus was a descendant of a noble family, born in Africa. His military career eventually carried him to the governorship of Britain. He was one of several commanders who revolted at the news of the assassination of Pertinax in 193 A.D. The Pannonian general Septimius Severus was the first to reach Rome and win recognition from the Senate. He offered Albinus the title of Caesar, implying that he was first in the line of succession, in order to pacify the west while he disposed of Pescennius Niger in the east (see preceding). During the two years of their association, Severus produced coinage for Albinus from the Roman mint. This coinage may thus reflect Severus' rather than Albinus' propaganda purposes.

Albinus' portrait conforms to a new model introduced to the coinage by Severus, featuring a round head, short nose and shortish beard. Albinus was older than Pescennius Niger, but his coin portraits hint at this only through the wrinkles on his forehead, which are actually more suggestive of worry than of advanced years. In either case they constitute an obvious foil to the youthfully smooth skin of Severus himself (see following).

It is hard to escape the suspicion that we are seeing two intentionally contrasted versions of the same portrait, especially as Albinus' own coinage, produced later at the Lugdunum mint, depicts a somewhat different countenance whose strong character makes this likeness seem vacuous by comparison.

The reverse type of this very rare aureus features an agricultural god, Deus Frugiferus (in Greek, Aion Karpophoros), who was worshiped at Albinus' native town of Hadrumetum. This god is often identified with the Egyptian Osiris and indeed is represented with Osirian attributes on a companion aureus to this piece. An alternate conception, perhaps derived from Punic sources, occurs here and also on the civic bronze coinage of Hadrumetum. The issue of coins honoring Albinus' home town parallels Severus' own coinage with the patron gods of his natal city Lepcis Magna, also in Africa.

139 AUREUS OF SEPTIMIUS SEVERUS

Regnal dates: 193–211 A.D.

OBVERSE:

SEVERVS AVG—PARTH MAX, laureate bust of Septimius Severus right with aegis, dotted border.

REVERSE:

IVLIA AVGVSTA, draped bust of Julia Domna right, dotted border.

Weight 7.20 gm; diameter 20 mm.↓

Rome mint, struck 200–201 A.D., first dynastic issue.

Published: Glendining (Ryan collection 1, 1951), lot 1819.

Equivalent coins, various dies: Jameson 2 (1913), 169; P. V. Hill, *The Coinage of Septimius Severus and His Family at the Mint of Rome* (London, 1964), p. 26, 503; *BMCRE* 5 (1975), p. 192, 192. Variant: Cohen p. 98, 1.

Rare.

The reign of Septimius Severus is one of the pivotal periods of Roman history, for this vigorous emperor challenged and permanently changed the basic power relationships he had inherited. Commander of Upper Pannonia (Hungary) at the time of Pertinax's murder, he was acclaimed by his troops and became the first of several competing rebels to reach Rome and gain senatorial recognition. He campaigned nearly constantly, first against imperial rivals and then aggressively on the Roman frontiers. He strengthened and democratized the army, openly basing his rule upon military power. His deathbed advice to his sons was: "Enrich the soldiers and despise the rest!" And indeed Severus treated the Senate with contempt and reduced its partnership in the imperial administration, so that from his reign we can trace the steady transformation of the Principate into an autocracy. Finally Severus undercut the privileged status of Rome and Italy, opening the way for decentralization which in the course of the third century produced fragmentation instead. His own roots in Roman Libya and his marriage to a Syrian made him especially receptive to oriental religious and political ideas, which from his reign onward exercised an increasing influence over imperial policy.

Severus' portraiture strongly revives the theme of apotheosis with complex iconographical references. He had himself portrayed with characteristics of the deified emperors Antoninus Pius and Marcus Aurelius. The portrait on this aureus is of the Antoninus Pius variety, with high, domed forehead, raised eyebrows and an almost angelic expression. In another portrait type Severus' hair is dressed in corkscrew curls across his forehead in imitation of the Graeco-Egyptian god Sarapis, for whom he professed a special devotion. Sarapis was an imperial god and a beneficent miracle worker. He was thus an ideal symbol for Severus' program of fusing Roman and oriental ideas and for his promise of political rebirth for the empire. In the present portrait Severus also wears the aegis, an attribute of Zeus symbolic of his invulnerability in battle. Severus was not the first emperor to affect divine attributes, but he was the first to coordinate them with successful imperial policy. Their acceptance demonstrates how effectively he moved Rome in the direction of eastern political culture.

Severus' dynastic policy gave unusual prominence to his family on coinage and in other media. The reverse of this aureus shows his wife Julia Domna, the daughter of the hereditary priestly family of the sun god Elagabalus in Syrian Emesa, whom Severus married because her horoscope forecast that her husband would be a king. Julia Domna was an intellectual woman with religious and philosophical interests and a strong enough character to influence even the forceful Severus. From this point of view her early coin portraits are uncommunicative, for they give us a merely charming young girl with a strong physical resemblance to her husband, far removed from the intense, meditative woman of oriental appearance who appears in most of her sculptures. The gemlike miniaturism of both coin portraits is typical of the numismatic portraiture of the reign.

140 AUREUS OF MACRINUS

Regnal dates: 217–218 A.D.

OBVERSE:
 IMP C M OPEL SEV MACRINVS AVG, laureate, draped and cuirassed bust of Macrinus right, dotted border.

REVERSE:
 PONTIF MAX TR P II COS II P P, Felicitas standing left, holding long caduceus and cornucopia, dotted border.

Weight 7.20 gm; diameter 21.5 mm. ↗

Rome mint, struck January 218 A.D., second issue.

Published: Stack's (H.P. Ward, Jr. collection, 1964), lot 61; Leu 10 (1974), lot 253.

Same dies: *BMCRE* 5 (1975), p. 503, 56, pl. 79, 19 = C.L. Clay, "The Roman Coinage of Macrinus and Diadumenian," *NZ* 93 (1979), p. 35, Die 2. Variants: Cohen 92; *RIC* 4, part 2 (1938), p. 8, 40.

Macrinus was a Mauretanian of humble birth who nevertheless rose through the ranks of the imperial household. As praetorian prefect he accompanied the emperor Caracalla on his Parthian campaign. In Mesopotamia he organized an assassination and assumed the purple himself. He evidently intended a restoration of constitutional government under civilian control, but he inherited virtually insoluble problems—a depleted treasury, crushing debts and a spoiled, undisciplined army. To Macrinus' credit he attempted the necessary reforms, but he was soon dethroned by a young pretender from the family of Julia Domna who claimed to be an illegitimate son of Caracalla.

Macrinus' portraiture attempts a revival of the old civilian image of the emperor as a noble human being portrayed with expressive realism. But his drawn face also introduces a typical third-century motif, the depiction of the emperor as anxious and tormented by the enormity of his responsibilities; for the same world-weary content in a non-imperial portrait, [54]. Typologically Macrinus' portrait combines features from two phases of his numismatic iconography: it has the short-cropped beard of the early type and the careworn face of the second. The existence of these two portrait types, which are associated with aurei of different weights, formerly led to the attribution of the mature portrait group to Antioch. But die links demonstrate that the entire coinage was minted at Rome, and the heavier weight of the later aurei, including this one, must have some relation to Macrinus' fiscal reforms.

Like all new emperors Macrinus sought to characterize his reign with coin types primarily drawn from the larger repertory of personified abstractions. Felicitas or Good Luck had several temples at Rome, the oldest dating back to the middle of the second century B.C. Her name had definite connotations of fertility, and with the development of the cult of imperial virtues she came to symbolize the flowering of nature as well as human happiness under the rule of a beneficent emperor. Felicitas was frequently invoked in the prayers and poems which celebrated the beginning of the year. As a coin type too she is particularly associated with New Year's issues, especially for those years in which the emperor held the consulship, as did Macrinus in 218 A.D.

This extremely rare aureus can be rather precisely dated by its reference to Macrinus' second consulship. The emperor's earliest coinage referred to him as consul because he had been granted honorary consular ornaments as praetorian prefect under Caracalla. His consulship of 218 was actually his first. But Macrinus was still in the east, and the mint was uncertain how best to indicate the state of affairs. It opted for the flattering formula COS II ("consul for the second time"). When coinage bearing this legend reached the emperor in the east, he repudiated the usage and ordered the mint to restore the old legend COS. Thus the inscription COS II appeared on his coinage only from 1 January 218 until his negative response reached the mint, perhaps in February.

141 AUREUS OF DIADUMENIAN

Regnal dates: Caesar 217–218 A.D.

OBVERSE:
   M OPEL ANT DIADVMENIAN CAES, bare-headed, draped and cuirassed bust of Diadumenian right, dotted border.

REVERSE:
   SPES PVBLICA, Spes walking left, holding flower and lifting skirt, dotted border.

Weight 7.18 gm; diameter 20 mm. ↑

Rome mint, struck early March to mid-June 218 A.D., third issue.

Published: Naville-Ars Classica 3 (Evans collection, 1922), lot 106; Glendining (Platt Hall collection, 1950), lot 1767.

Same dies: Hirsch 24 (Consul Weber collection, 1909), lot 1964 = Hess-Leu (ESR collection, 23 March 1961), lot 282. Equivalent coins, various dies: Cohen 22; C.L. Clay, "The Roman Coinage of Macrinus and Diadumenian," *NZ* 93 (1979), p. 22.

Ex A.J. Evans collection, London; H. Platt Hall collection, London.
Extremely rare.

Macrinus' son Diadumenian was only nine years old at the time of his father's usurpation. But he was acclaimed Caesar or heir apparent by the troops when they saluted his father as Augustus. The army had revered the murdered emperor Caracalla and was largely ignorant of the circumstances of his death. Macrinus implied a moral if not biological kinship with him by bestowing Caracalla's regnal name of Antoninus on Diadumenian, while he himself assumed the name Severus. Both of these names appear among the abbreviations of their obverse legends.

Diadumenian is depicted bare-headed, as was conventional for a Caesar. With the exception of the Flavian dynasty [130] the laurel wreath was the prerogative of the Augustus. As was common with child portraits, Diadumenian is not strongly characterized on his coinage. The *Historia Augusta* reports that he was an exceptionally beautiful boy, tall, dark-eyed and strikingly blond despite his father's Moorish blood. Diadumenian's coin portraits are not in fact as appealing as those of the sons of Septimius Severus, but the difference is largely the consequence

of a sentimental, idealizing approach for the Severan boys as opposed to a more objective realism in the case of Diadumenian.

The personification on the reverse of this extremely rare aureus is Spes, Hope. She had had a temple at Rome since the First Punic War, and her cult symbolized the importance of the younger generation. Under the empire she had been specifically associated with the designation of an heir. Her imagery is unusually charming for a Roman virtue: she carries a flower suggesting the freshness of youth and the promise of a fruitful maturity, while her raised skirt conveys the eager haste of the young. The type of Spes had already been used on coins of Titus, Commodus and the Severan boys, but it acquired a particular prominence in this reign because it was one of only two types employed for Diadumenian as Caesar.

142 BRONZE MEDALLION OF SEVERUS ALEXANDER

Regnal dates: 222–235 A.D.

OBVERSE:
IMP CAES M AVREL SEV ALEXANDER AVG, laureate, draped and cuirassed bust of Severus Alexander right, dotted border.

REVERSE:
LIBE—RALITAS AVG—VSTI II, emperor seated left on platform flanked by figure of Liberalitas and two attendants, on left citizen climbing ladder to receive his portion, dotted border.

Weight 38.78 gm; diameter 39 mm.↑

Rome mint, struck 224 A.D., special issue for the consecration of the Temple of Jupiter Ultor.

Equivalent coins, various dies: Cohen 121; Gnecchi 2, p. 80, 9 and pl. 98, 9 = *BMC* 6 (1962), p. 134, 210.

Very rare.

A medallion is a coin-like work of art, produced with special care by the mint and intended for presentation by the emperor to some honored personage. Medallions are larger and heavier than regular coinage, and all but the latest specimens are characterized by a wide, sometimes ornate border. These imperial gifts display the finest artistry of which the mint was capable. Because of their personal association with the emperor, medallion portraits are highly significant for the nuances of imperial image-making as directed toward influential people.

At his accession Severus Alexander was only a child, managed by his formidable mother and grandmother, both relations of the Syrian Julia Domna [139]. They characterized his reign as a restoration of constitutional government and old-fashioned Roman mores after the oriental excesses of Severus' cousin and predecessor Elagabalus. This portrait, from early in the reign, conforms to those claims. The young emperor's attributes and short military haircut are correctly traditional, and the psychological sensitivity of the portrait revives the values of the best imperial portraiture of the second century [133, 134, 135]. The fat cheek indicates that the emperor is still in his early adolescence, while the innocent soulful eye speaks eloquently of his premature earnestness. This ranks among the most expressive child portraits of Roman numismatic art.

The reverse of the medallion depicts a *congiarium* or public largess. This was a distinctive Roman institution, a voluntary distribution of wine, oil or money to the poor of Rome. Under the Republic such a convenient public relations tool could be employed by any magistrate or candidate for public office. Under the Principate, as was only natural, the emperor reserved the right to authorize such largesses in his own name. They were generally associated with some joyous event, such as a succession, imperial birthday or marriage, a victory or the like. Three of Severus Alexander's five largesses celebrate his consulships. The occasion for the second largess, commemorated here, is not recorded, but it should probably be connected with the dedication of the Temple of Jupiter Ultor in 224 A.D.

The elaborate type seemingly depicts the actual distribution, a traditional manner of commemorating such events on coins of large module. The emperor is seated on a curule chair atop a platform ornamented with a frieze on its base. He is accompanied by two assistants and a figure of Liberality (a statue?) identical with the personification which commemorates largesses on smaller coins. A citizen climbs a ladder at left to receive his portion from the emperor's own hand. It is permissible to suspect that the depiction is symbolical rather than historical, for similar scenes on second-century sestertii show the emperor present but not working, and the number of citizens entitled to receive these distributions numbered in the tens of thousands.

Severus Alexander is the first emperor known to have commemorated his largesses on medallions as well as on his regular currency. It is believed that such medallions were bestowed on the magistrates or others who aided the emperor in the work of distribution.

143 GOLD MEDALLION OF GALLIENUS

Regnal dates: 253–268 A.D.

OBVERSE:
   IMP GALLIENVS P F AVG, laureate head of Gallienus right, dotted border.

REVERSE:
   VICT—OR—IA GERMANICA, Gallienus standing right in military attire, crowned by Victory and flanked by bound captives, dotted border.

Medallion of 6 aurei (?), weight 13.51 gm; diameter 28 mm.↓

Rome mint, struck 257 A.D., sixth issue.

Unrecorded variety. Cf. R. Göbl, "Aufbau V/1: Valerianus und Gallienus (253–260)," *NZ* 74 (1951), p. 26f, sixth emission, C (bronze medallion).

Unique.

After the reign of Severus Alexander the Roman empire entered a period of deep crisis. The army, which had been strengthened at the expense of other institutions, now discovered its unbridled power to make or break emperors. The nominees of various frontier units followed one another in rapid succession, coping desperately with the triple dangers of barbarian invasion, rival pretenders to the throne and the murderous fickleness of their own troops. Economic life withered, and the currency was repeatedly debased in an effort to meet mounting military costs in a rapidly shrinking economy.

The disasters mounted to a crescendo during the reign of Valerian I and his son Gallienus. A new conqueror, Shapur I, arose in Persia and laid waste the empire's eastern provinces. In 256 A.D. Valerian traveled east to confront him, and in 260 he was captured and carried off to Persia. Gallienus, who had remained in the west, struggled to preserve the territorial integrity of the European empire. Although he had some success against the Germanic tribes, the usurper Postumus (see following) detached Gaul, Britain and Spain from the empire. Nevertheless Gallienus must be counted a great emperor, for his reign of fifteen years is far the longest of any soldier-emperor of the mid-third century, and he did in the end hold most of the empire together in the face of powerful centrifugal forces.

Ironically there are indications that Gallienus was a man of some culture who would have preferred to preside over an artistic and intellectual renaissance. One surprising sign of his taste is a sudden flowering of precious-metal medallions, assorted multiples of the aureus or denarius in a system comprising graded values. Another is the introduction of a softer and richer portrait style for medallions and sculptures, though it must be confessed that Gallienus' regular currency approaches the aesthetic nadir of Roman coinage. A third mark of Gallienus' sophistication appears in his predilection for obscure attributes and recondite legends, many associated with portraits of the emperor in apotheosis. The revival of this theme after two decades of unpretentious and hard-bitten military portraits represents a straining for a higher cultural level.

This gold multiple commemorates the victories of 256–257 A.D. in which Gallienus recovered territory between the Rhine and the Danube which had been overrun by Germanic tribes. The portrait is an early example of the emperor in apotheosis, with relatively subtle marks of godhead: longish hair, a slightly elevated chin and a commanding but tormented expression. This multiple is of extreme importance for the iconography of Gallienus because it demonstrates that the delicate but rather pinched features of the supposedly late portrait type in fact developed rather early in his reign.

The medallion's reverse type celebrates the German victories with an allegorical scene of a sort first developed on sestertii of Vespasian commemorating the end of the Jewish War. The armed emperor is crowned by Victory and holds a *parazonium*, a short sword symbolic of martial valor. The depiction of two captives at his feet betrays a contempt for the barbarian; Romans defeated in civil war are never so displayed on coinage. The type thus includes a complex of military themes—armor, courage, victory, the humiliation of the vanquished—which are never entirely absent from Roman coinage but become dominant in the numismatic propaganda of the late empire.

144 AUREUS OF URANIUS ANTONINUS

Dates of usurpation: 253–254 A.D.

OBVERSE:
   L IVL AVR SVLP VRA ANT[ONINVS], laureate, draped and cuirassed bust of Uranius Antoninus right, dotted border.

REVERSE:
   CONSERVATO—R AVG, quadriga left in which Stone of Emesa carved with eagle relief and flanked by parasols, dotted border.

Standard of Severus Alexander, weight 6.15 gm; diameter 20 mm.↑

Emesa mint, struck October–November 253 A.D., third issue.

Same dies: H.R. Baldus, *Uranius Antoninus, Münzprägung und Geschichte, Antiquitas* 3, 11 (Bonn, 1971), pl. 7, 69 (III/12); R. Delbrueck, "Uranius of Emesa," *NC* 1948, p. 17, fig. 8 (obverse) and p. 15, 3 (reverse). Equivalent coins, various dies: Cohen 2; *RIC* 4, part 3 (1949), p. 205, 2.

Extremely rare.

Uranius Antoninus is one of the rash of obscure usurpers who so threatened the stability of the Roman empire toward the middle of the third century. Ironically, these rebellions were not always treasonable in intent. Sometimes a frontier unit, hard pressed by barbarian movements, felt the need of the emperor's personal leadership, yet a single emperor could not be everywhere in the vast, trouble-ridden expanse of the Roman empire. Often, then, the response was to create an emperor out of a popular commander to stiffen local morale. The usurpation of Uranius Antoninus in the Syrian city of Emesa was probably such an emergency measure, for about this time Shapur I of Persia invaded Syria and indulged in intentional, terrifying cruelty against the city of Antioch. Presumably Uranius Antoninus organized his people in defiance of the Sasanid invader, and he may have done so more in the character of local priest-king than as a Roman military man. The absence from his obverse legends of the traditional imperial titles—Caesar, Imperator, Augustus—tends to support such a view.

Uranius' likeness here combines features of the established soldier-emperor portrait type with a distinct Syrian style. The short, military haircut and armor glimpsed under the cloak are of course Roman. But Syrian practice has influenced the vacant, frontal eye, the eyebrow textured as a spiral, the hard modeling and a conception of facial structure not much different from that of archaic Greece [58]. The awkward and uneven lettering is also provincial.

The reverse type of this aureus honors the chief god of Emesa, Sol Invictus Elagabalus, who was worshiped in the form of a meteoritic stone. The fetish is depicted here in a ceremonial chariot, presumably illustrating its participation in local religious festivals, with a legend identifying the stone as the emperor's protector. Such propaganda is essentially local in appeal but also highly appropriate to the army, for Elagabalus had been the patron of the legions since the reign of the emperor of the same name. The type also constitutes an allusion to the heritage of the Severan dynasty, for a similar design had been employed by the emperor Elagabalus in 218 A.D. Furthermore the weight of Uranius' aurei reinforces the link, for it revives the standard of Severus Alexander with a weight of about 6.15 gm at a time when contemporary Roman aurei generally weighed less than 3 gm. But it must be emphasized that any serious claim to the whole empire must be couched in different terms, for the meteoritic Stone of Emesa had acquired a very unsavory reputation at Rome during the reign of Elagabalus.

145 AUREUS OF POSTUMUS

Regnal dates: 260–269 A.D.

OBVERSE:
POSTVMVS PIVS FELIX AVG, jugate heads of Postumus and Hercules left, both laureate, dotted border.

REVERSE:
HERCVLI NEMAEO, nude Hercules, viewed from behind, strangling Nemean lion, club at feet, dotted border.

Weight 5.75 gm; diameter 20 mm. ↓

Colonia Augusta (Cologne) mint, struck mid-269 A.D., decennalian issue.

Published: Naville-Ars Classica 3 (Evans collection, 1922), lot 1772; Elmer 522, pl. 7, 12; P. Bastien, "Les travaux d'Hercule dans le monnayage de Postume," *RBN* 1958, p. 75, 3 and pl. 4, 3.

Equivalent coins, various dies: Cohen 131; *RIC* 5, part 2 (1933), p. 359, 274.

Ex A.J. Evans collection, London.

Extremely rare.

———

It is perhaps inevitable that the chaos of the third century and the simultaneous claims of various pretenders should have led to a major secession from the Roman empire. In 259 A.D. or more probably in the middle of 260 an officer named Postumus established a separate empire in the province of Gaul, winning the allegiance of the governors of Britain and Spain as well. The Gallic empire flourished for more than a decade as a separate entity, experiencing an economic and cultural revival which can be verified by comparing its coinage with contemporary Roman currency. The Gallic aureus outweighs Gallienus' gold. Postumus' aurei are artistically polished and innovative, frequently employing facing portraits and jugate busts, which are both quite scarce in the main Roman series.

Completely unprecedented is Postumus' manner of joining an imperial and a divine image. Postumus was not the first emperor to advertise a special relationship with Hercules, but the divine hero had a special resonance for the third century because he symbolized the perpetual and courageous struggle against evil and injustice. Curiously, the use of jugate busts suggests that

Hercules is not so much Postumus' patron as a companion or co-ruler, with the hero assigned the rear position symbolizing junior status. He is also engraved more weakly to achieve a background effect.

Postumus' own portraiture revives the hirsute look which had been out of favor for half a century and which had civilian and cultural associations in contrast to the short military crop and stubbly beard. The inspired, upward gaze is handled rather subtly here, consisting of the slightest elevation of the chin and raised eyebrows. Postumus totally avoids the worried or spiritual expressions often associated with this pose in the mid-third century [54, 143].

This extremely rare aureus belongs to an especially interesting series which emphasizes Postumus' devotion to Hercules by portraying all of the hero's labors on its reverses. The issue was probably minted in 269 for the emperor's decennalia or tenth anniversary in power, which fell in the middle of that year. Aurei with the labors of Hercules were presented like medallions to high-ranking officers and civil administrators, while less valuable versions in bronze were produced for lower functionaries. This particular reverse with its striking rear view derives from a venerable Greek original probably attributable to Lysippus. The mere allusion is indicative of Postumus' cultural level, and the plasticity of the coin type is vastly superior to the sketchy technique of most contemporary Roman reverses.

146 AUREUS OF TETRICUS I

Regnal dates: 270–273 A.D.

OBVERSE:
    IMP TETR—ICVS AV—G, laureate and cuirassed bust of Tetricus
    left, holding shield with gorgoneion device on near shoulder and
    spear over far shoulder, dotted border.

REVERSE:
    VIRTVS AVG, emperor in military attire standing left, holding
    globe and parazonium, captive at feet, dotted border.

Weight 4.73 gm; diameter 19 mm.↑

Colonia Augusta (Cologne) mint, struck 1 January–9 December 271
    A.D., second issue.

Published: Feuardent (de Quelen collection, 7 May 1888), lot 1799;
    Bourgey (Tacamier collection, 2 March 1926); Elmer 820; Soth-
    eby's (Barnes collection, 1974), lot 39.

Ex Vicomte de Quelen collection; Tacamier collection; Barnes
    collection.

Probably unique.

After almost a decade of firm rule by Postumus, the Gallic army reverted to that destructive interference in politics which had contributed so significantly to the crisis of the third century. After undoing Postumus and three successors in short order, the soldiery seemed slightly daunted by its own lawless power. In the breach the Gallic Senate appointed a civilian bureaucrat named Tetricus as the new ruler of the secessionist empire. Gallic power declined precipitously under Tetricus, and there is some reason to think that he was a reluctant emperor, essentially the captive of his generals. For when Aurelian invaded Gaul in 273 Tetricus is supposed to have sent a secret message begging to be rescued from his plight. His troops tried to force him to make a stand at Chalons-sur-Marne, but Tetricus surrendered to Aurelian and abdicated. He was paraded in Aurelian's triumph at Rome along with the Palmyran queen Zenobia, but after this humiliation he was granted a high post in the Italian civil administration and lived the rest of his life in honor and comfort at Rome.

The reduced weight of this aureus testifies to the deteriorating situation in Gaul. Tetricus' pacifist convictions are not readily apparent in its typology and iconography, however, for it was after all probably intended as military pay or, more precisely, as a donative or imperial bonus to a soldier. It belongs to an issue probably struck for Tetricus' assumption of his first consulship at Cologne on 1 January 271. The emperor appears in dress armor, holding a shield with gorgoneion device, another Medusa adorning his corselet. The gorgoneion was, in the latter third century, a symbol of universal power transmitted to the emperor by Jupiter, and the shield itself had cosmic significance in imperial iconography. Tetricus' longish, richly textured hair and beard, elegant features and serene expression derive from the portraiture of his predecessor Victorinus. The fervid originality of Gallic coinage under Postumus has spent itself. However the coinage still displays a high technical level.

The reverse type of this aureus invokes Virtus or martial valor, one of the most important of the imperial virtues in a time of constant military threat. Virtus was originally personified as a female of Amazonian type, probably reflecting a golden cult

statue which stood at Rome until melted down by Alaric. (For a Roma resembling Virtus, see [126]). With the passage of time there is an increasing tendency to illustrate the concept with the activities of the emperor himself, as here. The change in emphasis is definitely related to the religious trends of the third century. The cult of the imperial virtues had constituted a form of indirect emperor worship. The relation of these virtues to the emperor himself was similar to the philosophical model of third-century Neoplatonism, which postulated a series of spiritual powers emanating from the One. Just as the contemplation of these emanations could lead the philosopher to union with the true ground of being, the shift of focus from the emperor's personified virtues to the divine emperor himself could—ironically—appear as a higher and more internal form of the imperial cult.

147 AUREUS OF QUINTILLUS

Regnal dates: July (?) –September (?) 270 A.D.

OBVERSE:
IMP C • M • AVR • QVI—NTILLVS AVG, laureate, draped and cuirassed bust of Quintillus right, dotted border.

REVERSE:
FIDES EXERCITI, Fides standing left, holding two military standards.

Weight 5.18 gm; diameter 21 mm.↓

Mediolanum (Milan) mint.

Published: J. Lafaurie, "Trésor d'un navire romain trouvé en Méditerranée," *RN* 1958, p. 103, no. 24 and pl. 9, 24; H. Huvelin and J. Lafaurie, "Trésor d'un navire romain trouvé en Méditer-ranée. Nouvelles découvertes," *RN* 1980, p. 101, no. 54 and pl. 8, 54.

Same obverse die: Jameson 4 (1932), 520; Huvelin and Lafaurie nos. 50–53. Same reverse die: Canakklé hoard no. 2615 (antoninianus).

From a Roman shipwreck off the coast of Corsica, with coins found along the east coast of the island.

Unique. One of seven known aurei of Quintillus, six from the same obverse die.

Quintillus was the younger brother of Claudius II Gothicus (268–270 A.D.), an energetic ruler of the central Roman empire who devoted himself to combating disruptive Germanic tribal migrations until his premature death from plague. Quintillus, left in command of the garrison at Aquileia, was proclaimed emperor at the news of Claudius' demise. But his elevation merely served as a signal for rebellion. Zenobia, queen of Palmyra, occupied Syria and Egypt in the name of her son Vabalathus, while the army at Sirmium created an imperial rival in its commander Aurelian. Quintillus' troops showed such preference for Aurelian that they refused to be exhorted into battle against him. Quintillus chose the honorable escape of suicide after a reign of only a few months.

This unique aureus bears a likeness of Quintillus which must be counted one of the finest portraits of the late third century in any medium. It is almost the last appearance of the soft but realistic modeling of the Greek tradition, with its pathetic overtones. The hollow cheek, the infinite focus of the eye and the lightly furrowed brow give the face a melancholy expression. The iconographical concept of the emperor oppressed by his burdens was popularized by Gallienus [143], but this image of Quintillus has none of the authority, none of the marks of apotheosis of Gallienus' portrait. Its brooding humanity is seemingly at odds with the emperor's military attire and indeed with the dominant iconographical trends of the period.

The reverse type honors Fides or Good Faith, yet another personified virtue. She had a temple on the Capitoline Hill near that of Jupiter, and her cult was closely related to his. As the army came to play a dominant role in the elevation and removal of emperors, its loyalty became an issue of extreme concern to each reigning emperor. Thus in the periods of civil war and especially in the troubled third century there is a proliferation of coin types affirming or appealing to the good faith of the army. The type showing Fides holding legionary standards was first devised for Macrinus (217–218 A.D.) and was used by virtually every succeeding emperor.

There is at this period a chasm separating the carefully executed aurei from the debased and inartistic antoniniani which constituted the vast bulk of the imperial coinage. A similar aesthetic contrast can be observed between the obverses and reverses of the aurei. Evidently three different artists were involved in the production of the dies: a very accomplished one for the portrait and two less skilled engravers for the lettering and reverse figures. Significantly, the reverse dies of five of the other known aurei of Quintillus were also used for antoniniani. The weight of this aureus, like the gold of Claudius II Gothicus, shows that the Roman emperors ultimately adopted the heavy aureus weight of the Gallic empire.

148 AUREUS OF FLORIAN

Regnal dates: June (?)–August 276 A.D.

OBVERSE:
  VIRTVS F—LORIANI A—VG, laureate and cuirassed bust of
  Florian left, holding shield with aegis device on near shoulder and
  spear over far shoulder, dotted border.
REVERSE:
  VICTORIA PERPET, Victory standing right, inscribing $x^x x$ on
  shield attached to tree trunk, dotted border.
Weight 4.65 gm; diameter 20 mm.↑
Rome mint.
Published: *RIC* 5, part 1 (1927), p. 352, 23 and pl. 9, 157.
Equivalent coin, various dies: Cohen 92.
Ex British Museum.

Florian was the half-brother of Tacitus, an elderly senator who was frivolously acclaimed emperor by the Senate after the assassination of the great Aurelian in 275 A.D. The beleaguered empire scarcely needed such a leader, and Tacitus died of exhaustion in the course of his first military campaign. Florian, who had accompanied Tacitus, promptly seized power and was recognized by the Senate and the western provinces of the empire. At first he pursued the campaign against the barbarian invaders. But he was soon confronted by a rival emperor, Probus, who had been elevated by the Syrian army. Before a decisive battle could take place Florian's troops deposed and arrested their own candidate. Florian was put to death after a reign of just over two months.

Florian's aurei maintain the high technical standards of his recent predecessors. This one features a new variety of obverse legend proclaiming "The Courage of the Emperor Florian" instead of listing his name and titles in the conventional manner. This practice, first introduced under Claudius II Gothicus, carries even further the process of "reabsorption" of the imperial virtues already described under Tetricus [146]. The portrait presents a burly officer, all physical power with no trace of the melancholy sensitivity of Quintillus. The depiction is a bit schematized, with intensity expressed only by the parallel wrinkles across the forehead. This new "stereometric" style may reflect the influence of Palmyrene artists who emigrated to Antioch and even Rome after Aurelian's destruction of their city in 273 A.D. It remained in favor with the Illyrian soldier-emperors until the time of Constantine the Great. As on the aureus of Tetricus, the armor has more than military significance: both shield and cuirass are ornamented with a pattern representing the aegis, another symbol of universal power deriving from Jupiter.

The reverse type of this aureus commemorates the imperial prayers for a long reign. On accession public vows were made (*vota suscepta*) promising certain observances on the completion of ten years in power. On the appropriate anniversary the vows were fulfilled (*soluta*) with great public festivities and new ones were undertaken. From the time of Commodus the type of Victory inscribing numerals on a shield was used to record the imperial vows. The votive numerals may refer to either sort of

vow, but where two sets of numerals appear the smaller number represents the old vows fulfilled and the larger number the new ones undertaken. The inscription $x^x x$ here probably does not represent the number thirty, an absurdly premature projection of Florian's tricennalia, but parallels the inscription VOTIS X ET XX ("ten and twenty year vows") on a bronze medallion of Tacitus. Apparently with the brief reigns of these two brothers we meet a curious new phenomenon, the celebration of the fulfillment of the decennalian vows only a few months after accession and new prayers offered for twenty-year reigns. This practice continued in the reign of Probus, who celebrated his decennalia in 279 or 280, anticipating the correct date by six or seven years. After him it cannot be identified again, although in the fourth century votive numerals were sometimes falsified for other reasons, for example to coordinate the anniversary celebrations of imperial colleagues or to indicate seniority.

The legend "Perpetual Victory" beautifully illustrates the fact that in these votive contexts the goddess of Victory appears not in a military sense but as an expression of the triumphant nature of the imperial anniversary celebrations.

149 GOLD MEDALLION OF PROBUS

Regnal dates: 276–282 A.D.

OBVERSE:
   IMP C M AVR PROBVS P F AVG, radiate bust of Probus left,
   wearing consular toga picta and holding eagle-tipped sceptre,
   dotted border.

REVERSE:
   TEMP FELICI—TAS, Aeternitas standing right, holding sceptre
   and resting hand on zodiacal frame from which emerge the Four
   Seasons, on right genius or New Year with cornucopia, SIS in
   exergue, dotted border.

Medallion of 1 1/2 aurei, weight 7.86 gm; diameter 24 mm.↓

Siscia mint, struck at the end of 277 A.D., consular New Year's issue.

Published: Cohen 710; Gnecchi 1, p. 10, 7; *RIC* 5, part 2 (1933), p. 80,
   598; Toynbee pl. 2, 9; M&M 25 (1962), lot 638.

Same obverse die: Toynbee pl. 2, 10. Variant: Toynbee pl. 2, 11.

Formerly Cabinet des Médailles, Paris; stolen in a major theft of
   medallions in 1831.

Unique.

A typical occasion for the presentation of medallions was the
New Year. This was a holiday which normally involved the
exchange of gifts (*strenae*). Imperial New Year's gifts frequently
took the form of medallions, especially in years when the emperor held the consulship. Since assumption of the consular
office occurred on New Year's Day, the medallion types frequently commemorate that auspicious event.

The types of this unique medallion clearly associate it with an
imperial consular New Year. Probus is depicted with the eagle-

tipped sceptre and richly embroidered *toga picta,* paraphernalia
of the consular office. The decoration of the toga picta is engraved here with astonishing precision. This detail is characteristic of the increased emphasis on ceremonial costumes on
third-century medallions, a reminder how far the principate
had evolved in the direction of oriental absolutism. Probus' portrait revives the motif of the lean and careworn emperor but
expresses it in the new stereometric style. The facial structure is
very similar to that of Quintillus [147], with fine straight nose,
delicate eye and sharply defined cheekbone. However the modeling is drier for Probus, with sharp parallel creases lined up
across his forehead. This hardness sacrifices some of the realism
and most of the emotional appeal of the Quintillus portrait, but
the coin portrait is still refined and realistic in comparison with
the highly expressionistic sculpture of the day.

The connection between the New Year, fertility and the virtue
Felicitas has already been touched on in relation to the aureus of
Macrinus [140]. On this medallion this complex of ideas is
given allegorical form according to conventions well established
in antique art. Time or Eternity holds the frame of the zodiac,
through which the Four Seasons pass in their ordained cycle.
Each holds fruit or a horn of plenty, as does the New Year,
symbolizing the promise of abundance implicit in the cosmic
order. Related scenes occur on sarcophagi, in mosaics and on
other imperial medallions. On some of the latter it is the emper-
or who holds the zodiacal frame, implying a comparison with

149 GOLD MEDALLION (continued)

the gods who control the seasons, such as the sun or Eternity. There is a clear suggestion that the rule of the emperor is not only beneficent but a part of the order of nature. Thus the association of the emperor with the Four Seasons in panegyrics as well as in programmatic art is yet one more metaphor conducing to or justifying his deification. In Probus' case there may also be a topical reference to his policies for the expansion of agriculture.

The divine claims of Probus and contemporary emperors are different in character from those of pre-crisis princes. Nero, for example, was a megalomaniac out of touch with the sensibilities of his time, and his divine pretensions were interpreted as expressions of personal vanity despite the authority of the historical models. Probus on the other hand was a genuinely simple man, renowned for eating the same vegetable ration as a common soldier. His affectation of divine attributes was a matter of imperial policy, a political response to the religious needs of the day. In the case of Probus the contrast between his actual character and his sacred office is apparent in the portraits, but we shall see on the following coins an increasing tendency to submerge the individual in the trappings of rank.

150 AUREUS OF PROBUS

Regnal dates: 276–282 A.D.

OBVERSE:
    IMP PROBVS INV AVG, jugate busts left of Sol, radiate and draped, and Probus, laureate and cuirassed with gorgoneion device on armor, dotted border.

REVERSE:
    SECVRI—TAS SAECVLI, Securitas enthroned left, holding sceptre and resting left hand on head, SIS in exergue, dotted border.

Weight 6.55 gm; diameter 22 mm. ↑

Siscia mint, struck 277 A.D.

Published: Kent-Hirmer 548.

Same obverse die: Leu 25 (1980), lot 412. Equivalent coin, various dies: *RIC* 5, part 2 (1933), p. 80, 596.

Very rare.

During the third century the Roman world was groping its way toward monotheism. Its religious yearnings tended to focus on the sun as an appropriate symbol for the lord of the universe. Many solar cults coexisted and were facilely identified with one another. Several had even made explicit claims of universality. Most notable were the orgiastic Syrian cult of Elagabalus [144], briefly the official religion of the empire in the Severan period; and the Persian cult of Mithras, a mystery religion with seven degrees of spiritual advancement, perennially popular within the military. Both of these cults employed the title Sol Invictus, "the Invincible Sun," alluding to the sun's daily triumph over the powers of darkness and implying that his invincibility could be transmitted to his devotees. The recognition of the problem of evil and the theme of perpetual struggle made the solar cults particularly resonant for the troubled souls of the third century.

In 274 A.D. the emperor Aurelian introduced a new solar cult designed to foster moral and religious unity throughout the empire. Its intentionally vague central ideas were borrowed from the cult of Elagabalus—a syncretistic monotheism and the promise of a blissful afterlife. But the ritual and institutions were modeled on the traditional Roman state cult or on popular Graeco-Roman practices: for example the priesthoods were lay political offices modeled on the priestly colleges of the Roman state cult, and the god's birthday on 25 December was celebrated with chariot races.

What differentiated the cult of Sol Invictus from the traditional state religion was its relationship to Aurelian's ideal of political absolutism. Sol Invictus was officially recognized as the chief god of the Roman pantheon. The other gods were by no means repudiated, but worshipers were invited to understand them as personified aspects of the One God, Sol. He especially epitomized their protective functions and thus allegorically represented the emperor, supreme ruler and guardian of the state. Furthermore Sol had a special guardianship of the emperor which shaded into companionship and even identification. This intimate tie tended to justify the centralized despotism of the late third century. All of Aurelian's successors continued to promote this convenient official cult and advertised it on their coinage.

The obverse of this great rarity employs the jugate busts popularized by Postumus [145]. There is a conscious contrast between the schematized anguish of Probus' portrait and the soft, idealized likeness of Sol. The epithet Invictus has here been transferred to the emperor himself, suggesting an assimilation to the god. The rich armor serves to underline the essentially military nature of Sol's protection: he had been the patron of the legions since the reign of Elagabalus. The gorgoneion device [146] is associated in this period with Apollo-Sol as well as Jupiter, evidence of syncretism among these cosmic gods.

The reverse depicts Securitas or Security, an imperial virtue symbolizing the emperor's power to insure the stability of the state. She is normally portrayed in an attitude of repose, either leaning against a column or, as here, resting her head on her hand. Typically she was invoked when great danger had been averted or the succession insured. Here she may allude to the strengthening of the Rhine frontier or the failure of any of several pretenders. The execution of the type is crude and provincial, illustrating the difference in skill between obverse and reverse die engravers [147].

151 AUREUS OF CARINUS

Regnal dates: 282–285 A.D.

OBVERSE:
   IMP CARINVS P F AVG, laureate, draped and cuirassed bust of
   Carinus right, dotted border.

REVERSE:
   VIRTV—S AVG, Hercules standing right, holding lion skin and
   resting on club, dotted border.

Weight 4.33 gm; diameter 20 mm.↑

Rome mint, struck mid-November 284 A.D., festal (consecration)
   issue.

Same obverse die: Leu 10 (1974), lot 378; Leu 18 (1977), lot 383.
   Equivalent coins, various dies: Cohen 160; *RIC* 5, part 2 (1933), p.
   168, 233.

Rare.

Carinus was the elder son of the emperor Carus, whose reign (282–283 A.D.) marked a new stage in the evolution of the Principate toward an undisguised autocracy. Like virtually all of the soldier-emperors, Carus was elevated by his troops; but he was the first to neglect the gesture of applying to the Senate for confirmation. This ended the Senate's constitutional authority over the imperial succession and made raw military power the theoretical as well as the actual basis of government.

Following the model of Valerian and Gallienus, Carus immediately divided the empire with the thirty-year-old Carinus, whom he placed in charge of the province of Gaul. He then hastened to realize the plan of his predecessor Probus for an invasion of Parthia, departing Rome in 283 with his younger son Numerian and entrusting the stability of the west to Carinus. First Carus and then Numerian died under mysterious circumstances in the course of the eastern campaign. The returning army elevated Diocletian, actually no match for Carinus' considerable military gifts, but Carinus was assassinated by one of his own officers.

This rare aureus belongs to a festal issue struck in connection with the triple consecration of Carus, Numerian and the child Nigrinian (probably Carinus' son), celebrated by Carinus at Rome in November of 284. The emperor's portrait, while still stereometric in conception, is decidedly idealized when compared with that of Probus [149, 150]. Firm flesh, smooth skin and a carefully dressed beard eliminate the haunted, ascetic look. This is in contrast to Carinus' portrait busts in the round, which employ the typical expressive devices of overlarge eyes and furrowed brow. The coin portrait hints more subtly at world-weariness through the swollen flesh under the eye.

The reverse type offers yet another example of the vague, allusive quality of the symbols pertaining to the deified emperor. The legend speaks of the emperor's valor, but the type is neither the personification Virtus nor the emperor himself but the weary Hercules, depicted according to the formula of the Hercules Farnese, a statue type developed by Lysippus in the late fourth century and popularized at Rome by Commodus. This particular juxtaposition of Virtus and Hercules suggests an identification between the emperor and the hero or perhaps even implies that Hercules is a sort of manifestation or emanation from the emperor, who is thus elevated to a Jovian level. The persistent recourse to Hercules in imperial programmatic art of the third century must be inspired in part by the fact that the hero's apotheosis after his labors tended to prefigure and thus to justify the divinization of the emperor. Furthermore both relate to the theory called euhemerism which asserted that all the gods were originally great men whose achievements caused them to be worshiped by a grateful posterity. Though Euhemerus proposed his theory in early hellenistic times, it found its greatest acceptance among Roman intellectuals and surely contributed to a religious climate in which rather ordinary military men could be raised to the by now somewhat tarnished level of the pagan gods.

152 AUREUS OF MAGNIA URBICA

Regnal dates: wife of Carinus, 282–285 A.D.

OBVERSE:
MAGNIAE V—RBICAE AVG, diademed and draped bust of Magnia Urbica right, dotted border.

REVERSE:
CONCOR—DI—A AVGG, Concordia enthroned left, holding patera and double cornucopia, dotted border.

Weight 5.03 gm; diameter 19 mm.↑

Siscia mint, struck late summer 284 A.D.

Published: Jameson 2 (1913), 304.

Equivalent coins, various dies: Cohen 1; *RIC* 5, part 2 (1933), p. 185, 304; K. Pink, "Magnia Urbica, Gattin des Carinus," *NZ* 79 (1961), p. 7, no. 2b.

Ex Jameson collection, Paris.

Very rare.

Magnia Urbica was long known to history only from her very rare coinage. A few coins and medallions of Carinus feature her portrait as a reverse type, proving that she was the wife of this soldier-emperor. Her position has been further corroborated by inscriptions.

This aureus is part of a festal issue struck for the planned re-union of the brothers and co-emperors Carinus and Numerian in 284 A.D. after the death of their father Carus. The meeting never took place, however, for Numerian was assassinated at Perinthus on the homeward march from Persia.

Magnia Urbica wears a bejeweled but severe coiffure very typical of the late third century. It has been described as a sort of feminized helmet, appropriate to these Spartan empresses who accompanied their husbands on all their campaigns and proudly bore the title *Mater Castrorum*, "Mother of the Camps." It is not uncommon to see these ladies portrayed with the features of their husbands. Magnia Urbica, for example, here has a profile very similar to that of Carinus as well as the same pronounced pouch under the eye. In addition she has the pinched and world-weary expression of many third-century emperors,

though it is eschewed on the Roman coinage of Carinus. The modeling is rudimentary, creating a dry effect particularly pronounced at the mint of Siscia [149, 150].

The reverse of the aureus features a personification of Concord who also appears on the aureus of Aelius [135]. This was a conventional reverse type for empresses, symbolizing the harmony of the imperial marriage. Comparison with the Aelius aureus demonstrates how much the figure has become schematized. The imperial mints always endeavored to maintain the highest standards for imperial portraiture on the gold coinage, but in the latter third century the reverse types generally range from perfunctory to barbarous. As noted above [147], they must have been entrusted to different artists.

153 GOLD MEDALLION OF MAXIMIAN

Regnal dates: first reign, 286–305 A.D.

OBVERSE:

IMP C M AVR VAL MAXIMIANVS P F AVG, head of
Maximian right in lion skin headdress, dotted border.

REVERSE:

VIRTVTI A—VGG V ET IIII COS, Hercules standing right,
holding bow, crowned from behind by Roma, at feet river god
reclining left, SMT in exergue, dotted border.

Medallion of 5 aurei, weight 26.87 gm; diameter 32 mm.↓

Ticinum mint, struck for 1 January 293 A.D., consular New Year's
issue.

Published: Gnecchi 1, p. 13, 7 and pl. 5, 8; L. Laffranchi, "L'XI anno
imperatorio di Costantino Magno," *APARA* 1921, p. 422, 40; K.
Pink, "Die Goldprägung des Diocletianus und seiner Mitregen-
ten," *NZ* 1931, p. 24; *Trau* 3459.

Found in 1885 at O Szöni, Hungary (ancient Brigetio); ex F. Trau
collection, Vienna.

Unique.

The emperor Diocletian (285–305 A.D.), though a camp-made
sovereign, was not a great soldier, and he furthermore perceived
that the empire's parlous condition could never be remedied by
a single ruler, no matter how energetic. In 286 he therefore
selected as his colleague the brilliant commander Maximian
and placed him in charge of the western half of the empire. By
293 the partnership absorbed two more able generals as Caesars.
These junior partners were responsible for active military work,
while the senior emperors devoted themselves to administration. However the tetrarchy also involved a territorial division
of responsibility: Diocletian held the east, alternating his seat
between Nicomedia and Antioch; Maximian presided over Italy and Africa with his court at Milan or Aquileia; Galerius
patrolled the Danube provinces; and Constantius Chlorus saw
to the security of Gaul, Britain and Spain.

Diocletian and Maximian adopted the patronage of Jupiter and
Hercules respectively, and these gods virtually displaced all others from their coinage. This rare medallion of five aurei depicts
Maximian as Herculius, that is not merely as a protege of the
hero but assimilated to him. The style is ambitious, with very
bold relief and elaborate modeling, though the wide staring
eye—a mark of divine inspiration—is by realistic standards less
accomplished than the other features. Comparison with other
tetrarchic portraits shows that this likeness does not depict Maximian as an individual so much as an ideal type—the same
alert, bull-necked and bullet-headed military man as we saw
already on the aureus of Florian [148]. This blockiness is absolutely typical of tetrarchic sculpture, which is however starkly
abstract in contrast to this richly modeled portrait with its variously textured surfaces and decorative arabesques. It is significant that none of these textures is soft: the lion skin helmet for
example has a metallic quality quite unlike its Greek prototypes [79, 100].

The reverse legend records the sharing of the consulships of
293: it was Diocletian's fifth and Maximian's fourth. The legend is expressed in a slightly unusual order, with the numerals
preceding the consular office; [120, 121, 130, 132, 133, 134, 135,
136, 138, 140] for the conventional form in which the numerals
follow the office. The distinction indicates that the medallion
was struck to celebrate the consulships in question, as opposed
to merely recording the emperor's accumulated magistracies
and honors (the imperial *cursus honorum*). This was probably
then a New Year's medallion, distributed on the occasion of the
consular procession like [149]. The allegorical type depicts Hercules as the personification of the emperor's valor as on [151],
crowned by Roma and worshiped by a river god.

Diocletian and Maximian undertook a gradual overhaul of the
coinage, which was improved with respect to intrinsic value,
workmanship and mint administration. The administrative aspect of the reform involved the opening of many additional
mints and the development of a coherent system of mintmarks.
The letters in the exergue of the reverse stand for *Sacra Moneta*,
"holy coinage," exemplifying the divinization from the reign
of Aurelian onward of everything relating to court life. The
letter T identifies the issuing mint as Ticinum.

154 GOLD MEDALLION OF MAXENTIUS

Regnal dates: 306–312 A.D.

OBVERSE:
IMP MAXENTIVS P F AVG, head of Maxentius left in lion skin headdress, dotted border.

REVERSE:
CONSERVA—TO—R VRB SVAE, emperor in military attire standing right before Roma enthroned left, together holding globe, P*R in exergue, dotted border.

Medallion of 2 aurei, weight 10.53 gm; diameter 26 mm. ↑

Attributed to the First Engraver. Rome mint, struck late in 308 A.D., consular New Year's issue(?).

Published: Carson "Treasure" p. 71, no. 112 or 113.

Same dies: Alföldi *CG* 28 = R.A.G. Carson, "Gold Medallions of the Reign of Maxentius," *Atti*, CIN 1961 (Rome, 1965), 9, pl. 27, 8 = *RIC* 6 (1967), p. 372, 166 = C.C. Vermeule, *Roman Medallions* (second edition, Boston, 1975), pl. 9, 87 = Carson "Treasure" pl. 7, 111. Hoard also published: R.A.G. Carson, "The Greatest Discovery of Roman Gold Pieces since the Great Find at Arras," *Illustrated London News*, 14 November 1959, p. 650f.

Ex Parthenico hoard, 1958.

One of three specimens known.

Diocletian's tetrarchic system included a mechanism for the orderly transfer of power, involving voluntary abdication of the Augusti after twenty-year reigns. This notion failed its first test. Maximian abdicated with great reluctance on 1 May 305. The following year on 28 October he staged a *coup* at Rome in which his son Maxentius was also elevated to imperial rank. So strong was their position in Rome that they were able to survive attacks in 307, first by the legitimate Caesar of the west, Severus II, and then by the western Augustus Galerius. In April of 308 Maxentius and Maximian quarreled, and the older man took refuge with his son-in-law Constantine. Maxentius ruled alone in Italy until 312, when Constantine marched against Rome.

Maxentius' rare medallions are of particular interest because little other major official art of this reign survives. This medallion demonstrates that the revival of a classicizing style often associated with the western mints under Constantine is equally attributable to Maxentius. In fact M.R. Alföldi hypothesizes that the chief engraver of the Roman mint, blending his own refined style with that of Treveri (see following), went on to become the vehicle for the stylistic renaissance of the Roman coinage which moved from western to eastern mints in the course of Constantine's long reign. The lion skin headdress and its implied identification with Hercules is adopted from Maximian (see preceding). But Maximian's bold masculinity has been superseded by fine bone structure, soft, expressive modeling and a gentle, inward expression, all traits associated with the hellenizing strain within the Roman portrait tradition [121]. The affecting upward gaze recalls the iconography of Gallienus, one of the last exponents of classicism [143]. Maxentius' portrait seems especially virtuistic because accomplished within the constraints of an extremely low relief.

Maxentius' reverse types not surprisingly emphasize his possession of the Eternal City and draw upon traditional Roman themes. The type featuring the emperor and the goddess Roma, usually in a temple, is the most common of Maxentius' bronze coinage and also occurs on coins issued in the names of Maximian and Constantine, dating its introduction to the period of their short-lived alliance against Galerius. The type celebrates Maxentius' restoration of the Hadrianic Temple of Roma [137], which was badly damaged by fire in 307, and his dedication of a new cult statue, Dea Roma, which became the basis for most numismatic depictions of the goddess thereafter. The wolf and twins device on Roma's shield refers to the Roman foundation legend and had in the course of the third century acquired an association with the concept of the eternity of the empire. The legend names Maxentius as the city's savior, praising his services to her cult but also alluding to his success in resisting the attacks of Severus and Galerius in the course of 307. In a broader sense it may also comment on the passage between Maxentius and Roma of the globe, symbol of world sovereignty. This theme must surely have played to the natural resentment felt in Rome over the transfer of government functions to provincial cities under the tetrarchy.

The changing titulature and shifting alliances of the early phase of Maxentius' revolt are reflected on his coinage and enable it to be dated rather precisely. This two-aureus multiple is related by its Herculian obverse type to medallions struck for Maxentius' first consulship, which he assumed on 20 April 308 after his father's attempted *coup*. But the mint mark ties it even more closely to another consular medallion struck later in the year, perhaps in preparation for Maxentius' second consulship in 309.

155 GOLD MEDALLION OF CONSTANTINE THE GREAT

Regnal dates: 306–337 A.D.

OBVERSE:
  IMP CONSTANTINVS PIVS FELIX AVG, laureate, draped and cuirassed bust of Constantine right, dotted border.

REVERSE:
  PRINCIPI IVVENTVTIS, Constantine standing right in military attire, holding globe and spear, PTR in exergue, dotted border.

Medallion of 9 solidi, weight 40.03 gm; diameter 42 mm. ↘

Treveri (Trier) mint, struck for 25 July 310, quinquennalian issue.

Published: J. Babelon and A. Duquénoy, "Médaillons d'or du trésor d'Arras," *Arethusa* 1924, p. 52, 9 and pl. 8, 9; E. Bourgey, *Les Médaillons d'or du Trésor d'Arras* (Paris, n.d.), 9; Toynbee pl. 9, 5; Alföldi *CGT* p. 126, 57, pl. 5, 1; Alföldi *CG* 324; *RIC* 6 (1967), p. 220, 801; *IRI* 3 (1972), pl. 69, 240; P. Bastien and C. Metzger, *Le trésor de Beaurains (dit d'Arras)*, NR 10 (Wetteren, 1977), 446. Mentioned: A. Chastagnol, "À propos des *quinquennalia* de Constantin," *RN* 1980, p. 113.

Ex Arras hoard, 1922.

Unique.

This splendid multiple of nine solidi was found in the famous Arras hoard, an enormous gold treasure from the tetrarchic period which was especially rich in medallions and other donative issues. The portrait is roughly contemporary with that of Maxentius preceding, with which it shares a low relief, elegant soft modeling and a transparent bone structure. However the content of Constantine's portrait is less psychological or spiritual; his impassive features express a new iconographical concept, that of the divine ruler who projects not the force of his own personality so much as the power of his office. The remnants of classical technique were perhaps transmitted through the mint tradition of the Gallic emperors [145, 146]. A similar revival of classical forms to express a refined militarism may be seen in the portraits on the Arch of Constantine, recarved upon existing work of the Antonine period some five years after the issue of this multiple.

The hoard context makes it fairly clear that this medallion belongs to an issue minted for Constantine's quinquennalia or fifth anniversary in power, which was celebrated in Trier on 25 July 310. The reverse type of *Princeps Iuventutis* is traditional for the coinage of a Caesar. It alludes to an honor devised by Augustus for his young grandsons Gaius and Lucius when he wished to designate them as his heirs: the honorary leadership of the youth corps of the Roman knightly order. The type was used for Constantine after his acclamation and confirmation as Caesar in 306. However in the following years his position became quite cloudy. In 307 he was elevated to the rank of Augustus by the renegade emperor Maximian, who was in revolt against the senior Augustus Galerius. The latter not unnaturally refused to recognize this promotion, and there ensued a period of cold relations in which Constantine used the imperial title on his own authority. Final, formal recognition as Augustus came later in 309 or perhaps as late as 310. During this period Constantine may have continued to use the Princeps Iuventutis type, and he certainly gave it a renewed emphasis on his quinquennalian coinage despite its Caesarian connotations. It has

been suggested that the type was employed as an intentional appeal to old Roman traditions, for by 310 Constantine was already planning the conquest of the imperial city. The type perhaps implies that he regarded the confirmation of the Roman body politic as the true source of legitimacy and thus hints at his ultimate ambition of overthrowing the tetrarchy and restoring the dynastic principle.

The proportions of the Princeps figure are quite similar to those of several colossal military statues of the Constantinian period, which themselves belong to a long tradition deriving from the Primaporta statue of Augustus. Interestingly, the obverse portrait is designed as if to appear a close-up version of the same figure.

156 GOLD MEDALLION OF CRISPUS

Regnal dates: Caesar 317–326 A.D.

OBVERSE:
   FL IVL CRISPVS NOB CAES, laureate, draped and cuirassed bust of
   Crispus right, holding spear and globe, dotted border.

REVERSE:
   GAVDIVM ROMANORVM around, ALAMANNIA in exergue,
   Alamannia seated left in mourning under trophy, dotted border.

Medallion of 1 1/2 solidi, weight 6.68 gm; diameter 23 mm.↓

Treveri (Trier) mint, struck 319–320 A.D.

Published: Jameson 2 (1913), 358; *RIC* 7 (1966), p. 185, 237.

Same dies: Alföldi *CGT* p. 125, 20, pl. 8, 2. Equivalent coin, various
   dies: Gnecchi 1, p. 23, 3 = Alföldi *CG* 152.

Ex Jameson collection, Paris.

Perhaps the third specimen known.

Crispus was the son of Constantine by his first wife Minervina.
He was elevated to the rank of Caesar in 317 A.D. along with
his young half-brother Constantine Junior and Licinius Junior,
holding consulships in 318 and 321. He distinguished himself
in a campaign against the Franks and Alamanni in Gaul in 320,
and he commanded the Flavian fleet in the final war against
Licinius. His brilliant future was aborted through the jealousy
of his step-mother Fausta, who wished to clear the way for the
advancement of her own much younger sons. In 326 Fausta
tricked Constantine into executing the Caesar for treason. On
discovering the deceit, the grieving emperor had her suffocated
in a boiling bath.

This gold multiple dates from shortly after the Gallic victory of
320, in which Crispus' personal valor turned the tide in the
decisive battle. The Caesar is portrayed in military attire, with a
pose and attributes that also allude to his position as Princeps
Iuventutis (see preceding). In many respects the portrait seems
an echo of the likeness of Constantine the Great preceding, but
it reflects stylistic developments within Constantinian portraiture in its lower relief and simpler modeling. Also characteristic
of the middle Constantinian style is the transformation of the
military crop into a smooth, wavy cap of hair with rounded
bangs curling low over the forehead. Just as Constantine's earlier portraiture alludes discreetly to Augustan models, this coiffure invites comparisons with Trajan, another beloved emperor
[132]. But if these are elements of classical revival, the distortion
of the half-length figure reveals a new aesthetic, with symbolic
attributes taking priority over both realism and idealized canons
of proportion.

The reverse type commemorates the victory even more directly. The legend GAVDIVM ROMANORVM, "joy of the Ro-
man people," refers to an officially decreed public rejoicing. The
type of a grieving captive seated under a battlefield trophy is
conventional, dating back to the time of Vespasian. However
the treatment is quite extraordinary as an illustration of the
tendency toward physical dissolution inherent in late antique
art. There are no volumes, only lines and rows of pellets. The
use of scratchy parallel lines to represent drapery is not new on
Roman coinage, but the strong outlines attest to a novel artistic
conception.

157 GOLD MEDALLION OF CONSTANTINE THE GREAT

Regnal dates: 306–337 A.D.

OBVERSE:
D N CONSTANTINVS MAX AVG, radiate, draped and cuirassed bust of Constantine left, raising right hand and holding globe, dotted border.

REVERSE:
CRISPVS ET CONSTANTINVS NOBB CAESS COSS II, confronted busts of Crispus on left and Constantine II on right, each laureate, wearing *toga picta* and holding eagle-tipped consular sceptre, SIRM in exergue, dotted border.

Medallion of 2 solidi, weight 8.77 gm; diameter 25 mm.↓

Possibly a work of the First Engraver. Sirmium mint, struck 321 A.D., consular issue.

Equivalent coins, various dies: Christie's (19 October 1970), lots 197–199; N. Duval, "Un grand médaillon monetaire du IVe siècle," *RLouvre* 1973, no. 6, pp. 367ff. Variants: *RIC* 7 (1966), p. 682, 37 (Antioch mint, late 324 A.D.) and Christie's, lot 200 (COS III).

The fourth recorded specimen.

The Christian historian Eusebius strongly implies that Constantine converted to Christianity after the miracle of the Milvian Bridge in October of 312, and certainly this view is substantiated by the emperor's pro-Christian legislation, his numerous gifts and church foundations, his intense interest in ecclesiastical affairs and the prominence of Christians in his court and administration. The coinage however makes emphatic use of imagery deriving from the cult of Sol Invictus [150] from 310, when Constantine reported a miraculous vision of the god, until shortly before his final confrontation with Licinius in 324. Even afterward there was occasional allusion to the solar cult. Its prominence on coinage may be explained in part by the cult's deep roots in military life, for much of the imperial coinage was paid out to the soldiery. But it seems clear that Constantine employed solar imagery in official art in the belief that it was equally acceptable to pagans and Christians. Christian writers, after all, had long made use of solar metaphors for Christ, and there survives a depiction of Christ himself with attributes of Sol in the tombs of the Julii at Rome. Constantine's solar imagery represents a personal form of syncretism which he doubtless took for a true understanding of Christianity, as when he ordained the Day of the Sun a weekly day of rest.

Constantine appears on the obverse of this medallion personified as Sol Invictus. The radiate crown, raised right hand and the globe in the left hand are all attributes of Sol as depicted on the reverse of the Constantinian bronze coinage. As on the preceding multiple of Crispus, this symbolic complexity is achieved at the cost of anatomical distortion. The style of the portrait is increasingly hard and flat, with a linear and planar conception replacing the earlier soft and subtle modeling. The result is light, elegant and decorative, and incidentally quite opposite to the heavy brutality of Constantine's best-known colossal sculptures.

The reverse of this multiple commemorates the sharing of the consulships of 321 by Constantine's two oldest sons, Crispus and Constantine II. It was the second consulship for each. The two boys are portrayed in their rich consular regalia, with the embroidered *toga picta* and eagle-tipped sceptre [149]. There is considerable charm to these portraits: Crispus is allowed a physical resemblance to his father, while Constantine Junior is given the pudgy cheeks and pert nose of his mother Fausta. Furthermore the two half-brothers are distinguished in terms of their age. Crispus in his middle adolescence is poised and dignified, but the six- or seven-year-old Constantine can scarcely suppress a smile as he meets his brother's eyes. The treatment is slightly more plastic than on the obverse, while the distortion of the bodies is less evident both because of the pose and because of the age of the subjects.

Medallions of this sort were probably distributed on New Year's Day of 321, the start of the consular year, like [149]. None were produced at Antioch, however: Licinius did not recognize this monopoly of the consulships by Constantine's family, which violated the practice of sharing these honors between the two houses after the joint elevation of the Caesars in 317 A.D. Significantly, Constantine had these types recapitulated on gold multiples and solidi at Antioch in late 324, after he had absorbed Licinius' empire.

158 AUREUS OF LICINIUS JUNIOR

Regnal dates: Caesar 317–324 A.D.

OBVERSE:
D N VAL LICIN LICINIVS NOB C, facing bust of Licinius Junior, draped and cuirassed, dotted border.

REVERSE:
IOVI CONSER—VATORI CAES, Jupiter enthroned facing on platform inscribed SIC • V • /SIC • X •, holding sceptre and small Victory on globe with wreath, on left corner of platform an eagle with wreath in beak, SMNΓ in exergue, dotted border.

Weight 5.31 gm; diameter 21 mm.

Nicomedia mint, struck 321–322 A.D., quinquennalian issue.

Published: Leu 10 (1974), lot 406.

Equivalent coins, various dies: Cohen 28; *RIC* 7 (1966), p. 607, 42.

Very rare.

Though the collapse of the tetrarchic system spawned a brood of rival emperors, their wars and mutual treacheries rapidly thinned their ranks so that by 313 A.D. only two were left, Constantine in the west and Licinius I in the east. On 1 March 317 they formally established the dynastic principle, simultaneously promoting to the rank of Caesar Constantine's two oldest sons, Crispus and Constantine Junior, and Licinius' son Licinius Junior. The last was the legitimized offspring of a slave-concubine. Although he shared the consulship of 319 with Constantine the Great, Licinius Junior was too young to play any role in the following breach and warfare between the two Augusti. After the death of his father in 324 the youngster was returned to his original servile status and sent to work in an imperial weaving factory in Carthage. He was finally executed about 337, probably as part of the succession purge of Constantine's sons.

This aureus was struck to celebrate the Caesar's quinquennalia or fifth anniversary in power. The types are closely modeled on those of Licinius the elder for his own decennalian coinage of 317–318. The most striking feature of this aureus is its use of a facing bust of the Caesar, aged about nine, which most perfectly illustrates the triumph of the stereometric style in the east. The block-like head with features more incised than sculpted and the huge, hypnotic eyes with strong lower lid and tormented scowl are paralleled on the famous tetrarchic portraits in porphyry from Antioch and Alexandria. Both the abstraction and the compelling quality of this frontality are eastern features, the artistic expression of the equally oriental tendency to divinize the ruler which became paramount in this period.

The reverse type illustrates Licinius' own interpretation of the edict of Milan (313 A.D.) according to which he and Constantine committed themselves to tolerate Christianity and to promote monotheism. The prominence of Jupiter on Licinius' entire coinage suggests that he favored a syncretistic monotheism viewing Jupiter Optimus Maximus as the source of godhead, the other gods being, as it were, emanations or aspects of his perfection. This was a religious propaganda designed to appeal to the military, an answer to Constantine's own identification with Sol Invictus (see preceding). The type probably depicts a

copy of the Phidian statue of Zeus Olympios installed at Daphne near Antioch by Antiochus IV (Ammianus Marcellinus 22.13.1). Here again the eastern principle of frontality is more powerful than Roman numismatic tradition, which depicted seated figures in profile.

The inscription on the pedestal relates to Licinius' quinquennalian festival. As noted in connection with [148], vows were undertaken at accession for ten-year periods. The custom gradually arose of "partially" fulfilling the vows at the mid-term with a quinquennalian celebration, but this practice did not receive official recognition on coinage until the fourth century. Technically both of these numerals record the vows undertaken (*suscepta*) rather than fulfilled (*soluta*). The slightly unusual acclamatory form of the inscription echoes the popular invocation by which the citizens wished the emperor continued rule.

159 SILVER MEDALLION OF CONSTANTINE II

Regnal dates: Caesar 317–337 A.D.

OBVERSE:
  CAESAR, bare head of Constantine II right, dotted border.
REVERSE:
  X X within wreath, SIS in exergue, dotted border.

Medallion of 4 siliquae, weight 13.05 gm; diameter 38 mm.↓

Siscia mint, struck 336–337 A.D., vicennalian issue.

Equivalent coins, various dies: Toynbee pl. 14, 1; Lafaurie "Médaillons" p. 46, no. 6; *RIC* 7 (1966), p. 459, 260. Variant: Gnecchi 1,
  pl. 33, 15–16.

Extremely rare.

This magnificent silver medallion celebrates the vicennalia or twenty-year anniversary of one of Constantine's sons, calculated from his recognition as Caesar. Scholarly opinion is divided as to the identity of the Caesar and the date and occasion of issue. The least tortured interpretation of the obverse type argues that the multiple was designed and struck while the younger Flavians were still Caesars—that is, before the death of Constantine the Great on 22 May 337, or at the latest during the four-month interregnum which followed. On this dating the Caesar represented could only be the eldest of Constantine's surviving sons, Constantine II, whose vicennalia fell in 337 A.D. The portrait here indeed bears a close resemblance to other likenesses of Constantine II including the juvenile portrait on [157]. This resemblance, which is not apparent on all specimens of this medallic issue, tends to confirm the attribution to Constantine II.

The portrait of Constantine II belongs to the mature Constantinian style, which is flatter and more linear than ever before but which revives much of the hallowed iconography of apotheosis. The long strands of hair with thick locks upon the nape of the neck comprise a tidier version of the coiffure of Augustus in his most strongly hellenizing portraits [121], and ultimately it derives from the leonine locks of the deified Alexander and his successors [102, 103, 104, 113]. The large, radiant eye was also repeatedly used in hellenistic times to express spirituality. This is one of the most attractive versions of the motif, conveying a confident serenity rather than rhetorical inspiration. As is often the case with such gently spiritual expressions the viewer is reminded of Apollo, the ultimate model for the iconographical type of the perpetually young ruler. Given that a Christian royal iconography did not exist, Apollo offered the best traditional model for the Christian virtues of gentleness and inwardness. The richly folded neck truncation hints at heroic nudity, an allusion particularly notable in an era obsessed with ceremonial garb. The simple legend and its unusual position recall the Augustan coinage, whose influence is equally strong on the associated medallion which follows.

The reverse bears a conventional design for commemorating the imperial anniversaries. The Roman numeral indicates the number of years for which vows were fulfilled or undertaken. It is surrounded by a wreath deriving ultimately from the vicennalian bronze issue of Augustus [122] and depicted here with exceptional fullness and realism. The scheme was developed on

coinage of the tetrarchy. This is probably its first appearance on silver, inaugurating a strong association between that metal and votive types in the coinage of the late empire. The increasing emphasis on the emperor and his office, as opposed to commentary on his ideals and achievements, is most characteristic of late Roman coinage and reflects the growth of political absolutism.

160 SILVER MEDALLION OF CONSTANTINE THE GREAT

Regnal dates: 306–337 A.D.

OBVERSE:
AVGVSTVS, rosette-diademed head of Constantine right, dotted border.

REVERSE:
CAE • SAR in laurel wreath, SIS • in exergue, dotted border.

Medallion of 4 siliquae, weight 13.04 gm; diameter 37 mm. ↗

Siscia mint, struck 336–337 A.D.

Equivalent coins, various dies: Gnecchi 1, p. 64, 4 and pl. 31, 8 = Lafaurie "Médaillons" p. 46, 4 = *RIC* 7 (1966), p. 459, 259 = Kent-Hirmer 657; Lafaurie "Médaillons" p. 46, 5 = A.R. Bellinger, *Roman and Byzantine Medallions in the Dumbarton Oaks Collection*, DO Papers 12 (1958), p. 134, 12.

The fourth published specimen.

This impressive silver medallion is a companion piece to the preceding. The style is closely connected, and indeed the two medallions are probably the work of the same hand. This image of Constantine the Great exemplifies the official portrait type of his late reign. Its chief distinguishing characteristic is the diadem, a symbol of divine kingship adopted by Constantine in 324; this ornate example may be compared with the simpler versions of the hellenistic period on [102ff]. The mature Constantinian portrait also features luxuriant hair, an elongated head and, on coins, a decorative linear style. Despite the essential reticence of the manner, the heads on these two coordinate multiples are differentiated with respect to age and majestic presence, so that one feels little doubt in identifying the diademed Augustus as the elder Constantine. The reminiscence of Augustan coinage is particularly significant in Constantine's tricennalian year, for he was only the second emperor since Augustus to achieve a reign of thirty years.

The interpretation of these related medallions is controversial, but one widely accepted theory holds that both were issued for the vicennalia of Constantine II. The reverse type of this medallion indeed condenses the symbolism of the preceding, and other interpretations are difficult in view of the established role of the wreath in imperial *vota* coinage. It has also been suggested that the close association on these medallions of the Augustus with his oldest son may indicate a desire to establish his primacy among the four heirs that Constantine had by now designated. The known specimens hail principally from western mints under the control of Constantine II and his adolescent brother Constans with few from the east where Constantine the Great was in residence. Thus it would appear that the association, whatever its implications, was promoted more vigorously by the Caesar than by the Augustus.

A rival theory maintains that the AVGVSTVS medallions celebrate the promotion of the sons of Constantine from Caesar to Augustus, a step that was delayed until four months after Constantine's death to allow for the massacre of possible imperial rivals and their supporters. The considerable variability in the portraits from one medallion to the other may result from the fact that several individuals are represented. Alternatively, these may not be portraits at all but images of the emperor as an ideal type.

161 FESTAUREUS OF CONSTANTIUS II

Regnal dates: 337–361 A.D.

OBVERSE:
   FL IVL CONSTAN—TIVS PERP AVG, pearl-diademed, draped
   and cuirassed bust of Constantius II left, dotted border.

REVERSE:
   Emperor standing in facing quadriga, head turned to left, holding
   eagle-tipped sceptre and distributing coins, Christogram in upper
   right field, SMAN in exergue, dotted border.

Equivalent to 1 1/4 solidi, weight 5.33 gm; diameter 24 mm.

Antioch mint, struck probably 350 or 353/4 A.D.

Published: Leu 13 (1975), lot 503; *RIC* 8 (1980), p. 518, 78 (but
   described as having legend GLORIA ROMANORVM).

Variants: Jameson 4 (1932), 534 and Toynbee pl. 2, 17 (both with
   reverse legend).

Extremely rare variant of a very rare denomination.

Constantius II was the second of the three sons of Constantine the Great by Fausta, raised to the rank of Caesar in 324 at the age of seven. He was apparently responsible for the massacre of a collateral line of the family after Constantine's death in 337, whereupon he and his two brothers divided the empire more or less according to the portions they had already governed as Caesars. By the time of this issue, however, Constantius had become sole Augustus through the deaths of his brothers, Constantine II having been killed in the course of war with Constans, and Constans murdered by the usurper Magnentius [162]. Constantius' portrait is executed in a style by now familiar, though it has become even more delicate and indeed almost effete. It is interesting that this originally western style achieves its most exquisite refinement at Antioch, formerly the center of stereometric abstraction.

The reverse type illustrates a public largess distributed in quite different fashion from the *congiaria* of previous centuries [142]. The design of the emperor tossing coins from a facing quadriga was developed by Constantine the Great in an intentional echo of a long tradition of depictions of Sol or Helios [77]. Its formal and very artificial composition was developed in the fourth century B.C., but the proximate model may have been a reverse type of Probus labeled SOLI INVICTO. This is perhaps a witty type, for it seems possible that the coin itself was intended to be so distributed in the manner it illustrates. The type was regularly associated with the festaureus which was also issued by Constans, by Valentinian I and II and by Eugenius.

The figure ☧ in the upper right field is the monogram of Christ, a symbol strongly associated with Constantine's conversion to Christianity. According to Eusebius' *Ecclesiastical History*, before the battle of the Milvian bridge Constantine had a vision in which he was instructed to display this sign upon the shields of his men when he met Maxentius in battle. The result was the "miracle" by which Constantine won possession of Rome with an army only a quarter the size of his opponent's. The Christogram is virtually the only Christian symbol used on coinage of the early Christian empire, and as Constantine's own creation it was probably felt to be more a part of imperial than of Christian iconography. The conjunction of Christogram and quadriga is another example of the Flavians' use of solar imagery to express Christian ideas [154].

Strictly speaking this piece is not a medallion but an aureus, the historic gold denomination which was replaced by the solidus during the reign of Constantine the Great, about 312 in the west and 324 in the east. The aureus was revived only for ceremonial purposes, especially the commemoration of an imperial largess. We do not know the occasion for this particular distribution, but the celebration of Constantius' tricennalia or thirtieth anniversary in 353/354 is a likely possibility.

162 GOLD MEDALLION OF MAGNENTIUS

Regnal dates: 350–353 A.D.

OBVERSE:
  IMP CAES MAG—NENTIVS AVG, bare-headed, draped and cuirassed bust of Magnentius right, dotted border.

REVERSE:
  LIBERATOR • REI • PVBLICAE, nimbate emperor on horseback right, greeted by city goddess bowing left, holding scroll(?) and cornucopiae, SMAQ in exergue, dotted border.

Medallion of 3 solidi, weight 13.50 gm; diameter 35 mm. ⁄

Aquileia mint, struck March 350 A.D., first issue.

Published: A. Jeločnik, "Les multiples d'or de Magnence découverts à Emona," *RN* 1967, p. 214, probably no. 4 or no. 8.

Same dies: P. Bastien, *Le monnayage de Magnence*, NR 1 (Wetteren, 1964), pl. 10, 302 = Jeločnik pl. 35, 2. Equivalent coins, various dies: Cohen 26; Gnecchi 1, p. 33, 1; Kent-Hirmer 669; *RIC* 8 (1981), p. 326, 122.

Probably from the Emona hoard, 1956.

Extremely rare: about ten specimens known.

Magnentius was a leading officer of the unpopular Constans (337–351 A.D.). He was acclaimed emperor in 350 by a band of conspirators at a birthday party in Autun in the very presence of the incumbent. The support of the army and the local populace was decisive: Constans fled and was killed. Magnentius was quickly recognized throughout most of the western empire, though his usurpation was resisted by kinsmen of Constans at Rome and in Illyricum. Magnentius' invasion of the latter province in 351 unleashed a war with the eastern emperor Constantius II which led ultimately to the defeat and suicide of the usurper at Lyons in 353.

This medallion of three solidi gives us an interesting example of the application of the refined and subtle style of late antique coinage to a man of gross appearance. However the raised eyebrow and tight lips seem to represent an attempt at characterization, giving Magnentius a virile mien totally lacking from the portraits of the sons of Constantine. The absence of a diadem bespeaks Magnentius' hope of obtaining recognition from Constantius II. The elaborate reverse type celebrates the "liberation" of the grateful polity from the hated Constans. Magnentius arrives on horseback, nimbate like a Christian saint—a reminder that the iconography of holiness was developed first for the emperors and only gradually became the exclusive property of religion. The kneeling personification who welcomes the emperor represents the state in general but also perhaps the city of Aquileia, which became Magnentius' headquarters late in 350 and served as the base for his invasion of Illyricum the following year. The scarf-like object which she holds has been tentatively identified as a scroll, presumably containing the text of a welcoming panegyric addressed to the liberator. The type is based upon an even more elaborate medallion of Constantius I depicting his arrival at the city of London. Quite possibly Magnentius found an advent type of Constans from the Aquileia mint (although none has come down to us) and adapted it to his own medallions.

The occasion for the first issue of this medallion was probably Magnentius' formal state entry into Aquileia in early 350. It was repeated with a consular portrait for Magnentius' assumption of the consulship in the same city on 1 January 351, and again at the beginning of 352. Seven of these multiples were found together in a hoard in Ljubuljana in 1956, and the possession of so many specimens by what is presumed to be a single owner suggests that they were perhaps not true medallions in the sense of unique imperial gifts, but rather circulating currency of high value.

163 GOLD MEDALLION OF CONSTANTIUS GALLUS

Regnal dates: Caesar in the east, 351–354 A.D.

OBVERSE:
D N CONSTANTI—VS NOB CAES, bare-headed, draped and cuirassed bust of Constantius left, dotted border.

REVERSE:
GLORIA RO—MANORVM, Constantinopolis enthroned left, holding filleted thyrsus and globe with small Victory who crowns her, left foot resting on prow, SMANT in exergue, dotted border.

Medallion of 4 1/2 solidi, weight 20.14 gm; diameter 39 mm. ↘

Antioch mint, struck May 351 A.D., accession issue.

Published: *RIC* 8 (1981), p. 517, 71A.

Variants: Gnecchi 1, pl. 9, 13 (Constans) and pl. 11, 9–10 (Constantius II).

Unique.

Constantius Gallus was a nephew of Constantine the Great who was spared in the purge of 337 A.D. because of his tender years and precarious health. Reared in seclusion on a Cappadocian estate, he was suddenly elevated to the rank of Caesar in March 351 to insure the stability of the east while Constantius II did battle with Magnentius in the west. But his cruel and capricious rule led to his recall and execution in 354, once the crisis in the west had been resolved.

This medallion of 4 1/2 solidi was probably struck in 351 to commemorate Gallus' entry into his capital city of Antioch in mid-May. The portrait is an elongated and even more elegant version of Constantius II [161]. The bare head confirms the hint from the silver medallion of Constantine II [159] that the imperial diadem was the prerogative of the Augustus alone, as had once been the case with the laurel wreath [141].

The reverse type is a splendid portrayal of the city goddess of Constantinople, based upon a statue created on Constantine's order for the inauguration of his new capital in 330 A.D. This figure was an intentional parallel to the ancient personification of Roma [137] and in fact was housed in a temple together with her. On coins the details of her iconography vary. But she is always depicted resting her foot on a prow to symbolize the decisive naval victory of Constantine the Great over Licinius in the Hellespont in 324, a victory soon commemorated by the foundation of Constantinople itself. A curious feature of the versions on the gold multiples of circa 348–360 is that Constantinople holds a thyrsus, an attribute of Bacchus (Dionysus), the conqueror of the east. It is surprising to find a pagan symbol associated with a city which was deliberately characterized as Christian from its very foundation. However we must remember that Constantine permitted pagan temples and pagan religious art in his capital for their cultural significance, though public worship was prohibited. Furthermore some time was required to develop a visual language free of allusions to pagan symbols.

The treatment of Constantinople on this medallion demonstrates the primacy of the Antioch mint in late Roman numismatic art. The work is so fine that it is possible to delight in the beauty of the goddess's tiny face and curly hair, worn in hellenistic fashion. Details such as the lion's head ornament on the prow are lost from most examples of the type.

164 GOLD SOLIDUS OF PROCOPIUS

Dates of usurpation: 365–366 A.D.

OBVERSE:
   D N PROCO—PIVS P F AVG, pearl-diademed, draped and cuirassed bust of Procopius right, dotted border.

REVERSE:
   REPARATI—O FEL TEMP, emperor in military attire standing facing, holding spear and shield, CONS in exergue, dotted border.

Weight 4.46 gm; diameter 22 mm.↓

Constantinople mint.

Published: Naville-Ars Classica 3 (Evans collection, 1922), lot 223; Glendining (Platt Hall collection 2, 1950), lot 2069; M&M 12 (1953), lot 878; Leu 10 (1974), lot 430.

Equivalent coins, various dies: Cohen 5; *RIC* 9 (1933), p. 209, 2a; Kent-Hirmer 699.

Ex A.J. Evans collection, London; H. Platt Hall collection, London.

Very rare.

Procopius was a scion of the house of Constantine. He was one of the generals of the Persian expedition of Julian II (the Apostate), but he was clearly not a member of the cabal of dissident officers which may have assassinated his kinsman. In fact the new emperor Jovian found a convenient pretext to remove the grieving Procopius from his command by assigning him the transport of Julian's body to Tarsus and the organization of the funeral observances. By the next year Jovian was dead, and yet another of Julian's generals, Valentinian, had assumed the purple, appointing his brother Valens to govern the eastern half of the empire. When Valens set forth to renew the war with Persia, Procopius staged an uprising in Constantinople and had himself crowned emperor (28 September 365). He seized Thrace and parts of Asia Minor, but the following year he was defeated by Valens. He was executed on May 27.

Procopius' portrait is more virile in concept and a little rougher in execution than most we have seen from the fourth century. In a largely clean-shaven era, its most striking feature is the beard. In late antiquity a beard is usually a sign of devotion to the intellectual life, either philosophy or religion. As such, it is generally inappropriate to imperial iconography, although there are a few exceptional bearded emperors. Julian's beard was of course regarded as a mark of his devotion to philosophy, which was synonymous with paganism; and the same could be true of Eugenius (392–394) who was the last emperor to attempt a revival of official paganism. On the other hand the beard could be a token of mourning and a vow of vengeance in the cases of Nepotian and Vetranio (both 350), Flavian family members who revolted against the murderer of Constans. The latter interpretation is possible for Procopius in view of the suspicious circumstances of Julian's death and the presence of Valentinian among his high officers.

The reverse of this solidus revives a theme from the coinage of Constans and Constantius II, the "restoration of happy times." It was associated with the introduction of a new bronze denomination in 348 and presumably referred to the celebration in that year of the eleven-hundredth anniversary of Rome's foundation. The revival of the legend is no doubt intended as a remind-

er of Procopius' blood ties to the Flavian dynasty, which constituted the basis of his claim to the throne.

The emperor-militant was the standard solidus reverse type in this period and was also employed by Valentinian and Valens, against whom Procopius was in revolt. Normally the emperor holds a *labarum* or standard bearing the monogram of Christ, but Procopius' version not only lacks any allusion to Christianity but displays a solar symbol on the shield by the emperor's side. An association with Julian is suggested by the fact that the similar motif of a star on a shield had appeared on his Antiochene coinage as Caesar under Constantius II. It would clearly be rash to read anti-Christian sentiment into the use of these solar symbols in view of the strong and recent Flavian tradition to the contrary [157, 161]. However there are hints of dissolution of the solar-Christian nexus. Solar imagery disappears from the coinage at about this time, and a silver cup from Kertch shows the emperor Valentinian on horseback, trampling just such a shield as is depicted here while an attendant displays a shield bearing the Christian monogram.

165 GOLD MEDALLION OF VALENTINIAN I

Regnal dates: Emperor of the west, 364–375 A.D.

OBVERSE:

D N VALENTINI—ANVS P F AVG, pearl-diademed, draped and cuirassed bust of Valentinian right, dotted border.

REVERSE:

VICTORIA—ROMANORVM, Roma and Constantinopolis enthroned facing, each helmeted and holding globus nicephorus, Roma holding spear, Constantinopolis holding sceptre and resting foot on prow, Christian monogram between heads, ANTOB in exergue, dotted border.

Medallion of 2 solidi, weight 8.82 gm; diameter 27 mm.↓

Antioch mint, struck 374–375 A.D., decennalian issue.

Published: NFA 2 (1975), lot 475.

Variants: NFA 2 (1975), lot 477 (Valens); RIC 9 (1933), p. 275, 13 and 16 (with reverse legend GLORIA ROMANORVM).

Unique.

Valentinian, a staunchly Christian general under Julian the Apostate, was elevated to imperial rank on 26 January 364 after the accidental suffocation of the emperor Jovian. On 28 March he associated his brother Valens in his rule, leaving him to govern the east while he devoted himself to the defense of the Rhine frontier. Both reigns were characterized by nearly incessant military activity against the restless barbarians and against the rival kingdoms of the east.

This double solidus was issued at Antioch for the decennalia or tenth anniversary of Valentinian and Valens. Since Antioch was Valens' headquarters from 370 onwards, similar medallions were issued in his name. In fact, those of Valentinian are so much scarcer that they hint at a coolness between the two brothers at this point.

The reverse type pairs the empire's twin capitals in a manner designed to emphasize their parallelism rather than their distinctiveness. The figure of Roma shows a general derivation from the Maxentian cult statue of Dea Roma [154], although it is reasonable to suppose the proximate model was the cult statue of Roma installed by Constantine at the dedication of Constantinople. The personification of Constantinople however has acquired Roma's helmet, and her thyrsus-like sceptre is here so reduced as to be nearly indistinguishable from Roma's spear. She is thus transformed from an oriental city-Tyche, as on [163], into a warrior goddess. Roma's position on the proper right and Constantinople's deferential gaze give Roma the primacy. The type symbolizes the division of the empire into eastern and western halves, theoretically of equal importance, an arrangement which was to persist to the fall of Rome in 476 A.D. The Christian monogram perhaps implies that the new state religion was the basis of the theoretical unity of this divided empire.

The type of Roma and Constantinople enthroned was a specialty of the Antioch mint. It was first introduced for the vicennalia of Constantius II and promptly became the invariant reverse type for gold medallions of two solidi. This rigid stereotyping of a coinage which had once been varied and informative parallels the divinization of the imperial office per se and the disregard

for the emperor as an individual personality. Significantly the obverse legend of all coins now regularly begins with D N for Dominus Noster, "Our Lord." The focus on eternal verities was reassuring and indeed necessary when current events were so frequently bleak and threatening.

Although the type of Roma and Constantinople is routine for the double solidus, the usual legend is GLORIA ROMANORVM. The substitution here of VICTORIA ROMANORVM thus represents a major variation within a coinage of such marked uniformity. The association of Victory with imperial anniversaries has already been commented on in connection with [122, 148]; but the motive for this change of legend remains obscure in view of the fact that similar multiples with the GLORIA inscription were apparently also used for the same occasion.

The letters OB at the end of the mint mark stand for obryzum, "pure" (gold). This assurance was added to the coinage after the fiscal reform of 366/367 A.D. which required that taxes be paid in the form of bullion rather than coin.

166 GOLD SOLIDUS OF MAJORIAN

Regnal dates: Emperor in the west, 457–461 A.D.

OBVERSE:
D N IVLIVS MAIORI—ANVS P F AVG, helmeted, draped and cuirassed bust of Majorian right, holding spear and shield ornamented with Christian monogram, dotted border.

REVERSE:
VICTORI—A AVGGG, emperor in military attire standing facing, holding long cross and globus nicephorus and resting foot on human-headed serpent, R—V across field, CONOB in exergue, dotted border.

Weight 4.44 gm; diameter 21 mm.↓

Ravenna mint.

Equivalent coins, various dies: Cohen 1; O. Ulrich-Bansa, *Moneta mediolanensis* (Venice, 1949), pl. L, q.

Rare.

From the reign of Theodosius I (379–395 A.D.) the eastern half of the empire, wealthier and more populous, enjoyed a kind of political primacy. A series of weak emperors in the west allowed the all-important function of military command to slip from their own hands into those of hired professional soldiers. Long periods of bad relations with the eastern court left the west isolated both culturally and militarily. In the fifth century it experienced catastrophic losses as the result of barbarian migrations. Gaul was overrun by Germanic tribes in 406, Spain in 409; the Vandals occupied Africa in the 430's; and Italy itself was invaded on several occasions. Under these circumstances real power passed from the emperor to the head of the army, by now often of barbarian descent himself.

By the middle of the fifth century the west was on the verge of institutional as well as territorial disintegration. From 455 the military leader was Count Ricimer, a grandson of the Visigothic king Wallia. He provided the continuity under a succession of hapless emperors whom he found all too easy to depose when they displeased him. Majorian was the most promising of these figures. An energetic soldier of old Roman family, he reunited much of Gaul to the empire and aspired to the reconquest of Africa. However his fleet was destroyed at anchor through treachery, and this setback provided the pretext for his removal.

With increasing isolation the western mints developed their own traditions with respect to style and type choice. This solidus from the Ravenna mint shows the clear influence of the alien cultural tide which had swept the west. The workmanship is rough and the style well on the way to abstraction. But underlying the exotic surface are venerable and significant types. The obverse bust of the late Roman coinage is by now not usually a portrait but a symbolic representation of the ideal emperor. The bust holding spear and shield descends from types such as [146, 148], in which the shield is ornamented with symbols suggesting the divine source of the imperial power. Under the Christian empire this scheme was used only rarely as a setting for Christian symbols. Constantius II was the first to place the Christian monogram on his shield on solidi issued for his tricennalia or thirtieth anniversary in power. The type was revived by the western emperors Honorius (393–423) and Valentinian III (425–455) for their respective tricennalia. These three prototypes employed a facing bust, but Majorian's mint reverted to the more conventional profile. However in the third and fourth centuries such shield-bearing busts were usually depicted facing left when the shield bore a significant device in order to display it to the best advantage. Majorian's rightward profile is not unprecedented, but it invariably results in anatomical distortion and a weak display of the shield. It goes without saying that the tricennalian associations of the type were misunderstood or ignored, for Majorian was very far from celebrating such an occasion himself.

The reverse type on the other hand is a commonplace of western solidi of this period. It derives ultimately from a painting installed by Constantine over the entrance to his palace at Constantinople, depicting Christ trampling a human-headed dragon, an allegorical representation of his own victory over the pagan "serpent" Licinius. In its fifth-century revival the type promises victory over the enemies of the empire with a discreet allusion to the Arian heresy of the Goths and Vandals—and incidentally, of Ricimer himself.

Notes for Coin Entries

55 NUMISMATIC LITERATURE. Evolution and date of first man-made coinage: E. S. G. Robinson, "The Coins from the Ephesian Artemision Reconsidered," *JHS* 71 (1951), pp. 156ff; Robinson, "The Date of the Earliest Coins," *NC* 1956, pp. 1ff; L. Weidauer, *Probleme der frühen Elektronprägung*, Typos 1 (Friburg, 1975), pp. 72ff; *ACGC* pp. 20ff. General artistic sources: Weidauer, *op. cit.*, pp. 80ff; Weidauer, "Die Elektronprägung in der orientalisierenden Epoche frühgriechische Kunst," *SNR* 60 (1981), pp. 7ff. ARTISTIC PARALLELS. Published comparisons: *Kunstfreund* p. 9. Bronze griffin heads: Jantzen *GGK*, First Hammered Group, see especially no. 9. Derivation from Aramaeanizing late Neo-Hittite models: E. Akurgal, *The Art of Greece, Its Origins in the Mediterranean and Near East* (New York, 1968), p. 185f, pl. 15a and figs. 16, 17.

56 NUMISMATIC LITERATURE. Phanes stater: *Traité* 1, 2 (1907), 64, pl. 2, 19 and cols. 60ff. ARTISTIC PARALLELS. Published comparisons: *Kunstfreund* p. 8. Lionesses: on gemstones, *GGFR* 91, 138, 182, 390, 419; *AGG* 411, 427, 433, 446, 449; on coins, Kraay-Hirmer 692. Rhodian animal style: *AGA* 37. Early comparanda: J. D. Beazley, *The Development of Attic Black-Figure* (Berkeley-Los Angeles, 1951), pl. 1; CVA *France* 1 (Paris, 1922), Attico-Corinthian pl. 1, fig. 1 and pl. 2, figs. 3, 6, 7, 10, 12; E. Akurgal, *The Art of Greece, Its Origins in the Mediterranean and Near East* (New York, 1968), pls. 46, 50, 51, 54, figs. 128, 135; Becatti *Orificerie* p. 175, no. 236, pls. 47, 48; H. Gabelmann, *Studien zum frühgriechischen Löwenbild* (Berlin, 1965), no. 50, pl. 6, fig. 3.

57 NUMISMATIC LITERATURE. Incuse fabric: W. Schwabacher, "Zur Prägetechnik und Deutung der inkusen Münzen Grossgriechenlandes," *Atti*, CIN 1961 (Rome, 1965), pp. 107ff; *ACGC* p. 168; C. H. V. Sutherland, "The 'Incuse' Coinage of South Italy," *ANSMusN* 3 (1948), pp. 15ff; P. Naster, "La technique des monnaies incuses de Grand-Grèce," *RBN* 1947, pp. 5ff; C. Seltman, "The Problem of the First Italiote Coins," *NC* 1949, pp. 1ff. Regional system: G. Gorini, *La monetazione incusa della Magna Graecia* (Bellinzona, 1975). Poseidonia: P. Ebner, *La monetazione di Poseidonia-Paestum* (Salerno, 1964); S. Pozzi, "Ripostigli di monete greche rinvenuti a Paestum," *AIIN* 9–11 (1962–64), pp. 75ff. ARTISTIC PARALLELS. Published comparisons: P. Gardner, *The Types of Greek Coins, an Archaeological Essay* (Cambridge, 1883), p. 86; D. J. Finn, "The Chigi Athena," *JHS* 32 (1912), p. 50f. Bronze Poseidon statues: *CGA* 113 = Robertson 1, p. 183 and note 45; *CGA* 146 = Robertson 1, p. 196 and note 69. Archaistic Poseidon on hellenistic coinage: E. T. Newell, *The Coinages of Demetrius Poliorcetes* (London, 1927), pl. 2 and passim. Heraldic character of types: *ACMG* p. 29. Oblique abdominal muscles: Lullies and Hirmer 62–65.

58 NUMISMATIC LITERATURE. Collected material: Seltman. Chronology: C. M. Kraay, "The Archaic Owls of Athens: Classification and Chronology," *NC* 1956, pp. 43ff; W. P. Wallace, "The Early Coinages of Athens and Euboea," *NC* 1962, pp. 23ff; Kraay, "The Early Coinage of Athens: A Reply," *NC* 1962, pp. 417ff; E. J. P. Raven, "Problems of the Earliest Owls of Athens," *Essays Robinson*, pp. 40ff; *Asyut* pp. 61ff; H. A. Cahn, "Dating the Early Coinages of Athens," *Kleine Schriften zur Münzkunde und Archäologie* (Basle, 1975), pp. 81ff; Cahn, "Asiut" (review), *SNR* 56 (1977), p. 284f. Types: L. Lacroix, "La chouette et le croissant sur les monnaies d'Athènes," *AC* 34 (1965), pp. 130ff. ARTISTIC PARALLELS. Published comparisons: H. A. Cahn, *Griechische Münzen archaischer Zeit* (Basle, 1947), p. 17; Seltman *Masterpieces* p. 31; *Kunstfreund* p. 36; Cahn "Dating" p. 88, figs. 5a, 5b. Receding plane of face: H. Payne and G. M. Young, *Archaic Marble Sculptures from the Acropolis*, second ed. (New York, 1950), pl. 11c, pl. 24, 3–4 and pl. 56, 3. Peplos Kore: Lullies and Hirmer 43–45; Robertson 1, p. 101f and note 63. Discobolos fragment: Lullies and Hirmer 39; Robertson 1, p. 109 and note 82. Owl: Richter *Animals* pl. 62, figs. 207- 208.

59 NUMISMATIC LITERATURE. Early history of Achaemenid coinage: S. P. Noe, *Two Hoards of Persian Sigloi*, NNM 136 (New York, 1956); E. S. G. Robinson, "The Beginnings of Achaemenid Coinage," *NC* 1958, pp. 187ff. Robinson records four darics of this type, none of them die-linked. Persian coins of Croeseid type: Noe, *op. cit.*, pl. 12. ARTISTIC PARALLELS. Persian heroes on Achaemenid seals: A. Upham Pope, *A Survey of Persian Art* 1 (Tehran, 1964–65), pl. 123, A, B, C, D, L, M and pl. 124, B, D, F, L; Graeco-Persian style, *GGFR* 824, 829, 849, 877, 878. An uncertainty has arisen among numismatists as to whether the coin type really represents the Great King, because the hero's crenelated headdress is unlike the royal cidaris depicted in architectural reliefs, but this seems not to be a problem within the field of Achaemenid archaeology *per se*, see Upham-Pope, *op. cit.*, Chapter 20, C. J. Gadd, "Achaemenid Seals: A. Types," p. 384f.

60 NUMISMATIC LITERATURE. Die study with historical background: J. M. F. May, *The Coinage of Abdera, 540–345 B.C.* (London, 1966), see especially p. 71. Dates revised in light of hoard evidence: *Asyut* p. 37. Griffin as anti-Persian symbol: G. F. Hill, "Alexander the Great and the Persian Lion-Gryphon," *JHS* 43 (1923), pp. 156ff. ARTISTIC PARALLELS. Jantzen *GGK*, Seventh Cast Group, see especially no. 143; but the bronze attachments lack spiral locks as well as the other decorative details of this Abderan griffin.

61 NUMISMATIC LITERATURE. Die study: T. Gerassimov, "Nacholka ot dekadrachme na trako-makedonskoto pleme derone," *Izvestia na archeologicheskia institut* 11 (1938), pp. 249ff. Derrones: W. Schwabacher, "Zur Silberprägung der Derroner," *SM* 3 (1952), pp. 1ff; T. Gerassimov, "A Hoard of Decadrachms of the Derrones from Velitchkovo (Bulgaria)," *NC* 1938, pp. 80ff. Tribal coinage: *Traité* 1 (1907), cols. 1033ff and 1039ff; H. Gaebler, *Die antiken Münzen Nordgriechenlandes* 3. *Makedonien und Paionia* (Berlin, 1935); Y. Youroukova, *Coins of the Ancient Thracians*, BARSS 4 (Oxford, 1976), pp. 4ff. Date of issue: *Asyut* p. 29. Interpretation of obverse type: A. Fol and I. Mazarov, *Thrace and the Thracians* (New York, 1977), p. 30. ARTISTIC PARALLELS. Figure style: *TAT* figs. 157, 239, 245, 248, 250, 285, 286, 289, 290.

62 NUMISMATIC LITERATURE. Die study with historical background: J. Desneux, "Les tétradrachmes d'Akanthos," *RBN* 95 (1949), pp. 5ff. Later date for issues bearing θ: *Asyut* p. 41f. Regional system: H. A. Cahn, "Skione—Stagira—Akanthos," *AK* 9 (1963), pp. 7ff. ARTISTIC PARALLELS. Published comparisons: Desneux, "Sur quelques représentations du 'lion à la proie' en glyptique et en numismatique antiques," *RBN* 106 (1960), pp. 1ff; Desneux, "Akanthos," pp. 9ff, pls. 2–4. Development of lion fight motif: *AGG* p. 121ff. Bas relief from Thessaloniki: Desneux "Akanthos," pl. 4 = Richter *Animals* pl. 5, fig. 13; various reliefs, F. Hölscher, *Die Bedeutung archaischer Tierkampfbilder* (Würzburg, 1972), pl. 2, fig. 2, pl. 5, fig. 2, pl. 11, fig. 3. Gemstones: *AGG* 391, 407 (pl. 29 and pp. 128ff), 440, 450; *GGFR* 86 (Minoan), 387.

63 NUMISMATIC LITERATURE. Die studies with historical background and artistic commentary: Boehringer, see especially pp. 14ff; H. Scharmer, "Die Meister der spätarchaischen Arethusaköpfe," *AK* 10 (1967), pp. 94ff. ARTISTIC PARALLELS. Published comparisons: quadriga, C. C. Vermeule, "Chariot Groups in Fifth-Century Greek Sculpture," *JHS* 75 (1955), p. 106 and fig. 3; horses, Rizzo *Saggi* p. 15, fig. 7 and p. 16, fig. 9; Victory, G. Taddei, "La Vittoria in volo," *IN* 3 (March 1950), p. 18; Arethusa head, E. Langlotz, *Zur Zeitbestimmung der strengrotfiguren Vasenmalerei und der gleichzeitigen Plastik* (Leipzig, 1920), p. 94 and pl. 2, 1; Boehringer p. 13, note 13 and figs. 3a, 3b, p. 14, note 14; Rizzo *Saggi* p. 22, fig. 12. Akragantine goddess: Langlotz and Hirmer no. 44, color pl. 8; profile view, Langlotz, *Studien zur nordostgriechischen Kunst* (Mainz, 1975), pl. 22.1. Coiffure on other West Greek terracottas: Langlotz and Hirmer pls. 29, 35, 36–37, 38. Ludovisi Acrolith: Langlotz and Hirmer pls. 62–63. Decorative treatment of hair: *AGC* fig. 51; this example also suggests the Ionian influence on the facial type. Profile view of Euthydikos Kore: H. Payne and C. M. Young, *Archaic Marble Sculptures from the Acropolis*, second ed. (New York, 1950), pl. 85, 2. Crude ear: L. Weidauer, *Probleme der frühen Elektronprägung*, Typos 1 (Fribourg, 1975), pl. 19, 174 and pl. 27, 1 and 3. Nike: *TST* 37.

64 NUMISMATIC LITERATURE. Die studies with historical background and artistic commentary: Boehringer, see especially pp. 36ff; *Demareteion*. Interpretation of types: R. R. Holloway, "Damarete's Lion," *ANSMusN* 11 (1964), pp. 1ff. Revised dating with historical background: Kraay-Hirmer p. 288; "Hieron's Aitna" pp. 67ff; C. M. Kraay, "The Demareteion and Sicilian Chronology," Chapter 2 of *Greek Coins and History* (London, 1969); R. T. Williams, "The Demareteion Reconsidered," *NC* 1972, pp. 1ff (in defense of the traditional date); Kraay, "The Demareteion Reconsidered: A Reply," *NC* 1972, pp. 13ff. Boehringer, *loc. cit.*, and Holloway, *art. cit.*, pp. 1ff regard the artist of the decadrachm as a regular mint worker of old-fashioned taste who must have died shortly after executing the dies for the Demareteion issue since his style disappears from the series. ARTISTIC PARALLELS. Published comparisons: B. Ashmole, "Manners and Methods in Archaeology," *JHS* 58 (1938), p. 246; Seltman *Masterpieces* p. 49; *Demareteion* pp. 14ff, pls. 2, 4 with further bibliography on p. 27f; *Boston Sculpture* p. 17, no. 25. Coiffure: W. Schuchardt, "Köpfe des Strenge Stils," *Festschrift für Carl Weickert*, ed. G. Bruns (Berlin, 1955), figs. 9, 10; waves at temples, Langlotz and Hirmer pl. 41; spiral lock, Käppeli D10.

65 NUMISMATIC LITERATURE. Historical background and date of issue: "Syrakus und Leontinoi"; "Hieron's Aitna." ARTISTIC ANALYSIS AND PARALLELS. Pfeiff *Apollon* p. 65. Ludovisi Throne: Lullies and Hirmer pls. 134–137; Robertson 1, pp. 203ff and note 90. Piombino Apollo: Lullies and Hirmer pls. 92–95; Robertson 1, pp. 183ff, p. 560 and note 148. West Greek facial type: Langlotz and Hirmer pls. 54–55, 57, 58–59, 70, 71, 88, 95; H. Prückner, *Die Lokrischen Tonreliefs, Beitrag zur Kultgeschichte von Lokroi Epizephyrioi* (Mainz, 1968), pl. 2, 1 and pl. 12, 4. Coiffure: B. S. Ridgway, *The Severe Style in Greek Sculpture* (Princeton, 1970), figs. 74, 94–95; wavy lock behind ear, A. Greifenhagen, *Griechische Eroten* (Berlin, 1957), figs. 8, 46, 48.

66 NUMISMATIC LITERATURE. Catalogue of known specimens: C. G. Starr, *Athenian Coinage, 480–449 B.C.* (Oxford, 1970), pp. 33ff. Early theories of occasion of issue: Seltman p. 106f; *Traité* 2 (1910), col. 770. Revised dating: F. Mainzer, "Das Dekadrachmon von Athen," *ZfN* 36 (1926), pp. 37ff; Starr, *op. cit.*, pp. 38ff.

67 NUMISMATIC LITERATURE. Series, mint identification, Carian script: H. A. Troxell, "Winged Carians," *Essays Thompson* pp. 257ff; E. S. G. Robinson, "A Find of Archaic Coins from South-West Asia Minor," *NC* 1936, pp. 265ff. ARTISTIC PARALLELS. Eros on gemstones: *AGG* 171, 172, 250, 272, 274, 321. Eros on vases: A. Greifenhagen, *Griechische Eroten* (Berlin, 1957), pls. 1–4, 13, 41, 49. Eros as a death god: E. Vermeule, *Aspects of Death in Early Greek Art and Poetry*, SCL 46 (Berkeley-Los Angeles-London, 1979), pp. 155ff. Contorted poses on gemstones: Furtwängler *AG* pl. 8, 15–23, 35–37, pl. 9, 1, 3, 20, 24, pl. 15, 21–30, pl. 16, 32–62, pl. 23, 5, 9, 10, 17, 25ff; Cypriote examples, *GGFR* 367, 369. Eros and lion associated: Greifenhagen, *op. cit.*, p. 26 and no. 25 = *ARV* p. 264, no. 67. Sinuous East Greek lions: Summa, *Auction 1* (1981), lots 58, 59. Mane: H. Gabelmann, *Studien zum frühgriechischen Löwenbild* (Berlin, 1965), no. 2, pl. 1, figs. 2–3, no. 127, pl. 26, fig. 1, no. 134, pl. 28, figs. 2–3; on Carian coins, *ACGC* 99, 100.

68 NUMISMATIC LITERATURE. Die study with historical background and artistic analysis: Cahn, see especially pp. 42ff. Aetna tetradrachm by the same artist: Kraay-Hirmer color pl. 2. ARTISTIC PARALLELS. Published comparisons: Furtwängler *Masterpieces* p. 108; Rizzo *Saggi* p. 67f and figs. 48ff, p. 70, fig. 55; Cahn pp. 43ff with notes 4–9, pl. 10, O–U; Seltman *Masterpieces* pp. 55, 57; Robertson 1, p. 211. Facial features of bearded god: *CGA* 113 = Robertson 1, p. 183 and note 45; Lullies and Hirmer pls. 129, 132; Langlotz and Hirmer pl. 73. Analysis of Silenus figure: B. Ashmole, "Manners and Methods in Archaeology," *JHS* 58 (1938), p. 246, see especially note 23. Squatting figures: *ARVAP* figs. 68, 84, 174, 220, 262.2; F. Brommer, *Satyrspiele* (Bonn, 1944), figs. 54, 55. Treatment of abdominal muscles: *ARVAP* figs. 22, 23, 145.

69 NUMISMATIC LITERATURE. Die study: unpublished corpus by E. Boehringer, see "Hieron's Aitna" p. 95, note 77 and "Syrakus und Leontinoi" p. 7, note 1. Problems of dating: Gulbenkian p. 73f, nos. 215–219. ARTISTIC PARALLELS. Tomba del Tuffatore: M. Napoli, *La Tomba del Tuffatore* (Bari, 1970), see especially the kottabos player of color plate 13. Small head from metope of Temple E at Selinus: Rizzo *Intermezzo* p. 68, fig. 19. Coiffure: B. Pace, "Arti ed artisti della Sicilia antica," *Atti Acc. Lincei* 15 (Rome, 1917), p. 525, fig. 36; Lullies and Hirmer p. 123 with bibliography p. 74. Lion head architectural ornaments: Langlotz and Hirmer pls. 77–79; *CGA* 59, 60, 62.

70 NUMISMATIC LITERATURE. Die study with historical background: J. M. F. May, *Ainos, Its History and Coinage* (Oxford, 1950), see especially pp. 57ff. ARTISTIC PARALLELS. Published comparisons: Lacroix pp. 44ff; Seltman *Masterpieces* p. 50; *Kunstfreund* p. 194; Robertson 1, p. 212. Development of beardless Hermes: P. Raingeard, *Hermès Psychagogue, essai sur les origines du culte d'Hermès* (Rennes, 1934), pp. 380ff with many examples cited; P. Zanker, *Wandel der Hermesgestalt in der attischen Vasenmalerei* (Bonn, 1965), pls. 4, 6a. Hermes Perpheraios: C. Picard, "Le sculpteur Epeios: du cheval de Troie au taureau de Phalaris," *RN* 1942, pp. 1ff and fig. 1; Lacroix p. 47, notes 1, 2; May, *op. cit.*, p. 272f and note 1 on both pages.

71 NUMISMATIC LITERATURE. Die study: Schwabacher pp. 30ff. Interpretation of types: A. H. Lloyd, "The Coin Types of Selinus and the Legend of Empedocles," *NC* 1935, pp. 73ff; Rizzo *Intermezzo* pp. 49ff; L. Lacroix, *Monnaies et colonisation dans l'occident grec* (Brussels, 1965), p. 30f. Sicilian river cults: B. Pace, *Arte e civiltà della Sicila antica* (Rome-Naples, 1945), pp. 496ff; E. Ciaceri, *Culti i miti nella storia dell'antica Sicilia* (Catania, 1911), pp. 252ff. ARTISTIC PARALLELS. Published comparisons: quadriga, Schwabacher p. 35, note 1; river god, C. Waldstein, "Pythagoras of Rhegion and the Early Athlete Statues," *JHS* 2 (1881), pp. 347, 348; Waldstein, *Essays on the Art of Pheidias* (Cambridge-New York, 1885), p. 370 and fig. 23; Schwabacher pp. 77ff; B. Ashmole, *Late Archaic and Early Classical Greek Sculpture in Sicily and South Italy*, from *PBA* 20 (London, 1934), p. 25f, fig. 70; P. W. Lehmann, *Statues on Coins of Southern Italy and Sicily in the Classical Period* (New York, 1946), pp. 15ff; Robertson 1, p. 212. Related statue types: Robertson 1, p. 194f, with illustrations on pls. 61c, 61d; *CGA* 108, 109.

72 NUMISMATIC LITERATURE. Die study with historical background: Boehringer, see especially pp. 63ff. ARTISTIC PARALLELS. Published comparisons: quadriga, G. B. Waybell, "A Four-Horse Chariot Relief of the Fifth Century B.C.," *ABSA* 62 (1967), pp. 19ff; Arethusa, Rizzo *Saggi* p. 41 and fig. 27; *Problemi fidiaci* p. 203 and pl. 97, fig. 296; NFA 5 (1978), lot 47. Artemis on east pediment of Parthenon: Lullies and Hirmer pl. 157. Pheidian Aphrodite: Furtwängler *Masterpieces* pp. 66ff, figs. 20, 21b; *Problemi fidiaci* pl. 99; Schrader *Phidias* pl. 29–34.

73 NUMISMATIC LITERATURE. Die study with historical background and artistic analysis: Cahn, see especially pp. 56ff. ARTISTIC PARALLELS. Published comparisons: Furtwängler *Masterpieces* p. 108; Cahn p. 59, pl. 11 (Dresden Zeus also plated, implying another comparison). Pheidian style: *Parthenonfries* pls. 14, 64, 180 (Poseidon), 183, 184. Corkscrew curls: New York athlete, Richter *SSG* p. 79 with note 55, fig. 195 = *Problemi fidiaci* pls. 80–81, figs. 245ff; Vienna Zeus head, Schrader *Phidias* p. 61, figs. 38, 39. Elderly Silenus: M. Robertson, *Greek Painting* (Geneva, 1979), p. 125. Loose drawing: *ibid.* pp. 154ff; *CGA* 301ff.

74 NUMISMATIC LITERATURE. Die study: S. P. Noe, *The Mende (Kaliandra) Hoard*, NNM 27 (New York, 1926). Primitive Dionysiac coinage of Thraco-Macedonian region: *Traité* 1 (1907), cols. 1033ff; "Héllenisme primitif" pl. 5, 17–24, pls. 6, 7, 8. ARTISTIC PARALLELS. Drunken Dionysus: on vases, *Dionysos griechische Antike*, exhibit at Ingelheim, 1–30 May 1965, 18, 25; Melian relief, P. Jacobsthal, *Die melischen Reliefs* (Berlin, 1931), 86.

75 NUMISMATIC LITERATURE. Die engraver: *Euainetos* (flawed by outdated chronology), Catanian drachms: Rizzo p. 15, fig. 4 and pl. 14, 7, 8. Syracusan tetradrachm: Tudeer reverse die 24. ARTISTIC ANALYSIS AND PARALLELS. Published comparisons: quadriga, Rizzo *Saggi* p. 101, figs. 81, 82; C. C. Vermeule, "Chariot Groups in Fifth-Century Greek Sculpture," *JHS* 75 (1955), p. 108, p. 111 and note 24, figs. 13–18; Lullies and Hirmer pls. 188, 193–194; Richter "Phiale" p. 375 = Richter *MMH* p. 96f with note 44, pls. 78a, 78b, p. 132 and pl. 112d; fillet, *Kunstfreund* p. 128. Development of mature quadriga: Vermeule, *art. cit.*, pp. 104ff; G. B. Waybell, "A Four-Horse Chariot Relief of the Fifth Century B.C.," *ABSA* 62 (1967), pp. 19ff; Robertson 1, pp. 157, 224 with note 119, p. 416 with notes 150f; *Kamarina* pp. 45ff. Other quadrigas: in sculpture, Käppeli A5; in painting, *CGA* 316, 328; phiale, *TAT* p. 364, nos. 170–172. Analysis of Apollo head: Pfeiff *Apollon* p. 114f. Coiffure: on vases, Pfeiff *Apollon* pls. 13, 14b, 2 Beilage, fig. 4, pl. 40; H. Walter, *Griechische Götter, ihr Gestaltwandel aus dem Bewusstseinsstufen des Menschen dargestellt an den Bildwerken* (Munich, 1971), fig. 302; on transitional tetradrachms of Catana, Rizzo *Intermezzo* figs 1–4. Rich style on Attic vases: *CGA* pp. 269ff, pp. 279ff and nos. 308, 311, 312, etc. Copy(?) of this Apollo head in vase painting: *CGA* 363. Fillet: A. R. Bellinger and M. A. Berlincourt, *Victory as a Coin Type*, NNM 149 (New York, 1962), pl. 3, 4 (obverse).

76 NUMISMATIC LITERATURE. Die study with artistic comment: "Akragantine Decadrachms." Mirror image of obverse die: Tudeer obverse dies 22 and 25. Identification of engravers: Myr . . ., R. Weil, *Die Künstlerinschriften der sicilischen Münzen*, Winckelmannsprogramm 44 (Berlin, 1884), 13; "Signatures de graveurs" p. 298f; Jongkees pp. 40ff; "Akragantine Decadrachms."

77 NUMISMATIC LITERATURE. Die sequences with artistic commentary: Jongkees pp. 66ff; "Akragantine Decadrachms." Much of the remaining literature on these great coins derives from a politically-inspired attack by Axis scholars on the authenticity of specimens in Allied countries and is refuted by Jongkees. ARTISTIC PARALLELS. Published comparisons: *Agamemnon*, B. V. Head, *Historia Numorum* (Oxford, 1911), p. 121f; Jongkees p. 66; M. Bock, "Aischylos und Akragas," *Gymnasium* 65 (1958), pp. 402ff; Amaltheia relief and other works featuring eagle with hare, Bock, *art. cit.*, p. 404 and pl. 15. Quadriga of Helios in vase painting: *CGA* 313 = *ARV* p. 1338, Naples 2883; Robertson 1, p. 420 and note 160.

78 NUMISMATIC LITERATURE. Die study: Schwabacher, see especially p. 62f. Syracusan prototype of obverse: Schwabacher p. 59f; Tudeer pl. 2, 15. ARTISTIC PARALLELS. Published comparisons: C. Waldstein, *Essays on the Art of Pheidias* (Cambridge-New York, 1885), p. 370, fig. 23; Schwabacher p. 81f; Richter *SSG* p. 57 and figs. 43, 44, 45; P. W. Lehmann, *Statues on Coins of Southern Italy and Sicily in the Classical Period* (New York, 1946), pp. 15ff and pls. 3, 4. River god type on gemstones, G. Horster, *Statuen auf Gemmen*, HDD (KA) 3 (Bonn, 1970), pl. 13, 1–2.

79 NUMISMATIC LITERATURE. Die study with historical background and artistic analysis: *Kamarina* pp. 41ff. Athena as charioteer on other Sicilian coins: *Kamarina* p. 43 and pl. 18. Die engraver: *Euainetos* (flawed by outdated chronology); the attribution to Euainetus is the author's. ARTISTIC PARALLELS. Published comparisons: quadriga, Richter "Phiale" pp. 363ff = Richter *MMH* p. 96f and note 44, pl. 78a, 78b; *Kamarina* pp. 41ff, p. 45f and pl. 19, 10. Iconography of Heracles: *Kamarina* p. 55f and pl. 18.

80 NUMISMATIC LITERATURE. Die study with historical background and artistic analysis: *Kamarina* pp. 58ff. Artist attribution: Ly, *Kamarina* p. 59f, following S. Hurter, Leu 13 (1975), lot 46 note; Exakestidas, Hurter *loc. cit.*; Euainetus' signature on facing head didrachm, *Kamarina* pl. 21, 162. Interpretation of reverse type: *Kamarina* pp. 66ff. Sicilian water deities: S. Mirone, "Les divinités fluviales sur les monnaies antiques de la Sicile," *RN* 1917, pp. 1ff; F. Imhoof-Blumer, "Fluss- und Meergötter auf griechischen und römischen Münzen," *SNR* 23 (1923), pp. 173ff; L. Lacroix, "Fleuves et nymphes éponymes sur les monnaies grecques," *RBN* 1953, pp. 1ff. ARTISTIC PARALLELS. Published comparisons: *Kamarina* pp. 66ff, pls. 26–29. Diadoumenos and related sculpture types: Furtwängler *Masterpieces* pp. 238ff with plates passim; Robertson 1, p. 331f and notes 93–96. Diademed youth with features of Eros(?): E. Paribeni, *Museo Nazionale Romano. Scultore greche del V secolo, originali e repliche* (Rome, 1953), p. 46. Pheidian Eros: Furtwängler *Masterpieces* p. 69 and note 3, fig. 21a. Aphrodite on swan or goose: *Kamarina* pls. 26, 27; W. Züchner, *Griechische Klappspiegel* (Berlin, 1942), pp. 5ff; E. Simon, *Die Geburt der Aphrodite* (Berlin, 1959), pp. 32ff and figs. 18, 20, 21; *Intaglios and Rings* 36; *Boston Sculpture* p. 32, no. 43. Velificatio motif: G. E. Rizzo, "Aurae velificantes," *BCAR* 67 (1939), pp. 141ff; Simon, *op. cit.*, fig. 15.

81 NUMISMATIC LITERATURE. Die study with artistic comment: Tudeer especially pp. 157f, 220ff. Die engraver: Rizzo *Saggi* pp. 79ff = "Eukleidas," *Boll. d'Arte* February 1938. Relation of type to Syracusan traditions: *ACGC* p. 222. ARTISTIC ANALYSIS AND PARALLELS. Published comparisons: Rizzo *Saggi* pp. 88ff and figs. 69, 71, 72, 73; Lacroix p. 268f and pl. 13; *Kunstfreund* p. 172; Erhart p. 195f. Pheidian Athena Parthenos: N. Leipen, *Athena Parthenos, a Reconstruction* (Ontario, 1971); Robertson 1, pp. 311ff and notes 45–47. Athena head motif in other media: Leipen, *op. cit.*, no. 38, fig. 42, no. 39, fig. 43, no. 53, fig. 52, no. 57, fig. 54, no. 58, fig. 55, nos. 59–61, fig. 56, nos. 62, 63, figs. 57a, b, nos. 65–67; on Calene kylix, R. Pagenstecher, *Die calenische Reliefkeramik*, JDAI Ergänzungsheft 8 (Berlin, 1909), p. 24, pl. 21; jewelry and terracotta medallions, Jongkees p. 96 with notes 4, 5; Koul Oba medallions and various, Lacroix *loc. cit.*; on gemstones, *GGFR* color pl. p. 217, no. 3 and pl. 762. Athena head motif on coins: Lucanian Velia and Heraclea, *ACGC* 702, 738; Lycian dynasts, *ACGC* 988; Cilician civic and satrapal coinage, *ACGC* 1029, 1046. Coiffure: *CGA* 171, 331.

82 NUMISMATIC LITERATURE. Die study: Tudeer pp. 183ff, 232ff; Jongkees pp. 60ff, which deduces from the pattern of die use that this was an occasional coin rather than a regular issue. Catanian tetradrachm signed Choirion: Gulbenkian 193. ARTISTIC PARALLELS. Published comparisons: Rizzo *Saggi* p. 97; *GR Bronzes* pp. 176ff; Richter *MMH* p. 96; Jongkees p. 96. Three quarter heads in Parthenon sculptures: *Parthenonfries* pl. 10, fig. W II, pl. 56, fig. N IV, pl. 108, fig. N XLII, pl. 182, fig. O VI; Lullies and Hirmer pls. 149, 156. Three quarter heads on mirror covers: W. Züchner, *Griechische Klappspiegel* (Berlin, 1942), KS 100ff, especially KS 106 and (for the Catanian example) KS 100 (= Richter *loc. cit.* note 38, pl. 77c and note 39, pl. 77b). Imitations of type: on coins, Rizzo pp. 217ff; L. Mildenberg, "Kimon in the Manner of Segesta," *Proceedings*, CIN 8, New York-Washington 1973 (Paris-Basle, 1976), pp. 113ff; Larissa, see [93]; on South Italian Calenian ware pottery, G. M. A. Richter, "Calenian Pottery and Classical Greek Metalware," *AJA* 63 (1959), pl. 52, fig. 10; in jewelry and terracotta medallions, Jongkees p. 96, notes 2, 3. Echelos and Basile relief: Lullies and Hirmer 188.

83 NUMISMATIC LITERATURE. Erhart pp. 152ff; Rizzo *Saggi* pp. 95ff; *ACGC* p. 224f. Amphipolis: *Traité* 4 (1932), cols. 677ff, pl. 320, 10–17 and pl. 321, 1–4; *ACGC* p. 151f, nos. 568–570; Kraay-Hirmer 414–418. Clazomenae: *Traité* 2 (1910), cols. 1143ff and pl. 155, 20–32; *ACGC* p. 258, nos. 929–930; Kraay-Hirmer 608. Dies of issue: Gulbenkian 190–192. ARTISTIC ANALYSIS AND PARALLELS. Published comparisons: *GR Bronzes* p. 177. Analysis: Pfeiff *Apollon* p. 113f. Attic sculpture: G. Traversari, *Sculture del V -IV secolo a.C. del Museo Archeologico di Venezia* (Rome, 1973), 27; G. M. A. Richter, *Catalogue of Greek Sculptures in the Metropolitan Museum of Art* (New York, 1954), 71 and pl. 57, d-f; Pfeiff *Apollon* pp. 119ff and pl. 51a. Style choice a feature of hellenistic art: J. Onians, *Art and Thought in the Hellenistic Age. The Greek World View, 350–50 B.C.* (London, 1979).

84 NUMISMATIC LITERATURE. Die study with artistic analysis: Jongkees. Date and occasion of issue: "Syracusan 'Medallions' " pp. 205ff, influential but disproven by the accumulated hoard evidence; ACGC p. 223f; also points stressed by L. Mildenberg in a lecture delivered at the J. Paul Getty Museum, Malibu, 6 January 1983 (to be published). ARTISTIC ANALYSIS AND PARALLELS. Published comparisons: Furtwängler Masterpieces p. 108; Problemi fidiaci p. 51 and pl. 7, figs. 18–19, although Becatti plates a decadrachm of Euainetus [86]. Horses: Markman pp. 81ff. Laborde head: Problemi fidiaci pp. 48ff. Stele of Hegeso: Lullies and Hirmer 187.

85 NUMISMATIC LITERATURE. Die study with artistic analysis: Jongkees. Stylistic contrasts between Cimon's first and second types: Jongkees Ch. 7. False artists' signatures: Jongkees Chs. 8–10.

86 NUMISMATIC LITERATURE. Die study and catalogue: A. Gallatin, Syracusan Dekadrachms of the Euainetos Type (Cambridge, Mass., 1930). Date and economic context: C. Boehringer, "Zu Finanzpolitik und Münzprägung des Dionysios von Syrakus," Essays Thompson p. 13f, correcting the influential but unscientific "Syracusan 'Medallions'." Types imposed by Dionysius: suggestion of L. Mildenberg in a lecture delivered at the J. Paul Getty Museum, Malibu, 6 January 1983 (to be published). Copies of Arethusa head on coinage: ACGC 321, 322, 387, 610, 625, 681, 685, 714, 868, 870, 873, 874, 877 (not an exhaustive list). ARTISTIC PARALLELS. Published comparisons: Laborde head, Problemi fidiaci p. 51, figs. 17–19. Copies of Arethusa head in other art forms: Tarentine goddess, L. von Matt, Magna Graecia (New York, 1962), pl. 193; gold plaque from Braganza, Becatti Orificerie 463, pl. 130; on Calene kylikes, "Syracusan 'Medallions' " pp. 114ff; R. Pagenstecher, Die calenische Reliefkeramik, JDAI Ergänzfolgung 8 (Berlin, 1909), pp. 16ff (28 examples); Richter "Phiale" fig. 30; VMG 103 with full bibliography for the form. The numismatic information cited in these archaeological contexts is unfortunately out of date.

87 NUMISMATIC LITERATURE. Die study with artistic parallels: G. de Ciccio, Gli aurei siracusani di Cimone e di Evaneto (Rome, 1957), often useless because of the poor quality of the plates. Evidence for later date of issue: G. K. Jenkins, "Electrum Coinage at Syracuse," Essays Robinson p. 145, note 2; C. Boehringer, "Zu Finanzpolitik und Münzprägung des Dionysios von Syrakus," Essays Thompson, p. 18, note 33. ARTISTIC ANALYSIS AND PARALLELS. Published comparisons: gemstone from Catana, "Syracusan 'Medallions' " p. 321, pl. 13, 5 = Furtwängler AG pl. 9, 49 = di Ciccio, op cit., fig. 1; terracotta antefix, ACMG p. 133. Development of Herakles and lion composition: ACMG p. 56; Euainetos p. 33f, of lesser value because the chronology of the coins cited has been revised. Herakles and lion motif in other media: silver phalera from Pangyurishte treasure, TAT 293; gold repoussé ornaments, TST fig. 218. Arethusa's coiffure: CGA 171 = Robertson 1, p. 309f and note 43.

88 NUMISMATIC LITERATURE. Die study: D. Bérend, "Les tétradrachmes de Rhodes de la première période," SNR 51 (1972), pp. 1ff. ARTISTIC PARALLELS. Published comparisons: Furtwängler Masterpieces p. 410 and fig. 177; Naples fragment, Erhart p. 165 and note 380. Prior expressionism in Colossi of Monte Cavallo: Furtwängler Masterpieces pp. 95ff and fig. 42. Previous representations of Helios: CGA 313 = ARV p. 1338, Naples 2883; Robertson 1, p. 420 and note 160. Rhodian works depicting Helios: Bieber Hellenistic Sculpture p. 123f and fig. 488; Lullies and Hirmer 263; Robertson 1, p. 476.

89 NUMISMATIC LITERATURE. Catalogue by dies of known "Alliance" coins: S. Karwiese, "Lysander as Herakliskos Dragonopnignon," NC 1980, pp. 1ff. Date and nature of alliance: G. L. Cawkwell, "A Note on the Herakles Coinage Alliance of 394 B.C.," NC 1956, pp. 69ff; J. M. Cook, "Cnidian Peraea and Spartan Coins," JHS 81 (1961), pp. 66ff; Cawkwell, "The ΣΥΝ Coins Again," JHS 83 (1963), p. 152f; Karwiese, art. cit., pp. 7ff. ARTISTIC PARALLELS. Published comparisons: Karwiese, art. cit., pp. 12ff and pl. 2. Infant Herakles motif: O. Brendel, "Der schlangenwürgende Herakliskos," JDAI 47 (1932), pp. 191ff. Amulets: ACMG p. 60.

90 NUMISMATIC AND HISTORICAL LITERATURE. K. Regling, "Phygela, Klazomenai, Amphipolis," ZfN 33 (1922), pp. 55ff; Traité 4 (1932), cols. 677ff. Apollo at Amphipolis: J. Papastravrou, "Amphipolis," Klio N.F. 24, Beiheft 1936, p. 51. Athenian suppression of allies' coinage: E. S. G. Robinson, "The Athenian Currency Decree and the Coinage of the Allies," Hesperia Suppl. 8 (1949), pp. 324ff. ARTISTIC PARALLELS. Published comparisons: Furtwängler Masterpieces pp. 410ff. Amphipolitan Apollo and Parthenon pediment: coins, Regling, art. cit., pl. 2, 12; Kraay-Hirmer 415; Parthenon, Lullies and Hirmer 156. Kassel Apollo: Pfeiff Apollon pp. 81ff and pls. 31–32. Tiber Apollo: Pfeiff Apollon p. 101f and pls. 36–38. Apollo Citharode: statue, G. M. A. Richter, Three Critical Periods in Greek Sculpture (Oxford, 1951), p. 46 with bibliography in note 15 and fig. 87; on vases, CGA 356 = VMG 15 (with further bibliography); CGA 361 = A. D. Trendall, Frühitaliotische Vasen (Leipzig, 1938), p. 42, no. 97.

91 NUMISMATIC LITERATURE. Traité 4 (1932), cols. 701ff, 715ff, 727ff. Early staters: Traité 1 (1907), cols. 1195f and pl. 55, 18–21, 24–26. ARTISTIC PARALLELS. Published comparisons: Traité 4 (1932), cols. 727f; G. le Rider, Guide de Thasos (Paris, 1968), p. 64, fig. 24; Kunstfreund p. 270. Fifth-century Dionysus herm: G. M. A. Richter, 'Aspasios I and II," Studies D. M. Robinson 1, pp. 720ff and pl. 86, a, b, c and f. Herakles bas relief: RA 1 (1885), p. 472; A. Joubin, "Relief archaïque de Thasos," BCH 1894, p. 64 and pl. 16. Kneeling Herakles as potters' hallmark: A. Dumont, Inscriptions ceramiques de la Grèce, pl. 5, 24 and 40.

92 NUMISMATIC LITERATURE. This excessively rare stater is not included in either of the corpora of the Cyzicene electrum, W. Greenwell, Electrum Coinage of Cyzicus (London-Paris, 1887) and H. von Fritze, "Die Elektronprägung von Kyzikos," Nomisma 9 (1914). First published: K. Regling, "Die griechische Goldschatz von Prinkipo," ZfN 41 (1931), p. 21. Economic role of Cyzicene electrum: R. Bogaert, "Le cours du statère de Cyzique aux Ve et IVe siècles avant J-C," AC 32 (1963), pp. 85ff; Bogaert, "Encore le cours du statère de Cyzique," AC 33 (1964), pp. 121ff. ARTISTIC PARALLELS. Published comparisons: Regling, art. cit., p. 21; Kunstfreund p. 301. Gambling figures in various media: J. Dörig, "Tarentinische Knochelspielerinnen," Museum Helveticum 16 (1959), pp. 29ff and figs. 1–19, especially figs. 3–5 which approximate this pose; GGFR 543, 604, 726; G. M. A. Richter, A Handbook of Greek Art, seventh ed. (London-New York, 1974), fig. 317; CGA 319; HA 118.

93 NUMISMATIC LITERATURE. F. Herrmann, "Die Silber-münzen von Larissa in Thessalien," *ZfN* 35 (1925). Revised dating: A. R. Bellinger, *Atti*, CIN 1961 (Rome, 1965), pp. 57ff; C. M. Kraay, *Greek Coins and History* (London, 1969), p. 15f. ARTISTIC PARALLELS. Cult statue of nymph Larissa: Pliny, *NH* 34.68. Heavy features: *HA* 212; Robertson 1, p. 513 and note 25. Soft brow line: *HA* 224–225; Robertson 1, p. 462 and note 39. Horse: Markman pp. 93ff and fig. 59.

94 NUMISMATIC LITERATURE. Die study with historical back-ground: G. le Rider, *Le monnayage d'argent et d'or de Philippe II* (Paris, 1977). Panhellenic propaganda in coins types: A. B. West, "The Early Diplomacy of Philip II of Macedon Illustrated by His Coins," *NC* 1923, pp. 169ff; S. Perlman, "The Coins of Philip II and Alexander the Great and their Pan-Hellenic Propaganda," *NC* 1965, pp. 57ff. ARTISTIC PARALLELS. Published comparisons: M. Collignon, *Phidias* (Paris, 1886), p. 111. Zeus on Olympian coins: C. Seltman, *The Temple Coins of Olympia* (Cambridge, 1921), pl. 6, CE, CG, CH, CJ. Pheidian cult statue: Schrader *Phidias* pp. 44ff, figs. 13 and 14 and pp. 55ff, figs. 36–39; *Problemi fidiaci* pp. 131ff and figs. 215–221, 224–225; Lacroix pp. 259ff and pl. 22. Cyrene Zeus head: *CGA* 154. Zeus of Mylasa: *CGA* 237 = *Boston Sculpture* p. 33, no. 44. Horse on Bryaxis statue base: Markman fig. 57.

95 NUMISMATIC LITERATURE. Die study: S. P. Noe, *The Coinage of Metapontum*, NNM 32 (New York, 1927) and NNM 47 (New York, 1931), but this coin is not included. Signature ΚΑΛ: A. J. Evans, "The 'Horsemen' of Tarentum," *NC* 1889, p. 105f; "Signatures de graveurs" pp. 6ff; M. P. Vlasto, "Alexander, son of Neoptolemos, of Epirus," *NC* 1926, pp. 186ff and pl. 11, 10–20; as magistrate's signature, *ACMG* pp. 67ff; G. K. Jenkins, "A Tarentine Footnote," *Essays Thompson* p. 111. ARTISTIC ANALYSIS AND PARALLELS. Asymmetry and sharp cutting in stone sculpture: Langlotz and Hirmer pp. 290, 291 and pls. 132, 135. Coiffure: *CGA* 348. Dionysiac funerary art: South Italian vases, *VMG* p. 32 with bibliography p. 317, IV.2; Derveni crater, *CGA* 236 = Robertson 1, pp. 482ff and notes 93, 94; B. Barr-Sharrar, "Towards an Interpretation of the Dionysiac Frieze on the Derveni Krater," *Bronzes hellénistiques et romaines: tradition et renouveau, Actes du Ve Colloque international sur les bronzes antiques* (1979); sarcophagi, F. Matz, *Die dionysische Sarkopha-gen*, 4 vols. (Berlin, 1968–1975).

96 NUMISMATIC LITERATURE. Die study: G. K. Jenkins, "Coins of Punic Sicily, Part 3," *SNR* 56 (1977), pp. 5ff, see especially pp. 24ff. Interpretation of types: female head, *ibid.* pp. 26ff; palm tree, *ibid.* Part 2, *SNR* 53 (1974), p. 27; the traditional explanation that the palm tree is a Greek pun for Phoenicia (palm tree = φοῖνιξ in Greek) seems weak and contrived, for the language of the Carthaginians was not Greek. ARTISTIC PARALLELS. Published comparisons: Jenkins, *art. cit.*, Part 3, p. 28 with notes 82–86. Terracottas of goddess with lion and palm tree: P. Orlandini, "Typologia e cronologia del materiale archeologico di Gela della nuova fondazione di Timoleonte all'età di Ierone II," *ArchClass* 9 (1957), pl. 14, 1–2; M. J. Vermaseren, *Cybele and Attis, the Myth and the Cult* (London, 1977), p. 67f. Lion: W. L. Brown, *The Etruscan Lion* (Oxford, 1960), p. 150 and note 1.

97 NUMISMATIC LITERATURE. Die study with historical back-ground: M. P. Vlasto, "Les monnaies d'or de Tarente," *JIAN* 2 (1889), pp. 303ff. Identification of head: Vlasto, *art. cit.*, pp. 311ff; P. Wuilleumier, *Tarente des origines a la conquête romaine*, BEFAR 148 (Paris, 1939), p. 511. Date: G. K. Jenkins, "Note sur quelques monnaies d'or de Tarente," *Bulletin du cercle d'études numismatiques* 11 (1974), pp. 2ff; Gulbenkian p. 30, no. 39. Types of silver coinage: O. E. Ravel, *The Collection of Tarentine Coins formed by M. P. Vlasto* (London, 1947), 258ff. ARTISTIC PARALLELS. Tarentine goddess: Langlotz and Hirmer p. 290, no. 132. Veils in funerary art: F. Matz, ΔΙΟΝΥΣΙΑΚΗ ΤΕΛΕΤΗ, *Archäologische Untersuchungen zum Dionysoskult in hellenis-tischer und römischer Zeit* (Mainz, 1963), pl. 3; W.-H. Schu-chardt, *Das Orpheus-Relief* (Frankfurt, 1964), fig. 14. Veil and stephane in iconography of Persephone: *CGA* 129 = B. Ashmole, *Late Archaic and Early Classical Greek Sculpture in Sicily and South Italy* from *PBA* 20 (London, 1934), pl. 8, 28.

98 NUMISMATIC LITERATURE. K. Regling, "Die griechische Goldschatz von Prinkipo," *ZfN* 41 (1931), pp. 1ff; *ACGC* p. 252. Lion griffin as anti-Persian symbol: G. F. Hill, "Alexander the Great and the Persian Lion-Gryphon," *JHS* 43 (1923), p. 158f. ARTISTIC PARALLELS. Published comparisons: Silenus, *Kunst-freund* p. 266; griffin, Hill, *art. cit.*, p. 159, fig. 2. Pan: F. Brommer, *Pan in 5. und 4. Jahrhundert v. Chr.* from *Marburger Jahrbuch für Kunstwissenschaft* 15 (1949/50) pp. 5ff. Silenus: Thracian, *TAT* p. 361 and pl. 168; Tarentine, P. Wuilleumier, *Tarente des origines a la conquête romaine*, BEFAR 148 (Paris, 1939), pl. 38, 8. Greek depiction of Scyths: *TST* pls. 170, 195, 196, 198 and 226–229, especially the figure having his leg bandaged on pl. 229. Lion griffins: Graeco-Scythian, *TST* pl. 170; Tarentine, R. Lullies, *Der vergoldete terrakotta Appliken aus Tarent*, MDAI(R) Ergänzung-sheft 7 (Heidelberg, 1962), pls. 8.2 and 11.2; Käppeli C15; K. Schefold, "Der Löwengreifen von Augst," *JSGU* 35 (1944), p. 148f. Motif of lion holding a broken spear: G. Hafner, "Das Siegel Alexanders des Grossen," *Festschrift Brommer*, pp. 139ff and pl. 40, figs. 1–4; *ACMG* p. 66, note 3; W. L. Brown, *The Etruscan Lion* (Oxford, 1960), p. 151, note 1 and pl. 55, a. Tarentine influence: Käppeli *loc. cit.*

99 NUMISMATIC LITERATURE. G. le Rider, *Monnaies crétoises du Ver au Ier siècle av. J.C.* (Paris, 1966); P. Naster, "La légende ΣΙΒΡΥΤΤΙΩΙ sur des monnaies de Sybrita," *RBN* 1947, pp. 35ff. ARTISTIC PARALLELS. Published comparisons: *Traité* 3 (1914), col. 1014; Johnson *Lysippos* p. 172; Rizzo p. 302f; G. Horster, *Statuen auf Gemmen*, HDD(KA) 3 (Bonn, 1970), p. 30f. Dionysus on panther motif: derivation from fifth-century painting, Robert-son 1, p. 423f and note 168; Pella mosaic, *HA* 97 = Robertson 1, p. 487f and note 108; mosaic from the House of the Masks at Delos, *HA* 192 = Robertson 1, p. 579 and note 209; gemstone, Furtwäng-ler *AG* pl. 28, 23; sarcophagi, F. Matz, *Die dionysische Sarkopha-gen* 3 (Berlin, 1969), 162–166, 168. Panther: Richter *Animals* pl. 10, figs. 33, 34. Hermes' sandals: P. Raingeard, *Hermès Psychago-gue, essai sur les origins du culte d'Hermès* (Rennes, 1934), pp. 397ff. Lysippean Hermes tying his sandal: G. M. A. Richter, *Three Critical Periods in Greek Sculpture* (Oxford, 1951), fig. 26; Johnson *Lysippos* pp. 170ff, pls. 30, 31. Earlier sandal-tying motif: *Parthenonfries* pl. 44, fig. W XV; Horster *loc. cit.* and pl. 7, 2 = Furtwängler *AG* pl. 61, 35, III 130 note 1; *Intaglios and Rings* 135, 164. Expressionist figure style: *HA* 214 = Robertson 1, p. 451 and note 13.

100 NUMISMATIC LITERATURE. Extant examples: Mitchiner 1, p. 11. Date of the related Babylonian tetradrachms: N. M. Waggoner, "Tetradrachms from Babylon," *Essays Thompson* p. 271ff. Dr. Waggoner has informed me that the decadrachm falls precisely into the transition between tetradrachm series II and III, implying a date of about 327/326 B.C. I am greatly indebted to Dr. Waggoner for personal communication sharing her understanding of the economic function of the Babylonian coinage and other technical numismatic information on which this entry is based. She reports twelve decadrachm specimens known to her (others suspected) from four obverse dies, all intricately die linked, indicating a small issue produced over a short period of time. Find sites: *ICGH* 1749 (Babylon, 1849) and 1750 (Nippur, Mesopotamia, c. 1890) and *Coin Hoards* 1 (1975), 10, 1–3 (Babylon, 1973). Types: B. V. Head, *Historia Numorum* (Oxford, 1911), pp. 220ff; P. Lederer, *SNR* 28 (1941); Bellinger *Essays* pp. 13ff, 21ff; S. Perlman, "The Coins of Philip II and Alexander the Great and Their Pan-Hellenic Propaganda," *NC* 1965, pp. 57ff. ICONOGRAPHY AND ARTISTIC PARALLELS. Alexander portraits on his silver coinage: K. Gebauer, "Alexanderbildnis und Alexandertypus," *MDAI(A)* 63–64 (1938–39), pp. 2ff; Bieber *Alexander* pp. 50ff and bibliography p. 48, note 31; K. Lange, "Zur Frage des Bildnisgehaltes bei Köpfen auf Münzen Philipp II. und Alexanders III. des Grossen, von Makedonien," *WAdnG* 1951, pp. 27ff; E. Sjöqvist, "Alexander-Heracles: a Preliminary Note," *BMusB*, June 1953, pp. 30ff; Bellinger *loc. cit.*

101 NUMISMATIC LITERATURE. Die study with historical background and interpretation of types: M. J. Price, "The 'Poros' Coinage of Alexander the Great: A Symbol of Concord and Community," *Essays in Honor of P. Naster* (forthcoming), pp. 75ff. Mint attribution: Uncertain Mesopotamian mint, Price, *art. cit.*, p. 83f; Babylon, personal communication from Dr. N. M. Waggoner; Bactra, Mitchiner 1, p. 20. Indigenous Indian coinage: M. Mitchiner, *The Origins of Indian Coinage* (London, 1973), especially pp. 54ff. Finances of Alexander's eastern campaign: Bellinger *Essays* pp. 70ff; personal communication from Dr. Waggoner. ICONOGRAPHY AND ARTISTIC PARALLELS. W.B. Kaiser, "Ein Meister der Glyptik aus dem Umkreis des Alexanders des Grossen," *JDAI* 77 (1962), pp. 230ff, correcting much earlier literature. Gemstone of Pygoteles: Kaiser, *art. cit.*, fig. 9 with bibliography noted. Graeco-Bactrian elephant: Becatti *Orificerie* p. 206, no. 457, pl. 129.

102 NUMISMATIC LITERATURE. Mint attribution: M. Thompson, "The Mints of Lysimachus," *Essays Robinson*, pp. 163ff. Horn of Ammon: on Ptolemaic tetradrachms, Svoronos, pls. 1, 2, 4–6 passim; on a few rare Seleucid coins, E. T. Newell, *The Coinage of the Eastern Seleucid Mints*, NS 2 (New York, 1941), 291, 294–296, 459–460. ICONOGRAPHY AND ARTISTIC PARALLELS. Published comparisons: Bieber *Alexander* p. 27; K. Gebauer, "Alexanderbildnis und Alexandertypus," *MDAI(A)* 63–64 (1938–39), p. 21. Alexandrine iconography: Bieber *Alexander*; L'Orange *Apotheosis* pp. 19ff; E. G. Suhr, *Sculptured Portraits of Greek Statesmen*, Johns Hopkins University Studies in Archaeology 13 (Baltimore-London, 1931), pp. 73ff; J. J. Bernoulli, *Die erhaltenen Darstellung Alexanders des Grossen, Griechische Ikonographie* 3 (Stuttgart, 1905); T. Schreiber, "Studien über das Bildnis Alexanders des Grossen, ein Beitrag zur Alexandrinischen Kunstgeschichte," *ASGW* 21, 3 (1903); for the most recent bibliography see [36]. Comparable Alexander portraits: Geneva head, Johnson *Lysippos* p. 214, frontispiece and pl. 45; Rondanini Alexander, Bieber *Alexander* p. 25 with note 16, figs. 6–7; romanticized portrait in Athens, *HA* 219. Copies of coin type: on cameos, Gebauer, *art. cit.*, p. 32, pl. 4, 14, 15; on gemstone, *GGFR* 998; in other media, Gebauer, *art. cit.*, p. 21; on South Italian cups, G. Grimm, "Die Vergöttlichung des Alexanders des Gr. in Ägypten," *Ptolemäische Ägypten* fig. 72. Seated goddesses: Cnidian Demeter, *HA* 218 = Robertson 1, p. 462 and note 39; Tyche of Antioch, *HA* 251 = Robertson 1, p. 470f with notes.

103 NUMISMATIC LITERATURE. Collected material: Svoronos 1, pp. 32ff, listing four examples of the octodrachm denomination with monograms ꟿ (198), ⵗ (209), and Ⅺ (233); G. K. Jenkins, "An Early Ptolemaic Hoard from Phacous," *ANSMusN* 9 (1960), pp. 17ff adds four more specimens with two new monograms, A (pl. 5, 1) and ꟿ (pl. 5, 3). Interpretation of types: D. Salzmann, "Überlegungen zum Schild auf den Münzen des Ptolemaios Philadelphos und verwandten Denkmälern," *SM* 118 (1980), pp. 33ff. ICONOGRAPHY AND ARTISTIC PARALLELS. Kyrieleis pp. 4ff, see especially the Copenhagen mask A4; G. H. McFadden, "The Portrait of Ptolemy I Soter," *Studies D. M. Robinson* 1, pp. 713ff; Pfuhl pp. 6ff. Apotheosis: hellenistic savior type, L'Orange *Apotheosis* pp. 39ff; overlarge eyes, L'Orange *Apotheosis* pp. 110ff. Eagle on thunderbolt motif: *GGFR* 996.

104 NUMISMATIC LITERATURE. Die study with historical background: E. T. Newell, *The Pergamene Mint under Philetaerus*, NNM 76 (New York, 1936). ICONOGRAPHY AND ARTISTIC PARALLELS. E. G. Suhr, *Sculptured Portraits of Greek Statesmen*, Johns Hopkins University Studies in Archaeology 13 (Baltimore-London, 1931), pp. 156ff; Pfuhl pp. 4ff. Bronze portrait of Seleucus, Bieber *Hellenistic Sculpture* p. 49, note 93 and figs. 141–143 = Johnson *Lysippos* p. 230f, pl. 49. Apotheosis: hellenistic savior type, L'Orange *Apotheosis* pp. 39ff.

105 NUMISMATIC LITERATURE. Alexandrine prototype: Bellinger *Essays* pp. 3ff with further bibliography in notes, pl. 1, 4, 5. Agathoclean staters: Gulbenkian 339–341. Contemporary Nikai on coins: A. R. Bellinger and M. A. Berlincourt, *Victory as a Coin Type*, NNM 149 (New York, 1962), p. 24, pl. 6, 6 and p. 27f, pl. 7, 1. Oak wreath: J. Babelon, "Le roi Pyrrhos," *ANS CentPubl*, p. 64. ARTISTIC PARALLELS. Lysippean dancer: Bieber *Hellenistic Sculpture* p. 39 and note 38, figs. 90–92 = Johnson *Lysippos* p. 249f and pl. 61. Dancing Nike motif: Langlotz and Hirmer p. 294, no. 140; T. M. Marshall, *Catalogue of the Jewellery, Greek, Etruscan and Roman in the Departments of Antiquities, British Museum* (London, 1911), p. 199f, nos. 1845–1846 and pl. 32. Possibly relevant is A. Reinach, "Pyrrhus et la Niké de Tarente," *Neapolis* 1 (1913), pp. 19ff, which I have not seen. Transparent drapery: Lullies and Hirmer, pl. 178 = Robertson 1, p. 287f and note 227; Richter *SSG* fig. 638 and p. 243 with note 221.

106 NUMISMATIC LITERATURE. Collected material: Svoronos 1, pp. 64ff, 98ff, 107ff, 115, 116f, 119, 123, 135, 141ff, 161ff, etc.; also Svoronos 4, p. 151. Cult of deified Arsinoe: D. B. Thompson, *Ptolemaic Oinochoai and Portraits in Faience—Aspects of the Ruler-Cult* (Oxford, 1973), pp. 71ff with bibliography in notes 4–6, pp. 117ff; L. Robert, "Sur un décret d'Ilion et sur un papyrus concernant des cultes royaux," *Essays in Honor of C. Bradford Wells*, American Studies in Papyrology 1 (New Haven, 1966), pp. 175ff; D. B. Thompson, "A Portrait of Arsinoe Philadelphus," *AJA* 59 (1955), p. 201f which translates the text of a stele associating Arsinoe and Mendes. Coinage of Berenice I: Svoronos 1, 314ff; O. Mørkholm, *SNG Copenhagen: Egypt: The Ptolemies* (Copenhagen, 1977), 428ff. Parallel Roman series: Svoronos 4, pp. 142ff; H. Mattingly, "The 'Diana/Victory' Didrachms and the Decadrachms of Arsinoe," *NC* 1946, pp. 63ff. ICONOGRAPHY AND ARTISTIC PARALLELS. E. Brunelle, *Die Bildnisse der Ptolemäerinnen* (Stuttgart, 1976), pp. 10ff; Kyrieleis pp. 78ff, see especially J4, J8, J11; Thompson, *art. cit.*, pp. 199ff and pl. 54, figs. 1–2 (identified by Kyrieleis as Berenice II) and pl. 55, figs. 7–8 (possibly Berenice II, in the author's opinion). Other sculptured portraits: Macurdy, *art. cit.*, pl. 5b; *AMGB* 2, p. 330, pl. 108, 17. Overlarge eye as sign of divinity: L'Orange *Apotheosis* pp. 110ff.

107 NUMISMATIC LITERATURE. Collected material: Svoronos 1, pp. 178ff. Interpretation of attributes: Svoronos 4, p. 198f; W. Huss, "Ptolemaios III als Sarapis?" *JNG* 26 (1976), pp. 31ff. Ptolemaic ancestor worship: E. Winter, "Der Herrscherkult in den Ägyptischen Ptolemäertempeln," *Ptolemäische Ägypten*, pp. 147ff; Kyrieleis pp. 138ff. Isolation of Ptolemaic currency system: G. K. Jenkins, "Monetary Systems in Early Hellenistic Time," *Proceedings*, CIN 1963 (Jerusalem, 1967), pp. 53ff. Non-Ptolemaic octodrachms: D. H. Cox, "Gordion Hoards III, IV, V and VII," *ANSMusN* 12 (1966), pp. 51ff and pl. 21, 4, 5; E. T. Newell, *The Coinage of the Western Seleucid Mints*, NS 4, revised edition (New York, 1977), 1074, 1097. ICONOGRAPHY AND ARTISTIC PARALLELS. Kyrieleis pp. 25ff, see especially C1, C2, C13; Pfuhl pp. 32ff; *Boston Sculpture* p. 279, no. 450. Tarentine influence at Alexandria: Langlotz and Hirmer p. 294 (with bibliography).

108 NUMISMATIC LITERATURE. Collected material: Svoronos 1, p. 136, 145, 148, 150ff, 177. Dating: Kyrieleis attributes Berenice's entire portrait coinage to her early lifetime. The traditional arrangement (Svoronos 4, pp. 163ff and pp. 190ff) makes most of it posthumous. This seems preferable from the point of view of stylistic coherence, and it also avoids the incongruity of attributing a major portrait coinage to a queen whose husband lacked one. The lifetime coinage is all from Asian mints (Svoronos 4, pp. 163ff), and the dates are assumed to depend upon Ptolemaic possession of the cities in question. In fact, however, the Ptolemaic royal cult existed independently of Ptolemaic political control, at least at some cities; and thus it is possible that Berenice's Asian coinage could also be posthumous. ICONOGRAPHY AND ARTISTIC PARALLELS. Kyrieleis pp. 78ff; Bieber *Hellenistic Sculpture* figs. 346–347, identified as Arsinoe II by Kyrieleis (his J8), but the resemblance to Berenice's coin portraits is compelling; *AMGB* 2, p. 334; *Intaglios and Rings* 59.

109 NUMISMATIC LITERATURE. A. A. Boyce, "The Gold Staters of T. Quinctius Flamininus in History," *Hommages à Albert Grenier* 3, ed. R. Marcel, (Brussels-Berchem, 1962), pp. 342ff; R. A. G. Carson, "The Gold Stater of Flamininus," *BM Quarterly* 1955, pp. 11ff; Carson, "Roman Coins Acquired by the British Museum, 1939–1959," *NC* 1959, p. 4; Crawford p. 544, with bibliography on other honors tendered Flamininus. Locations of the other known specimens: M&M 61 (1982), lot 104 note. ICONOGRAPHY AND ARTISTIC PARALLELS. Iconography: J. Babelon, "L'Effigie de Flamininus," *RBN* 1970, pp. 59ff and pl. 2; *RHP* p. 5f; F. Chamoux, "Un portrait de Flamininus à Delphes," *BCH* 89 (1965), pp. 214ff and figs. 1, 4, 5, 9. Hellenistic savior type: L'Orange *Apotheosis* pp. 39ff. Influence of coinage of Philip of Macedon: *MitthellMünzserien* p. 137 and pls. 7–8. Portraits of Antiochus III: E. T. Newell, *The Coinage of the Western Seleucid Mints*, NS 4, revised ed. (New York, 1977), pls. 30–32; Bieber *Hellenistic Sculpture* p. 87 with note 69 and figs. 319, 320.

110 NUMISMATIC LITERATURE. *MitthellMünzserien* pp. 14ff; N. F. Jones, "Wreathed Tetradrachms of Magnesia," *ANSMusN* 24 (1975), pp. 63ff. Tetradrachms of Athens: M. Thompson, *The 'New-Style' Coinage of Athens* (New York, 1961), pls. 1 and 2. Monetary liturgies: *ibid.* pp. 593ff.

111 NUMISMATIC LITERATURE. Reported specimens: K. Regling, "Hellenistischer Münzschatz aus Babylon," *ZfN* 38 (1928), pp. 124ff for the first four specimens of this rarity, all from a single obverse die and signed by the magistrate Nikostratos; two new specimens from the same obverse die but with magistrate Eurylochos have recently appeared on the market: Leu 30 (1982), lot 183 and M&M 61 (1982), lot 149; see the latter for locations of all published specimens. ARTISTIC PARALLELS. Published comparisons: J. Six, "Asklepios by Bryaxis," *JHS* 42 (1922), p. 32 and fig. 2. Asclepius statuettes: P. Wolters, "Darstellungen des Asklepios," *MDAI (A)* 1892, pp. 3ff., figs. 1, 2. Aphrodite Anadyomene: D. M. Brinkerhoff, *Hellenistic Statues of Aphrodite, Studies in the History of Their Stylistic Development* (Diss. Harvard, 1958), pp. 56ff and pls. 40, 42, 48. Coiffure: *ibid.* pl. 36; R. Lullies, *Die kauernde Aphrodite* (Munich, 1954), figs. 9, 15. Small features in middle hellenistic art: *HA* 315. HISTORICAL BACKGROUND. E. J. and L. Edelstein, *Asclepius* (Baltimore, 1945).

112 NUMISMATIC LITERATURE. Die study with historical background and artistic comment: A. Houghton, "A Tetradrachm of Seleucia Pieria at the Getty Museum: An Archaizing Zeus and the Accession of Alexander Balas in Northern Syria," *JPGMJ* 10 (1982), pp. 153ff; the catalogue entry also owes much to personal discussion with Mr. Houghton but does not necessarily represent his final views on the subject. ARTISTIC PARALLELS. Libyan locks: Pfuhl pp. 43ff; Bieber *Hellenistic Sculpture* p. 89f and figs. 328ff, with bibliography; on the Farnese cup, *HA* 336; Kyrieleis pls. 100, 104, 105, 108; for Cleopatra Thea, Pfuhl figs. 26, 28; on coins of Cleopatra Thea, E. T. Newell, *Late Seleucid Mints in Ake-Ptolemais and Damascus*, NNM 84 (New York, 1939), pl. 2, 7–9 and pl. 15, 86–88. Libyan locks on Semitic coinages: Nabataea, *BMC Arabia* pl. 1, 5 and 6, pl. 49, 4; Himyarites of southern Arabia, *BMC Arabia* pl. 8, 1ff; Characene in the Mesopotamian delta, *BMC Arabia* pl. 43, 2ff, pl. 44, 1ff, pl. 54, 4ff and pl. 55, 10ff. Fifth-century Zeus with corkscrew curls: F. Kupferberg, *Zeus* (1967), p. 87 and pls. 28–29; bronze Zeus head in Vienna, Schrader *Phidias* p. 61, figs. 38, 39.

113 NUMISMATIC LITERATURE. Die study with historical background: K. V. Golenko and P. J. Karyszkowski, "The Gold Coinage of King Pharnaces of the Bosporus," *NC* 1972, pp. 25ff. Coinage of Mithradates VI: W. H. Waddington, E. Babelon and T. Reinach, *Recueil général des monnaies grecques d'Asie Mineure*, 1: *Pont et Paphlagonie* (Paris, 1904), pls. 1–3. ICONOGRAPHY AND ARTISTIC PARALLELS. Influence of Alexander portraiture: L'Orange *Apotheosis* pp. 39ff; D. Michel, *Alexander als Vorbild für Pompeius, Caesar und Marcus Antonius*, Latomus 94 (1967).

114 NUMISMATIC LITERATURE. Date and attribution: J. W. Curtis, "The Coinage of Pharaonic Egypt," *JEA* 43 (1957), pp. 71ff; G. K. Jenkins, "Greek Coins Recently Acquired by the British Museum," *NC* 1955, pp. 148ff. Hieroglyphs: E. Chassinet, "Une monnaie d'or à légendes hiéroglyphes trouvée en Egypte," *BIAO* 1 (1901), pp. 78ff; M. Jungfleisch, "L'Hiéroglyph ⚖ en numismatique," *RN* 1931, pp. 129ff.

115 NUMISMATIC LITERATURE. Die study with historical background: G. K. Jenkins, "Coins of Punic Sicily, Part 4," *SNR* 57 (1978), p. 36f and pl. 15–20. Symbolism of Punic types: G. K. Jenkins and R. B. Lewis, *Carthaginian Gold and Electrum Coins*, RNS Special Publication 3 (London, 1963), p. 11f. Pegasus: on Corinthian coins, G. K. Jenkins, "A Note on Corinthian Coins in the West," *ANS CentPubl* pp. 367ff; on South Italian vases, *VMG* 32, 33, 40, 70, 80, 90 with bibliography under no. 32.

116 NUMISMATIC LITERATURE. Corpus with historical background: L. Kadman, *Corpus Nummorum Palaestinensium* 3. *The Coins of the Jewish War of 66–73* (Jerusalem, 1960). Symbolism of types: Kadman, *op. cit.*, pp. 83ff; E. W. Klimowsky, *On Ancient Palestinian and Other Coins, Their Symbolism and Metrology* (Tel Aviv, 1974), pp. 28ff, 33ff, 71ff. Dating: C. Roth, "The Year-Reckoning of the Coins of the First Revolt," *NC* 1962, pp. 91ff. My thanks to Dr. Leo Mildenberg for information regarding the other extant specimens of this rare coin. Reported finds: C. S. Lewis, "Shekel of the Year Five," *NC* 1876, p. 322; J. Baramki, "Coins in the Palestine Archaeological Museum, Part 3," *QDAP* 8 (1939), p. 77; A. Spijkerman, "Trésor de sicles juifs trouvé au Mont des Oliviers à Jerusalem," *SM* 11, 42 (1961), p. 32, no. 14; *Israel Numismatic Bulletin* 1 (January–March 1962), p. 18; Y. Yadin, *IEJ* 15 (1965), pl. 19, F; T. Becker, "Coins at Masada," *Coinage* 14, 8 (August, 1978). Locations of other specimens: British Museum (*NC* 1876); Rockefeller Museum, acquired 1937 (Baramki, *QDAP*); Museum of the Studium Biblicum Franciscanum, Jerusalem, found 1961 (*SM*); and five in the Israel Bank Collection, one found in Jerusalem in 1964, one found at Masada prior to the excavation (*IEJ*), and three found in the course of the Masada excavations.

117 NUMISMATIC LITERATURE. Origins of Roman coinage: R. Thomsen, *Early Roman Coinage*, 3 vols. (Copenhagen, 1957–62). Decussis: Thomsen 2, p. 42f; Crawford pp. 43, 626ff. Griffin helmet: *MitthellMünzserien* pp. 118ff. Symbolism of the prow: Crawford p. 719, note 2. Connection with Antigonus Doson: Thomsen 3, pp. 147ff.

118 NUMISMATIC LITERATURE. Bahrfeldt pp. 64, 68; Crawford p. 741, note 3. ICONOGRAPHY AND ARTISTIC PARALLELS. *RHP* p. 62f, see especially fig. 88 (marble head in the Prado) = O. Vessberg, *Studien zur Kunstgeschichte der römischen Republik*, SIR Skrifter 8 (Lund, 1944), pp. 125ff and pl. 46, 1–2 (there hypothetically identified as Flamininus) = H. Möbius, *Studia Varia, Aufsätze zur Kunst und Kultur der Antike mit Nachträgen*, ed. W. Schiering (Wiesbaden, 1967), pp. 210ff and pl. 45, figs. 3–4; Bernoulli 1 (1882), pp. 187ff and pl. 19; *Roman Portraits* 9–11.

119 NUMISMATIC LITERATURE. Die study: H. A. Cahn, "L'aureus de Brutus avec EID · MAR," *Actes*, CIN 1953 (Paris, 1957), pp. 214ff. ICONOGRAPHY AND ARTISTIC PARALLELS. *RHP* p. 62f. Classical hellenizing style: B. Schweitzer, *Die Bildniskunst der römischen Republik* (Leipzig, 1948), pp. 134ff, see especially no. 147; Poulsen 1, nos. 1, 6. Brutus portrait with elevated gaze: *Roman Portraits* 10.

120 NUMISMATIC LITERATURE. Bahrfeldt pp. 95ff. ICONOG-RAPHY AND ARTISTIC PARALLELS. Antony: *RHP* pp. 41ff; G. Grimm, "Zu Marcus Antonius und C. Cornelius Gallus," *JDAI* 85 (1970), pp. 158ff, figs. 1ff; D. Michel, *Alexander als Vorbild für Pompeius, Caesar und Marcus Antonius*, Latomus 94 (1967), pp. 109ff; O. Brendel, "The Iconography of Marc Antony," *Hommages à Albert Grenier* 1, ed. R. Marcel (Brussels-Berchem, 1962), pp. 359ff; Bernoulli 1 (1882), pp. 203ff; Kingston Lacy head, *AMGB* 2, p. 330f; Aquileia dish, H. Möbius, "Der Silberteller von Aquileia," *Festschrift für Friedrich Matz*, eds. N. Himmelmann-Wildschütz and H. Biesantz (Mainz, n.d. [c. 1962]), pp. 80ff, pls. 24ff; *GGFR* 1013; gemstone with horn of Ammon, *Ptolemäische Ägypten* pl. 81. Antyllus: *RHP* p. 59, no. 80.

121 NUMISMATIC LITERATURE. Mints and issues of Octavian: *BN* 1, Chs. 1, 2; *EAC* pp. 34ff; *BMCRE* 1 (1923), pp. xiiiff; Kent-Hirmer p. 18 , p. 276f. Development of Augustan numismatic portraiture: *SMACA* pp. 65ff; *RHP* pp. 51ff with bibliography. Capricorn: K. Kraft, "Zum Capricorn auf den Münzen des Augustus," *JNG* 17 (1967), pp. 17ff. ICONOGRAPHY AND ARTISTIC PARALLELS. O. Brendel, *Ikonographie des Kaisers Augustus* (1931), Type C; C. Weikert, "Augustus Bild und Geschichte," *Die Antike* 14 (1938), pp. 202ff; P. Zanker, *Studien zu den Augustus-Porträts*, 1. *Der Actium-Typus*, AAWG (PH) Folge 3, 85 (Göttingen, 1973), see especially the head from Fondi, pp. 29ff, pls. 22ff = E. Buschor, *Das hellenistische Bildnis*, second ed. (Munich, 1971), 226, pl. 75. Other idealizing portraits of Brendel Type C: Capitoline bust, Weikert, *op. cit.*, pl. 23 = G. Rodenwaldt, *Kunst um Augustus* (Berlin, 1943), p. 20, figs. 8–9; in Konya Museum, J. Inan and E. Rosenbaum, *Roman and Early Byzantine Portrait Sculpture in Asia Minor* (London, 1966), p. 59, no. 9 and pl. 6, 3–4; *Roman Portraits* 18.

122 NUMISMATIC LITERATURE. Propaganda content of Augustan bronze: M. Grant, *From Imperium to Auctoritas* (Cambridge, 1946); K. Kraft, "S(enatus) C(onsulto)," *JNG* 1962, pp. 7ff; A. Bay, "The Letters S C on Augustan *Aes* Coinage," *JRS* 62 (1972), pp. 111ff; *EAC* pp. 13ff with further bibliography. Denomination, date, occasion of issue: *BN* 1, p. 43; M. Grant, *Roman Imperial Money* (Edinburgh, 1954), pp. 100ff; *RAI* p. 21; K. Pink, "Die Triumviri monetales unter Augustus," *NZ* 71 (1946), p. 117f; *BMCRE* 1 (1923), p. xlix; H. Willers, *Geschichte der römischen Kupferprägung vom Bundesgenossenkrieg bis auf Kaiser Claudius* (Leipzig-Berlin, 1909), p. 152f. Pax and Victoria: J. Gagé, "Un Thème de l'Art impérial romain: la Victoire d'Auguste," *MEFR* 1932, pp. 61ff; C. H. V. Sutherland, *Coinage in Roman Imperial Policy, 31 B.C. to A.D. 68* (New York, 1978 reprint of London, 1951 original), p. 28f. ICONOGRAPHY AND ARTISTIC PARALLELS. O. Brendel, *Ikonographie des Kaisers Augustus* (1931). Primaporta statue: H. Kähler, *Die Augustusstatue von Primaporta* (Cologne, 1959). *Roman Portraits* 24, 27.

123 NUMISMATIC LITERATURE. Coin types, style and imperial propaganda: C. H. V. Sutherland, *Coinage in Roman Imperial Policy, 31 B.C. to A.D. 68* (New York, 1978 reprint of London, 1951 original), pp. 105ff; *EAC* pp. 112ff. ICONOGRAPHY AND ARTISTIC PARALLELS. West 1, pp. 201ff; V. Poulsen, "Portraits of Caligula," *AArch* 29 (1958), pp. 175ff, see especially figs. 3–4; Bernoulli 2, 1 (1886), pp. 301ff. Gaius' neurotic quality is pronounced in the later Copenhagen bust, Poulsen 1, 54.

124 NUMISMATIC LITERATURE. Die study with analysis of types, artistic commentary: W. Trillmich, *Familien-propaganda der Kaiser Caligula und Claudius—Agrippina Maior und Antonia Augusta auf Münzen*, AMuGS 8 (Berlin, 1978) supplemented by H. Jucker, "Methodisches zur Kunstgeschichtlichen Interpretation von Münzbildnissen der Agrippina Maior und der Antonia Minor," *SM* 23, 90 (May 1973), pp. 55ff. Carpentum: M. Bernhart, "Consecratio. Ein numismatischer Beitrag zur römischen Kaiserkonsekration," *Orientalische Studien, Festschrift für Fritz Hommel* 2 (Leipzig, 1918), pp. 160ff. Tiberius' use of carpentum: *RIC* 1 (1923), p. 106, 21. ICONOGRAPHY AND ARTISTIC PARALLELS. West 1, pl. 44, figs. 191–194; of particular interest is no. 229, which depicts Agrippina at full length holding a patera and sceptre, the attributes of Vesta; Bernoulli 2, 1 (1886), pp. 242ff, especially pl. 15.

125 NUMISMATIC LITERATURE. Date, sequence of issues, mint practices: D. W. MacDowall, *The Western Coinages of Nero*, NNM 161 (New York, 1979). Reverse type: A. A. Boyce, "The Harbor of Pompeiopolis," *AJA* 62 (1958), pp. 67ff; Boyce, "Nero's Harbor Sestertii," *AJA* 70 (1966), p. 65f. G. Fuchs, *Architekturdarstellungen auf römischen Münzen der Republik und der frühen Kaiserzeit*, AMuGS 1 (Berlin, 1969), see especially p. 63; R. Meiggs, *Roman Ostia* (Oxford, 1960), pp. 54ff. ICONOGRAPHY AND ARTISTIC PARALLELS. Poulsen 1, pp. 32ff; L'Orange *Apotheosis* pp. 57ff; West 1, pl. 62, figs. 255, 272, 273; Bernoulli 2, 1 (1886), pp. 385ff. Coiffure *in gradus formata*: J. M. C. Toynbee, "Ruler Apotheosis in Ancient Rome," *NC* 1947, p. 137; on a circus charioteer, West 1, pl. 66, fig. 289. Harbor in wall painting: A. Maiuri, *Les fresques de Pompéi et d'Herculaneum* (Paris, n.d. [c. 1942]), pl. 33 = Fuchs pl. 20.

126 NUMISMATIC LITERATURE. Die study with historical background: C. M. Kraay, *The Aes Coinage of Galba*, NNM 133 (New York, 1956). ICONOGRAPHY AND ARTISTIC PARALLELS. E. Fabbricotti, *Galba*, SA 16 (Rome, 1976), pp. 41ff, see especially p. 59, I, pl. 8, 1 and p. 73, VIII, pl. 16; H. Jucker, "Ein Aureus und der Kopf des Kaisers Galba," *JBHM* 43–44 (1963–64), pp. 261ff, especially p. 291, fig. 43 (= Fabbricotti I) and p. 292, fig. 44 (= Fabbricotti VIII); Bernoulli 2, 2 (1891), pp. 1ff. Roma: R. Mellor, ΘΕΑ ΡΩΜΗ, *The Worship of the Goddess Roma in the Greek World* (Göttingen, 1975); standing Roma type, Vermeule *Roma* pp. 101ff, see especially pl. 11 illustrating a statuette of Virtus from the Terme Museum which shows many points of similarity to the Roma depicted here.

127 NUMISMATIC LITERATURE. Collected material with historical background: R. Mowat, "Le monnayage de Clodius Macer," *RIN* 1902, pp. 165ff; A. Gara, "La monetazione di Clodius Macer," *RIN* 1970, pp. 63ff. Centenary revival of Antonian types: *RAI* p. 86; Antonian legionary coinage, Crawford p. 539ff, no. 544.

128 NUMISMATIC LITERATURE. Die study with mint attributions, analysis of types and historical background: P.-H. Martin, *Die anonymen Münzen des Jahres 68 nach Christus* (Mainz, [Diss. Frankfurt], 1971). Older views of propaganda content and issuing authority: C. M. Kraay, "The 'Military Class' in the Coinage of the Civil Wars of A.D. 68–69," *NC* 1952, pp. 77ff; H. Mattingly, "Revolt and Subversion: The So-Called 'Military' Coinage of A.D. 69 Re-examined," *NC* 1952, pp. 72ff; J.-F. Jaquier, *BSFN* January 1969.

129 NUMISMATIC LITERATURE. Personifications: Mattingly "Virtues." ICONOGRAPHY AND ARTISTIC PARALLELS. Bernoulli 2, 2 (1891), pp. 1ff and pls. 5, 6.

130 NUMISMATIC LITERATURE. Type revivals: *RAI.* Augustan prototype: *RIC* 1 (1923), p. 64, 60 and 61, also p. 88, 327. ICONOGRAPHY AND ARTISTIC PARALLELS. Wegner *Flavier* pp. 18ff and 85ff, see especially pls. 13, 14, 18; West 2, pp. 14ff, see especially pl. 3, figs. 6–8 and pl. 4, figs. 9–10; Bernoulli 2, 2 (1891), pp. 31ff, especially pl. 11a–b.

131 NUMISMATIC LITERATURE. Claudian prototype of obverse: *RIC* 1 (1923), p. 131, 78 and 79. ARTISTIC PARALLEL. B. M. Felletti Maj, *La tradizione italica nell' arte romana* 1, SA 3 (Rome, 1977), p. 330f with notes 83, 84 and fig. 162 (in this stadium the *velarium* is in place) = C. L. Ragghianti, *Pittori di Pompei* (Milan, 1963), pl. 85.

132 NUMISMATIC LITERATURE. P. V. Hill, "The Bronze Coinage of A.D. 103–111," *NC* 1970, pp. 57ff. Style of architectural reverse types: D. F. Brown, *Temples of Rome as Coin Types,* NNM 90 (New York, 1940), pp. 26ff. ICONOGRAPHY AND ARTISTIC PARALLELS. Hill, *art. cit.,* style Eii; West 2, pp. 61ff, see especially pl. 16, fig. 57 and pl. 18, figs. 64, 66; Bernoulli 2, 2 (1891), pp. 73ff. Atmospheric effects: in architectural murals, *HA* 170, 174, 177; in bas relief, Brown *loc. cit.*

133 NUMISMATIC LITERATURE. Date: Hill *Undated Coins* p. 40f. ICONOGRAPHY AND ARTISTIC PARALLELS. Wegner *Hadrian* pp. 74ff, see especially the Terme bust, p. 119f and pls. 32b, 33; West 2, pp. 75ff, see especially pl. 19, figs. 70–73; Bernoulli 2, 2 (1891), pp. 92ff, see especially pl. 30.

134 NUMISMATIC LITERATURE. Other specimens from the same dies: a) Museum of Fine Arts, Boston: C. C. Vermeule, *Roman Medallions,* second ed. (Boston, 1975), 24 = *Trau* 1267 = M&M 17 (1957), lot 451; b) Hirsch 31 (1912), lot 1325 = Naville 2 (Vautier collection, 1922), lot 732 = Glendining (Ryan 5, 1952), lot 2548; c) M&M 43 (1970), lot 343. Obverse die a medallion die: Toynbee p. 32. Alphaeus Master: C. Seltman, "Greek Sculpture and Some Festival Coins," *Hesperia* 17 (1948), pp. 71ff. Date and vicennalian issue: Hill *Undated Coins* p. 67. ICONOGRAPHY AND ARTISTIC PARALLELS: Wegner *Hadrian* pp. 7ff, see especially the Stazione Termini type, pp. 8ff with parallels p. 108, pl. 3 and p. 96f, pl. 4; West 2, pp. 111ff; Bernoulli 2, 2 (1891), pp. 105ff.

135 NUMISMATIC LITERATURE. Hill *Undated Coins* pp. 3, 72. ICONOGRAPHY AND ARTISTIC PARALLELS: West 2, pp. 141ff; Bernoulli 2, 2 (1891), pp. 134ff, see especially pls. 42, 43; Delbrueck *Bildnisse* pl. 24.

136 NUMISMATIC LITERATURE. Die study: A. M. Woodward, "The Coinage of Pertinax," *NC* 1957, pp. 84ff. Ops as anniversary revival: *RAI* p. 113; for bibliography on Ops see note 8. Antonine prototypes: *RIC* 3 (1930), p. 35, 77 and p. 109, 612 and 613. ICONOGRAPHY AND ARTISTIC PARALLELS. Bernoulli 2, 3 (1894), pp. 1ff, see especially pl. 2.

137 NUMISMATIC LITERATURE. Mints: J. van Heesch, "Les ateliers monétaires de Pescennius niger," *RBN* 124 (1978), pp. 57ff. Alexandrian attribution: portrait style, W. E. Metcalf, "New and Noteworthy from Roman Alexandria: Pescennius Niger-Diadumenian," *Essays Thompson* pp. 173ff, pl. 19, 1; inscription P P, *RIC* 4, 1 (1936), p. 19, p. 25, 12 and p. 174, 613. Roma and Jupiter as accession types: T. V. Buttrey, " 'Old Aurei' at Palmyra and the Coinage of Pescennius Niger," *Berytus* 14 (1963), pp. 117ff. Roma as an anniversary revival: *RAI* p. 114. Antonine prototypes: Hill *Undated Coins* p. 185, 310, p. 186, 329, 349, 350, 351, 358 and p. 94. ICONOGRAPHY AND ARTISTIC PARALLELS. Bernoulli 2, 3 (1894), pp. 15ff. Eastern style: M. A. R. Colledge, *The Art of Palmyra* (Boulder, Colo., 1976), pls. 64, 65, 76, 85, 91 and especially 123. Hadrianic cult statue of Roma: Vermeule *Roma* pp. 35ff, p. 107; for bibliography on the cult of Roma, see *RAI* p. 114, note 2.

138 NUMISMATIC LITERATURE. V. Zedelius, *Untersuchungen zur Münzprägung von Pertinax bis Clodius Albinus* (1977), which I have not seen. Deus Frugiferus: *RIC* 4, 1 (1936), p. 41f. ICONOGRAPHY AND ARTISTIC PARALLELS. J. Balty, *Essai d'iconographie de l'empereur Clodius Albinus,* Latomus 85 (Brussels, 1966), see especially figs. 10, 13, 14; Bernoulli 2, 3 (1894), p. 19.

139 NUMISMATIC LITERATURE. Date and issue: P. V. Hill, *The Coinage of Septimius Severus and His Family at the Mint of Rome, A.D. 193–217* (London, 1964); however Hill describes the aegis as a lion skin. Severus portrait style: Hill, "The Coin Portraiture of Severus and His Family from the Mint of Rome," *NC* 1979, pp. 36ff, group Mii. Julia portrait style: *ibid.* group E. ICONOGRAPHY AND ARTISTIC PARALLELS. Severus: D. Söchting, *Die Porträts des Septimius Severus* (Diss. Bochum, 1972); A. M. McCann, *The Portraits of Septimius Severus,* MAAR 30 (Rome, 1968), Type 5, pp. 95ff and pp. 136ff, see especially nos. 46 and 74; Bernoulli 2, 3 (1894), pp. 21ff. Apotheosis in portraiture of Antoninus Pius and Marcus Aurelius: L'Orange *Apotheosis* pp. 66ff. Corkscrew curls and Sarapis: L'Orange *Apotheosis* pp. 77ff. Julia: Bernoulli 2, 3 (1894), pp. 35ff; *Roman Portraits* 89.

140 NUMISMATIC LITERATURE. Die study and sequence of issues: C. L. Clay, "The Roman Coinage of Macrinus and Diadumenian," *NZ* 93 (1979), pp. 21ff, revising K. Pink, *Aufbau* 1, "Die Zeit des Septimius Severus," *NZ* 66 (1933), pp. 50ff. ICONOGRAPHY AND ARTISTIC PARALLELS. Wigger-Wegner pp. 131ff and pls. 32, 33; Bernoulli 2, 3 (1894), pp. 74ff; Poulsen 2, no. 138, presumably a three-dimensional example of the earlier of Macrinus' two numismatic portrait types. Felicitas: G. M. A. Hanfmann, *The Seasons Sarcophagus in Dumbarton Oaks,* CRHSAA 2 (Cambridge, Mass., 1951), pp. 163ff.

141 NUMISMATIC LITERATURE. Sequence of issues: C. L. Clay, "The Roman Coinage of Macrinus and Diadumenian," *NZ* 93 (1979), pp. 21ff, revising K. Pink, *Aufbau* 1, "Die Zeit des Septimius Severus," *NZ* 66 (1933), pp. 50ff. ICONOGRAPHY AND ARTISTIC PARALLELS. Bernoulli 2, 3 (1894), pp. 84ff and pl. 24.

142 NUMISMATIC LITERATURE. Largess medallions: Toynbee p. 110. Date and occasion of issue: K. Pink, *Aufbau 3*, "Von Alexander Severus bis Philippus," *NZ* 68 (1935), pp. 12ff, see especially p. 13. Temple of Jupiter Ultor: D. F. Brown, *Temples of Rome as Coin Types*, NNM 90 (New York, 1940), p. 16. ICONOGRAPHY AND ARTISTIC PARALLELS. C. C. Vermeule, "Adolescent Power," *Iconographic Studies* (Boston, 1980), pp. 35ff; Wigger-Wegner pp. 177ff and pls. 46, 47; *IRI* 2, pp. 83ff, see especially pl. 1, fig. 4 and pl. 3, fig. 6 = Poulsen 2, no. 140; Bernoulli 2, 3 (1894), pp. 97ff.

143 NUMISMATIC LITERATURE. Date and issue: R. Göbl, *Aufbau 5, 1*, "Valerianus und Gallienus (253–260)," *NZ* 74 (1951), pp. 8ff (this multiple is not listed but can be seen to fit into the sixth emission); the portrait style would certainly seem to belong to Gallienus' sole reign, but *Aufbau 5, 2*, "Gallienus als Alleinherrscher," *NZ* 76 (1953), pp. 5ff lists only numbered victories. Denomination: L. C. West, "The Relation of Subsidiary Coinage to Gold under Valerian and Gallienus," *ANSMusN* 7 (1957), pp. 95ff, see especially p. 100. Flavian prototype of reverse: *RIC* 2 (1926), p. 67, 418, 419 and p. 77, 525. ICONOGRAPHY AND ARTISTIC PARALLELS. L. S. B. MacCoull, "Two New Third-Century Imperial Portraits in the Ny Carlsberg Glyptothek, Copenhagen," *Berytus* 17 (1967–68), pp. 65ff (the medallion portrait corresponds to her Type 5); *IRI* 2, pp. 220ff and figs. 137ff; A. Alföldi, *Studien zur Geschichte der Weltkrise des 3. Jahrhunderts nach Christus* (Darmstadt, 1967), see especially pl. 67, figs. 1 and 2, pl. 71, figs. 1 and 2, pl. 72, figs. 1 and 2 and pl. 78, fig. 1; L'Orange *Apotheosis* pp. 86ff; Bernoulli 2, 3 (1894), pp. 165ff.

144 NUMISMATIC LITERATURE. Die study with historical background: H. R. Baldus, *Uranius Antoninus, Münzprägung und Geschichte*, Antiquitas Series 3, 11 (Bonn, 1971), revising R. Delbrueck, "Uranius of Emesa," *NC* 1948, pp. 11ff. Stone of Emesa reverse on coins of Elagabalus: *RIC* 4, 2 (1938), p. 32f, 61, 62, 64, 65, p. 37, 143, 144. ARTISTIC PARALLELS. Portrait style: M. A. R. Colledge, *The Art of Palmyra* (Boulder, Colo., 1976), see especially fig. 29.

145 NUMISMATIC LITERATURE. Labors of Hercules series: P. Bastien, "Les travaux d'Hercule dans le monnayage de Postume," *RBN* 1958, pp. 59ff, revising the arrangement of Elmer. Chronology of reign: J. Lafaurie, "La chronologie des empereurs gaulois," *RN* 1964, pp. 91ff; Lafaurie, "L'empire gaulois. Apport de la numismatique," *Aufstieg und Niedergang der römischen Welt 2, Principat 2*, ed. H. Temporini (Berlin-New York, 1975), pp. 986ff; P. Bastien, *Le monnayage de bronze de Postume*, NR 3 (Wetteren, 1967), pp. 13ff; M. Thirion, "Les dates de Postume," *Oppedragen aan A. N. Zadoks-Josephus Jitta bijhaar zeventigste veerjaardag*, SAG (Groningen, 1976), pp. 573ff. ICONOGRAPHY AND ARTISTIC PARALLELS. *IRI* 2, pp. 251ff. Hercules and lion motif: A. von Salis, *Löwenkampfbilder des Lysipp*, Winckelmannsprogramm 112 (Berlin, 1956), figs. 1, 4, 5 and 6; Johnson *Lysippos* p. 190f.

146 NUMISMATIC LITERATURE. Succession of issues: Elmer, revised on the basis of hoard evidence by J-B. Giard, "Les premières émissions de Marius et de Tétricus père à Cologne," *BSFN* 17, 2 (July 1962), p. 178f. Imperial virtues and Neoplatonism: Mattingly "Virtues." ICONOGRAPHY AND ARTISTIC PARALLELS. *IRI* 2, p. 258f; B. Haarlov, *New Identifications of Third Century Roman Emperors*, OUCS 7 (Odense, 1975), p. 20f and note 60, pls. 23, 25. Gorgoneion: Bastien "Egide." Shield as cosmic symbol: Bastien *"Clipeus."*

147 NUMISMATIC LITERATURE. Aurei of Quintillus: J. Lafaurie, "Trésor d'un navire romain trouvé en Méditerranée," *RN* 1958, pp. 79ff, updated by H. Huvelin and J. Lafaurie, "Trésor d'un navire romain trouvé en Méditerranée. Nouvelles découvertes," *RN* 1980, pp. 75ff. Known specimens: the Montacara specimen, now at Oxford; the Jameson specimen (vol. 4, p. 108, no. 520); and five from the shipwreck, including the Hunt specimen. ICONOGRAPHY AND ARTISTIC PARALLELS. *IRI* 2, p. 264f. World-weary expression: L'Orange *Studien* figs. 206–209.

148 NUMISMATIC LITERATURE. Anticipatory votive coins: bronze medallion of Tacitus with reverse legend VOTIS X ET XX and an allegorical type including Victory holding a shield inscribed VOTIS XX, Cohen 174; coins of Probus with VOTIS X ET XX, Cohen 945ff, and VOTA SOLVTA X, Cohen 952; Cohen 948f are dated by Probus' third consulship to 279–280 A.D. ICONOGRAPHY AND ARTISTIC PARALLELS. *IRI* 2, p. 275f; Bernoulli 2, 3 (1894), p. 186f. Palmyrene sources of stereometric style: Vermeule "Tetrarchs" p. 59. Aegis: Bastien "Egide" pp. 247ff.

149 NUMISMATIC LITERATURE. This variety is not listed in the standard reference, K. Pink, "Die Medaillonprägung unter Kaiser Probus," *NZ* 76 (1955), pp. 16ff. ICONOGRAPHY AND ARTISTIC PARALLELS. *IRI* 2, pp. 276ff and figs. 192–194; Bernoulli 2, 3 (1894), pp. 188ff. Four Seasons: G. M. A. Hanfmann, *The Season Sarcophagus in Dumbarton Oaks*, CRHSAA 2 (Cambridge, Mass., 1951), especially pp. 163ff, pl. 44, fig. 108 and pl. 142; J. M. Charbonneaux, "Aion et Philippe L'Arabe," *MEFR* 72 (1960), pp. 263ff.

150 NUMISMATIC AND HISTORICAL LITERATURE. History and theology of solar cult: G. H. Halsberghe, *The Cult of Sol Invictus* (Leiden, 1972). ICONOGRAPHY AND ARTISTIC PARALLELS. Solar imagery: "Sol Invictus Imperator," *Likeness and Icon* pp. 325ff. Gorgoneion: Bastien "Egide" pp. 272ff; Bastien *"Clipeus"* p. 340f.

151 NUMISMATIC LITERATURE. Sequence of issues: K. Pink, *Aufbau 6, 2*, "Carus und Söhne," *NZ* 80 (1963), pp. 1ff. ICONOGRAPHY AND ARTISTIC PARALLELS. *IRI* 2, pp. 282ff and figs. 203, 204; Bernoulli 2, 3 (1894), pp. 191ff. Hercules Farnese: Johnson *Lysippos* pp. 197ff and pls. 37, 38.

152 NUMISMATIC LITERATURE. Sequence of issues: K. Pink, "Magnia Urbica, Gattin des Carinus," *NZ* 79 (1961), pp. 1ff. Identity of Magnia Urbica: Pink, *art. cit.*, p. 1; *RIC* 5, 2 (1933), p. 181, 334 and 355. ICONOGRAPHY AND ARTISTIC PARALLELS. *IRI* 2, p. 285f. Coiffure: *Likeness and Icon* pp. 62ff and figs. 14, 15.

153 NUMISMATIC LITERATURE. Parallel multiple for Diocletian: Gnecchi 1, pl. 4, 10. *Cursus honorum* versus commemorative dating: L. Laffranchi, "L'XI anno imperatorio di Costantino Magno," *APARA* 1921, p. 422f. ICONOGRAPHY AND ARTISTIC PARALLELS. *IRI* 3, pp. 16ff, pp. 119ff and pls. 22–30, 81; Bernoulli 2, 3 (1894), pp. 197ff; Vermeule "Tetrarchs," see especially figs. 8–10. Maximian Herculius: J. A. Straub, *Vom Herrscherideal in der Spätantike* (Stuttgart, 1964 reprint of 1939 original), p. 42f. Stereometric style in late antique portraiture: L'Orange *Studien*; L'Orange, *Art Forms and Civic Life in the Late Roman Empire* (Princeton, 1965), pp. 110ff and figs. 54–63.

154 NUMISMATIC LITERATURE. Maxentian multiples: R. A. G. Carson, "Gold Medallions of the Reign of Maxentius," *Atti*, CIN 1961 (Rome, 1965), pp. 347ff; and again, Carson "Treasure." Sequence of mintmarks: C. E. King, "The Maxentian Mint," *NC* 1959, pp. 47ff, see especially p. 69. Style of the Roman mint: Alföldi *CG* pp. 24ff. First Engraver: Alföldi *CG* pp. 12ff. ICONOGRAPHY AND ARTISTIC PARALLELS. *IRI* 3, p. 30f, pp. 188ff; Alföldi *CG* pp. 53ff, see especially pl. 25, fig. 289; L'Orange *Studien* 52ff; Bernoulli 2, 3 (1894), pp. 207ff. Cult statue of Dea Roma: Vermeule *Roma* pp. 42ff, 107f. Association of wolf and twins with Aeternitas: Bastien "*Clipeus*" p. 342f.

155 NUMISMATIC LITERATURE. Arras hoard: P. Bastien and C. Metzger, *Le trésor de Beaurains (dit d'Arras)*, NR 10 (Wetteren, 1977). Quinquennalian issue: A. Chastagnol, "A propos des *quinquennalia* de Constantin," *RN* 1980, pp. 106ff; Bastien and Metzger, *op. cit.*, pp. 193ff and especially p. 200f; P. Brunn, "Constantine's *dies imperii* and *quinquennalia* in the Light of the Early Solidi of Trier," *NC* 1969, pp. 177ff. Princeps Iuventutis type: *RIC* 6 (1967), p. 111; Alföldi *CGT* p. 108; Toynbee p. 115. ICONOGRAPHY AND ARTISTIC PARALLELS. *IRI* 3, pp. 32ff, pp. 209ff, especially no. 128 = H. P. L'Orange and A. von Gerkan, *Der spätantike Bildschmuck des Konstantinsbogen* (Berlin, 1939), pp. 168ff, pl. 43 = L'Orange *Studien* figs. 120–122; "ConstPort" pp. 79ff, see especially p. 91f which compares the early numismatic style to the Arch of Constantine and the Lateran statue; *SpätKaisPor* pp. 110ff; Bernoulli 2, 3 (1894), pp. 211ff. Military statues of Constantine: L'Orange *Studien* figs. 157–158.

156 NUMISMATIC LITERATURE. Alföldi *CGT* p. 112. ICONOGRAPHY AND ARTISTIC PARALLELS. *IRI* 3, p. 60, pp. 272ff and pl. 95, no. 335, pl. 96, pl. 97, no. 347; "ConstPort" pp. 79ff; *SpätKaisPor* pp. 132ff; Bernoulli 2, 3 (1894), pp. 232ff. Trajanic imagery: Alföldi *CG* pp. 57ff. Lowered chin and upward gaze: *SpätKaisPor* pp. 118ff, pls. 33–34, pp. 132ff, pl. 45 = *IRI* 3, no. 132, pl. 78, 256; L'Orange *Studien* no. 75, figs. 146–147 = *IRI* 3, no. 140, pl. 78, 273.

157 NUMISMATIC LITERATURE. The other three recorded specimens of this multiple come from the Sidi bu Said hoard, were sold by Christie's and acquired by the Cabinet des Médailles, Paris; Dumbarton Oaks; and a private collection. The COS III multiple also went to Dumbarton Oaks. All are mounted in jewelry. First Engraver: Alföldi *CG* pp. 12ff. Numismatic style of Sirmium mint: Alföldi *CG* pp. 78ff. ICONOGRAPHY AND ARTISTIC PARALLELS. Constantine: *IRI* 3, p. 211f and pl. 69, 238; "ConstPort" pp. 79ff; *SpätKaisPor* pp. 110ff; Bernoulli 2, 3 (1894), pp. 211ff. Solar symbolism: *Likeness and Icon* p. 231 and figs. 4, 5. Solar symbolism and Christianity: J. A. Straub, "Constantine as ΚΟΙΝΟΣ ΕΠΙΣΚΟΠΟΣ: Tradition and Innovation in the Representation of the First Christian Emperor's Majesty," DOPapers 21 (Washington–Cambridge, Mass., 1967), pp. 39ff; Straub, *Vom Herrscherideal in der Spätantike* (Stuttgart, 1964 reprint of 1939 original), pp. 129ff; J. Karayannopoulos, "Konstantine der Grosse und der Kaiserkult," *Historia* 5 (1956), pp. 341ff; T. Preger, "Konstantine-Helios," *Hermes* 36 (1901), pp. 457ff. Christ as Sol Iustitiae: Straub *art. cit.*, p. 43, note 31. Sons of Constantine: Bernoulli 2, 3 (1894), pp. 232ff. Crispus: *IRI* 3, p. 60, pp. 272ff; L'Orange *Studien* fig. 59. Constantine II: *IRI* 3, p. 62, pp. 280ff, see especially no. 116/196, pl. 94, 357 and no. 197, pl. 100, 359 (= *SpätKaisPor* pp. 136ff, pls. 48–49), also no. 130, pl. 72, 251 (identified as Constantine I); L'Orange *Studien* figs. 148–149.

158 NUMISMATIC LITERATURE. Licinian prototype: *RIC* 7 (1966), p. 602, 18 and pl. 20, 41, p. 678, 20 and pl. 23, 32. Licinius' monotheism: A. H. M. Jones, *Constantine and the Conversion of Europe* (New York, 1964 edition of London, 1948 original), p. 111f. Votive inscription: *RIC* 9 (1933), p. xxxviif. ICONOGRAPHY AND ARTISTIC PARALLELS. *IRI* 3, p. 207f. Stereometric tetrarchic portraits: L'Orange *Studien* pls. 32–35, 42; D. M. Brinkerhoff, *A Collection of Sculpture in Classical and Early Christian Antioch* (New York, 1970), pp. 19ff and nos. 22–23, 25, 26–27, 29; Vermeule "Tetrarchs."

159 NUMISMATIC LITERATURE. Date and attribution: Lafaurie "Médaillons" pp. 35ff; arguments for regarding these multiples as a commemorative issue of somewhat later date will be presented by P. Bastien, *Le monnayage de l'atelier de Lyon* 4 (forthcoming); much earlier literature follows Colson, "Médaillon d'argent du César Constantius Gallus," *RN* 1857, p. 407f. Augustan models: *SMACA* pl. 2, 4 and pl. 3, 6 and 7. ICONOGRAPHY AND ARTISTIC PARALLELS. *IRI* 3, p. 62, pp. 280ff, see especially no. 203 (juvenile, = L'Orange *Studien* no. 159); Bernoulli 2, 3 (1894), pp. 232ff; L'Orange *Studien* fig. 188 (= *IRI* 3, no. 234, identified as Constans) and figs. 229, 231 (not identified as imperial). Mature Constantinian style: "ConstPort" pp. 92ff; Alföldi *CG* pp. 112ff. Apollo as model for young ruler type: "ConstPort" p. 95.

160 NUMISMATIC LITERATURE. Dating and interpretation: Lafaurie "Médaillons" pp. 35ff; A. R. Bellinger, *Roman and Byzantine Medallions in the Dumbarton Oaks Collection*, DOPapers 12 (Washington-Cambridge, Mass., 1958), p. 134, 12; for dissenting views, Kent-Hirmer p. 332, 657 and P. Bastien, *Le monnayage de l'atelier de Lyon* 4 (forthcoming). Augustan models: *SMACA* pl. 14, 2–7. Mints: The known mints of this issue include Trier, Lyons, Arles, Aquileia, Siscia, Thessalonica, Constantinople(?) and Nicomedia. Other published specimens from the Siscia mint: Lafaurie "Médaillons" p. 46, 4 and 5 (the Dumbarton Oaks specimen) and M&M 61 (1982), lot 494; the authenticity of the last has been questioned. ICONOGRAPHY AND ARTISTIC PARALLELS. Published comparisons: Colossal head in Palazzo dei Conservatori, "ConstPort" p. 92f; bronze head in Belgrade, Alföldi *CG* p. 129. Mature portrait: "ConstPort" pp. 92ff; Alföldi *CG* pp. 122ff; L'Orange *Apotheosis* pp. 90ff. Diademed bronze head in Belgrade: "ConstPort" figs. 1, 2 = Alföldi *CG* pl. 35, fig. 298 = *SpätKaisPor* p. 119ff, pl. 36.

161 NUMISMATIC LITERATURE. Date: *RIC* 8 (1981), p. 507. Festaureus denomination: Toynbee p. 40; *RIC* 8 (1981), p. 55f. ICONOGRAPHY AND ARTISTIC PARALLELS. *IRI* 3, pp. 62ff, 299ff; L'Orange *Studien* p. 141; *SpätKaisPor* pp. 132ff and pl. 74; Bernoulli 2, 3 (1894), pp. 232ff. Pearl diadem: Alföldi *CG* p. 142f. Quadriga of Helios: G. Hafner, *Viergespanne in Vorderansicht, die repräsentative Darstellung der Quadriga in der griechischen und der späterer Kunst* (Berlin, 1938), p. 61, nos. 162ff and pl. 3, pp. 117ff (type C); T. M. Marshall, *Catalogue of the Jewellery, Greek, Etruscan and Roman in the Departments of Antiquities, British Museum* (London, 1911), p. 239, no. 2108, pl. 40 and p. 369, no. 3097, pl. 71; on coins of Probus, *RIC* 5, 2 (1933), pl. 1, 13, pl. 5, 1, 9, 10. Christogram: Alföldi *CG* pp. 139ff.

162 NUMISMATIC LITERATURE. Multiples of Magnentius: A. Jeločnik, "Les multiples d'or de Magnence découverts à Emona," *RN* 1967, pp. 209ff. Circumstances of issue, interpretation of types: *RIC* 8 (1981), pp. 9ff and p. 309f; Kent-Hirmer p. 54f and p. 333, no. 669. Entire coinage of Magnentius with historical background: P. Bastien, *Le monnayage de Magnence*, NR 1 (Wetteren, 1964). Theme of liberation in the coinage of Magnentius: W. Kellner, *Libertas und Christogramm, Motivgeschichtliche Untersuchungen zur Münzprägung des Kaisers Magnentius (350–353)* (Karlsruhe, 1968), pp. 15ff. Prototype of Constantius I: P. Bastien and C. Metzger, *Le trésor de Beaurains (dit d'Arras)*, NR 10 (Wetteren, 1977), 218. ICONOGRAPHY AND ARTISTIC PARALLELS. *IRI* 3, pp. 358ff; *SpätKaisPor* pp. 175ff, pls. 76, 77 = *IRI* 3, no. 253; Bernoulli 2, 3 (1894), pp. 238ff.

163 NUMISMATIC LITERATURE. Date and occasion of issue: *RIC* 8 (1981), p. 13 and p. 39. Similar medallions for Constans and Constantius II on the occasion of Constantius' twenty-fifth anniversary: *RIC* 8 (1981), pp. 51, 517; for Constantius II in the course of his reign: *RIC* 8 (1981), pp. 275, 388, 415, 480, 525. ICONOGRAPHY AND ARTISTIC PARALLELS. *IRI* 3, p. 72, pp. 353ff; *SpätKaisPor* p. 158f and pl. 75, 1; L'Orange *Studien* figs. 146–147 (not identified as Gallus). Constantinopolis: J. M. C. Toynbee, "Roma and Constantinopolis in Late-Antique Art from 312 to 365," *JRS* 37 (1947), pp. 135ff, which demonstrates that Constantinopolis was a syncretistic creation with borrowings from several pagan sources; A. Alföldi, "On the Foundation of Constantinople: A Few Notes," *JRS* 37 (1947), pp. 10ff, especially pl. 1, 7 which apparently establishes an identification between Crispus, actual victor of the naval campaign against Licinius, and Bacchus.

164 NUMISMATIC LITERATURE. FEL TEMP REPARATIO coinage: *RIC* 8 (1981), pp. 34ff. Militant emperor type for Valentinian and Valens: *RIC* 9 (1933), p. 13, nos. 1–2 and passim. Votive star: *RIC* 8 (1981), pp. 525ff. ICONOGRAPHY AND ARTISTIC PARALLELS. Possible portrait of Procopius: L'Orange *Studien* figs. 194–195 = *IRI* 3, no. 249 (identified as Constantius Gallus). Kertch cup: *SpätKaisPor* pp. 147ff, figs. 45–47, pl. 57.

165 NUMISMATIC LITERATURE. Decennalian function: *RIC* 9 (1933), p. 265. ICONOGRAPHY AND ARTISTIC PARALLELS. Valentinian: *SpätKaisPor* pp. 178ff, especially p. 178, pl. 78; L'Orange *Studien* fig. 150; Delbrueck *Bildnisse* pls. 40, 41; Bernoulli 2, 3 (1894), pp. 251ff. Roma and Constantinopolis: J. M. C. Toynbee, "Roma and Constantinopolis in Late-Antique Art from 312 to 365," *JRS* 37 (1947), pp. 139ff; Toynbee, "Roma and Constantinopolis in Late-Antique Art from 365 to Justin II," *Studies D. M. Robinson* 2, pp. 261ff; Vermeule *Roma* pp. 48ff.

166 NUMISMATIC LITERATURE. Prototypes with tricennalian associations: A. A. Boyce, *Festal and Dated Coins of the Roman Empire: Four Papers*, NNM 153 (New York, 1965), pp. 54ff, p. 76 and pl. 9, 84 and pl. 13, 123. ICONOGRAPHY AND ARTISTIC PARALLELS. Shield-bearing busts: Bastien "Clipeus," with discussion of the Christogram device on p. 348f. Painting of Christ trampling serpent: Eusebius *Vita Constantini* 3.3. Similar motif on Constantinian bronze: Cohen 551f.

Abbreviated Titles of References

AA	*Archäologischer Anzeiger.* Berlin.
AArch	*Acta Archaeologica.* Copenhagen.
AAWG(PH)	*Abhandlungen der Akademie der Wissenschaften in Göttingen, Philologisch-Historische Klasse* Gottingen.
ABKPM	*Amtliche Berichte aus den königlichen preussichen Museen.* Berlin.
ABSA	*Annual of the British School at Athens.* London.
ABV	Beazley, J. D., *Attic Black-Figure Vase-Painters.* Oxford, 1956.
ABVP	Boardman, J., *Athenian Black Figure Vases.* Oxford, 1974.
AC	*L'Antiquité Classique.* Louvain-la-Neuve.
ACGC	Kraay, C. M., *Archaic and Classical Greek Coins.* Berkeley and Los Angeles, 1976.
ACMG	Holloway, R. R., *Art and Coinage in Magna Graecia.* Bellinzona, 1978.
AFLL	*Annali della Facoltà di Lettere di Lecce.* Lecce.
AGA	Charbonneaux, J., Martin, R., and Villard, F., *Archaic Greek Art.* London, 1971. English translation of *Grèce archaïque*, Paris, 1968.
AGC	Jenkins, G. K., *Ancient Greek Coins.* London, 1972.
AGG	Boardman, J., *Archaic Greek Gems.* Evanston, 1968.
AIIN	*Annali dell'Istituto Italiano di Numismatica.* Rome.
AJA	*American Journal of Archaeology.* New York, Archaeological Institute of America.
AK	*Antike Kunst.* Olten, Vereinigung der Freunde antiker Kunst in Basel.
"Akragantine Decadrachms"	Seltman, C., "The Engravers of the Akragantine Decadrachms," *NC* 1948, pp. 1ff.
Alföldi *CG*	Alföldi, M. R., *Die constantinische Goldprägung.* Mainz, 1963.
Alföldi *CGT*	Alföldi, M. R., "Die constantinische Goldprägung in Trier," *JNG* 9 (1958), pp. 99ff.
Alsop	Alsop, J., *The Rare Art Traditions. The History of Art Collecting and Its Linked Phenomena Wherever These Have Appeared.* New York, 1982.
AMGB 2	Vermeule, C. C., and von Bothmer, D., "Notes on a New Edition of Michaelis: Ancient Marbles in Great Britain, Part 2," *AJA* 60 (1956), pp. 321ff.
AMIIN	*Atti e Memorie dell'Istituto Italiano di Numismatica.* Rome.
AMuGS	Series: Antike Münzen und geschnittene Steine. Berlin, Deutsches Archäologisches Institut.
ANS	American Numismatic Society, New York.
ANS CentPubl	*Centennial Publication of the American Numismatic Society*, edited by H. Ingholt. New York, 1958.
ANSMusN	*American Numismatic Society Museum Notes.* New York.
Antiquitas	Series: Abhandlungen zur Vor- und Frühgeschichte, zur Klassischen und Provinzial-römischen Archäologie und zur Geschichte des Altertums, edited by A. Alföldi, J. Straub and K. Tackenberg. Bonn.

APARA	*Atti della Pontifica Accademia romana di archeologia.* Rome.
ArchClass	*Archaeologia Classica, Rivista della Scuola nazionale di Archeologia.* Rome, Istituto di Archeologia e Storia dell'arte greca e romana e di Etruscologia e antichità italiche dell'Università di Roma.
ARV	Beazley, J. D., *Attic Red-figure Vase-Painters.* 3 vols. Second edition. Oxford, 1963.
ARVAP	Boardman, J., *Athenian Red Figure Vases: The Archaic Period.* London, 1975.
AsGW	*Abhandlungen der sächsischen Gesellschaft der Wissenschaften.* Leipzig.
Asyut	Price, M. J., and Waggoner, N. M., *Archaic Greek Silver Coinage—The "Asyut" Hoard.* London and Encino, 1975.
Atti. Acc. Lincei	*Memorie della Regia Accademia Nazionale dei Lincei. Classe di Scienze Morali, Storiche e Filologiche.* Rome.
Aufbau	Göbl, R., and Pink, K., *Der Aufbau der römischen Münzprägung in der Kaiserzeit,* a continuing series of articles in *Numismatische Zeitschrift,* Vienna.
Bahrfeldt	von Bahrfeldt, M., *Die römische Goldmünzprägung während der Republik und unter Augustus.* Halle, 1923.
BARSS	British Archaeological Reports, Supplementary Series. Oxford.
Bastien "Clipeus"	Bastien, P., "Clipeus et buste monétaire des empereurs romains," *NAC* 10 (1981), pp. 315ff.
Bastien "Egide"	Bastien, P., "Egide, Gorgonéion et buste impérial dans le monnayage romain," *NAC* 9 (1980), pp. 273ff.
BCAR	*Bullettino della Commissione Archeologica Comunale in Roma.* Rome.
BCH	*Bulletin de Correspondance Hellénique.* Paris.
Becatti *Orificerie*	Becatti, G., *Orificerie antiche dalle minoiche alle barbariche.* Rome, 1955.
BEFAR	Series: Bibliothèque des Écoles françaises d'Athènes el de Rome. Paris.
Bellinger *Essays*	Bellinger, A. R., *Essays on the Coinage of Alexander the Great,* NS 11. New York, 1963.
Bernoulli	Bernoulli, J. J., *Römische Ikonographie.* 4 vols. Stuttgart, 1882–1894.
BIAO	*Bulletin de l'Institut français d'Archéologie Orientale.* Cairo.
Bieber *Alexander*	Bieber, M., *Alexander the Great in Greek and Roman Art.* Chicago, 1964.
Bieber *Hellenistic Sculpture*	Bieber, M., *The Sculpture of the Hellenistic Age.* Revised edition. New York, 1961.
BM Quarterly	*Quarterly of the British Museum.* London.
BMC	*A Catalogue of the Greek Coins in the British Museum.* 29 vols. London, 1873–1927.
BMCRE	Mattingly, H., and Carson, R. A. G., *Coins of the Roman Empire in the British Museum.* 6 vols. London, 1923–1962.
BMCRR	Grueber, H. A., *Coins of the Roman Republic in the British Museum.* 2 vols. London, 1910.
BMusB	*Bulletin of the Museum of Fine Arts, Boston.* Boston.
BJ	*Bonner Jahrbücher des Rheinischen Landesmuseums in Bonn and des Vereins von Altertumsfreunden im Rheinlande.* Bonn.
BN	Giard, J.-B., *Bibliothèque Nationale. Catalogue des monnaies de l'empire romain.* Vol. 1. *Auguste.* Paris, 1976.

Boehringer	Boehringer, E., *Die Münzen von Syrakus*. Berlin, 1929.
Boston Sculpture	Comstock, M. B., and Vermeule, C. C., *Sculpture in Stone. The Greek, Roman and Etruscan Collections of the Museum of Fine Arts*. Boston, 1976.
Brendel	Brendel, O., *Etruscan Art*. Harmondsworth, England and New York, 1978.
BSFN	*Bulletin de la Société française de Numismatique*. Paris, Cabinet des Médailles.
Cahn	Cahn, H. A., *Die Münzen der sizilischen Stadt Naxos*. Basle, 1944.
Carson "Treasure"	Carson, R. A. G., "A Treasure of Aurei and Gold Multiples from the Mediterranean." In *Mélanges de numismatique, d'archéologie et d'histoire offerts à J. Lafaurie*. Paris, 1980.
CGA	Charbonneaux, J., Martin, R., and Villard, F., *Classical Greek Art*. London, 1972. English translation of *Grèce classique*, Paris, 1969.
Charbonneaux	Charbonneaux, J., *Les bronzes grecs*. Paris, 1958.
CIN	Congrès international numismatique, held at Brussels, 1906; London, 1936; Paris, 1953; Rome, 1961; Jerusalem, 1963; New York and Washington, 1973.
Clain-Stefanelli	Clain-Stefanelli, E. E., *Numismatics, an Ancient Science*, Bulletin 229, *Contributions from the Museum of History and Technology*, Paper 32, Smithsonian Institution. Washington, 1965.
Cohen	Cohen, H., *Description historique des monnaies frappées sous l'empire romain*. 8 vols. Paris, 1880–1892.
Coin Hoards	*Coin Hoards*. London, Royal Numismatic Society.
"ConstPort"	Harrison, E. B., "The Constantinian Portrait." In *DOPapers* 21. Cambridge, Mass. and Washington, 1967.
Crawford	Crawford, M. H., *Roman Republican Coinage*. 2 vols. Cambridge, 1974.
CRHSAA	Catalogue of the Representations of the Horae and the Seasons in Ancient Art. Cambridge, Mass.
CVA	*Corpus Vasorum Antiquorum*. Various places and dates of publication.
Delbrueck *Bildnisse*	Delbrueck, R., *Bildnisse römischer Kaiser*. Berlin, 1914.
de Luynes	Babelon, J., *Catalogue de la collection de Luynes*. 4 vols. Paris, 1924–1936.
Demareteion	Schwabacher, W., *Das Demareteion*, Opus Nobile 7. Bremen, 1958.
Doeringer	*Art and Technology*, edited by S. Doeringer et al. Cambridge, Mass., 1970.
Dörig	Dörig, J., *Art antique. Collections privées de Suisse Romande*, Editions archeologiques de l'Université de Genève. Mainz, 1975.
DOPapers	*Dumbarton Oaks Papers*. New York.
EAA	*Enciclopedia dell'arte antica, classica e orientale*. 7 vols. Rome, 1958–1966.
EAC	Sutherland, C. H. V., *The Emperor and the Coinage, Julio-Claudian Studies*. London, 1976.
Elmer	Elmer, G., "Die Münzprägung der gallischen Kaiser in Köln, Trier und Mailand," *BJ* 146 (1941).
Erhart	Erhart, K. P., *The Development of the Facing Head Motif in Greek Coinage*. Diss. Harvard, 1978.
Essays Robinson	*Essays in Greek Coinage Presented to Stanley Robinson*, edited by C. M. Kraay and G. K. Jenkins. Oxford, 1968.

Essays Thompson	*Greek Numismatics and Archaeology, Essays in Honor of Margaret Thompson*, edited by O. Mørkholm and N. M. Waggoner. New York, 1979.
Euainetos	Liegle, J., *Euainetos*. Berlin, 1941.
Festschrift Brommer	*Festschrift für Frank Brommer*, edited by U. Höckmann and A. Krug. Mainz, 1977.
Furtwängler *AG*	Furtwängler, A., *Die antiken Gemmen*. Leipzig, 1900.
Furtwängler Masterpieces	Furtwängler, A., *Masterpieces of Greek Sculpture*. London, 1895.
GBA	*Gazette des Beaux-Arts*. Paris.
GGFR	Boardman, J., *Greek Gems and Finger Rings, Early Bronze Age to Late Classical*. New York, 1972.
Gnecchi	Gnecchi, F., *I medaglioni romani*. 3 vols. Milan, 1912.
Götter Griechenlands	Lange, K., *Götter Griechenlands, Meisterwerke antiker Münzkunst*. Weihnachten, 1940.
GR Bronzes	Lamb, W., *Greek and Roman Bronzes*. London, 1929.
GRBS	*Greek, Roman and Byzantine Studies*. Durham, N. C., Duke University.
Gulbenkian	Robinson, E. S. G., *A Catalogue of the Calouste Gulbenkian Collection of Greek Coins*, Part 1. *Italy, Sicily, Carthage*. Lisbon, 1971.
HA	Charbonneaux, J., Martin, R., and Villard, F., *Hellenistic Art*. London, 1973. English translation of *Grèce hellénistique*, Paris, 1970.
HASB	*Hefte des Archäologischen Seminars der Universität Bern*. Bern.
HDD(KA)	Habelts Dissertationsdrucke, Reihe Klassische Archäologie. Bonn.
Hellénisme primitif	Svoronos, J. N., *L'hellénisme primitif de la Macédoine, prouvé par la numismatique et l'or du Pangée*. Paris and Athens, 1919.
Hess-Leu	Joint auctions of A. Hess A.G., Lucerne and A.G. Bank Leu and Company, Zurich.
"Hieron's Aitna"	Boehringer, C., "Hieron's Aitna und das Hieroneion," *JNG* 13 (1968), pp. 67ff.
Hill *Undated Coins*	Hill, P. V., *The Dating and Arrangement of the Undated Coins of Rome, A.D. 98–148*. London, 1970.
Hunter collection	Macdonald, G., *Catalogue of Greek Coins in the Hunterian Collection*. 3 vols. Glasgow, 1899–1905.
ICGH	*An Inventory of Greek Coin Hoards*, edited by M. Thompson, O. Mørkholm and C. M. Kraay. New York, 1973.
IEJ	*Israel Exploration Journal*. Jerusalem, Israel Exploration Society.
Intaglios and Rings	Boardman, J., *Intaglios and Rings, Greek, Etruscan and Eastern, from a Private Collection*. London, 1975.
IRI 2	Felletti Maj, B. M., *Iconografia romana imperiale da Severo Alessandro a M. Aurelio Carino (222–285 d.C.)*, Quaderni e Guide di Archeologia 2. Rome, 1958.
IRI 3	Calza, R., *Iconografia romana imperiale da Carausio a Giuliano (287–363 d.C.)*, Quaderni e Guide di Archeologia 3. Rome, 1972.
Jameson	*Collection R. Jameson*. 4 vols. Paris, 1913–1932.
Jantzen	Jantzen, U., *Bronzewerkstätten in Grossgriechenland und Sizilien*, *JDAI* Ergänzungshefte 13. Berlin, 1937.

Jantzen *GGK*	Jantzen, U., *Griechische Greifenkessel.* Berlin, 1955.
JBHM	*Jarhbuch des Bernischen Historischen Museums.* Bern.
JDAI	*Jahrbuch des Deutschen Archäologischen Instituts.* Berlin.
JEA	*Journal of Egyptian Archaeology.* London, The Egypt Exploration Society.
JHS	*Journal of Hellenic Studies.* London.
JIAN	*Journal International d' Archéologie Numismatique.* Paris and Athens.
Johnson *Lysippos*	Johnson, F. P., *Lysippos.* Durham, N. C., 1927.
JNG	*Jahrbuch für Numismatik und Geldgeschichte.* Kallmünz.
JŒAI	*Jahreshefte des Österreichischer Archäologischen Instituts.* Vienna.
Jongkees	Jongkees, J. H., *The Kimonian Dekadrachms.* Utrecht, 1941.
JRGZ	*Jahrbuch des römisch-germanischen Zentral-Museums.* Mainz.
JRS	*Journal of Roman Studies.* London.
JSGU	*Jahrbuch der Schweizerischen Gesellschaft für Ur- und Frühgeschichte.* Basle.
Käppeli	Käppeli, R., and Cahn, H. A., *Kunstwerke der Antike, Sammlung R. Käppeli.* Basle, n.d. (c. 1963?).
Kamarina	Westermark, U., and Jenkins, G. K., *The Coinage of Kamarina,* Royal Numismatic Society Special Publication 9. London, 1980.
Kent-Hirmer	Kent, J. P. C., Hirmer, M., and Hirmer, A., *Roman Coins.* New York, 1978. Revised edition of J. P. C. Kent, B. Overbeck and A. U. Stylow, *Die römische Münze,* Munich, 1973.
Kraay-Hirmer	Kraay, C. M., and Hirmer, M., *Greek Coins.* New York, 1961.
Kunstfreund	*Griechische Münzen aus der Sammlung eines Kunstfreundes,* joint auction of Bank Leu and Münzen und Medaillen A. G., Zurich, 28 May 1974.
Kyrieleis	Kyrieleis, H., *Bildnisse der Ptolemäer.* Berlin, 1975.
Lacroix	Lacroix, L., *Les représentations des statues sur les monnaies grecques.* Paris, 1949.
Lafaurie "Médaillons"	Lafaurie, J., "Une série de médaillons d'argent de Constantine I et Constantine II," *RN* 1949, pp. 35ff.
Langlotz and Hirmer	Langlotz, E., and Hirmer, M., *The Art of Magna Graecia.* New York, 1965. English translation of *Die Kunst der Westgriechen,* 1963.
Latomus	*Latomus. Revue d'études latines.* Brussels.
LCS	Trendall, A. D., *The Red-figured Vases of Lucania, Campania and Sicily.* 2 vols. Oxford, 1967.
Leu	Bank Leu A. G., Zurich, Numismatische Abteilung (dealer).
Likeness and Icon	L'Orange, H. P., *Likeness and Icon. Selected Studies in Classical and Early Mediaeval Art.* Odense, 1973.
L'Orange *Apotheosis*	L'Orange, H. P., *Apotheosis in Ancient Portraiture.* Instituttet for sammenlignende kulturforskning, Series B, 44. Oslo and Cambridge, Mass., 1947.
L'Orange *Studien*	L'Orange, H. P., *Studien zur Geschichte des spätantiken Porträts.* Instituttet for sammenlignende kulturforskning, Series B, 22. Oslo and Cambridge, Mass., 1933.
Lullies and Hirmer	Lullies, R., and Hirmer, M., *Greek Sculpture.* Revised edition. New York, 1960.

MAAR	*Memoirs of the American Academy in Rome.* Rome.
Markman	Markman, S. D., *The Horse in Greek Art.* Diss. Columbia, 1943.
Master Bronzes	Mitten, D., and Doeringer, S., *Master Bronzes from the Classical World.* Mainz, 1967.
Mattingly "Virtues"	Mattingly, H., "The Roman 'Virtues'," *Harvard Theological Review* 30 (1937), pp. 103ff.
MBNG	*Mitteilungen der Bayerischen Numismatischen Gesellschaft.* Munich.
McClean	Grose, S. W., *Catalogue of the McClean Collection of Greek Coins.* 3 vols. Cambridge, 1923–1929.
MDAI(A)	*Mitteilungen des Deutschen Archäologischen Instituts, Athenische Abteilung.* Berlin.
MDAI(R)	*Mitteilungen des Deutschen Archäologischen Instituts, Römische Abteilung.* Mainz.
MEFR	*Mélanges d'Archéologie et d'Histoire de l'École Française de Rome.* Paris.
Metropolitan Bronzes	Richter, G. M. A., *Greek, Etruscan and Roman Bronzes.* New York, 1915.
Mildenberg	*Animals in Ancient Art from the Leo Mildenberg Collection*, edited by A. Kozloff. Cleveland, 1981.
Mitchiner	Mitchiner, M., *Indo-Greek and Indo-Scythian Coinage.* 9 vols. London, 1975–1976.
Mitthell Münzserien	Boehringer, C., *Zur Chronologie Mittelhellenisticher Münzserien, 220–160 v. Chr.*, AMuGS 5. Berlin, 1972.
Mon. Piot	*Monuments et Mémoires publiés par l'Académie des Inscriptions et Belles-Lettres (Fondation Piot).* Paris.
M&M	Münzen und Medaillen A. G., Basle dealer.
NAC	*Numismatica e Antichità classiche. Quaderni Ticinesi.* Lugano.
NC	*Numismatic Chronicle.* London, Royal Numismatic Society.
NFA	Numismatic Fine Arts, Beverly Hills dealer.
NNM	Series: Numismatic Notes and Monographs. New York, American Numismatic Society.
NR	Series: Numismatique Romaine. Essais, recherches et documents. Wetteren.
NS	Series: Numismatic Studies. New York, American Numismatic Society.
NSc	*Notizie degli Scavi di Antichità.* Rome, Accademia dei Lincei.
NZ	*Numismatische Zeitschrift.* Vienna, Numismatische Gesellschaft.
OUCS	Series: Odense University Classical Studies.
Para.	Beazley, J. D., *Paralipomena. Additions to Attic Black-Figure Vase-Painters and to Attic Red-Figure Vase-Painters.* Oxford, 1971.
Parthenonfries	Brommer, F., *Der Parthenonfries.* Mainz, n.d. (c. 1977).
PBA	*Proceedings of the British Academy.* Oxford.
PCG	Hill, G. F., *Principal Coins of the Greeks.* London, 1965.
Pfeiff *Apollon*	Pfeiff, K. A., *Apollon, die Wandlung seines Bildes in der griechischen Kunst.* Frankfurt, 1943.
Pfuhl	Pfuhl, E., "Ikonographische Beitrage zur Stilgeschichte der hellenistischen Kunst," *JDAI* 45 (1930), pp. 3ff.
Pomerance	*The Pomerance Collection of Ancient Art.* Brooklyn, 1966.

Poulsen	Poulsen, V., *Les portraits romains*. 2 vols. Copenhagen, 1973–1974.
Pozzi	*Monnaies grecques antiques provenant de la collection de feu le Prof. S. Pozzi*, auction catalogue Naville-Ars Classica 20, Geneva, 4 April 1921.
Problemi fidiaci	Becatti, G., *Problemi fidiaci*. Milan, 1951.
Ptolemaische Agypten	*Das Ptolemäische Ägypten*, edited by H. Mahler and V. M. Strockna, Akten des internationalen Symposions, 27–29 September 1976 in Berlin. Mainz, 1978.
QDAP	*Quarterly of the Department of Antiquities, Palestine*. Jerusalem.
RA	*Revue Archéologique*. Paris.
RAI	Grant, M., *Roman Anniversary Issues*. Cambridge, 1950.
RBN	*Revue Belge de Numismatique et de Sigillographie*. Brussels.
RE	*Paulys Real-Encyclopädie der classischen Altertumswissenschaft*. Stuttgart, various dates.
REA	*Revue des Études anciennes*. Talence, Demaine University, section d'histoire.
Regling	Regling, K., *Die antike Münze als Kunstwerke*. Berlin, 1924.
Rép. stat.	Reinach, S., *Répertoire de la statuaire grecque et romaine*. 6 vols. Paris, 1897–1930.
RHP	Toynbee, J. M. C., *Roman Historical Portraits*. Series: Aspects of Greek and Roman Life. Ithaca, 1978.
RIC	Mattingly, H., et al., *The Roman Imperial Coinage*. 9 vols. London, 1923–1981.
Richter *Animals*	Richter, G. M. A., *Animals in Greek Sculpture*. Oxford, 1930.
Richter *MMH*	Richter, G. M. A., *Metropolitan Museum of Art. Handbook of the Greek Collection*. Revised edition. Cambridge, Mass., 1953.
Richter "Phiale"	Richter, G. M. A., "A Greek Silver Phiale in the Metropolitan Museum of Art," *AJA* 45 (1941), pp. 363ff.
Richter *SSG*	Richter, G. M. A., *The Sculpture and Sculptors of the Greeks*. Second edition. New Haven, 1950.
RIN	*Rivista Italiana di Numismatica e di Scienze affini*. Pavia.
Rizzo	Rizzo, G. E., *Monete greche della Sicilia antica*. Rome, 1946.
Rizzo *Intermezzo*	Rizzo, G. E., *Intermezzo*. Rome, 1939.
Rizzo *Saggi*	Rizzo, G. E., *Saggi preliminari su l'arte della moneta nella Sicilia greca*. Rome, 1938.
RLouvre	*La Revue du Louvre et des Musées de France*. Paris, Conseil des Musées nationaux.
RN	*Revue Numismatique*. Paris.
RNS	Royal Numismatic Society, London.
Robertson	Robertson, M., *A History of Greek Art*. 2 vols. Cambridge, 1975.
Rolley *Bronzes*	Rolley, C., *Monuments graeca et romana 5. Greek Minor Arts*. Fasciculus 1. *The Bronzes*. Leiden, 1967.
Roman Portraits	Richter, G. M. A., *Roman Portraits*. Exhibit catalogue, New York, 1948.
Roscher	Roscher, W., *Ausführliches Lexikon der griechischen und römischen Mythologie*. 6 vols. Leipzig, 1884–1937.
RVAp	Trendall, A. D., and Cambitoglou, A., *The Red-Figured Vases of Apulia*. 2 vols. and indices. Oxford, 1978–1982.

SA	Series: Studia Archaeologica. Rome.
SAG	Series: Scripta Archaeologica Groningana. Groningen.
Schrader *Phidias*	Schrader, H., *Phidias.* Frankfurt, 1924.
Schwabacher	Schwabacher, W., "Die Tetradrachmenprägung von Selinunt," *MBNG* 43 (1925), pp. 1ff.
SCL	Series: Sather Classical Lectures. Berkeley, University of California.
SE	*Studi Etruschi.* Florence.
Seltman	Seltman, C., *Athens, Its History and Coinage Before the Persian Invasion.* Cambridge, 1924.
"Signatures de graveurs"	Forrer, L., "Les signatures de graveurs sur les monnaies grecques," *RBN* 61 (1905), pp. 1ff, 387ff.
SIR	Svenksa Institutet i Rom. Rome.
SM	*Schweitzer Münzblätter.* Basle.
SMACA	Grant, M., *The Six Main Aes Coinages of Augustus.* Edinburgh, 1953.
SNG	*Sylloge Nummorum Graecorum,* a multivolume survey of the world's major collections, arranged by nation. Various places and dates of publication.
SNG ANS	*Sylloge Nummorum Graecorum: The American Numismatic Society.* 5 vols. New York, 1969 and continuing.
SNG Copenhagen	*Sylloge Nummorum Graecorum: The Royal Collection of Coins and Medals, Danish National Museum.* Copenhagen, 1942 and continuing.
SNG Lloyd	*Sylloge Nummorum Graecorum: Great Britain 2, The Lloyd Collection.* 4 vols. 1933–1937.
SNG Lockett	*Sylloge Nummorum Graecorum: Great Britain 3, The Lockett Collection.* 5 vols. 1938–1949.
SNG Oxford	*Sylloge Nummorum Graecorum: Great Britain 5, Ashmolean Museum, Oxford.* 3 vols. 1962 and continuing.
SNG Spencer Churchill	*Sylloge Nummorum Graecorum: Great Britain 1, 1, Spencer Churchill and Salting Collections.* 1931.
SNR	*Schweizerische Numismatische Rundschau.* Bern, Schweizerische Numismatische Gesellschaft.
SpätKaisPor	Delbrueck, R., *Spätantike Kaiserporträts von Constantinus Magnus bis zum Ende des Westreichs.* Berlin, 1933.
Strack	Strack, P. L., *Untersuchungen zur römischen Reichsprägung des zweites Jahrhunderts.* 3 vols. Stuttgart, 1931–1937.
Studies D. M. Robinson	*Studies Presented to David Moore Robinson,* edited by G. E. Mylonas and D. Raymond. 2 vols. Saint Louis, 1951, 1953.
Svoronos	Svoronos, J. N., *Ta Nomismata tou Kratous ton Ptolemaion.* 4 vols. Athens, 1904–1908.
Sydenham	Sydenham, E. A., *The Coinage of the Roman Republic.* London, 1952.
"Syracusan 'Medallions' "	Evans, A. J., "The Syracusan 'Medallions' and Their Engravers," *NC* 1901, pp. 205ff.
"Syrakus und Leontinoi"	Chantraine, H., "Syrakus und Leontinoi," *JNG* 8 (1957), pp. 7ff.
TAT	Venedikov, I., and Gerassimov, T., *Thracian Art Treasures.* Sofia, 1975.
Toynbee	Toynbee, J. M. C., *Roman Medallions,* NS 5. New York, 1944.
Traité	Babelon, J., *Traité des monnaies grecques et romaines.* 4 vols. Paris, 1907–1932.

Trau	*Sammlung Franz Trau, Münzen der römischen Kaiser*, auction catalogue of Gilhofer and Ranschburg, Vienna, 22 May 1935.
TrésAth	Svoronos, J. N., *Trésor des monnaies d' Athenes.* Munich, 1923.
TST	Artamov, M. I., *Treasures from Scythian Tombs in the Leningrad Museum.* London, 1969.
Tudeer	Tudeer, L. O. Th., *Die Tetradrachmenprägung in der Periode der signierende Künstler.* Berlin, 1913.
Typos	Typos, Monographien zur antiken Numismatik. Series of the Schweizerische Numismatische Gesellschaft, edited by C. Martin, H. A. Cahn and L. Mildenberg.
Vasenlisten	Brommer, F., *Vasenlisten zur griechischen Heldensage.* Third edition. Marburg, 1973.
Vermeule *Roma*	Vermeule, C. C., *The Goddess Roma in the Art of the Roman Empire.* Cambridge, Mass., 1974 revision of 1959 original.
Vermeule "Tetrarchs"	Vermeule, C. C., "Tetrarchs True and False." In *Iconographical Studies.* Boston, 1980.
VMG	*The Art of South Italy: Vases from Magna Graecia*, edited by M. E. Mayo and K. Hamma, exhibit catalogue, Richmond, 1982.
WAdnG	*Wissenschaftliche Abhandlungen des deutschen numismatikertages in Göttingen.*
Wegner *Flavier*	Wegner, M., *Das römische Herrscherbild. Die Flavier. Vespasian. Titus. Domitian. Nerva. Julia Titi. Domitia. Domitilla.* Berlin, 1966.
Wegner *Hadrian*	Wegner, M., *Das römische Herrscherbild, 2, 3: Hadrian. Plotina. Marciana. Matidia. Sabina.* Berlin, 1956.
West	West, R., *Römische Porträt-Plastik.* 2 vols. Munich, 1933 and 1941, revised 1970.
Wiggers-Wegner	Wiggers, H. B., and Wegner, M., *Das römische Herrscherbild, 3,1: Caracalla bis Balbinus.* Berlin, 1971.
ZfN	*Zeitschrift für Numismatik.*

Glossary

Achaemenid—Persian dynasty, founded by Cyrus the Great (559–529 B.C.), who absorbed the Median, Neo-Babylonian and Lydian empires. His successors temporarily extended their rule into Europe and Egypt and retained the Asiatic core of the empire until the conquest of Alexander the Great, 331–325 B.C.

acrolith—a statue with the head and extremities of stone, attached to a body of another material such as wood or terracotta, fairly common in Greek Italy where stone was scarce.

Actium—Roman naval battle of 2 September 31 B.C., in which Marcus Agrippa decisively defeated Cleopatra's fleet, provoking a general desertion of Antony and assuring Octavian's ultimate control of the Roman world.

addorsed—back-to-back

aegis—an attribute of Zeus/Jupiter which conferred invulnerability in battle and which he frequently loaned to other gods, especially Athena/Minerva; iconographically it tends to be represented as a goatskin, often with a fringe of serpents and a gorgoneion in the center. See gorgoneion.

Amazon—in Greek mythology, one of a warlike race of women from Scythia who allegedly cut off their right breasts to improve their archery, exposed all male children at birth and consorted with men only briefly for purposes of procreation.

Ammon—a ram god with an oracle at the desert oasis of Siwah, whose recognition of Alexander the Great as his son was the first public step toward the conqueror's claim of divinity.

amphora—a pot with two handles and narrow bottom used for storing wine or oil. See Appendix A, *Shapes of Greek Vases.*

ampyx—a woman's headband, typically worn just at the hairline.

anastole—Alexander's characteristic cowlick, which caused the hair to rise above the forehead.

anguipede—serpent-footed, i.e., having a serpent's tail in place of the lower limbs.

antoninianus—a Roman base silver coin of the third century A.D. characterized by a radiate portrait for emperors and a bust upon a crescent for empresses. Theoretically a double denarius, it was subject to extreme debasement and devaluation.

apicate—having a pointed vertical projection.

apotheosis—deification, especially the moment of transformation from the human to the divine state.

aryballos—oil jar

as—originally a cast bronze coin weighing one Roman pound, reduced to a token coin of copper under the Principate and dropped from the monetary system in the course of the third century A.D. See Appendix F, *The Roman Monetary System.*

astragalos—a knucklebone, used in gambling and fortune telling much like modern dice.

Augustus, abbreviated AV, AVG—literally "revered one," an honorary title conferred by the Senate on Octavian in 27 B.C. and assumed as a title by succeeding emperors.

aulos—Greek flute.

aureus—the basic gold coin of Rome from the first century B.C. to the beginning of the fourth century A.D. It began with a weight of about 8 gm and ended at 5.25 gm, with considerable fluctuation even below these weights in the course of the third century. See Appendix F, *The Roman Monetary System.*

baldric—a shoulder strap from which a scabbard is suspended.

balsamarium—lidded container used for precious commodities such as unguents and perfumes.

bilingual—in vase painting, having some parts executed in black-figured technique and others in red-figured technique.

caduceus—a wand surmounted by two loops, the attribute of a divine messenger; Latin equivalent of Greek kerykeion.

Caesar, abbreviated C, CAE, CAES—the cognomen (surname) of Julius Caesar. As the adoptive name of Octavian it became the surname of the imperial family, assumed by successive dynasties in part because it implied a legitimate claim to the vast personal estate of the emperor. As an imperial title it was often contrasted with the title Augustus to indicate a designated heir.

cantharus—see kantharos

chiton—long garment with sleeves, worn by both Greek men and women, generally belted and often of sheer fabric. It was particularly associated with wealthy and luxurious societies such as that of sixth-century Ionia.

chlamys—a short mantle fastened on one shoulder, often worn by travelers and by the messenger god Hermes/Mercury.

chous—a form of oinochoe without a separate neck.

Christogram—the monogram of Christ, taking both the form ☧ and the form ✶; associated with posthumous accounts of the conversion of Constantine.

chryselephantine—of ivory overlaid with gold.

chthonic—pertaining to the earth (Greek *chthonos*) and thus generally combining fertility and underworld symbolism.

cidaris—flat-topped, ceremonial tiara of the Persian Great King.

cista—a wooden or metal box, or woven basket, especially one used in the mysteries for holding the sacred utensils.

city-Tyche—the specific goddess of a Greek city, often represented with the attributes of Tyche (Fortuna), namely a cornucopia and sometimes a rudder. The city-Tyche also typically wears a crown in the form of a city wall.

congiarium—a public distribution of food or money to the poor of Rome by a magistrate, undertaken at his own expense. Under the Principate this institution was the sole prerogative of the emperor, and the largess normally consisted of money.

consul, abbreviated COS—the highest magistracy of the Roman state. Under the Republic two consuls were elected annually and shared supreme executive and military power; their names, rather than numerals, were used to identify the year in the Roman calendar. Under the Principate the office was more honorary than effective but was nevertheless frequently held by the emperor and avidly sought by prominent men.

COS—see consul.

cuirass—armor for the torso.

cul—set-off convex area, here used of the handle zone of a calyx krater.

curule—a chair shaped like a camp stool but carved and inlaid with ivory, used by the highest Roman magistrates. Interlocking curved legs are a distinguishing characteristic.

daric—the standard gold coin of Achaemenid Persia. See Appendix E, *Greek Weight Standards and Denominations.*

decadrachm—Greek coin weighing ten drachmae, a rare and exceptional denomination. See Appendix E, *Greek Weight Standards and Denominations.*

decennalia—celebration by a Roman emperor of ten years in power.

decussis—an extraordinary Roman cast coin equivalent to ten asses. See Appendix F, *The Roman Monetary System.*

Deinomenid—Sicilian dynasty founded by the brothers Cleander and Hippocrates of Gela (505–491 B.C.), which at the height of its power controlled most of southern and eastern Sicily. The dynasty fell in 466 B.C.

Demareteion—a Syracusan coin of great value struck after the battle of Himera in 480 B.C. and named after the tyrant's wife Demarete, according to various ancient authors; traditionally identified with the earliest Syracusan decadrachm.

denarius—the basic Roman silver coin from the late third century B.C. through the first third of the third century A.D. Its original weight of 4.5 gm was rather quickly reduced to just under 4 gm, whence the denarius drifted gradually to a final weight of less than 2.5 gm. Originally it was equivalent to ten asses, later to sixteen. See Appendix F, *The Roman Monetary System.*

diadem—a flat band of cloth wound round the head indicating religious consecration. It was affected by victorious athletes and by Greek rulers who wished to imply divine authorization for their position. It entered Roman imperial iconography under Constantine the Great and was soon converted into a jewelled circlet.

diadochi—successors, especially the successors of Alexander the Great.

didrachm—Greek coin weighing two drachmae. A silver didrachm was roughly equivalent to a silver stater or nommos. See Appendix E, *Greek Weight Standards and Denominations.*

die—an engraved stamp for coining, in which the design is cut in intaglio. See Appendix B, *Notes on the Technique of Ancient Coin Production.*

die link—a visible relation between coins struck from the same die. See Appendix C, *Die Studies.*

dipinto—an inscription painted on a vase, usually after firing on the underside of the foot.

D N—abbreviation for *dominus noster*, "our lord," introduced early in the fourth century A.D. and illustrating the trend toward political autocracy in the later Roman empire.

Donations of Alexandria—dynastic arrangements announced by Marc Antony in 34 B.C., by which he divided the Orient among Cleopatra and her children. Cleopatra was proclaimed queen of Egypt, Cyprus, Libya and southern Syria; Caesarion (her son by Julius Caesar) was named her co-regent and King of Kings. Of Cleopatra's children by Antony, Alexander Helios received Armenia, Media and all territories east of the Euphrates; Cleopatra Selene received Cyrenaica and parts of North Africa; and Ptolemy Philadelphus northern Syria and Cilicia. The territories so distributed included independent foreign kingdoms, the realms of Roman client kings and actual Roman provinces.

donative—a military bonus, customarily paid under the Principate upon the accession of a new emperor, after victories, for imperial anniversaries and for other festive occasions involving the imperial house.

Dorian—Greek linguistic group that settled the Greek mainland in the twelfth century B.C., generally warlike and noted for their simple habits and severe taste in art.

drachma—literally a "handful," a Greek unit of weight around 4 gm which became the basis for several currency systems. See Appendix E, *Greek Weight Standards and Denominations.*

echinus—used here of the mouth or foot of a vase that is convex and spreads outward to a flat rim at either top or bottom (inverted echinus).

electrum—natural alloy of gold and silver, used for the earliest coinage in Asia Minor and subsequently manufactured for special non-civic "trade" currencies.

endromides—winged sandals.

ephebos—adolescent boy.

exergue—the portion of a round field (e.g., of a coin or the tondo of kylix) beneath the main device, often separated off by a ground line (the exergual line).

fillet—a skein of wool, often knotted, signifying religious consecration. A fillet was commonly tied to a lustral (purifying) branch or bound round the head of priests and victorious athletes.

Flavian—family name of two Roman dynasties, the first founded by Vespasian (69–79 A.D.), the second founded by Constantius Chlorus (305–306 A.D.) and firmly established by Constantine the Great (307–337 A.D.).

glyptic—pertaining to carving, especially small-scale intaglio engraving as of gemstones and coin dies.

globus nicephorus—a globe surmounted by a small figure of Victory (Greek Nike), employed in imperial iconography to symbolize world dominion.

gorgoneion—an emblem based upon the facing head of the Gorgon Medusa, whose ability to turn men to stone with a glance translated itself into the supposed apotropaic (protective) power of the image.

greaves—armor for the shins.

griffin—a fabulous beast of oriental origin, part lion and part eagle, sometimes also with serpentine elements; in myth, the fierce guardian of treasures and secret mineral deposits.

hecte—one-sixth stater, a denomination used in Greek electrum currency systems. See Appendix E, *Greek Weight Standards and Denominations.*

Herculius—surname assumed by Maximian indicating that he enjoyed the special patronage of Hercules.

herm—quadrangular pillar topped by a carved head or bust, used as a boundary marker, sign post, mile post, etc.

himation—a cloak or overgarment worn by Greek males and females. It consisted of a rectangular piece of cloth wrapped around the body.

hoard—a buried treasure of coins. See Appendix D, *Hoards.*

hoplite—a heavy-armed foot soldier who carried a large shield (Greek *hoplon*).

hoplitodromos—heavy-armed racer.

hydria—water jar with an oval body, narrow neck and three handles, two placed horizontally for carrying and the other placed vertically for pouring. See Appendix A, *Shapes of Greek Vases.*

imago, pl. imagines—official three-dimensional portrait supplied by the Roman government to its mint(s) to serve as a model for numismatic portraiture.

imperator, abbreviated IMP—military commander-in-chief. Originally the battlefield title of a consul, it later could be conferred on any general by his troops and remained permanently among his honorary titles. Under the Principate acclamation as imperator was equivalent to recognition as emperor.

imperatorial—adjective derived from imperator (see above) but referring particularly to the period of the Late Republic when power was concentrated in the hands of a few rival war lords.

imperium—the right of command, invested in Rome's head magistrates by the Senate and the people.

incuse—in coinage, depression caused by the tool used to force annealed metal into the obverse die. At first irregular in shape, it later assumes geometric form and still later is usually elaborated in decorative fashion or serves as the background for a reverse type.

infibulated—used of Greek athletes who protect their genitals while exercising with a ribbon-like tie.

Ionian—a Greek linguistic group which mainly inhabited the coast of western Asia Minor, noted for wealth and luxurious habits and for an ornate style in art.

Julio-Claudian—the first Roman imperial dynasty, reflecting the merger of Augustus' Julian line with the Claudian family of his wife Livia. The Julio-Claudians ruled the Roman empire from 27 B.C. to 68 A.D.

kalos name—a young man's name included in the formula *X kalos,* "X is beautiful," commonly inscribed on Attic red-figured vases in the later sixth and early fifth centuries B.C. Those names which appear repeatedly are presumed to belong to the most admired youths of the time.

kantharos—a stemmed drinking cup with high looping handles and relatively deep body, favored in the Greek West.

kerykeion—a wand surmounted by two loops, an attribute of a divine messenger; Greek equivalent of Latin caduceus.

kithara—Greek concert lyre.

kitharode—lyre player.

kore, pl. korai—young woman; in art, an archaic votive statue depicting a young woman standing facing and modestly dressed.

kottabos—a Sicilian game played at drinking parties, involving throwing the dregs of the wine from drinking cups into a metal basin.

kouros, pl. kouroi—youth; in art, an archaic votive statue of a nude youth striding forward, hands at his sides, characterized by a fundamentally geometrical analysis of the human anatomy.

krater—wide-mouthed vase used for mixing water and wine, as the Greeks did not drink their wine neat. There are several important varieties of krater, see Appendix A, *Shapes of Greek Vases.*

krobylos—a Greek style of hairdressing for either sex, in which the hair is combed over the ears and tucked up behind into a wreath, fillet or diadem.

krotalon—a rattle used in the worship of Dionysus and Cybele.

kylix—two-handled cup for drinking wine. See Appendix A, *Shapes of Greek Vases.*

laureate—wearing a crown of laurel leaves. Among the gods the laurel wreath is an attribute of Apollo and of Zeus/Jupiter. In Roman political life it was an honor awarded to successful military commanders along with the title imperator, and thus it became an attribute of the emperor symbolizing his aspect as commander-in-chief of the armed forces.

laver—wash stand

legate—a Roman provincial governor appointed by and directly subordinate to the emperor, independent of the senatorial administrative apparatus.

lekythos—a single-handled oil vessel with narrow neck and flaring lip.

Levant—the countries of the eastern Mediterranean littoral and adjacent islands.

litra—a small unit of weight employed by the prehellenic inhabitants of Sicily, later adopted by the Greek settlers. See Appendix E, *Greek Weight Standards and Denominations.*

liturgy—literally "service," especially the assumption of public duties at one's own expense, a common practice in the Graeco-Roman world.

maeander—a ribbon-like design composed of a series of continuous or interlocking angular elements.

maenad—frenzied female worshipper of Dionysus.

medallion—a coin-like work of art, usually larger and more imposing than the regular coinage and intended for presentation by a ruler to an honored personage.

metope—painted or carved panel between the triglyphs of a Doric frieze.

metrology—the study of weights and measures.

mnaieion—a large Ptolemaic gold denomination, weighing eight drachmae and equivalent in value to a silver mina (Greek *mna*). See Appendix E, *Greek Weight Standards and Denominations.*

mural crown—crown in the form of a city wall, typical headgear of a Graeco-Roman city goddess.

nommos—a silver denomination, weighing about eight gm, used in much of Greek Italy. See Appendix E, *Greek Weight Standards and Denominations.*

obverse—the major or "heads" side of a coin, struck from a die fixed in an anvil and slightly convex in appearance. See Appendix B, *Notes on the Technique of Ancient Coin Production.*

octodrachm—a Greek coin weighing eight drachmae, struck in either gold or silver; an unusually large denomination. See Appendix E, *Greek Weight Standards and Denominations.*

oinochoe—a one-handled pitcher for pouring wine.

omphalos—the navel or center of the world, supposedly located at Apollo's sanctuary at Delphi and represented in art as a basket-sized mound with its surface in lozenge pattern.

orant—praying figure.

orichalcum—brass.

Orphism—a Greek mystic cult which rejected physical life as unworthy, practiced self-abnegation through curious disciplines and promised purification and reward in the afterlife.

palaestra—wrestling school.

Palladium, Greek Palladion—a small statuette of Athena allegedly rescued from the sack of Troy by Aeneas and carried to the future site of Rome, where it became one of the relics of the city's foundation entrusted to the care of Vesta; more generally, the archaic image of Athena.

Panathenaic amphora—an amphora given as a prize at the Panathenaic festival, regularly decorated with Athena on one side and a depiction of the contest for which it was offered on the other. See Appendix A, *Shapes of Greek Vases.*

Panathenaic festival—an Athenian festival celebrated every year on Athena's purported birthday and every fourth year with special magnificence. It consisted of a procession, sacrifices and games.

parazonium—short Roman sword, symbolic of martial valor.

patera—a flat dish used to offer sacrifice; Roman equivalent of Greek phiale.

pelte—a small, light shield of leather.

peplos—belted outer garment for a Greek woman, especially favored by the Dorians and therefore the usual female dress in severe style art.

petasus—a broad-brimmed felt hat, especially popular in Thessaly and characteristic of the messenger god Hermes/Mercury.

P F—abbreviation for *Pius Felix,* "pious and happy," a title of the Roman emperors.

phalera—a boss or disc of metal used to adorn a helmet or the bridle of a horse, especially an ornament for a horse's forehead.

phiale—a flat dish used to offer sacrifice; Greek equivalent of Roman patera.

phorbeia—a leather strap placed round the mouth and head of a flute player to improve his embouchure (mouth position in playing).

pileus—a conical cap, especially associated with the Dioscuri; Latin equivalent of Greek pilos.

pilos—a felt skull cap; Greek equivalent of Latin pileus.

plektron (Latin plectrum)—a pick for a stringed instrument.

Pontifex Maximus, abbreviated P M, Pon(t) Max—high priest of Rome, responsible for the government of the Vestal Virgins and the general supervision of Roman religious life. The high pontificate was a lay political office for which candidates campaigned, but election was for life. It was Julius Caesar's first political success. Augustus assumed the office when it fell vacant in 12 B.C., and thereafter it was held by each emperor.

P P—abbreviation for *Pater Patriae,* "Father of his Country," an honorary title conferred by the Senate on Augustus in 2 B.C. and on other emperors at various points in their reigns but rarely automatically upon accession.

Praetorian Guard—a corps of nine battalions, each 500 strong, who served as bodyguards and orderlies to the Roman emperors.

praetorian prefect—commander of the Praetorian Guard, an extremely powerful officer who was often able to manipulate or even assassinate the emperor he was supposed to serve, particularly in the troubled third century A.D.

Princeps Iuventutis—honorary leader of the youth corps of the Roman knightly order (equites), an honor devised by Augustus for his young grandsons Gaius and Lucius Caesar when he adopted them as his heirs, and conferred thereafter on very young heirs designate.

Principate—the institution of government by a Princeps or "first citizen" in which the ruler's power is limited by constitutional forms and historical tradition. This was the form of government of the Roman empire from 27 B.C. to the latter third century A.D.

propraetor—a Roman magistrate who had formerly held the elective office of praetor, generally serving as a provincial governor by senatorial appointment.

protome—forepart of a figure, animal or human.

Ptolemaic—Macedonian dynasty in Egypt, founded by Alexander's general Ptolemy in 323 B.C. and terminated by Cleopatra's suicide in 30 B.C.

Punic—relating to the Phoenician colony of Carthage in North Africa.

pyrrhic—an armed dance performed at the Panathenaic festivals.

pyx, pyxis—box.

quadriga—four-horse chariot.

quinquennalia—celebration by a Roman emperor or heir designate of five years in power.

radiate—wearing a crown of rays symbolizing the sun.

rerebrace—armor for the upper arm.

reserved—in vase painting, an area showing the natural reddish color of the clay.

reverse—the minor or "tails" side of a coin, struck from a die which receives a direct hammer blow and somewhat concave in appearance. See Appendix B, *Notes on the Technique of Ancient Coin Production*.

rhyton—a horn-shaped drinking cup, often in the form of an animal's head.

rotelle—a small wheel-like disk, often a decorative element that rests on the mouth of a metal or terracotta oinochoe or hydria.

Saite—from the city of Sais, especially referring to the Twenty-Sixth through Thirtieth Dynasties of Egypt, the last period of Egyptian autonomy.

sakkos—a snood or cloth covering for a Greek lady's hair.

sarissa—Macedonian lance.

Sasanid—a Persian dynasty founded by Ardashir I (211/12–241 A.D.), which ruled the Persian empire until 636 A.D.

satrap—a governor of the Persian empire, either a great noble or a vassal king and nearly autonomous with respect to military powers, judicial and diplomatic authority and the right of coinage.

satyr—a mythical woodland creature with coarse face, human body but the ears, feet and tail of a horse or goat, a symbol of the animal passions in man and a companion of Dionysus; frequently indistinguishable from the silen.

S C—abbreviation for *Senatus consulto*, "by order of the Senate."

scarab—amulet or gemstone in the shape of a beetle.

Scylla—a predatory sea monster which barked like a dog and dwelt, according to some authorities, in the Straits of Messina.

Second Triumvirate—political alliance of Octavian, Marc Antony and Lepidus, given a specious constitutionality by the Lex Titia of 43 B.C. which conferred on them five years' consular power for the purpose of "setting the Republic in order." The triumvirate was renewed for a second five years in 37 B.C.

selinon—a form of wild celery which gave its name to the river and town of Selinus in western Sicily. The selinon leaf served as the city's civic badge.

sestertius—under the Roman Republic a silver coin equivalent to ¼ denarius; under the Principate a brass coin equivalent to four asses, the largest of the aes denominations until the middle of the third century A.D. when it was first supplemented by a double-sestertius denomination and then dropped from the currency system. See Appendix F, *The Roman Monetary System.*

shekel—a Semitic unit of weight, the basis of the monetary system in Phoenicia and Palestine; linguistically but not metrologically equivalent to the Persian siglos. See Appendix E, *Greek Weight Standards and Denominations.*

siglos—the standard silver denomination of Achaemenid Persia, linguistically cognate to the Semitic shekel. See Appendix E, *Greek Weight Standards and Denominations.*

silen—a mythical woodland creature with coarse face, human body and horse's ears, tail and feet, a symbol of the animal passions in man and a companion of Dionysus; also the possessor of arcane knowledge. Originally the silen was separate from the satyr, but the two were confused even by ancient authors.

siliqua—a Roman silver denomination of the fourth century A.D., ultimately struck at 144 to the pound. See Appendix F, *The Roman Monetary System.*

skyphos—a deep, stemless drinking cup with two horizontal handles.

solidus—the standard Roman gold coin from the fourth through the tenth centuries A.D., introduced by Constantine the Great and struck at 72 to the pound. See Appendix F, *The Roman Monetary System.*

spall—chip.

sphendone—literally "sling," a hair net or scarf to support a Greek lady's hair at the back of the head.

sphinx—a fabulous creature of oriental origin, possessed of a female head and torso with a lion's body and eagle's wings and like the griffin a guardian figure, notably of graves.

S P Q R—abbreviation for *Senatus populusque romanus,* "Senate and Roman people."

stamnos—a wide-bodied pot with horizontal handles, used for storing wine and other supplies. See Appendix A, *Shapes of Greek Vases.*

stater—a Greek unit of weight, ranging between approximately eight and twelve gm depending upon locality. It became the basis for several Greek currency systems. See Appendix E, *Greek Weight Standards and Denominations.*

stephanephorus—literally "wreath-bearer," a broad-flanned tetradrachm with a wreath encircling the reverse type, struck in the second century B.C. by Athens and various cities of Asia Minor.

stereometric—an adjective referring to the tendency to reduce the human physiognomy to blocky, geometric forms, typical of Palmyrene art and of Roman imperial portraiture of the late third century A.D.

stopped key pattern—a decorative pattern composed of a series of separate elements of key shape.

strigil—a metal scraper used in bathing.

taenia—a ribbon, especially a headband, worn in token of victory. In numismatic iconography it is distinguished from the diadem mainly by its narrow width and the lack of visible ties, which give it something of the appearance of a metal circlet.

Tarquins—dynasty of Etruscan kings who, according to tradition, ruled Rome from 616 B.C. until expelled in 509 B.C.

tetradrachm—a Greek coin weighing four drachmae, usually in silver; the major denomination of many Greek currency systems. See Appendix E, *Greek Weight Standards and Denominations.*

tetrarchy—a form of government with power shared among four colleagues, tried briefly from 293 A.D. until it disintegrated into a welter of competing claimants after 305 A.D.

thiasos—a band of revelers, especially one honoring Dionysus.

thymiaterion—incense burner.

thyrsus—staff surmounted by a pine cone, carried in Dionysiac revels and symbolic of fertility.

toga picta—embroidered toga originally reserved for the triumphal procession of a Roman military victor, later transferred to the consuls when the triumphal procession was assimilated to the consular procession which inaugurated the consular year.

toga virilis—the Roman garment of manhood, whose assumption marked the beginning of legal adult status. The transition to adulthood occurred at the father's discretion with the earliest legal age fixed at fourteen, but exceptions were often made for imperial children.

toreutic—relating to decorative metalwork, including chasing, embossing and other techniques.

torus—cushion-shaped molding, used of the mouth or foot of a vase that is flat on the top and bottom and convex on the edge.

tribunician power, abbreviated TR P (OT), TRIB POT, TRIBVNIC POT—the power of the tribune to intervene in government processes on behalf of the people, conferred on Augustus in large part because it carried a guarantee of personal inviolability. As an imperial power of all succeeding emperors it was renewed annually and thus constitutes a very specific basis for dating coins or inscriptions where it is recorded.

tricennalia—celebration by a Roman emperor of thirty years in power.

tridrachm—a Greek coin weighing three drachmae, an unusual denomination probably intended to facilitate exchange between incompatible weight standards.

triglyph—the vertical element of a Doric frieze, which flanks painted or carved panels (metopes). It consists of a number of plastic or painted vertical lines.

tripod—a three-legged stand for a large bowl (lebes), a typical dedication at Greek temples and one especially associated with Apollo and his sanctuary at Delphi.

triskeles—a radiate figure composed of three legs, usually a solar symbol but also, in Sicilian contexts, an emblem of that three-cornered island.

triumph—a procession through Rome celebrating a successful military campaign upon the return of the commander. Authorized by the Senate, it was regarded as the pinnacle of a Roman political career under the Republic. Under the Principate the honor was reserved for the emperor or members of the imperial family; other victors were granted only the right to wear the triumphal insignia.

triumvir—any Roman magistrate who held office jointly with two colleagues, but especially a member of the political alliances known as the First Triumvirate (Julius Caesar, Pompey and Crassus) and the Second Triumvirate (Octavian, Marc Antony, Lepidus).

trophy—a battlefield monument composed of the arms of the vanquished.

type—in numismatics, the device on a coin.

velificatio—the gesture of drawing the veil away from the face, especially associated with bridal and erotic scenes but also with females exposed to the wind, such as Nereids or goddesses riding on animals or in chariots.

vicennalia—celebration by a Roman emperor of twenty years in power.

Villanovan—prehistoric Italian culture spanning the transition from the Bronze Age to the Iron Age.

weight standard—the theoretical basis of an ancient currency system, involving a unit of a certain average weight with multiples and fractions thereof. See Appendix E, *Greek Weight Standards and Denominations,* and Appendix F, *The Roman Monetary System.*

MAPS

Origin of Objects in Wealth of the Ancient World

Appendix A

Vase Shapes Represented in Wealth of the Ancient World.

1 COLUMN-KRATER
Large footed bowl with two columnar handles; used for mixing wine with water [1].

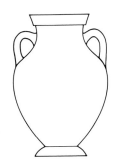

2 PANEL-AMPHORA
Two-handled jar with a narrow neck and decoration in panels on front and back; used for the storage and transportation of wine and other liquids [2].

3 KYLIX
Type A: two-handled cup with a stemmed foot and a molding between the bowl and foot; used for drinking wine [3].

4 NECK-AMPHORA
Two-handled jar similar to no. 2 except that the neck is offset and the decoration is continuous around the body; also used for the storage and transportation of liquids [4].

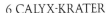

5 KYLIX
Type B: two-handled cup similar to no. 3 except that there is no molding between the bowl and the foot; also used for drinking wine [5, 7, 8, 11].

6 CALYX-KRATER
Modern name for a large footed bowl with an offset convex handle zone and arching handles set low on the body; used for mixing wine with water [6, 14, 15].

7 PANATHENAIC AMPHORA
Large one-piece jar with a narrow neck and sharply tapering body; used for the olive oil granted to victors in the Panathenaic games [9, 10].

8 STAMNOS
Modern name for a large pot with a wide-shouldered body, wide mouth and horizontal handles; thought to have been used for the storage and/or mixing of liquids [12].

9 PELIKE
Modern name for a pot similar to an amphora, but with a body broad at the base and a wide mouth; used for the same purposes as an amphora [13].

10 HYDRIA
Pot with an oval body, wide mouth and one vertical and two horizontal handles; used for carrying, dipping and pouring water [34].

Appendix B

Notes on the Technique of Ancient Coin Production

In antiquity coins were manufactured entirely by hand.

The Flan or metal blank upon which the coin was to be struck was normally prepared by casting molten metal in a mold. Since ancient coins were accepted on the basis of their weight, this factor had to be strictly controlled. Modern experiments suggest that for large denominations considerable accuracy could be achieved simply by carefully pouring the metal into a mold of pre-determined size. For gold coinage and for small denominations greater exactitude was the rule, and here the technique may have involved the use of small nuggets and/or powdered metal, first weighed and then heated in the mold. In emergencies, existing coins of the required weight might be overstruck with new designs.

Dies in antiquity were made of a hard bronze alloy with a high proportion of tin, or alternatively of iron. They were so far as we know individually engraved by hand, using the tools of the gem cutter. In a few cases, particularly in Roman coins, scholars suspect the use of a hub, a method of mass-producing dies: a punch bearing the type in relief would stamp out a series of similar dies, whose details were then added by hand.

Minting. The obverse ("heads") die was fixed into an anvil, while the reverse ("tails") die was attached to a punch. The metal blank, heated to make it malleable, was placed upon the obverse die, and the reverse die was struck into the flan by a hammer blow. No collar was used to control the spread of the flan under this blow, and as a result each coin has an individual and slightly irregular shape. In some cases the metal spread up around the reverse punch, so that the outline of the die is visible. In other cases the reverse die was prepared with a wide border to produce a flatter coin. Other irregularities of the finished coin may result from this hand striking procedure as well: flan cracks from insufficient heating of the blank before striking; and double-striking, weak strikes and off-center designs from carelessness in the actual striking.

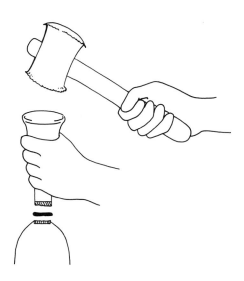

Appendix C

Die Studies

One of the most powerful tools of modern scientific numismatics depends upon the fact that obverse and reverse dies rarely had identical lifetimes. Typically, an obverse die lasted longer than a reverse die because it experienced less stress in striking. (Modern experiments using dies of the ancient variety have established that an obverse die of tetradrachm size can produce 10,000 to 16,000 coins with little sign of wear, whereas a reverse die becomes unusable after about 8000 coins.) In addition to normal deterioration, changes in mint administration might affect the lifetime of a die which bore a magistrate's name or symbol. Thus it happens that each obverse die was usually paired with several different reverses, and when it was retired the reverse die was often still in good condition and would continue to be used with the next obverse. The simplest pattern of die use at a mint might be schematized as follows:

Obverse dies:

Reverse dies:

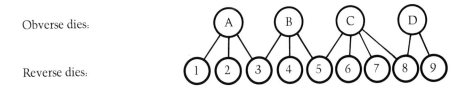

The correct sequence of the dies in a series can to some extent be determined on the basis of style, but this is only a very rough indicator. A more objective criterion is the deterioration of the die over its lifetime, producing flaws which are apparent on the struck coins and which become ever more conspicuous with continued use. Sometimes damaged dies were patched or re-cut to extend their lifetime, and these alterations too can be detected on the coins struck from them. For example, obverse die C might be in perfect condition while paired with reverse die 5. During its association with reverse die 6 it perhaps develops a minor crack, which widens into a major defect during use with reverse die 7. Then C is patched, enabling it to be used with reverse die 8.

There exist other, more complex patterns of die use than the one above, and most Roman issues are too vast to be easily organized into die sequences. On the other hand many Greek cities had a more manageable output, and where sufficient quantities of material can be collected it is often possible to reconstruct a detailed account of mint activity and of the artistic development of the coinage.

Appendix D

Hoards

A coin hoard is a buried treasure, usually the possession of a single owner which was buried for safe-keeping—there being no banks—and for some reason never recovered. When properly recorded hoards are a rich source of numismatic information. In the first place a hoard generally reveals a cross-section of the coinage available in a particular place at a given time, and the cumulative evidence of hoards allows us to reconstruct the patterns of circulation and perhaps the economic function of individual coinages, as well as illuminating the economic condition of different regions and periods of the ancient world. Secondly, hoards establish relative chronology. Coins which are found together in hoards are in most cases approximately contemporary, but the degree of wear will indicate which are older and which are newer. Hoard studies are essential in Greek numismatics, for few Greek coins bear objective dates, and the task of organizing this vast body of material and establishing its internal relations is work for several generations of numismatists. The field of Roman coins is less disorderly because imperial portraits and inscriptions generally suffice to date a coin to a particular reign. Nevertheless the sequence of issues within each reign and the role of coinage in Roman economic and military life can be clarified with the aid of hoard evidence.

Appendix E

Greek Weight Standards and Denominations

Originally, Greek coins were valued solely for their precious metal content. Bullion of high quality was employed, and thus the weight of the coin was a direct indicator of its value. Although many Greek mints appear to have used the same terminology for their coin denominations, the ideal weight of the basic unit—either the drachma or the stater—varies from place to place. Also the multiples and fractions generated from these basic units may vary from one mint to the next. A weight standard, then, is a currency system comprising various denominations whose weights are related mathematically. The following table gives the theoretical outlines of the weight standards represented in this exhibit.

Abderite standard

A local standard of Abdera

DENOMINATION	WEIGHT	EQUIVALENCY
octodrachm	29.5 gm	2 tetradrachms
tetradrachm	14.7 gm	

Aeginetic standard

Widely used in the Greek peninsula, the Aegean islands, Crete and Caria in southwest Asia Minor.

DENOMINATION	WEIGHT	EQUIVALENCY
stater	12.2 gm	2 drachmae
drachma	6.1 gm	2 triobols
triobol	3 gm	3 obols
obol	1 gm	

Attic (Euboic) standard

Used in Athens and Euboea, the Chalcidian peninsula of Macedon and in Sicily with a local system of subdivision. Its adoption by Alexander the Great made it the weight standard of most hellenistic kingdoms.

DENOMINATION	WEIGHT	EQUIVALENCY
gold stater	8.5 gm	24 drachmae
decadrachm	43.0 gm	10 drachmae
tetradrachm	17.2 gm	2 didrachms
didrachm	8.6 gm	2 drachmae
drachma	4.3 gm	6 obols or 5 litrae
obol	0.72 gm	
litra (Sicilian)	0.86 gm	

Babylonian standard

Used in Mesopotamia after its conquest by Alexander the Great. The "Poros" decadrachm [101] may in fact be a 5-shekel piece on this standard.

DENOMINATION	WEIGHT	EQUIVALENCY
5-shekel piece	39 gm	roughly to Attic decadrachm
2-shekel piece	15 gm	roughly to Attic tetradrachm
shekel	7.5 gm	roughly to Attic didrachm

Campanian standard

One of several weight standards used in southern Italy, primarily by the cities of Campania on the west coast.

DENOMINATION	WEIGHT	EQUIVALENCY
silver stater	7.4 gm	2 drachmae
drachma	3.7 gm	6 obols
obol	0.6 gm	

Chian (Rhodian) standard

Widely popular around the Aegean in the fourth century B.C.

DENOMINATION	WEIGHT	EQUIVALENCY
tetradrachm	15.6 gm	4 drachmae
drachma	3.9 gm	2 hemidrachms
hemidrachm	1.9 gm	

Italic-Tarentine standard

The weight standard of Tarentum, replacing the Achaean standard throughout most of southern Italy in the course of the fifth century.

DENOMINATION	WEIGHT	EQUIVALENCY
dinommos	15.6 gm	2 nommoi
nommos	7.8 gm	2 drachmae
drachma	4.0 gm	4 diobols
diobol	1 gm	

Persic standard

The weight standard of Achaemenid Persia, a slightly reformed version of the Lydian standard inherited from Croesus. Besides being used for the royal Persian coinage it was the usual standard for southern Anatolia and Cyprus and was also adopted by scattered cities in western Asia Minor, Macedon and Thrace.

DENOMINATION	WEIGHT	EQUIVALENCY
gold daric	8.35 gm	20 silver sigloi
silver stater	11.0 gm	2 sigloi
siglos	5.5 gm	

Phocaic standard

One of two weight standards for the early electrum coinage, retained for electrum trade currencies in Asia Minor after this alloy was generally superseded by silver.

DENOMINATION	WEIGHT	EQUIVALENCY
electrum stater	16.1 gm	6 hectae
electrum hecte	2.6 gm	

thereafter divisions by halves: twelfth staters, twenty-fourths, forty-eighths and ninety-sixths; however the denominations smaller than the hecte were rarely issued after the earliest period.

Phoenician standard

The weight standard of Phoenicia, properly based upon the silver shekel. Tetradrachms of compatible weight were produced at other places, for example in Macedon and Ptolemaic Egypt. These are conventionally called "Phoenician" but probably represent independent developments rather than the adoption of an existing standard.

DENOMINATION	WEIGHT	EQUIVALENCY
4-shekel piece	28 gm	2 double shekels
double shekel	14 gm	2 shekels
shekel	7 gm	2 half shekels
half shekel	3.5 gm	

"Phoenician" standard of Macedon

Indigenous(?) silver standard to which Philip II added a range of gold denominations on the Attic standard.

DENOMINATION	WEIGHT	EQUIVALENCY
gold stater	8.5 gm	24 drachmae
gold hemistater	4.3 gm	12 drachmae
gold quarter stater	2.15 gm	6 drachmae
tetradrachm	14.45 gm	4 drachmae

The fractions are complicated, involving divisions into didrachms and drachmae, but also retaining from an earlier currency system a series of multiples based on the obol—octobols, tetrobols, triobols, diobols—whose weights are incompatible with the drachma multiples.

Ptolemaic ("Phoenician") standard

The weight standard of the Ptolemaic kingdom, seemingly developed to hinder trade with the rest of the hellenistic world, which was almost unified in its use of the Attic standard. The purpose was presumably to prevent the outflow of bullion from the kingdom and to enhance the profitable royal monopoly on foreign exchange.

DENOMINATION	WEIGHT	EQUIVALENCY
gold mnaieion or octo- drachm	27.7 gm	2 gold tetradrachms
gold tetradrachm	13.6 gm	2 gold didrachms
gold didrachm	6.8 gm	
silver decadrachm	35.4 gm	2½ silver tetradrachms
silver octodrachm	27.7 gm	2 tetradrachms
silver tetradrachm	13.6 gm	4 drachmae

Thasian standard

One of several competing weight standards of archaic Thraco-Macedonian coinage. Their relation is complex and obscure, and the complete range of denominations is not found at any single mint.

DENOMINATION	WEIGHT	EQUIVALENCY
dodecadrachm	39 gm	12 drachmae
octodrachm	29 gm	8 drachmae
stater	9.8 gm	3 drachmae?
hemistater	4.9 gm	1½ drachmae?
drachma	3.3 gm	

Appendix F

The Roman Monetary System

The Roman monetary system evolved considerably over its nine centuries of existence. The outlines of its development are presented in Arthur Houghton's essay. The following table is but a sampling of the system at various stages in its development which are particularly relevant to coins exhibited in *Wealth of the Ancient World*. There was a general and persistent tendency to devalue the currency by reducing its weight and/or by debasing its precious metal content. This tendency was interrupted from time to time by reforms which often involved the introduction of new denominations. The weights given here therefore represent the ideal weights at the inception of each system, with some indication of the levels to which they declined if the system was long-lived.

Bronze standard,

c. 289–211 B.C.

DENOMINATION	WEIGHT (AVERAGE)	EQUIVALENCY
as	310 gm–250 gm	12 unciae
semis	165 gm–134 gm	6 unciae
triens	115 gm–89 gm	4 unciae
quadrans	86 gm–66 gm	3 unciae
sextans	54 gm–43 gm	2 unciae
uncia	28 gm–21 gm	
semuncia	15 gm–10 gm	½ uncia

Augustan system,

c. 23 B.C.–235 A.D.

DENOMINATION	WEIGHT (AVERAGE)	EQUIVALENCY
gold aureus	7.80 gm–6.55 gm	25 denarii
silver denarius	3.80 gm–3.10gm	4 sestertii
orichalcum sestertius	25 gm	2 dupondii
orichalcum dupondius	12.5 gm	2 asses
copper as	11 gm	4 quadrantes
copper quadrans 3 gm discontinued c. 100 A.D.	3 gm	
silver antoninianus introduced 214 A.D.	5 gm	2 denarii

Reform of Aurelian

c. 270 A.D.

DENOMINATION	WEIGHT (AVERAGE)	EQUIVALENCY
gold aureus	6.50 gm	20 antoniniani(?)
silver-washed antoninianus	4.40 gm	
bronze denarius	*	*
bronze sestertius	*	*
bronze as	*	*

Weights and equivalencies have not yet been deduced for these rare and short-lived denominations.

	DENOMINATION	WEIGHT (AVERAGE)	EQUIVALENCY
Tetrarchic system *c. 294–309 A.D.*	gold aureus	5.35 gm	24 argentei
	silver argenteus	3.2 gm	5 folles
	follis	10 gm, steadily declining	5 bronze denarii
	bronze post-reform radiate (antoninianus) (soon discontinued)		2 bronze denarii

	DENOMINATION	WEIGHT (AVERAGE)	EQUIVALENCY
Constantinian system *c. 309–fifth century A.D.*	gold solidus	4.5 gm	2 semisses, 18 miliarensia, 24 siliquae
	gold semis	2.25 gm	9 miliarensia
	gold 1½ scripulum	1.70 gm	9 siliquae
	silver milarense	4.5 gm	1⅓ siliquae
	silver siliqua (argenteus)	3.1 gm	¾ miliarense
	bronze follis	5–3 gm	
	bronze centenionalis introduced 348 A.D.	4.50 gm	2 folles
	gold tremissis introduced by Theodosius I to replace the 1½ scripulum	1.50 gm	6 miliarensia, 8 siliquae
	silver reduced siliqua, introduced 355 A.D.	2 gm	½ miliarense

Index 1

Artists Represented in Wealth of the Ancient World

The spelling of ancient names and term varies according to the background and preferences of the several contributors

Index 2

Mint Cities

Index 2 (continued)

Index 3

Gods, Mythological Figures and Personifications depicted on Objects in Wealth of the Ancient World

Index 4

Rulers and Historical Personages

*denotes the issuing authority of a coin exhibited in *Wealth of the Ancient World* or a historical personage depicted on a coin or object.

Index 4 (continued)